T0323409

Demystifying China's Innovation Machine

Demystifying China's Innovation Machine

Chaotic Order

Marina Yue Zhang, Mark Dodgson,
and David M. Gann

OXFORD
UNIVERSITY PRESS

OXFORD
UNIVERSITY PRESS

Great Clarendon Street, Oxford, OX2 6DP,
United Kingdom

Oxford University Press is a department of the University of Oxford.
It furthers the University's objective of excellence in research, scholarship,
and education by publishing worldwide. Oxford is a registered trade mark of
Oxford University Press in the UK and in certain other countries

© Marina Yue Zhang, Mark Dodgson, and David M. Gann 2022

The moral rights of the authors have been asserted

First Edition published in 2022

Impression: 1

Published in the United States of America by Oxford University Press
198 Madison Avenue, New York, NY 10016, United States of America

British Library Cataloguing in Publication Data

Data available

Library of Congress Control Number: 2021942896

ISBN 978-0-19-886117-1

DOI: 10.1093/oso/9780198861171.001.0001

Printed and bound by
CPI Group (UK) Ltd, Croydon, CR0 4YY

To Rowena and Ingrid

Preface

China is at a unique time in its history, undertaking a massive transformation—driven by innovation—that is complex, multilayered, and sometimes mystifying. People with diverse values, interests, and concerns interpret this transformation differently. What is indisputable is that China has increased its capacity for innovation at a scale and speed unmatched in the history of the world. To understand China and its relationship with the rest of the world, we believe it is important to appreciate the nature of China's innovation, its strengths and weaknesses, its contributions to the domestic and global economy, and how it might impact future sustainability. Understanding innovation in China is a very challenging task, requiring insights from historical, cultural, institutional, geopolitical, and technological perspectives.

Our journey in producing this book has been long and involved. For Marina it has been deeply personal. This book is not just meant to help others demystify China's innovation but is also the product of her journey to understand a major transformation of the country of her birth. She was born and brought up in China but left the country in her youth to pursue education and freedom. She has lived and worked between China, Hong Kong, Singapore, the United Kingdom, and Australia since then. In the past thirty years, her professional experience with blue-chip corporations and start-ups in the technology industry in Asia and her academic inquiry into innovation have been driven by a personal mission of seeking to demystify China's innovation. Since the beginning of her career, she has been keen to understand why China lost its global competitiveness in innovation after the sixteenth century, and how it intends to regain it.

Marina and Mark began working together on innovation over twenty years ago. They have continued to research and publish together and separately on China and innovation ever since. They were joined by David for their extensive studies of Chinese technology firms. Mark and David have researched and published on innovation together for over thirty years. The current volume pulls together many decades of the authors' collaborative work on innovation, built upon an extensive review of the literature on innovation in China (including relevant academic journals, books, think tank reports, and industry reports), analysis of statistical data and policy, case studies, and interviews.

Marina is the lead author and intellectual inspiration of the book and has also been its key researcher. Mark and David's role has been in adding their perspectives and insights, and contributing to the lengthy discussions about, and extensive drafting of, the arguments in the book. Mark wishes to particularly thank Shulin Gu, Lan Xue, Lei Guo, and Bengt-Ake Lundvall for improving his knowledge of innovation in China. David would like particularly to thank the participants at the World

Economic Forum meetings in Tianjin and Dalian from 2016 to 2019. The major effort, intellectual drive, and emotional commitment to the book are Marina's, and she offers her personal list of thanks and acknowledgements below.

Marina Zhang
Mark Dodgson
David Gann

July 2021

Personal Acknowledgements from Marina Zhang

There is a long list of people I should thank apart from my coauthors, who have been my mentors, supporters, and inspirations. First of all, my husband Bruce has been an anchor in my life—his unconditional love and support indulge me to undertake adventures and offer a 'harbour' when I am tired and vulnerable. My daughters Rowena and Ingrid are the sources of my inspiration for pursuing truth and lifelong learning. When Rowena was back home from her study at Oxford University during the Covid-19 pandemic in the middle of 2020, she helped with data collection and analysis. Ingrid's optimistic and joyful nature brings me laughter and hope, despite her being a demanding teenager. Of course, I am deeply grateful to my parents, who not only gave me life, but also planted a seed in my mind to understand technology and how new and complex things work. Their dedication to, and service for, China's telecommunication industry during their entire career was exemplary. I must also mention my two cats—TimTam and Toulouse—elegant and quiet creatures who like to pretend they are 'philosophers', lost in deep thought when sitting next to me as I ponder what I will find next in the 'black box' of China's innovation machine.

Together with my research collaborators—including colleagues and students from Tsinghua University, UNSW, and Swinburne University, as well as former colleagues at IBM, Ericsson, and the start-up firms I co-started and worked in—I have conducted a large amount of empirical research, especially case studies of Chinese firms in the telecommunication, internet, semiconductor, biopharmaceutical, manufacturing, and other technology sectors. I owe a great deal to all of you. I am also greatly indebted to my friends and many anonymous interviewees, who were (and, in many cases, still are) in positions that enabled them to share valuable insights with me. Your perspectives helped me demystify China's innovation machine every time I got lost within the 'black box'.

Some of the individuals from whom I benefited for this book include (in alphabetic order) Simon Barker, Hong Cai, Satish Chand, Jin Chen, Minzhang Cheng, Shijuan Cui, Yongji Dong, Xueqian Du, Wei Fan, Jian Gao, Lei Guo, Michael Gilding, Peter Jen, Jizhen Li, Zhenfeng Li, Wenchen Lin, Shaun Liu, Xielin Liu, Yigong Liu, Hailong Luo, Wenjun Ouyang, Gordon Redding, Michaele Ricks, Curt Shi, Bruce Stening, Bill Wang, Qiang Wang, Yi Wang, Dong Wei, Wensheng Wei, Tao Wen,

Peter Williamson, Qing Wu, Yu Xia, Debiao Xiong, George Yang, Haidong Yang, Wei Yang, Xing Yang, Jing Ye, Shaker Zahra, Charles Zhang, Huiying Zhang, Wei Zhang, Haiping Zhao, Qing Zhou, and Hengyuan Zhu.

These people who contributed to the research for this book represent a diverse range of expertise in China's innovation, from multinational firms, technology firms/start-ups, venture incubators and accelerators, think tanks, venture capitalists and other investors, entrepreneurs, scientists and innovators, legal professionals, diplomats, researchers, professors, and policymakers. The list is nowhere near exhaustive. Apart from those who do not want their names made public, if I have forgotten anybody, it is not because you are not important; it is simply because my memory is fading. However, I vividly remember those sparkling discussions we had over meals, tea, or coffee.

I would also like to express my great appreciation to the many of my WeChat groups. In particular, I would like to mention the WeChat group of my 130 Peking University classmates who entered the study of Life Sciences in the same year as me. This group is not only an important and credible source for a deep understanding of advances in innovation—as many of them work in leading global biotechnology or pharmaceutical labs/firms, start-ups in biopharmaceuticals, or as scientists or investors in gene editing, AI, big data analytics, and other future technologies, in both the United States and China—but also as a 'home' for my mind and soul to which I feel I belong. In this group, we have a rule that different opinions must be injected into the group discussion from time to time to avoid the possibility of an 'echo chamber' in a group of people with such homogeneous backgrounds.

The 'crowd wisdom' I obtained for this book has been a manifestation of the central idea in this book: the chaotic order that China's innovation machine is the result of bottom-up evolution, facilitated by top-down, but pragmatic and adaptive policies. In other words, China's innovation machine is most effective in a policy environment where the market prevails. However, policy intervention plays a significant role when market mechanisms derail.

The sweeping pandemic of Covid-19 has changed our lives. The lockdowns for billions, and the loss of loved ones for millions were devastating. With the scientific breakthroughs of vaccines against the virus, we can be more confident than ever that technology and global collaboration in science and innovation will bring health, prosperity, and hope.

Finally, I would like to dedicate this book to Rowena and Ingrid. When they were young, they learned from me; however, increasingly I find I learn more from them—their quick embrace of new concepts, their fresh perspectives of a generation born in the new millennium, their passion for, and preoccupation with, the environment, sustainability, justice, and diversity, and, most importantly, their quest for a global view that is unbiased, inclusive and kind. You are the hope, my angels!

Marina Zhang

July 2021

Contents

List of Abbreviations

5G	fifth-generation mobile communications system
AI	artificial intelligence
API	active pharmaceutical ingredient
ASEAN	Association of Southeast Asian Nations
B2B	business-to-business
B2C	business-to-consumer
BRI	Belt and Road Initiative
C2C	consumer-to-consumer
C2M	customer-to-manufacturer
CAD	computer-aided design
CARG	compound annual growth rate
CAS	Chinese Academy of Sciences
ChiNext	A NASDAQ-style subsidiary of the Shenzhen Stock Exchange
CNIPA	China National Intellectual Property Administration, known as Sino IP Office before August 2018
Covid-19	coronavirus disease of 2019
CPC	Communist Party of China
CPS	cyber physical system
CRO	contract research organization
CVC	corporate venture capital
DC/EP	Digital Currency/Electronic Payment (the official name of China's e-RMB)
DRAM	dynamic random-access memory
e-commerce	electronic commerce
EDA	electronic design automation
EU	Europe Union
EUV	extreme ultraviolet
EV	electric vehicle
FDI	foreign direct investment
GDP	gross domestic product
GVC	global value chain
IC	integrated circuit
ICT	information and communications technology
IDM	integrated device manufacturers
IMT-2000	International Mobile Telecommunications *2000*
IoT	internet of things
IP	intellectual property
IPO	initial public offering
ISIC	International Standard Industrial Classification of All Economic Activities
JV	joint venture
LCD	liquid crystal display

m-commerce	mobile commerce
MIIT	Ministry of Industry and Information Technology
MNC	multinational corporation
MoC	Ministry of Commerce
MoST	Ministry of Science and Technology
NDRC	National Development and Reform Commission
NEV	new energy vehicle
NFC	near field communication
NIS	national innovation system
O2O	online-to-offline
ODM	original design manufacturing
OECD	Organization for Economic Cooperation and Development
OEM	original equipment manufacturer
OLED	organic light emitting diode (or organic LED)
P2P	peer-to-peer or person-to-person
PBOC	People's Bank of China
PCT	Patent Cooperation Treaty
PDK	process design kit
PE	private equity
POS	point of sale
PRC	People's Republic of China
QR code	quick response code
RAN	radio access network
R&D	research and development
RMB	renminbi, the name of Chinese currency
S&T	science and technology
SEZ	Special Economic Zone
SME	small and medium-sized enterprise
SMS	short messaging service
SOE	state-owned enterprise
STAR	Shanghai Stock Exchange Science and Technology Innovation Board
STEM	science, technology, engineering and mathematics
TFP	total factor productivity
TFT-LCD	thin film transistor liquid crystal display
UAV	unmanned aerial vehicle, commonly known as 'drone'
UID	unique identifier
US	United States
USPTO	United States Patent and Trademark Office
VC	venture capital
VR/AR	virtual reality/augmented reality
WAP	wireless access point
WHO	World Health Organization
WIPO	World Intellectual Property Organization
WTO	World Trade Organization

List of Figures

List of Tables

Introduction

China's extraordinary economic development is explained in large part by the way it innovates. This book explains how it innovates, which has important implications not only for China, but also for the rest of the world. Contrary to widely held views, China's innovation machine is not created and controlled by an all-powerful government. Instead, it is a complex, interdependent system composed of hundreds of millions of elements, involving bottom-up innovation driven by innovators and entrepreneurs at different levels and highly pragmatic and adaptive top-down policy. Using case studies of leading firms and industries, statistics, and policy analysis, the book argues that China's innovation machine is similar to a natural ecosystem. Bottom-up innovations in technology, organization, and business model resemble genetic mutations which are random, self-serving, and isolated initially, but the best-fitting are selected by the market and their impacts are amplified by the innovation machine. This machine draws on China's massive number of small manufacturers, efficient and resilient supply chains, local innovation clusters, and highly digitally literate population, connected through supersized digital platforms. Although innovation in China suffers from a lack of basic research and reliance upon certain critical technologies from overseas, its scale (size) and scope (diversity) possess attributes that make it self-correcting and stronger in the face of challenges, such as Covid-19 and global political and trade tensions. China's innovation machine is most effective in a policy environment where the market prevails; policy intervention plays a significant role when market mechanisms are premature or fail. The book concludes that the future success of China's innovation will depend on continuing policy pragmatism, maintaining support and encouragement for mass innovation and entrepreneurship, and the development of the nation's 'digital, smart, and innovative' new infrastructures.

Chapter 1 places China's innovation machine in context. It introduces its characteristics, including massive numbers of innovators embedded in China's manufacturing and supply chains that offer efficiency, flexibility, and resilience; the emergence of the digital economy; and pragmatic government policies that have seen the nation progress from catching up with world leaders to leading in some fields. It explains the importance of Chinese culture for innovation, and the ability of the nation to operate with 'multiple institutional logics' of state control and market forces. Challenges confronting China's innovation machine are outlined, including in some areas of advanced technology and basic research, the fracturing of globalization, and the reascendancy of central planning.

Chapter 2 shows how much China has caught up in the global innovation race, using international indices of innovation performance, and data on R&D

Demystifying China's Innovation Machine: Chaotic Order. Marina Yue Zhang, Mark Dodgson, and David M. Gann, Oxford University Press. © Marina Yue Zhang, Mark Dodgson, and David M. Gann 2022.
DOI: 10.1093/oso/9780198861171.001.0001

expenditures, higher education, scientific outputs, and patents. Frameworks such as 'windows of opportunity' are used to explore how China catches up in innovation and is changing policies from importing innovation to developing 'indigenous innovation'. The bottlenecks confronting China's catch-up and leadership are examined using the case of semiconductors, Huawei, and 5G, and the chapter poses the question whether the country can overcome such bottlenecks in core technologies. To do so, it is argued that greater investment is needed in basic research, especially by enterprises.

Chapter 3 demonstrates the importance of manufacturing in China's innovation machine. It explains the history of China's industrialization and how it overcame early challenges to become the 'world's factory'. It argues that China has since progressed to become the 'world's workshop', with the capability and capacity to translating complex designs into products with engineering precision and with unmatchable speed and scale. Examples are provided of large overseas companies attracted to manufacture in China, such as Tesla and Apple. It also examines a new model of mass customization facilitated by the country's super e-commerce platforms such as Alibaba and Pinduoduo, which connects consumers with hundreds of millions of SME manufacturers, including China's 'hidden champions' in niche areas of manufacturing. Chinese manufacturing possesses significant strengths in its resilience and flexibility, building upon its highly skilled workforce and digital infrastructure. The chapter shows how China's manufacturing is benefiting from recent trends that have moved production in global value chains to countries with lower labour costs.

Chapter 4 explains the development and significance of China's mega supply chains, and their position in the global division of labour. It explains the importance of modularity, standardization, and complementarity in supply chains. It analyses how efficiencies and resilience are achieved and balanced in supply chains, and the importance of 'platforms', both geographical clusters, such as industrial bases in Shenzhen, Chengdu, and Suzhou, and digital platforms, such as Alibaba and Pinduoduo. The chapter also argues that China's mega supply chains have become regional hubs supplying intermediate products to manufacturing facilities in countries with lower labour costs. The chapter discusses the extent to which China is progressing towards 'Industry 4.0', with smart supply chains, and how the country is responding to the challenges from growing global trade tensions.

China has one of the most advanced digital economies in the world. Chapter 5 analyses the rise of China's digital economy and the transformational effect of digital innovation on consumers and throughout China's economy and society. The 'platform of platforms' created by leading firms is critical in China's digital infrastructure, and the user data generated on these platforms is a new factor in Chinese productivity. The ability of the digital economy to build and address demand in China's highly differentiated markets is shown in cases such as Xiaomi. The chapter reveals the zigzag pattern of iterative interactions between technology entrepreneurs and policymakers. It presents a detailed case study of mobile payments, explaining such dynamic interactions between firm strategies, user endorsements, and government policies. The rise of the 'platform of platforms' has raised concerns about user data safety and fair market competition. The chapter discusses the social and political implications arising from powerful platform firms in the digital economy. It concludes with discussion of the importance of future technologies, including artificial intelligence and the internet of things, especially their applications in the industry internet.

Chapter 6 examines the growth of technology entrepreneurship in China. Compared to other professions such as public service or academia, entrepreneurship was not regarded highly in Chinese culture and was banned in the Mao era as 'walking on the road of capitalism'. It has now become a key element of China's innovation machine, and being an entrepreneur is an attractive career. The reforms in China's capital market, including venture capital investment, together with policy support under the banner of 'mass entrepreneurship and innovation' such as access to science and research, incubators and accelerators, and entrepreneurship education, are described. The case of the emerging biotechnology/biopharmaceutical industry is used to illustrate the importance of combining technology, talent, capital, and policy in technology entrepreneurship. Selected large and rapidly growing 'unicorns' are profiled, illustrating how entrepreneurial firms aiming to develop future technologies emerge and grow.

Chapter 7 analyses the different 'institutional logics' surrounding China's innovation machine, including the 'visible hand' of the state, and 'invisible hand' of the market. The idea of innovation in China resulting from centralized decisions in government is shown to be a myth; instead, it results from the interaction of initial bottom-up innovations and subsequent top-down direction, support, or correction. The cultural roots of China's multiple institutional logics are explained, including the role of hierarchy, tolerance of ambiguity, and search for unity. Balance is sought within Chinese bureaucracies, between central and local governments, and between formal and informal authority. The chapter analyses Chinese policy frameworks for science and technology, innovation, intellectual property, education and talent, environment, industry, and the reform of state-owned enterprises. A case study of the car industry is provided, focusing particularly on how policy instruments are used to encourage carmakers to capitalize on the opportunities presented by the new technology trajectory of new energy vehicles.

Chapter 8 explores how order emerges from chaos in China's innovation machine. It emphasizes how innovation is emergent, evolutionary, and complex and cannot be centrally planned and controlled. Innovation involves experimentation, the initial growth of which requires certain protection, but the scale and scope of which can be rapidly amplified in an interdependent digital economy. The challenges facing the innovation machine are outlined. These include the impact of the Covid-19 pandemic and the impending clash of political ideology between China and the West manifested by a technology cold war over issues such as technological standards. The chapter argues that, despite numbers of shortcomings, China's innovation machine is remarkably successful and robust, and can even strengthen as result of external pressures. It does, however, face specific internal policy challenges, including whether the government can maintain the pragmatism of recent policies with continued development of the market and requiring greater transparency on the nature and purpose of China's approach to innovation, and the nation's greater assumption of leadership roles in international forums. How China handles these challenges will significantly impact the future of global economic development and political cooperation.

1
China's Innovation Machine

China would not have become a superpower without its capacity to absorb, create, and diffuse innovation. We call this capacity 'China's innovation machine'. The constitution and future performance of this innovation machine not only is critical for China but is of great consequence for the rest of the world.

In this chapter we explain the nature of China's innovation machine and how it has been a crucial element of China's economic success. Three major elements of China's innovation machine are introduced, which will be elucidated further in subsequent chapters. The first is the nature of innovation itself. The changing nature of innovation allows Chinese companies and entrepreneurs to experiment with innovative ideas, allied to the opportunities presented by digital technologies. The nation's manufacturing power and supply chains, as well as its digital technological advances, illustrate how bottom-up pressures, even using low levels of technology, can evolve into an effectiveness-based model of innovation. The second is China's pragmatic and adaptive policy environment. From cultural and historical perspectives, we explain China's multi-institutional logics. The policy approach displays the pragmatism of an authoritarian and centralized political system prepared to encourage bottom-up innovation at a local level, but use top-down initiatives to rectify mistakes when markets underperform or derail. The third is the interactions between bottom-up and top-down forces in an interdependent ecosystem. We argue that China's resilient and agile innovation machine, driven by 'chaotic', bottom-up innovation and entrepreneurship, supported by adaptable and pragmatic policies, has the ability to successfully deal with future global challenges and opportunities. We also identify the shortcomings of China's innovation machine and, if the conditions supporting it cannot be sustained, how they could lead it to break down.

We conclude that China's innovation machine, while undoubtedly impressive and powerful, will face some significant trials ahead if it is to continue on the trajectory that has contributed so much to the country's economic success. To become a leader in science, technology, and innovation, China will need to adjust the balance of its R&D investments towards more basic research, and enhance the paths for connecting that research to its application. Its innovation policies will need to continue to display the pragmatism that has allowed industrial and business realities to override political doctrines. And in a geopolitical environment where globalization is in retreat and the momentum is towards a technological schism between China and the West, China will benefit from improving its transparency and openness by

Demystifying China's Innovation Machine: Chaotic Order. Marina Yue Zhang, Mark Dodgson, and David M. Gann,
Oxford University Press. © Marina Yue Zhang, Mark Dodgson, and David M. Gann 2022.
DOI: 10.1093/oso/9780198861171.003.0001

following existing global rules on the one hand and contributing to making new ones on the other.

Some Context

Why 'Innovation Machine'?

The standard of living and quality of life of the population in any country is determined to a significant extent by its historical accumulation of innovations and its ability to innovate. It is innovation—the successful application of new ideas that add value—and the skills, processes, and resources that marshal it that improve the performance of businesses and governments and provide the means to afford social and economic advances.

China's innovation performance, like every nation's, results from the actions of innovators: organizations and individuals prepared to create and apply novel improvements in technologies and business models for innovative value propositions, as well as users that are willing to adopt and improve innovative products and services. These innovative actors operate within the context of what is commonly called national systems of innovation, defined by the composition of a country's institutions—for example, in research, education, finance, and law—and by the quality of social and business relationships, such as the level of trust between people and organizations.[1]

We prefer the metaphor 'innovation machine', as it is less reliant on describing various elements and is more active and dynamic. The machine is comprised of numerous components, and these can include institutions. It produces actions to a purpose, and these can include social and economic advance. It needs to be powered (fuelled), and its operation needs to be eased (oiled), which can be allied to social and business relationships. The innovation machine both guides and is animated by the activities of innovative people and organizations. One value of the metaphor is that machines can break down, quickly and unexpectedly, and we explore the ability of China's innovation machine to withstand shocks, using the examples of the Covid-19 crisis and current trade tension.

Research into national innovation systems shows that the appetite and ability to innovate are deeply embedded within the particularities of countries. While many nations have similar institutional structures and social and business mores, and technologies and some business behaviours are ubiquitous, countries differ in the way they encourage, apply, and use innovations. They have different innovation machines. This relates to their distinctive histories, politics, religions, and industrial

---

[1] R. R. Nelson and S. G. Winter (1982), *An Evolutionary Theory of Economic Change*, Cambridge, MA: Harvard University Press. B. A. Lundvall (1992), *National Innovation Systems: Towards a Theory of Innovation and Interactive Learning*, London: Pinter.

and social structures. For this reason, China's innovation machine is significantly different from other leading nations.

China's Size and Scale

In the broad sweep of history, China's greatest advantage in the world results from the sheer size of its population. The massive size of Chinese market is the engine for its economic growth, affecting the global economy and geopolitics.

China is the world's largest country by population: 1.4 billion; 18 per cent of the world's total. It has the second largest GDP after the United States (67 per cent of that of the US in 2019, and it grew at 2.3 per cent in 2020). Its size is also shown in the scale of its infrastructure and its industrial structure. China has four of the world's top twenty busiest airports by passenger numbers; seven of the top ten ports in shipment volume; twenty-two (plus five under construction) out of the world's seventy-one largest hydroelectricity power stations; and eighty-six (plus fifteen under construction) of the world's 107 highest bridges.[2] China also has the world's most extensive high-speed railway networks, over 39,000 km, which is 70 per cent of the world's total (by the end of 2020). China is the only country in the world that possesses all industry categories defined by the International Standard Industrial Classification of All Economic Activities (ISIC).

In 2019, on the list of Fortune 500 companies measured by revenue, 129 were from China (including ten from Hong Kong), the first time China had more firms listed than the US (which had 120 in total).[3] Although the majority of the mainland firms are state-owned enterprises (SOEs) in the banking, energy, and property sectors, several technology companies, including Huawei, were listed among the top 100. Together with Amazon, Alphabet (Google), and Facebook, China's Alibaba, JD, Tencent, and Xiaomi were listed as the world's top internet companies. Firms such as Sany Heavy Industry, Geely Automobile, and Haier are leaders in their respective industries in the global arena. A country's Fortune 500 companies can indicate its economic size and market strength.

One of the most striking elements of China's size advantages lies in its skilled workforce. China educates the largest number of graduates in STEM (science, technology, engineering, and mathematics), with more than the total of the next six countries combined (India, the US, Russia, Iran, Indonesia and Japan).[4] While China may have lost its low-cost labour advantage to countries such as Vietnam and Mexico, the vast pool of its engineers has become a new comparative advantage

---

[2] This list of highest bridges includes bridges with a deck height of at least 200 metres (660 ft). The *deck height* of a bridge is the maximum vertical drop distance between the bridge deck (the road, rail or other transport bed of a bridge) and the ground or water surface beneath the bridge span (https://en.wikipedia. org/wiki/List_of_highest_bridges, accessed 19 July 2021).

[3] See the full list at https://fortune.com/fortune500/, accessed 19 July 2021.

[4] See http://english.www.gov.cn/statecouncil/ministries/202012/01/content_WS5fc63051c6d0f72576 941058.html, accessed 19 July 2021.

which cannot be easily matched by any other country. The advantage lies in millions of engineers who can not only design products but adapt and manufacture them for the mass market. The scale advantage of engineers enables China to conduct large-scale experimentation and data collection in emerging industries, which provides great benefit, for example, in feeding AI applications with big data.

On the demand side, China's GDP per capita rose from about $3,300 to $10,000 during the 2010s. This means that about 400 million Chinese are middle-class consumers, the largest such market in the world, according to World Bank measures.[5] China's consumer market, however, is highly differentiated. It is multifaceted, dynamic, and complex, and traditional market segmentation categories do not apply. Each of its niche markets is massive and, in this sense, China's consumer market has both scale and scope.

China's e-commerce platform, Pinduoduo (PDD), which provides consumers with group-buying deals for better prices, is an example of the importance of niche but large markets. The company was established in 2015 when China's e-commerce market seemed well established and occupied by Alibaba and JD, among many specialized firms. Yet by 2018, PDD had attracted over 200 million users in the niche market of middle-aged consumers in smaller cities searching for deep discounts. This market niche led the company to be listed on the US stock exchange, NASDAQ, in 2018, three years after its founding. To appreciate the size of niche markets in China, the relatively small market of online gaming is larger in value than the substantial car industries in Turkey or Thailand. We will discuss how PDD expanded into those niche markets using AI algorithms and big data analytics, and pioneered the transformation of China's manufacturing to smart manufacturing, in Chapter 3.

In 2019, South Korea's Samsung closed its last factory in Huizhou, Guangdong province, moving its entire mobile handset manufacturing out of China. Part of the reason for the move was the search for cheaper labour in countries such as Vietnam, but it more broadly reflected how, once a top brand, Samsung had lost its battle in China's mobile phone market. Its market share dropped from 20 per cent in 2013 to less than 1 per cent in 2019.[6] Consumers in large cities are attracted by companies such as Apple and Huawei for their brands and features; consumers in smaller cities, counties, and towns are attracted by the price of Xiaomi, and other domestic brands such as OPPO and Vivo; and rural consumers have their own choices of non-branded copycat products. In China's administrative system, there are 33 provinces, 333 cities, 2,862 counties, 41,658 towns, and 662,238 villages. Multinational firms find it hard to reach any markets below second-tier cities. Chinese firms, in contrast, often start building their base in lower-tier cities, counties, and towns. Xiaomi's success, for example, was built on its nationwide county showrooms and village deliveries on its own e-commerce platform. The success of mobile handset brands Vivo and

[5] See https://www.worldbank.org/content/dam/Worldbank/document/MIC-Forum-Rise-of-the-Middle-Class-SM13.pdf, accessed 19 July 2021.
[6] See https://www.statista.com/statistics/430749/china-smartphone-shipments-vendor-market-share/, accessed July 19 2021.

OPPO was built on extensive sales channels at the township level. Samsung's retreat suggests that scale in China needs to be accompanied by disaggregated, fragmented, and local knowledge.

Covid-19

In 2020, the novel coronavirus Covid-19 pandemic broke out in China's central city, Wuhan. After an initial attempt by the local government to hide the virus from the public, the central government made a radical decision to lock down Wuhan days before the Chinese New Year national holiday. A pause button was pressed on the Chinese economy, not just on the 11 million citizens in Wuhan but the rest of the 1.4 billion Chinese who went into self-quarantine. Using centralized authority, the country contained the spread of the deadly virus at the cost of many lives in Wuhan and a suspension of the economy in the country. Wuhan is not only a supply centre for critical components in the car and pharmaceutical industries, but also a hub city connecting the country's supply chain networks. The lockdown of the city caused many enterprises nationwide to slow down or stop production because of shortages in the supply of critical components. Effectively, there was a two-month pause in China's supply chains.

The Chinese political system revealed its shortcomings and advantages during the outbreak of Covid-19. Local officials in Wuhan had incentives to hide the truth about the virus from their seniors and the people, as they feared news of the crisis could challenge their authority. Such a reaction is not unusual; as Francis Fukuyama argues, all governments, whatever their ideology and political values, have incentives to downplay the seriousness of any unknown virus.[7] What is unusual is the scale of the response by the central government. A short period of initial chaos was replaced by a long period of great discipline and order. We will explain this phenomenon using China's cultural roots and institutional logics in Chapter 7.

As they are likely to be profound, the consequences of Covid-19 for China's innovation machine will be discussed throughout this book. The virus provided, for example, an unwelcome stress test for the deep embeddedness of China in global supply chains and manufacturing capacity. Viruses do not respect national boundaries. When Covid-19 spread all over the world and became a pandemic, many countries imposed widespread restrictions on the mobility of people and goods. The direct impact of such restrictions caused serious shortages of supplies (essential medicines, personal protection equipment, including face masks, and critical medical equipment such as respirators and ventilators) for health systems in many countries. The crisis forced many nations to recognize the importance of independent

---

[7] F. Fukuyama (2020), 'The Thing That Determines a Country's Resistance to the Coronavirus: The major dividing line in effective crisis response will not place autocracies on one side and democracies on the other', *The Atlantic*, 30 March, https://www.theatlantic.com/ideas/archive/2020/03/thing-determines-how-well-countries-respond-coronavirus/609025/, accessed 19 July 2021.

supply chains and manufacturing capacity of their own or of their close allies. The question arises what future supply chains will look like, and, for example, if rebuilding or onshoring national manufacturing capacity is attempted, whether this strategy may help to rebuild the first few tiers of the global supply chain, while most components at the lower tiers of industrial production still remain in China.

Another immediate consequence of the virus for China was the way that, with its advanced digital platforms and sophisticated logistics networks, most people in the country maintained a relatively normal life during the quarantine by means of online education, conferencing/meeting, shopping, and socializing, supported by efficient delivery services. Covid-19 starkly revealed how being digital and being connected are the new normal in modern society.

It is often held in the West that the word 'crisis' in Chinese combines danger and opportunity. Irrespective of the accuracy of this interpretation, the Covid-19 crisis has, in addition to its diabolical consequences, also provided opportunities for Chinese firms. TikTok, for example, became a global product during the lockdown, and Alibaba entered new markets, providing competition for Amazon.[8]

The implications of Covid-19 on China's innovation machine will be discussed in Chapter 8.

China's Success Story

China was the world's most advanced technological power for most of human history. By the end of the seventeenth century, however, it had been overtaken by Europe, and since then has endured a 200-year interregnum in scientific and technological progress, due to wars, natural disasters, and internal turmoil. Since the 1980s, when the country started its economic reforms and opened up to the outside world, China has stepped back onto the world stage and is rapidly catching up in scientific and technological innovation. In this relatively short period, China has lifted over 750 million people out of poverty.[9] In absolute values in areas such as R&D expenditure and the number of researchers, patents, and publications, China is now ranked first or second in the world, with volumes that overshadow most high-income economies. Examples of its scientific and technological prowess include the development of the world's fastest supercomputer, its first single-aisle jet aircraft, high-speed rail networks, fifth-generation (5G) communication networks, and the ability to land a spaceship on Mars, along with a plethora of world-leading innovations in the digital economy.

According to the Global Innovation Index (GII) jointly published by the World Intellectual Property Organization (WIPO), Cornell University, and INSEAD, in

---

[8] R. McMorrow and N. Liu (2020), 'How a Pandemic Led the World to Start Shopping on Alibaba', *Financial Times*, 28 April.

[9] See https://www.cnbc.com/2021/03/01/chinas-spending-on-rd-hits-a-record-378-billion.html, accessed 19 July 2021.

2020 China was ranked the world's fourteenth most innovative country, out of 131.[10] In 2013, it was ranked thirty-fifth. This rapid catch-up in innovation is reflected in the acceleration in China's R&D intensity: the ratio of a country's total R&D spending to its GDP. According to the OECD, it takes a long time for a country to reach an R&D intensity of 1 per cent; however, once past this threshold, it is likely to see a take-off in R&D intensity, quickly approaching 2 per cent and then levelling off at around 2–3 per cent.[11] From around 1 per cent in 2000, it took China thirteen years to achieve about 2 per cent in R&D intensity. In 2020 China's R&D intensity reached 2.4 per cent.[12] This increase in expenditure, measured by absolute value, indicates a huge leapfrog in R&D spending, given China's GDP grew from $9.57 trillion to $14.7 trillion during the same period.[13]

Chapter 2 provides more statistics and analysis to explain China's technological catch-up.

Manufacturing and Supply Chains

In 2015 China's leaders announced a ten-year, $300 billion, strategy for upgrading China's manufacturing sector. *Made in China 2025* aims to build advanced manufacturing and make its semiconductor, new and electric vehicle, artificial intelligence, and other high-tech industries, as good as any in the world, if not better. It was a declaration that China was no longer content with being the world's factory.

Around the turn of this century, Western multinational corporations began increasingly to establish manufacturing facilities with joint venture partners as entry tickets to China's booming markets. They also invested because of low-cost labour and land. In recent years, however, skilled labour and land are no longer cheap in the Eastern coastal cities. The fact that many factories there did not move westwards to inland cities for cheaper options suggests that there are other factors underlying the success of China's manufacturing.

In Northern Huaqiang Street in Shenzhen—a city that grew out of what was a small fishing village in Guangdong province in the 1980s and today is home to over 20 million people and many of China's high-tech enterprises—it is easily possible to source and assemble a smartphone from scratch in a few hours. One can find designs and components for almost every kind of electronic products, from automatic translators to unmanned aerial vehicles/drones, in a street less than two kilometres long. Underlying this capacity is the development of China's supply chains and manufacturing capacity in electrical and electronic industries. Shenzhen's success was not

---

[10]   See https://www.wipo.int/edocs/pubdocs/en/wipo_pub_gii_2020/cn.pdf, accessed 19 July 2021.

[11]   See https://www.oecd-ilibrary.org/docserver/670385851815.pdf?expires=1612831575&id=id&accname=guest&checksum=F9D42D483FA89EAA6915B157A87EAA0A, accessed 19 July 2021.

[12]   See https://www.scmp.com/news/china/science/article/2189427/chinas-funding-science-and-research-reach-25-cent-gdp-2019, accessed 19 July 2021.

[13]   See https://data.worldbank.org/indicator/NY.GDP.MKTP.CD?locations=CN, accessed 19 July 2021.

due to the policies of central planning. Instead, Shenzhen has been one of the most market-oriented cities, where the city government has been praised for being the 'people's servants'.

Shenzhen was the first 'special economic zone' in China, and in the 1980s became home to the original equipment manufacturer (OEM) factories for many multi-nationals. A relaxed policy environment and fast economic development attracted not just foreign investment, but also Chinese entrepreneurs who were willing to take risks and were unafraid to start a new life in this brand-new city. Yuehai Subdistrict of Nanshan District (one of nine in Shenzhen), an area of about 15 square kilometres, is home of Shenzhen High-Tech Industrial Park, which hosts many Chinese technology firms, including Tencent, Huawei, and ZTE. Eighty-seven high-tech firms from this park have been listed on stock exchanges in China, Hong Kong, and the US. Its GDP exceeds that of many capital cities.[14] Unlike Beijing and Shanghai, China's political and financial centres respectively, which show a strong siphoning effect of talent, capital, and policy from their surrounding regions, Shenzhen is a city with strong spillover effects. Over the decades, the Greater Bay Area of the Pearl River Delta, with Shenzhen at its centre, has become a hub of China's supply chains and manufacturing power, connecting nine surrounding cities in Guangdong.

In November 2019, Tesla announced a $2 billion investment in China to produce its Model 3 and Model Y electric vehicles. Tesla's entry to China was controversial at the time: the tension of trade conflicts between the US and China was intense and China's domestic electric vehicle market was crowded. Reactions to Tesla's announcement differed, with speculation that the deal would either make or break the company. Numerous questions arose, from concern that the Chinese government would force Tesla to transfer its technology to local firms to whether it could avoid losing its core technology to Chinese rivals and achieve the mass production it sought. Despite all those doubts, Tesla fulfilled its promise by not only delivering its Model 3 and Model Y to China's market but also reducing their prices as more local suppliers were used. Tesla's success in Shanghai made its owner Elon Musk the richest man in the world by the end of 2020. What is clear is that Tesla's decision to build one of its largest electric vehicle mega factories in China is revealing of the risks prepared to be taken to access Chinese manufacturing capability and its extensive supply chains.

Apple's success with its iPhone is due primarily to its creative designs and marketing and sales. Without Chinese manufacturing, however, Apple's iPhone prices would be significantly higher. In 2015, thirty of Apple's thirty-three OEM factories were in China, sourcing 44.9 per cent of its supplies from local supply chains. In 2019, fifty-two of its fifty-nine OEM factories were in China, sourcing 47.6 per cent of the supplies locally. Foxconn, Apple's largest OEM partner, operates the world's largest yet most efficient and flexible factories and is one of the world's greatest users of advanced robotics. Foxconn has the engineering capability and capacity to mass-produce complex and advanced designs with precision. In such processes,

---

[14] See https://en.wikipedia.org/wiki/Nanshan_District,_Shenzhen, accessed 19 July 2021.

manufacturing is not simply assembly lines connecting together existing components following pre-specified instructions; they are workshops that allow experimentation in production and process innovation. This type of innovation involves tacit knowledge-based skills and craftsmanship at a mass scale. China's massive workforce with STEM degrees in those factories underlies its capacity for mass manufacturing complex-technology products with precision and at low cost.

The capacity to make things better, cheaper, faster, and more efficiently is a type of process innovation with an exploitation orientation, empowered by experienced engineers and workers, and holds the key to attracting foreign investors such as Tesla and Apple. In this process, innovators use a kind of effectiveness-driven mentality which enables firms to source, allocate, and match dispersed resources, raw materials, talented employees, and technologies (sometimes suboptimal or even obsolete ones from other countries), and translate them into products for the market in the shortest time and at the lowest costs. As an example, in 2008, Chinese wind turbine manufacturer Goldwind spent €41.2 million acquiring 70 per cent of the German wind turbine design firm Vensys and its core intellectual property. At the time of the acquisition, Goldwind was outbid by several European manufacturers, none of whom, however, could solve the problem of mass-producing Vensys' design, and were therefore unsuccessful in their bids. Five years after the acquisition, Goldwind became the world's largest wind turbine manufacturer and Vensys a global leader in wind turbine design.[15] This type of manufacturing capacity becomes a new hub connecting innovation with the market in the global value chain.

Alongside the scale of China's manufacturing capacity are its massive, flexible, and efficient supply chain networks. The country has the world's largest network of suppliers, comprised of countless small and micro enterprises. Each of these enterprises is highly specialized, which increases efficiency in production. Each is centred around a product family or industry value chain in regional clusters, connected to the national supply chain and logistic ecosystem by advanced digital platforms run by the country's technology giants such as Alibaba, Tencent, JD, and PDD.

The flexibility and efficiency of this network derives from matching supply and demand, and optimizing operations in production and logistics. The entire supply chains form interconnected and interdependent ecosystems, which increases their resilience. Within this system, many clusters have been formed to share R&D, operational knowledge, and sometimes customer experience on joint platforms. Although the size of the ecosystems may stay stable over time, their composition can change frequently. There are new entrants and business failures every day. This self-rectification upgrades innovation capability at the system level, with weaker firms failing and new entrants bringing progressive improvements. Chinese supply chain networks comprise hundreds of millions of innovators, entrepreneurs, engineers, and workers capitalizing on windows of opportunity opened by shifts in technological change and consumer demand at a global scale.

---

[15] See https://en.wikipedia.org/wiki/Goldwind, accessed 19 July 2021.

Since the US/China trade conflicts in 2018, Chinese manufacturing capacity has moved overseas, especially to Vietnam and India. But this is not a transfer of manufacturing capability; it is more accurately the spillover of Chinese supply chains into those countries for material, labour, and tariff advantages. In other words, manufacturing in those countries is still part of China's mega supply chain networks. Somewhat paradoxically, while the 2008 financial crisis was disruptive, it also consolidated and strengthened Chinese manufacturing by forcing it to move up the global value chain. Over the past decade, China has transformed from the 'world factory' making low-end goods to the 'world manufacturing laboratory' where creative innovations are translated into complex products for the mass market.

The contribution made by China's manufacturing capability in global innovation value chains has often been undervalued. In the traditional view of industry value chains (i.e. the smiley curve of value adding), manufacturing is on the lowest point, with the high points being R&D and design at the one end and marketing and sales at the other. The innovation in China's manufacturing sector has often been overshadowed by the brilliant designs that emerge elsewhere (the Chinese call these 'black technology'—a term used to describe technological advancements that are changing the ways we live and see the world). Yet China's unique manufacturing power is an inseparable part of the global innovation value chain. In the journey from research and design to product, China has many companies such as Foxconn that rapidly ramp up large-scale production of advanced-technology products and quickly bring innovations to market. China has become the world's workshop in translating technology into mass production. Relative to R&D-driven or design-based innovation, Chinese innovation has greater strengths in production and process innovation.

In Chapters 3 and 4, we uncover the myth of China's supposedly low-innovation manufacturing sector and its super supply chain networks, and analyse their contributions to China's innovation machine.

Digital Economy

There were over 989 million internet users in China, about one fifth of the world's total, with over 99.7 per cent accessing the internet via their smartphones by December 2020.[16] China's digital economy contributed 36 per cent of the country's GDP in 2019.[17] Its digital firms, including its sharing and platform-enabled businesses, characterize its technological success. Previously, such technology-based firms simply copied established business models from developed countries. The new generation of Chinese firms has emerged and thriven by means of technological

[16] China Internet Network Information Center (CNNIC) (2020), 'The 47th China Statistical Report on Internet Development', https://www.cnnic.com.cn/IDR/ReportDownloads/202104/P02021042055730 21 72744.pdf, accessed 20 July 2021.

[17] IMF (2019), 'China's Digital Economy: Opportunities and Risks', IMF Working Paper.

innovation, capital support from both domestic and global sources, and adept use of enthusiastic consumers of innovation connected via their mobile phones in the world's largest market.

Important in this journey was the launch of Weibo in 2009. Weibo is a Twitter-like microblog platform based on China's internet portal, sina.com. Weibo marked the beginning of what has been called China 2.0 when individuals became broad-casters and media contributors.[18] Weibo has around 450 million monthly users in China, where Twitter and Facebook are blocked by the government.

In 2011, Tencent, another internet giant, launched WeChat, its social media plat-form on mobile devices. WeChat disrupted the entire social media landscape in China. Weibo enables individuals to be connected with strangers, and hosts news, opinion, and endorsements, in a model of 'one to many'. WeChat, in contrast, opened a new era of 'pervasive connectivity', which enables individuals to be connected point to point in a massively connected network. WeChat had over 1.24 billion monthly active users by March 2021.[19]

In 2012, Xiaomi launched its smartphones. Xiaomi literally means 'millet', the small grain used to complement rice in Chinese diet. As a newcomer in the mobile phone business, where many incumbent global and domestic manufacturers com-pete fiercely, Xiaomi quickly won market share with its low-cost, but attractively designed products. Xiaomi's business model is based on its extensive ecosystem where its customers, suppliers, and app developers are connected and collectively contribute to product design and upgrades. Xiaomi has popularized smartphones among millions of Chinese and was the third largest mobile phone manufacturer in the world by the end of third quarter of 2020.[20] Xiaomi entered the Fortune 500 list in 2019 when it was only 9 years old.

The rapid adoption of smartphones helped the diffusion of WeChat, many mobile phone-based businesses, including the location-based services of ride-hailing com-panies such as Didi and Kuaidi (which were merged to become Didi Chuxing), and real-time lifestyle applications based on user-generated content such as Dazhong Dianping and Meituan (which were merged to become Meituan Dianping). TikTok is another product in this category, providing the means for users to create and share their own short videos. It is popular worldwide, with close to 700 million active users in January 2021, most of them aged between 16 and 24. TikTok is owned by the Chinese technology company, ByteDance, which was founded in 2012. Using advanced algorithms and AI technology, ByteDance began by launching its mobile phone-based news portal, Today's Headlines ('jin ri tou tiao'), which pushes news to individuals on the basis of their search history and personal preferences. 'Jin ri tou tiao' quickly disrupted the dominance of Baidu, a PC-based search engine and news

---

[18] M. Y. Zhang (2010), *China 2.0: The Transformation of an Emerging Superpower...and the New Opportunities*, Singapore: Wiley & Sons.

[19] See https://www.statista.com/statistics/255778/number-of-active-wechat-messenger-accounts/, accessed 19 July 2021.

[20] See https://www.idc.com/promo/smartphone-market-share/vendor, accessed 19 July 2021.

portal. In 2016, ByteDance launched its short-video platform, Douyin, in China, and in 2017, it introduced TikTok, Douyin's English version, globally. In 2019, ByteDance launched an enterprise product, Lark. In 2021, ByteDance's value was estimated as high as $140 billion, the highest-valued start-up in the world,[21] despite its global businesses having been affected by the political controversies surrounding TikTok in countries such as the United States.

These firms are not just innovators in technology and business models: they form interdependent ecosystems that have changed many industrial structures, including supply chains and manufacturing systems, as well as consumers' behaviour. China's digital economy has arisen through an evolutionary process driven by technological advances enabled by the bandwidth of the country's advanced communication infrastructures and adaptive policy support. As a result of the development of the digital economy, the power of discourse of issues related to the country and its people has shifted towards citizens. Collectively, they shape the trends of consumption, entertainment, and even culture.

In Chapter 5, we analyse the emergence and development of China's digital economy and discuss its significance in China's innovation machine.

Chinese Industry and Innovation Policy

After the foundation of the People's Republic of China in 1949, the government set out to build a new socialist country. As it emerged from two centuries of being suppressed and humiliated by what Mao Zedong called the 'three big mountains of imperialism, feudalism, and bureaucrat-capitalism', catching up with the developed world became an overarching ambition. Catching up with modern industry was needed to meet the country's enormous challenges of feeding and improving the living standards of a vast and growing population, as well as maintaining social stability.

Catching-Up Mentality

In the late 1950s and early 1960s, under Chairman Mao's mandate, China started a 'Great Leap Forward Campaign', aiming to fast-track its industrialization. Amongst its absurdities, millions of people were forced to sacrifice their cooking utensils to make iron and steel in 'home-made' blast furnaces. The result was a disaster. The campaign, intended to solve national problems through industrialization, was distorted, as ideology prioritized the theoretical over the practical.

---

[21] See https://www.statista.com/chart/19317/highest-valued-startup-companies-in-the-world/, accessed 19 July 2021.

There were, however, some significant scientific achievements in this period. Projects important to national defence and international reputation, or 'face', were launched, including nuclear, rocket, and satellite research, designated as the 'Two Bombs and One Satellite' programme. It was supported by state power and led by the country's top scientists, most of whom returned after being trained in the US or Europe, and China celebrated the success of its catch-up in nuclear power in 1964 and satellite launch in 1970, which demonstrated to the Soviets and the Americans that China was a peer in strategic technology and could independently deliver such scientific programmes.

China's progress in science and technology as an input to innovation, however, was completely curtailed during the disastrous decade of the Cultural Revolution. It was not until 1978 that the nation's paramount leader Deng Xiaoping claimed 'science and technology are primary productivity forces', recognizing the importance of science and technology above class struggle. The Communist Party of China (CPC) also realized that economic growth through catching up in science and technology is the means not only for achieving social prosperity and economic growth, but also for cementing its own legitimacy as the ruling party.

China is sometimes accused of taking a nationalist approach to innovation.[22] It is not the first country to do so. The Eisenhower administration in the US used federal funding, national laboratories, research institutes, and companies to support the development of technology for military purposes that also had commercial value. China's Asian neighbours, such as Japan and South Korea, all adopted this type of nationalist approach to develop their innovation capability for catching up in various industries. Kim Linsu, writing about South Korea's catch-up, suggested there are several distinctive stages a nation can take in catching up: transferring foreign technology, effectively diffusing imported technology and upgrading technological capability, developing local efforts to assimilate, adapt, and improve imported technology, and finally developing its own.[23] This model can be described as 'linkage-learning-leverage'.[24]

Learning from the policies of other Asian catching-up countries, such as Japan in the 1960s, South Korea in the 1970s, and Taiwan in the 1980s, China has developed its own pattern.[25] Before 2013, China's catch-up in innovation concentrated on developing production and basic innovation capability, which was largely achieved through the acquisition, adaptation, and application of existing knowledge. Inward foreign direct investment (FDI), largely in the format of Sino-foreign joint ventures,

[22] See, for example, S. Hansen (2014), 'Techno-Nationalism in China's Rise: The Next Gunpowder Moment', *The Strategist*, Australia Strategic Policy Institute, 14 October, https://www.aspistrategist.org.au/techno-nationalism-in-chinas-rise-the-next-gunpowder-moment/, accessed 19 July 2021.

[23] L. Kim (1997), *Imitation to Innovation: The Dynamics of Korea's Technological Learning*, Cambridge, MA: Harvard Business School Press.

[24] J. A. Mathews (2006), 'Dragon Multinationals: New Players in 21st Century Globalization', *Asia Pacific Journal of Management*, 23, 5–27.

[25] M. Dodgson (2009), 'Asia's National Innovation Systems: Institutional Adaptability and Rigidity in the Face of Global Innovation Challenges', *Asia Pacific Journal of Management*, 26, 589–609.

helped Chinese firms develop production technologies and expertise. Since this time, however, China has developed more advanced technological innovation capability in targeted and emerging industries, moving from 'creative adaptation' to 'creative innovation'. Success during this period can be attributed to the ability to 'learn quickly, upgrade quickly, and scale-up quickly'.

At the national level, using various institutional instruments, the government supports the development of innovation capabilities in strategic projects or industries, largely through being a follower of mature technologies in advanced countries. For emerging technologies, such as nanotechnology and quantum computing, the government aims to increase national technological capabilities through different forms of policy interventions.

For high-tech industries or projects significant to its national strategy, the Chinese government encourages developing independent innovation capability and indigenous technologies. For R&D projects in 5G networks, new energy sources, and electric vehicles, for example, the government provides support through public procurement, special tax incentives, and unconditional research grants, as well as subsidies at both the supply and the demand sides. After such projects have demonstrated their potential and reached a certain level of development, policies pragmatically let market forces determine their future direction. From the supply side, enterprises developing radical innovations are supported by policy instruments such as the use of national standards. In the early days of the electric vehicle (EV) industry, the government provided substantial subsidies to both electric vehicle manufacturers and consumers. As the market mechanism has kicked in, it is competition which will determine the winners and the losers at the supply side.

For complex product systems such as passenger jets, where China has little advantage, the dominant pattern of catching up is path-following of incumbents from advanced countries.

For lower-tech industries, the government uses different instruments to provide guidance and financial support, while encouraging competition to screen and identify champions. Low-tech, low-priced innovations often produce 'illegal' products. China's copycat mobile phone manufacturing industry was a case in point. In its early days, the government 'kept one eye shut, one eye open' to its development. After the sector developed basic production capability and innovative business models, the government started to break up illegal manufacturers through multiple judicial actions, whilst awarding those with key technologies. This policy led to the rise of global brands such as Huawei and Xiaomi. Less successful companies, such as Bird, turned to supply less developed markets in India and Africa. The least successful ones became component suppliers or went out of business.

China's rapid rise in strategically significant projects has been underpinned by an industrial policy characterized by 'concentrating strengths to do great things'. National interests are reflected in these projects in which the central government fully exerts its overall coordination role for allocating resources and influencing markets. This is done in the context of state ownership accounting for a major proportion of the Chinese economy, providing the foundation for a top-down approach to innovation. State ownership can guarantee the implementation of projects for which political importance overrides economic returns. This top-down approach gives leeway for the central government to intervene in, allocate public resources to, and monitor the economy when a market logic fails to deliver on its expectations, and empowers it to act during times of crisis or urgency. This top-down approach is like a 'visible hand' influencing firms' behaviour. It is not uncommon for firms to have rent-seeking behaviours by actively building personal connections (*guanxi*) with the government bureaucracy, hoping to be protected when needed. This 'visible hand' may rectify the market when it fails to work, but it may also lead to opportunism or unfair competition. This mentality only works when the target for catching-up is visible and its technological trajectory is stable. As China has now achieved its catch-up goals in production and basic innovation capabilities, a different and more diverse approach to innovation will be more effective in the future.

Mass Entrepreneurship and Innovation

A policy shift since the global financial crisis of 2008 has seen the rise of technology entrepreneurship as the government determined to offset the pressures of the economic slowdown, especially its result of increasing the unemployment of university graduates. Such a policy shift was a result of lessons learned from the success of innovative clusters such as Silicon Valley. The Chinese government has promoted entrepreneurial activity largely by providing financing and policy support, as well as reforming the investment community, including venture capital and private equity investment, and the nation's capital market.

In 2014, 'mass entrepreneurship and innovation' was proposed as an engine for China's growth. Between 2015 and 2018, the term entrepreneurship was closely linked with innovation in many State Council documents, aiming to stimulate creativity and develop innovation-driven entrepreneurship as a new national strategy for growth.

Successful ventures have emerged from entrepreneurial clusters in Beijing, Shenzhen, Hangzhou, and several other locations. As an illustration, there is a coffee shop named 'The Garage Coffee' on Entrepreneurship Road in Haidian District in Beijing, where the country's top universities, including Peking University, Tsinghua University, and many research institutes of the Chinese Academy of Sciences, are located. This is the first themed cafe that provides a place where young entrepreneurs can gather to discuss their start-up ideas with potential investors.[26] Most Chinese live in apartment blocks and do not have the mythical garage as start-up

---

[26] The Garage Coffee was visited by China's Premier Li Keqing on 21 May 2015. See reports on https://ihouse.ifeng.com/news/2015_05_21-50400306_0.shtml, accessed 19 July 2021.

venues, but the use of such imagery is indicative of the government's policy of encouraging 'mass entrepreneurship and innovation'.

In Chapter 6, we discuss China's approach to technology entrepreneurship and its significant implications for innovation.

Chinese Culture and Innovation

To understand innovation in China it is necessary to appreciate its cultural underpinnings. The legacy of Confucianism is real and strong in Chinese culture. Confucianism has deep roots in China's civilization, with high value placed on authority and harmonious relationships with extended family, community, and nature, along with long-term perspectives, high tolerance of ambiguity, and competitiveness with external groups. Confucian social harmony is maintained largely because of moral doctrines ensuring the enforcement of 'civilized conduct' by following hierarchical relationship rules. In this sense, Confucian morality, not just laws and rules, governs China.

Unity has been the single most important political value to define and maintain Chinese culture. The need for unity has been used by China's rulers for generations to defend against any threat from internal rebellions or external invasions. Relatedly, throughout Chinese history, outsiders were considered evil, which produced strong resistance to external forces and influences.

The Chinese language has been a bond maintaining unity. Despite speaking hundreds of regional dialects, the Chinese language has had only the one written form since the Qin Dynasty some 2,500 years ago. The pictographic nature of the language provides another foundation of Chinese civilization. Unlike alphabet-based languages that emphasize sequences of letters, the Chinese language focuses on wholeness of all elements in pictographic characters. Languages influence people's cognitions, with Chinese people tending towards more holistic processing of information.[27] While the Chinese language is rich in describing relations and degrees of emotions, it is vague in precision. For example, '*I*' has over twenty different expressions according to the context where '*I*' is relatively positioned. As examples of ambiguity, size in Chinese is '*da xiao*' (big or small) or '*chi cun*' (foot or inch).

High tolerance of ambiguity is not just manifested in the language. The 'middle way', the highest philosophical 'state of mind' in Taoism—a balanced state between *yin* (passive) and *yang* (active) forces—is the foundation of Chinese holistic cognition and pragmatic attitudes in life. This philosophy has pervasive effects on behaviours, which react against going to extremes: not too good or too bad, not too left or too right, not too black or too white. The best solution to any problem arises, in this world view, from a compromised solution which allows all sides to maintain valid

---

[27] See more in G. Redding (1990), *The Spirit of Chinese Capitalism*, Berlin: de Gruyter.

positions, even though they can be contradictory. Finding a middle way is the essence of Confucianism.

These cultural traits can limit innovation. They can be contrary to scientific progress, as power, relationships, holistic thinking, or a middle way often overshadow the pursuit of truth. In scientific research, evidential truth is elevated over compromise or balance. The way Confucianism constrains innovation was identified by Feng Youlan, a Chinese philosopher, in his provocative essay 'Why China Has No Science: An Interpretation of the History and Consequences of Chinese Philosophy' almost a century ago, and remains apposite today.[28]

The cultural influence in China can be traced back to Confucian education that teaches students to respect the status quo and never challenge authority. This eases organizations' compliance with political agendas, and bureaucratic hierarchies can still prevail over expertise, even in the higher education sector.

Multi-Logic Institutions

China is a one-party state that tolerates little opposition to, or dissent towards, its ruling party. Its current governance can be traced back to the logic of the 'omnipotent government' from the Qin Dynasty, which reached its pinnacle during Mao's time. Much of the order in Chinese society is maintained through a top-down chain of command. Historically, the ultimate head of state was the emperor—the 'son of heaven', who was endowed with inhuman superpowers to rule the country (*tianxia*), and govern its people. Such superpower, however, would periodically lose its legitimacy when the system failed to deal with population growth, social unrest, and economic recession, and led to a dissatisfied underclass overturning the regime in revolutions. Dynasty after dynasty, Chinese history has repeated itself in such a cycle of revolt, totalitarianism, and revolt again.[29]

Despite institutional reforms since the opening-up policy and economic reforms of the 1980s, the government still maintains centralized state power that allows it to allocate resources to achieve strategic goals considered to benefit the party and country, especially when facing a national crisis or under the threat of foreign 'invasion'. Such concentrated power imposes certain constrains on enterprises, especially SOEs, to operate.

As argued by Zhou Xue Guang, however, the fundamental institutional order in China is actually more complex and lies in the multi-logics in its system.[30] Chinese society, in this view, has been driven by the dynamic interplay of multiple logics,

[28] F. Youlan (1922), 'Why China Has No Science: An Interpretation of the History and Consequences of Chinese Philosophy', *International Journal of Ethics*, 32(3), 237–63.

[29] C. O. Hucker (1975), *China's Imperial Past: An Introduction to Chinese History and Culture*, Redwood City: CA: Stanford University Press.

[30] X. G. Zhou (2017), *Institutional Logics of Chinese Governance: An Organizational Perspective* [in Chinese], Beijing: Sanlian Press.

including official rank-oriented bureaucratic traditions, *guanxi*-based cultural values, central-planning logic, market economy logic, and many unwritten rules. The multi-logic institutional order influences China's economic policies and explains why many institutional reforms are, actually, bottom-up. According to Zhou, the highest order—top-down—policies are often vague in wording, which gives substantial leeway for local interpretations in implementation. In fact, it is often the practices from the bottom, as in the case of many innovative business models in the digital economy, that lead to institutional changes.

This approach has historic roots, contemporized by Deng Xiaoping when he described reforms as 'crossing the river by feeling the stones'. It has helped China's pragmatic policy approach using mechanisms that are temporary, flexible, and even tolerant of local deviations from central guidance. Reformers begin entrepreneurial activities which may challenge the status quo of existing rules and regulations. If their actions break existing (often obsolete) rules and regulations or enter an 'institutional void',[31] but bring benefits to the party and country, their practices can be endorsed by the government and legitimized in new rules and regulations. For example, a farming practice called 'production contracted to each household' in a small village in An'Hui province carried on by the earliest reformers was initially considered illegal, but legitimized and diffused to the entire country, and played an important role in stimulating rural economic reforms in 1978.

The multi-logics apply to relationships between central and local governments. In the implementation of policy, a central-local dual perspective is often allowed as an unwritten protocol. At the central level, while a policy often only provides general guidelines, its implementation is adaptable at the local level. In the emerging ride-hailing business, for example, the central government, together with multiple relevant ministries, issued a general and relatively relaxed regulation. At the local level, established taxi services provide an income source for local governments. When disadvantaged by competition from emerging car-hailing services, organized protests by taxi drivers imposed serious political pressure on some local governments. Therefore, when local conditions in different cities were taken into consideration, various but overall more strict and specific regulations were enacted and implemented for ride-hailing services. This central-local dual framework does not decentralize the power of the central government; instead, it is a top-down mandate that gives discretion to local officials on how to implement the policy to achieve the best results. This approach also gives the central government enough leeway to adjust policies if local experiments identify problems. The bottom line is that as long as the local governments maintain political correctness and social stability, they have room to use their discretion when implementing central government policies.

The multi-logic-based, pragmatic approach is manifested in 'experimental regulation' in emerging industries and businesses. Under this system, Chinese

---

[31] S. M. Puffer, D. J. McCarthy, and M. Boisot (2010), 'Entrepreneurship in Russia and China: The Impact of Formal Institutional Voids', *Entrepreneurship Theory & Practice*, 34, 441–67.

policymakers rely on experimentation to effectively respond to emerging challenges brought about by new economic opportunities. In industry policies, the central-local government connection becomes a central-sector dual model. This model can be characterized as inter-ministerial competition, marked by deep-rooted political involvement, frequent bureaucratic bargaining, and weak legal enforcement, especially at the central level. This has led to a situation where no single government agency of equal bureaucratic rank can exert complete authority in policymaking in a specific industry. This issue is particularly true for a nascent field from two or more industries which connect to different ministerial bureaucratic bodies.

Chinese multi-logic institutional order often imposes extra challenges on firms. Firms need to rationalize the dominant institutional logic in a certain context and make strategic decisions accordingly. Different institutional logics can be conflictual with or complementary to one another. For example, China's market economy logic is incomplete, as it is subject to interventions of multiple ministerial powers that retain discretion in their interpretation and implementation of specific policies. Firms may choose to follow a market economy logic in their strategic thinking, but may also need to adopt behaviours related to bureaucratic controls or *guanxi* that are necessary for them to create and maintain competitive advantages.

In recent years, the Chinese government has realized the drawbacks as well as the benefits of state intervention in innovation. Gradually, it has relaxed its control of many emerging industries. The central government tends to give general policy guidance, but leave local governments or other administrative authorities a certain freedom in their implementation. These variations in policy implementation accommodate local conditions in economic, industrial, and demographic differences, on the one hand, and encourage competition between local governments, on the other.

In Chapter 7, we discuss the implications of China's cultural roots in influencing innovation in individuals, organizations, and enterprises, as well as how they guide practices in research institutes and universities.

Shortcomings and Challenges

Reactions to China's rapid rise in global competitiveness through innovation have been mixed.[32] While some applaud China's catch-up and expect it to be a future global innovation leader, others are more sceptical. Some predict that innovation under a centralized political authority has little chance of becoming sustainable and China's growth, therefore, will slow down or enter the so-called 'middle-income trap': the common fate of countries that escape poverty but hit a wall at a GDP of around $10,000 per capita. Others believe that China's aggressive catch-up, supported by its policies focused on concentrated strengths and enabled by its

---

[32] X. Fu (2015), *China's Path to Innovation*, Cambridge: Cambridge University Press.

centralized political authority, is a threat to the technological advantages of the developed world.

Advanced Technologies and Basic Research

Building 'a science and technology giant' is not just a slogan in China. In well-funded, state-of-the-art laboratories and factories, the nation is on the path towards building itself into a scientific and technological as well as an economic superpower. It still, however, has many disadvantages. Developed countries may lag behind China's manufacturing volume and flexibility, but their advantages in research and certain core technologies and high-end manufacturing remain.

China's innovation achievements have been largely in the applications of digital technology, crucial to which are technology in semiconductors, telecommunications, software, and IT services. However, in core technologies, such as high-end chips, China is still a follower, and its catch-up will slow down due to the diminishing latecomers' advantage of speed, scale, and cost.[33] China relies on imported core technologies. It is, for example, the world's largest consumer of semiconductor products, which have been the single largest imported products for many years. In 2018, the country imported chips worth about $260 billion, double the value of imported crude oil.[34] The impact of technological sanctions against Huawei since it was included in the US government entity list—published by the US Department of Commerce aiming to prevent the use of US technology in companies on the list—was shown in Huawei's smartphone business in 2020. We analyze Huawei's reliance on global supply chains in the discussion of bottlenecks in China's catch-up in Chapter 2.

Without advanced technological capability and leading basic research it is difficult for Chinese latecomers to narrow the gap with global forerunners. The technology frontier is a moving target which can easily negate early successes in catch-up. Latecomer firms can only achieve sustained catch-up globally when they transition from being a technological follower to being part of global industry leadership. Sustained catch-up is a long-term and dynamic process; the goal of catching-up for latecomers is to obtain leadership so that they can define new technology frontiers by developing advanced technological capabilities on a par with or better than the forerunners.

While China's investment in R&D has been rapidly increasing, its focus on efficiency over creativity means it has made limited investment in basic research—the kind of long-term research likely eventually to have the greatest impact on society and the economy. In 2018, only 5.5 per cent of the country's total R&D expenditure

[33] K. Lee (2013), *Schumpeterian Analysis of Economic Catch-up: Knowledge, Path-creation, and the Middle-income Trap*, Cambridge: Cambridge University Press.
[34] See http://www.tisino.com/cn/statisticalwindow/20161202/MTQ4MDY0NJY5ODQ.html, accessed 19 July 2021.

was in basic research, with 11 per cent in application research, and 83.5 per cent in experiment and development. In the US, in contrast, in 2018, 16.6 per cent of its total R&D expenditure was in basic research—a threefold greater commitment.[35] China's R&D efforts dedicated to experiment and development are the closest and quickest way to create value generation in industry value chains. This indicates that China has chosen an easy way—catching-up, rather than leapfrogging—and this has constrained the country's development of its own original innovation capability from basic science, with its risk-taking and scientific exploration motivated by curiosity rather than profit.

Huawei's founder Ren Zhengfei has warned his company and the country that 'basic sciences, including mathematics, are the foundation to sustainable catch-up in the global value chain'.[36] Industry leadership in innovation-based sectors, he says, requires both physical and intellectual capital. In the semiconductor industry, for example, the process of producing high-end (e.g. nano-range) chips is incredibly complicated: there are over 1,000 steps involved in making a 7nm dynamic-random-access-memory (DRAM) chip. Technology leaders have spent billions of dollars and decades of often basic research experiments in developing their technical capabilities in products and precision production. Breakthrough innovations in this area require not just investment in machines, but long-term experiments, which can often fail, based on deep and complex tacit knowledge in scientists, engineers and workers, and complementary skills and other assets within an innovation ecosystem.

China has a long way to catch up in this regard. For the future, to sustain catch-up, especially in the global market, and to transit to an innovation leader, China must adjust its investment structure in R&D. More needs to be directed to basic research and future technologies. To do so, the government needs policies that enhance and reward those who pursue exploratory research which carries little immediate or short-term returns. Advanced technological innovation starts from basic research led by dispassionate inquiry with no specific purpose and driven by human curiosity. If China wishes to become a technology leader, its future investments should be based less on cost and more on a complex array of hard-to-recreate competencies—including basic research—at both the firm and ecosystem levels. China's innovation machine needs the rocket fuel of basic research.

Ascendant Central-Planning Logic?

Overall, since the economic reforms of the 1980s, China has made faster progress in science and technology when the government's 'visible hand' loosens its grip. Technological innovation increases when the institutional environment encourages

---

[35] See https://fas.org/sgp/crs/misc/R44307.pdf, accessed 25 May 2021.
[36] Economist (2019), 'A Transcript of Ren Zhengfei's Interview', *The Economist*, 12 September, https://www.economist.com/business/2019/09/12/a-transcript-of-ren-zhengfeis-interview, accessed 19 July 2021.

experimentation and tolerates failure. The challenge is to retain this momentum in innovation as there is increasing concern for political and social stability. President Xi Jinping's party-wide campaign of anticorruption and ideological renaissance launched in 2013 has affected all ranks of cadres. One of the consequences of this campaign is the rebalancing away from market logic and Western-style market reforms. This has resulted in SOEs enjoying more benefits from the country's economic policies. Bank loans to SOEs, for example, increased from 30 per cent to 70 per cent of total business loans from 2013 to 2019. Government can create unfair competition between enterprises when, for example, the enterprises they support produce less competitive products which are subsidized by the government and sold at a discounted price. Enterprises, especially state-owned ones, have strong incentives to have rent-seeking behaviours for short-term returns by building relationships with the government, rather than engaging in risk-taking, long-term-orientated innovation activities.

Most of China's largest firms are SOEs. Constrained by political obligations and vested interests, SOEs are unlikely to lead China's breakthrough innovation. Unlike many countries where small and medium-sized enterprises are engines of innovation, Chinese SMEs are not the source of radical innovations.

Despite the preponderance of SOEs and shortage of innovative SMEs, and the way the private sector has faced a more challenging institutional environment, a free market has arisen in emerging areas such as the digital economy and the consumer goods and services of new lifestyles enabled by digital platforms. A large number of capital-funded entrepreneurial firms in this field have been at the forefront of breakthrough innovations. There has also been some real regulatory liberalization, including administrative and judicial changes, to accommodate the growth of emerging industries and business models.

The question is what the implications for China's innovation machine of the relative adjustments and tensions within its multi-logics will be. We explore this issue in Chapter 7.

The Fracturing of Globalization

Economic activities have extended worldwide and become progressively globally embedded. The geographic footprint of supply chains has become global, and manufacturing has become interdependent and complex. Products have increasingly consisted of components sourced from intertwined global supply chains. The production of a complex product often involves multiple tiers of suppliers in its supply chain network, distributed in many countries. As a result, trade of final goods is becoming rarer; more trade involves intermediate products or components. In the early 1990s, 70 per cent of global trades were in final goods, but by 2018 this had decreased to about 30 per cent.[37] China, using its mass manufacturing capacity and massive supply

---

[37] See the World Bank trade data, https://data.worldbank.org/topic/21, accessed 19 July 2021.

chains, has strengthened its position as a hub connecting countries with technology, resources, and consumers in these complex, connected, and global networks.

In the 1980s and 1990s, globalization was driven by multinational enterprises, especially those from the developed world, which expanded through FDIs. Towards the end of 1990s, with the emergence of the internet and communication technologies, these firms concentrated more resources domestically on R&D, design, brands, marketing, and sales, but outsourced production. Outsourcing production provides them with access to cheap labour and land and proximity to markets and raw materials. It has, however, led to declining employment and prosperity amongst blue-collar workers in home markets. Two events—Brexit and Trump's presidency—are consequences of globalization that disadvantaged populations wanted to reverse.

China, on the other hand, has benefited greatly from globalization. Such benefits, however, have not been gained without paying a huge price, including environmentally. China's restructuring of its SOE sector in the late 1990s, for example, led to the loss of hundreds of millions of jobs. This reform created social unrest which challenged the legitimacy of China's ruling party. Reform of the SOEs happened almost at the same time as the West started outsourcing production. Meanwhile, China started the largest urbanization in human's history. A 1998 tax reform required local governments to transfer a proportion of their tax income to the central government, forcing them to make up lost income by attracting foreign investment by offering cheap land and other benefits to foreign investors. The land and labour accommodated the mushrooming growth of OEM factories for outsourced manufacturing capacity. This was a strategy of killing two birds with one stone: the factories absorbed laid-off SOE employees and migratory workers who lost their land during urbanization, as well as developing China's lower-tier supply chains and manufacturing capacity.

The start of China's global expansion can be attributed to when, in the early 2000s, China Telecom, together with French Telecom, laid a 39,000-kilometre optical submarine cable connecting South East Asia and Western Europe via the Middle East. Since then, Chinese companies have woven a growing web of cables around the globe covering more than 500,000 kilometres.[38] The government's Belt and Road Initiative is also expanding to build a new 'Digital Silk Road'.[39] In recent years, Chinese enterprises have increased their outward FDI in other developing or emerging countries and increasingly in developed ones, aiming to enter strategically important markets and to acquire advanced technologies. This 'Going-Out' national policy has borne fruit.[40] A group of Chinese multinational firms is not only gaining market share, but also becoming technological leaders in their respective industries, on the basis of their advanced innovation capability gained from overseas investments.

---

[38] See https://en.wikipedia.org/wiki/SEA-ME-WE_3, accessed 19 July 2021.

[39] J. Kurlantzick (2020), 'Assessing China's Digital Silk Road: A Transformative Approach to Technology Financing or a Danger to Freedoms?', 18 December, https://www.cfr.org/blog/assessing-chinas-digital-silk-road-transformative-approach-technology-financing-or-danger, accessed 19 July 2021.

[40] M. McKelvey and J. Jin (2020), *Innovative Capabilities and the Globalization of Chinese Firms*, Cheltenham: Edward Elgar.

5G, the fifth-generation of mobile networks, provides a good case in point. As a game-changing technology, the deployment of 5G has geopolitical implications. 5G is an important element of infrastructure that supports applications such as industry automation, self-driving cars, machine-to-machine communications, the internet of things, and smart cities. Plans for 5G are, therefore, critical for a country's future growth.

5G networks rely on standardization supported by patents and licensing agreements. China, collectively, owns over one-third of 5G's standard essential patents. History suggests that patent and standard holders in mobile communications benefit significantly from network effects. First movers can produce profits in the hundreds of billions of dollars over following decades. China lost its opportunities in 1G and 2G, paid a high cost learning from its failed attempt with its home-made 3G standard, and achieved a substantial degree of catch-up in 4G.[41] China was determined to catch up and lead in 5G. The generational transitions provided a window of opportunity for Chinese firms, which the country prepared for over decades.

For 5G technology to become a real global standard it needs to be widely diffused. This explains why the US puts pressure on its allies to reject Huawei's equipment for their 5G networks. Australia was the first Western country to announce Huawei was banned from its 5G networks. Following US pressure, the UK joined the ban, with more countries likely to follow suit, despite Huawei's product being more cost-competitive, providing more spectrum, and being more energy- and operationally efficient.

A major feature of globalization in recent decades is the ways in which innovation and production have become highly modularized and integrated into international value networks. In this system, countries with complementary capabilities can collaborate and push the innovation frontiers forward. The scale and pace of globalization and the integration of the world's economy are unprecedented. Such globalization, however, requires highly complex coordination and co-development, which makes it vulnerable to conflicts or crises, and involves winners, in this case China, and losers, including blue-collar workers in the West.

Since 2018, trade conflict between China and the US has not been just a concern for both countries but also for the rest of the world. The threat imposed by US-China conflicts exceeds economics and is a challenge to the world order established since the Second World War. As the former French prime minister Dominique de Villepin pointed out, Sino-US disputes are almost impossible to reconcile, because they are not trade disputes, but competition for global leadership.[42]

China's rise in economic power, especially through its innovation machine, has challenged the existing world order. Although a war between a rising power and an

---

[41] M. Y. Zhang (2016), 'Meso-Level Factors in Technological Transitions: The Development of TD-SCDMA in China', *Research Policy*, 45(2), 546–59.

[42] T. Sirekanyan (2021), 'World Order Established Following WWII Collapses—Former French PM Calls on to Understand Each Other on the Way to New World', *Armenpress*, 8 June, https://armenpress.am/eng/news/977753/, accessed 19 July 2021.

anxious hegemon—what Graham Allison called 'the Thucydides trap'[43]—is unlikely, a period of coexistence of segregated innovation machines is more likely to happen, that is, the world will develop two different scientific and technological systems and innovation ecosystems centred around China and the United States.

By prohibiting sales of high-technology products of US origin to Huawei and other Chinese technology companies, the US may have temporarily slowed down Huawei's global progress. It will, however, force Chinese companies to accelerate their own R&D on high-end chips, on the one hand, and, perhaps, also force US technology suppliers to reduce their own R&D for a smaller market. The sanction against Huawei will further segregate China's innovation machine from the one dominated by US technology, as it is not based on technological or economic rationales, but has become intensely political.

The danger of this mentality is that decoupling of the two systems would occur, leading to segregation of not just technology, but trade and capital, as well as human mobility. Unfortunately, Covid-19 has only accelerated this decoupling process.

China has returned to the world stage, not just in asserting its economic strength but also in its influence in global affairs. The focal point of future conflict lies less with military strength or territorial expansion. The control of a new world order lies with R&D, standards, and emerging technology. The dispute between the two superpowers creates unavoidable tensions. As the former US Secretary of State Mike Pompeo asserted amid the Covid-19 crisis, the United States and its allies must keep China in 'its proper place'. China inevitably sees its proper place rather differently from how Secretary Pompeo does.

The Covid-19 pandemic has the potential to further accentuate schisms in world technology and innovation, with detrimental effects. Separating China's innovation machine from the world would diminish the world's ability to deal with future crises and shocks and deliver the social and economic benefits it is capable of producing. Globalization or deglobalization post Covid-19 should not be based on ideology and values, but on technological advancement for humankind. For it to continue its part in global integration, post Covid-19, China's innovation machine and the policies that support it need to change. China has to become more open and transparent about its innovation ambitions, their purpose, and the means of achieving them.

We can identify the benefits of China's innovation machine for that country and the rest of the world, but we cannot predict its future. Growing insularity, parochialism, and authoritarianism around the world may win. We may see the tensions and inefficiencies of a polarized world, where innovation wars become trade wars, then most fearfully, responding to Thucydides' trap, real wars. The social and economic costs of such a schism will be enormous, and it will paralyse efforts to deal with global problems such as pandemics and climate change. While not uncritical of

---

[43] G. Allison (2017), *Destined for War: Can America and China Escape Thucydides's Trap?* Boston, MA: Houghton Mifflin Harcourt.

China's approach to innovation, we believe it has features that, with some adjustment, can play a crucially important role on the world stage.

The Future of Chinese Innovation in the Digital Economy

The contribution of innovation to economic growth and social progress is well established.[44] The nature of innovation, however, is changing, and China provides especial insights into emerging and different models of innovation based around digital technologies.

The World Economic Forum categorizes four stages of industrialization. The first stage was powered by water and steam, the second by electricity. About twenty years ago, when the internet and web-based technologies emerged and transformed society, we entered the third stage, using electronics and information technology to automate production. We are now, in this analysis, on the verge of the fourth stage of industrialization, which builds upon the third stage with more advanced digital technologies such as AI and quantum computing.[45]

Digital technologies have accelerated trends in the innovation process. These include the novel approaches to designing, producing, and delivering products and services which have blurred the boundaries between producers and users of technology, and between services and manufacturing.[46] Innovation relies not only on science and technology to create novelty, but also on the effective and rapid recombination of the new and existing, which can be assisted by digital technologies. Innovation is not bounded within the borders of enterprises, cities, or countries, but a collective effort of interdependent actors in complex ecosystems, again assisted by digital underpinnings. As claimed in the futurist book *The Future is Faster than You Think*,[47] convergence of future technologies will transform technologies, industries, and our lives at an exponential speed. Innovation empowered by future technologies is key in this transformation.

Simplistic 'science-push' and 'market-pull' views on innovation have been superseded, as many elements of the economy and society extensively interact around innovation. Innovation can result from large numbers of producers and users working interdependently in a dynamic and often iterative process, supported by multifaceted digital platforms. Flows of technology, capital, and talent are intertwined and

---

[44] J. Fagerberg (2006), 'Innovation: A Guide to the Literature', in J. Fagerberg and D. C. Mowery (eds.), *The Oxford Handbook of Innovation*, Oxford: Oxford University Press, 1-26..

[45] K. Schwab (2015), 'The Fourth Industrial Revolution: What It Means and How to Respond', *Foreign Affairs*, 12 December, https://www.foreignaffairs.com/articles/2015-12-12/fourth-industrial-revolution, accessed 26 May 2021.

[46] M. Dodgson and D. Gann (2014), 'Technology and Innovation', in M. Dodgson, D. Gann, and N. Phillips (eds), *The Oxford Handbook of Innovation Management*, Oxford: Oxford University Press..

[47] P. H. Diamandis and S. Kotler (2020), *The Future Is Faster than You Think: How Converging Technologies Are Transforming Business, Industries, and Our Lives* (Exponential Technology Series). New York: Simon & Schuster.

mutually reinforcing. In such systems, technological innovations, like species in natural ecosystems, are argued by evolutionary economists to be created following the rules of 'variation and selection', prior to the 'propagation' of favoured innovations.[48] Unlike evolution in biology, in human society connections with other elements in a system are key for a variation to be selected, retained, and expanded through co-creation and co-development.

These connections are supercharged by digital technologies. The digital world joins the cyber and physical world, enabling new lifestyles and new business models, and even new technological breakthroughs, with profound impacts on society. Empowered by digital platforms, individuals as customers and users have a widened stage on which they can play important roles in innovation: they cluster according to their common interests, not by their geographical proximities, and collectively generate disproportionly powerful influences on innovation compared to the simple addition of each individual.

Innovations develop quickly in connected innovation ecosystems because of their synergies and interdependencies. Thomas Friedman argues we are living in an 'age of accelerations'.[49] In such ecosystems, innovation can be complex and uncertain, where progress lies in connectivity and evolution. The potential consequences of small changes can be significant. Scale may not have its traditional value; new and small developments can overturn the status quo of incumbency. In this new world of innovation, there is a crucial role played by digital platforms that combine both demand and supply and have the potential to disrupt existing industry structures, such as with 'sharing' or 'on demand' economics. These types of new platform businesses are rapidly multiplying into many new services ranging from online education and shared rooms/kitchens/gyms/outfits to user-generated content that dominates the media and entertainment, as well as global industry value chains.

Unlike the digital economy in the US, which serves the global market (the largest proportion of the global market), the vast majority of China's digital economy addresses the domestic market. The growth of China's digital economy based on the current model, built upon independent but overlapping platforms led by major technology companies, will continue. China enjoys scale advantages from its large domestic market, as the country has a large and active digital-native population (25 years old or younger) who are eager to adopt new technologies and applications in life, learning, entertainment, socializing, and work. China's internet giants, such as Alibaba, Tencent, and Baidu, play an important role in China's digital economy, but a group of a younger generation of digital natives have emerged who are both founders of new internet firms with breakthrough applications, such as ByteDance, PDD, and Bilibili, and users of these applications. Government regulators, which provided room for innovation to thrive in the early days of China's digital economy, are now

---

[48] W. B. Arthur (2009), *The Nature of Technology: What It Is and How It Evolves*. London: Penguin Books.
[49] T. L. Friedman (2017), *Thank You for Being Late: An Optimist's Guide to Thriving in the Age of Accelerations*, London: Penguin Books.

pushing for investment and application of cutting-edge technologies to support China's fast-growing digital industry, on the one hand, and limit the monopoly of super platforms in order to promote innovation, on the other hand.

Once known for 'good enough' products at low cost, Chinese brands in electric consumer goods and white goods have upgraded to products with cost and quality advantage using customer-focused innovation strategies. The scale advantage of a connected digital ecosystem enables trial-and-error types of innovation and fast upgrades of new products, services, and business models. Xiaomi, the emerging producer of multiple technology products, including mobile phones, scooters, smart home and lifestyle products, runs interconnected 'open innovation' platforms, leveraging the scale advantage of its customer base and diverse product line. Like other customer-focused innovators in China, it uses the massive consumer market as a collaborator, rapidly refining its offerings through online feedback. This enables Xiaomi to produce cheaper and better products designed to offer hardware features as good as those from global brands but priced for the Chinese market.

One measure of innovativeness is the extent of disruption in an innovation's marketing and/or production process; the higher the disruption, the more radical the innovation.[50] Using this definition, Chinese digital firms are radical innovators. Their impacts are both at the macro (industry, city, and region) and micro (firm and individual) levels, as well as in the way they connect. They are also capable of massive social, economic, and political change, as seen in the case of mobile payments and other disruptive business models in the digital economy.

Evolution, Not Revolution

Innovation results when multiple actors (including both technology creators and users) work interdependently in a dynamic and sometimes recursive process in which micro-level elements of the economy and society interact with institutional elements. As in a natural ecosystem, innovations at the micro level, like genetic mutation, can evolve in the right niche. Institutional settings provide such niches if the mutation is selected by the market. In this process, flows of technology, capital, and talent are intertwined and mutually reinforcing. In this collective process, innovations resulting from bottom-up trial and error among a large enough pool of actors is akin to genetic mutations of individual organisms that can be passed on through reproduction of the fittest to the benefit of the entire population.

This evolutionary process underlies China's innovation machine. Chinese innovation is not just about novelty or efficiency: it aims to provide the right solutions to a specific user group at the right time; innovations delivering effective solutions that

---

[50] R. Garcia and R. Calantone (2002), 'A Critical Look at Technological Innovation Typology and Innovativeness Terminology: A Literature Review', *Journal of Product Innovation Management*, 19, 110–32.

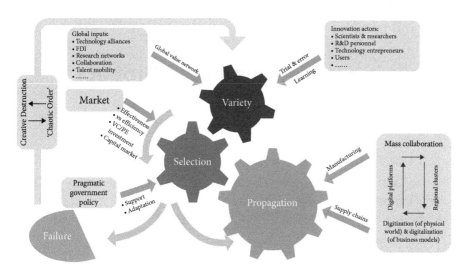

Figure 1.1 The evolution of China's innovation machine

have a chance of being selected and amplified in markets. This effectiveness-driven model allowed latecomer Chinese firms with limited technological capability to learn, catch up and sometimes disrupt, incumbent multinational firms. Through this process, incremental innovations can be propagated in China's innovation machine. This evolutionary process also enables China's innovation machine to possess self-correction and self-propagation attributes. Figure 1.1 illustrates the evolution of China's innovation machine.

We will explain the evolutionary aspect of China's innovation machine in Chapter 8.

We now turn to the question of whether China has caught up in the global innovation race.

2

Has China Caught up in the Global Innovation Race?

To understand how China's innovation machine works, we have first to establish where China stands in the global innovation race.

China was the world's most advanced technological power for most of human history.[1]

By the mid-eighteenth century, however, it remained an agrarian society when Europe embraced industrialization and led scientific advancement, the results of which have become the foundation of modern society. Since then China endured an interregnum of more than 200 years in scientific and technological progress due to wars, natural disasters, and internal turmoil. After the foundation of the People's Republic of China in 1949, the government set out to build a new socialist country. As it emerged from two centuries of humiliation of foreign powers, 'catching up and surpassing' the developed world became an overarching ambition. From Mao Zedong to Xi Jinping, technological progress is not just a means to economic development, but also an ideological end in itself in China.[2]

During the first decade following the foundation of the People's Republic of China (PRC), a national campaign under the slogan of 'surpassing Britain and catching up with America', led China onto the road of a Soviet model of industrialization.[3] In the subsequent decade, China's progress in science and technology as an input to innovation was completely curtailed during the disaster of the Cultural Revolution. In 1978, Deng Xiaoping, the nation's paramount leader, initiated the reform and opening-up of China's economy by recognizing the importance of science and technology above class struggle. His view was captured in his famous speech, 'emancipate the mind, seek truth from fact, and unite as one to face the future'. At this time the

---

[1] The 'Needham Question' or 'Needham Problem' refers to the guiding question behind Joseph Needham's (1900–95) massive *Science and Civilisation in China*, as well as his many other publications. As he phrased it (J. Needham (1969), "Science and Society in East and West." In *The Grand Titration: Science and Society in East and West*. pp. 190–217. London: Allen & Unwin), 'the essential problem [is] why modern science had not developed in Chinese civilization (or India) but only in Europe.' He went on to consider another quite different but equally important question and centered his historical research on it: 'why, between the first century BC and the fifteenth century AD, Chinese civilization was much more efficient than occidental in applying human natural knowledge to practical human needs' (p. 190).

[2] J. B. Gewirtz (2019), 'China's Long March to Technological Supremacy: The Roots of Xi Jinping's Ambition to "Catch Up and Surpass"', *Foreign Affairs*, 27 August, https://www.foreignaffairs.com/articles/china/2019-08-27/chinas-long-march-technological-supremacy, accessed 30 May 2021.

[3] C. Sorace, I. Franceschini and N. Loubere (Eds.), *Afterlives of Chinese Communism: Political Concepts from Mao to Xi* (pp. 275–280). Australia: ANU Press.

Demystifying China's Innovation Machine: Chaotic Order. Marina Yue Zhang, Mark Dodgson, and David M. Gann,
Oxford University Press. © Marina Yue Zhang, Mark Dodgson, and David M. Gann 2022.
DOI: 10.1093/oso/9780198861171.003.0002

Communist Party of China (CPC) realized that economic growth through catching up in science and technology is not only an ideological end, but also the means to achieving social prosperity and economic growth, and a way of maintaining its own legitimacy as the ruling party.

By catching up, China transformed itself from a predominantly rural, agricultural economy to an industrialized global manufacturing hub and the second-largest economy in the world.[4] Until recently, however, most Western observers considered China's catch-up in innovation as merely a copycat: imitating technologies and business models from the West and applying and amplifying them due to China's low-cost labour advantages.[5] Hardly anything from China was perceived as direct competition to the technology supremacy held by the West. This perception has changed rapidly as China climbed up on the industry value chain in the decades since the turn of the century, especially with its development in the digital economy.

When Fortune began to publish the world's largest 500 companies measured by revenue in 1995, 151 companies were from the US, 149 from Japan, and only 3 were from China. The 2020 list of Fortune 500 companies[6] included 124 from China (including Hong Kong) and 121 from the United States. China's list was dominated by state-owned banks and energy and property companies such as Sinopec, State Grid, and China National Petroleum, but technology firms such as Huawei, Alibaba, JD, Tencent, and Xiaomi were also listed. A country's Fortune 500 companies can indicate its economic size and market position in the world, but it is not necessarily an indicator of its innovation power. Examination of the list suggests that China's contributors tend to be lower-end in value-adding in the manufacturing value chain, and US companies are higher-end (including design, innovation, high-value manufacturing, and branding). Nine companies from Taiwan are also listed on the Fortune 500, most in high-end manufacturing, which is a significant tension point in competition between China and US in the technology industry, especially in the semiconductor sector.

China's digital economy accounts for over 36 per cent of the country's GDP. By the end of 2020, 989 million Chinese had access to the internet, an increase from fewer than 300 million in 2008. A total of 99.7 per cent of Chinese internet users have network access through their smartphones, over 86 per cent of them use mobile payments, and nearly 80 per cent use e-commerce services.[7] The annual volume of e-commerce trade grew more than thirty fold from 2004 to 2019, reaching $ 5.04 trillion, surpassing the combined total of Europe and the US.[8,9] E-commerce helps to

---

[4] World Bank Group (2019), *Innovative China: New Drivers of Growth*, Washington, DC: World Bank. doi: 10.1596/978-1-4648-1335-1.

[5] See, for example, World Bank Group, (2011), 'From Technological Catch-up to Innovation: The Future of China's GDP Growth', https://openknowledge.worldbank.org/handle/10986/12781, accessed 30 May 2021.

[6] See the full list at https://fortune.com/fortune500/, accessed 20 July 2021.

[7] China Internet Network Information Center (CNNIC) (2020), 'The 47th China Statistical Report on Internet Development', https://www.cnnic.com.cn/IDR/ReportDownloads/202104/P02021042055730 2172744.pdf, accessed 20 July 2021.

[8] We calculated the value using the average exchange rate of 1USD=6.91 RMB in 2019.

[9] E-commerce in China – Statistics and Facts. https://www.statista.com/topics/1007/e-commerce-in-china/, accessed 20 July 2021.

drive growth by enlarging the market reach of enterprises and helping them to manage their operations efficiently. The government's 'Internet Plus' strategy, introduced in 2015, aiming to roll out the applications of internet technology to all sectors of the economy, as in Internet + Finance, Internet + Health, Internet + Manufacturing, Internet + Logistics, and so forth, has transformed many industries.

China's rapid development in digital technology can be attributed in large part to the country's communications networks. China's three state-owned operators, China Mobile, China Telcom, and China Unicom, which are all Fortune 500 companies, offer relatively competitive prices for both fixed broadband and mobile connections compared with other Asia-Pacific countries and many high-income countries. On the infrastructure side, by the end of 2020 there were 5.75 million 4G base stations installed.[10] 4G base stations are installed even in the most distant villages without modern roads. For instance, a popular blogger from Sichuan province broadcasts her village life through 4G networks, attracting an audience of over 10 million on YouTube alone.[11] Since China granted 5G licences to its mobile operators in June 2019, 690,000 5G base stations were installed by October 2020, ahead of scheduled target, and rapid growth in these base stations is expected between 2021 and 2023.[12]

On the negative side, on 15 May 2020, the US Department of Commerce announced rules further targeting Chinese telecommunications company Huawei. The rules prohibit Huawei and its affiliates from using any products containing or produced with US technology or software. These rules specifically mean that no American tools can be used to make Huawei's products. Given the dominance of American technologies in the semiconductor industry, the impact of these rules is, in effect, 'to freeze Huawei out completely.'[13]

The ostensible reason for the US banning Huawei was that one of Huawei's former subsidiaries was involved in sanctions-busting with Iran, which led to a series of trade restrictions imposed on Huawei. The actual reason is, as the US Attorney General William Barr commented, 'China's current technological thrusts pose an unprecedented challenge to the United States.'[14] Mr Barr further explained why China's current focus on dominating 5G technology was of central concern. He said, '5G is an infrastructure business. It relies on a Radio Access Network (RAN). China has two of the leading RAN infrastructure suppliers: Huawei and ZTE. Together, they have already captured 40 percent of the market, and are aggressively pursuing the balance.'

---

[10] *Total number of telecommunication 4G mobile base stations in China from 2014 to 2020.* https://www.statista.com/statistics/989888/china-4g-mobile-base-station-number/. Accessed 20 July 2021.

[11] See more at https://en.wikipedia.org/wiki/Li_Ziqi_(vlogger), accessed 20 July 2021.

[12] According to the statistics of China's Ministry of Industry and Information Technology. http://english.scio.gov.cn/pressroom/2020-10/23/content_76835234.htm, accessed 20 July 2021.

[13] Economist (2020). 'Chip wars: A New Escalation in the Tech Conflict Illustrates the Limits of American Power', *The Economist*, 21 May, https://www.economist.com/leaders/2020/05/23/america-is-determined-to-sink-huawei, accessed 30 May 2021.

[14] US Department of Justice (2020), 'Attorney General William P. Barr Delivers the Keynote Address at the Department of Justice's China Initiative Conference, Thursday, Washington, DC. February 6, 2020', https://www.justice.gov/opa/speech/attorney-general-william-p-barr-delivers-keynote-address-department-justices-china, accessed 30 May 2021.

It is striking to see that a single private company, China's flagship technological corporation, has drawn such attention from the most powerful country in the world. The Huawei situation encapsulates a number of questions we shall address. Can we, for example, conclude that Huawei is really challenging US technology supremacy, indicating that China has caught up with the US in innovation? To answer these questions, we need to examine China's innovation achievements and weaknesses in the global context and analyse the logics, capabilities, and resources behind China's ambition of catching up in innovation.

Catch-Up Performance

Catch-up is a phenomenon by which latecomers (country/region, industry, or firm) shorten the distance between themselves and their particular forerunners by using more effective methods in a more compressed time frame.

International Index

The Global Innovation Index (GII) uses eighty indices, including traditional measures such as R&D expenditures and patent applications and emerging ones such as mobile applications and high technology exports, to measure national innovation performance. Among all the measures, in 2020 China ranked fourteenth out of 131 countries, and number seven in 'knowledge and technology outputs', but much lower in innovation infrastructure and institutions. China hosts seventeen of the top science and technology clusters worldwide—with Shenzhen–Hong Kong–Guangzhou ranked second and Beijing fourth.[15]

Similarly, in 2020, the Bloomberg Innovation Index ranked China fifteenth, using criteria in seven metrics, including R&D spending, manufacturing capability, and concentration of public high-tech companies. China scored highly on patent activity, high-technology density, tertiary efficiency, and in the middle of the range on R&D intensity (the ratio of R&D spending to GDP) and manufacturing value added. It was, however, lower on productivity and researcher concentration.[16]

The Global Competitiveness Index (GCI) compiled by World Economic Forum since 1979 uses an extensive set of indicators, including innovation capability, to measure economic competitiveness of 99 per cent of the countries in the world.[17] Introduced in 2018, GCI 4.0 provides a detailed map of the factors and attributes

---

[15] See https://www.wipo.int/edocs/pubdocs/en/wipo_pub_gii_2020/cn.pdf, accessed 31 May 2021.

[16] M. Jamrisco and W. Lu (2020), 'Germany Breaks Korea's Six-Year Streak as Most Innovative Nation', *Bloomberg Innovation Index*, January 18, https://www.bloomberg.com/news/articles/2020-01-18/germany-breaks-korea-s-six-year-streak-as-most-innovative-nation, accessed 31 May 2021.

[17] K. Schwab (ed.) (2019), *The Global Competitiveness Report: 2019*, Cologny, Switzerland: World Economic Forum, http://www3.weforum.org/docs/WEF_TheGlobalCompetitivenessReport2019.pdf, accessed 31 May 2021. Twelve pillars—institutions, infrastructure, ICT adoption, macroeconomic

that drive productivity, growth, and human development in the era of the 'Fourth Industrial Revolution'.[18] According to GCI 2019, China ranked twenty-eighth on overall competitiveness, unchanged compared to the previous five years (2014–18). China's strength lies in the sheer size of its market (first). In several areas, China's performance is almost on par with OECD standards. China, however, outperformed OECD countries on ICT adoption (eighteenth). On Innovation Capability, China was twenty-fourth, ahead of some more advanced countries, but lagging behind leading innovative economies, such as Germany and the US. China boosted its ranking on Business Dynamism to thirty-sixth by introducing a basket of policies encouraging entrepreneurship. The weakest areas in this index are Labour Market (seventy-second), Skills (sixty-fourth) and Institutions (fifty-eighth).

The Fourth Industrial Revolution emphasizes the contribution of human capital and innovation to economic growth.[19] In GCI 2019, China ranked second on the prominence of its research institutions, sixth on fibre Internet subscription per hundred population, eighth on percentage of domestic credit to private sector to GDP, and thirteenth on venture capital availability, thirteenth on scientific publications, and fifteenth on R&D intensity. These factors are all supportive of China's innovation machine.

R&D Expenditures

China has significantly increased its R&D spending over recent decades. Although growth rates varied, China's R&D spending contributed 8.6 per cent of the world total in 2009 and 18.7 per cent in 2019, second only after the US.[20] Figure 2.1 shows the growth of China's R&D expenditure by the total value and the percentage to the national GDP (R&D intensity), between 2009 and 2020.

As a result of increased investment in R&D in highly R&D-intensive industries, including aircraft manufacturing, pharmaceuticals, computers, electronic and optical products, and computer software, between 2003 and 2018, China's share in value-added output[21] increased from 6 per cent to 21 per cent, while the share of the US dropped from 38 per cent to 32 per cent. In medium-high R&D intensive industries, including the chemical industry (excluding pharmaceuticals), transportation

---

stability, health, skills, product market, labour market, financial system, market size, business dynamism, and innovation capability—are used as indicators.

[18] K. Schwab (2015), 'The Fourth Industrial Revolution: What It Means and How to Respond', *Foreign Affairs*, 12 December, https://www.foreignaffairs.com/articles/2015-12-12/fourth-industrial-revolution, accessed 26 May 2021.

[19] K. Roy (2019), 'How is the Fourth Industrial Revolution Changing Our Economy?' *World Economic Forum*, 26 November, https://www.weforum.org/agenda/2019/11/the-fourth-industrial-revolution-is-redefining-the-economy-as-we-know-it/, accessed 31 May 2021.

[20] World Bank Data, https://data.worldbank.org/indicator/NY.GDP.MKTP.KD.ZG?locations=CN/, accessed 31 May 2021.

[21] Value added is the difference between gross output and intermediate inputs and represents the value of labour and capital used in producing gross output.

(a)

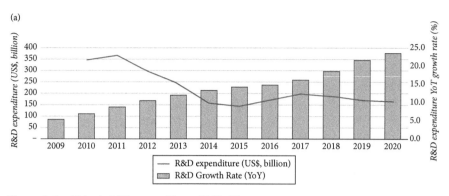

Figure 2.1a China's R&D expenditure, 2009–20

(b)

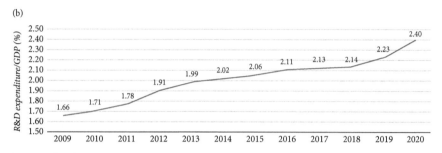

Figure 2.1b China's R&D intensity, 2009–20
Source: National Bureau of Statistics of China

equipment (excluding aircraft), electricity and other mechanical equipment, information technology services, and scientific instruments, China's share in value-added output increased from 7 per cent to 26 per cent from 2003 to 2018, while the share of the US dropped from 25 per cent to 22 per cent.[22]

Higher Education

China has one of the world's largest education systems. In the summer of 2020, 8.74 million people graduated from Chinese universities, a number expected to increase to 9.09 million in 2021.[23] This is compared to 17,000 when the PRC was founded. Unlike their counterparts in the 1950s, who were assigned 'official' jobs in government and SOEs, university graduates can find it difficult to be appointed to 'official'

[22] HIS Markit, special tabulations (2019) of the Comparative Industry Service. Indicators 2020: Industry Activities.

[23] State Council (2020), 'Chinese University, College Graduates to Exceed 9 Million in 2021', 1 December, http://english.www.gov.cn/statecouncil/ministries/202012/01/content_WS5fc63051c6d0f72576941058.html, accessed 31 May 2021.

jobs or, indeed, any jobs upon graduation. As a result, an increasing number of university graduates pursue entrepreneurial careers.

1999 marked a milestone in the development of China's higher education, as this was the year that universities substantially expanded student enrolments. The number of enrolments rose rapidly, with a near sevenfold increase between 1998 and 2016. STEM (science, technology, engineering, and mathematics) attracts about 40 per cent of enrolments across all levels of learning. For instance, China has produced the largest number of graduates with doctorate degrees in sciences and engineering (excluding medicine): in 2007 it surpassed the US (excluding foreign students) as the largest producer of doctoral degrees in natural science and engineering.[24] The number of doctoral graduates in science and engineering from 1997 to 2019 is shown in Figure 2.2.

China has also implemented programmes to attract high-quality overseas returnees—those originally from China who were educated in Western universities and benefited from working experience in the West—to join Chinese organizations. This group has played a catalytic role in transforming China's research environment. Attracted by Chinese human capital, with advanced degrees in STEM and the increasing returnee talent pool, many global firms, including IBM, GE, Siemens, Roche, and Microsoft, chose China as one of their research bases in China. Knowledge from these Chinese R&D labs of multinationals benefits both the domestic and global market.

One consequence of growing competition in the knowledge-based global economy is an international talent race in higher education, particularly in STEM. In this race, global university rankings have become, for better or worse, a tangible yardstick that influences government policies in higher education. Since 2000, China has made investment in higher education a major national priority, aiming to build world-class

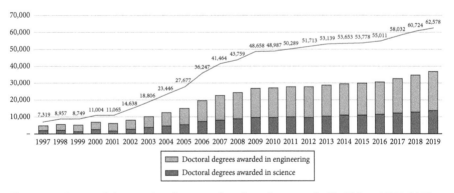

Figure 2.2 Doctoral degrees in science and engineering awarded in China, 1987–2019
Source: Ministry of Education of PRC

[24] According to the American Institute of Physics (2018), 'Rapid Rise of China's STEM Workforce Charted by National Science Board Report', 31 January, https://www.aip.org/fyi/2018/rapid-rise-china%E2%80%99s-stem-workforce-charted-national-science-board-report, accessed 31 May 2021.

universities measured by improved global rankings. China is not, of course, alone in this race. South Korea, for example, has adopted similar policies to stimulate research by universities, as they are viewed as key driving forces of economic development, especially in innovation.

Such policies strongly emphasize performance-driven accountability, for example in research publications, and in this regard it can be argued to have paid off. China's leading universities are climbing up the global rankings across three different world university ranking systems: QS World University Rankings (QS), Academic Ranking of World Universities (ARWU), and the Times Higher Education World University Rankings (THE). In 2003, when the ARWU ranking began, there was one Chinese university in the world's top 200; by 2020 there were twenty-two.[25] Tsinghua University and Peking University, are now ranked among the top 100 in the world by QS, ARWU, and THE.

Project 211 and Project 985 are among the best-known government initiatives to promote the country's higher education system, aiming to improve the stature of Chinese universities in the world and, in particular, to boost the world rankings of top-tier universities. The funding priorities of these government projects concentrate on STEM fields. In an effort to join the global elite universities, such as the Ivy League in the US or the Russell Group in the UK, the C9 League was established in China, comprising a group of nine research-focused universities. These are Tsinghua University, Peking University, Zhejiang University, Fudan University, Shanghai Jiao Tong University, University of Science and Technology of China, Nanjing University, Xi'an Jiaotong University, and Harbin Institute of Technology. All these institutions rose in the global rankings between 2016 and 2020.

China's rapid catch-up in university rankings is driven by institutional competition, large amounts of funding (in part to attract top-tier returnees), and concentration on STEM research. Project 985 invested $14.7 billion between 1999 and 2016 in thirty-nine universities. The top two universities, Tsinghua University and Peking University, each received extra funding of $1.1 billion from Project 985 in three stages. As a result, research funding per researcher at Tsinghua and Peking is 7.2 times higher than that in Germany, given that the government spending on tertiary education is only 0.87 per cent of GDP in China, much lower than that in OECD countries, where the ratio is between 5 and 6 per cent of GDP.

Whether China's performance-driven and ranking-driven catch-up models in higher education can generate the innovation the country requires for sustainable growth is uncertain. Such models focus on short-term incentives (e.g. research publications) rather than long-term knowledge accumulation based on academic curiosity and freedom. The question is whether it is possible for Chinese elite universities to compete with the top American and European universities without fundamental changes in their organizational models and incentive systems.

---

[25] See 2020 Academic Ranking of World Universities, https://www.shanghairanking.com/rankings/arwu/2020, accessed 31 May 2021.

Scientific Outputs

Although the Global Competitive Index ranked China thirteenth on scientific publications in 2019,[26] there is a question whether, funded by the central budget and concentrated efforts, China has achieved catch-up in quantity, rather than quality, in scientific outputs.

Nature Index, which tracks contributions to research articles published in eighty-two high-quality natural science journals chosen by an independent group of researchers, measures global research output and collaboration.[27] Four disciplines, chemistry, earth and environmental sciences, life sciences, and physics, are included in this index, which shows the quality of Chinese scientific publications is improving. In 2020, the top three performing countries were the US, China, and Germany. China, again, showed a rapid catch-up on this index: in 2013, the US index, measured by share (a fractional count allocated to an institution or country for an article where the maximum share is 1.0 if the article is a single-authored one), was 3.6 times that of China's; in 2020, the number was 1.53 times. From 2018 to 2020 alone, China's index jumped 15 per cent. China's advantages in scientific outputs are in chemistry, where it leads, followed by the US and Germany. In earth and environmental science, life science and and physics, China was second after the US.

The Chinese Academy of Sciences (CAS) was the top institution in Nature Index in 2021.[28] CAS is a massive organization, with over 100 research institutions, three universities, and 130 key state laboratories. It employs over 71,000 personnel, and has 64,000 research students. Size can count in research. The top Chinese universities ranked by Nature Index were Peking University, ranked tenth, and University of Chinese Academy of Sciences, ranked ranked twelfth.

Under the current reward system in China's higher education, grassroots initiatives and the freedom for young researchers to pursue fresh research ideas which have the potential to push science to its limits with high risk, but may not carry immediate or short-term results, are not encouraged. Evaluating research is linked primarily to the quantity of publications and patents, as well as their potential commercial value. Bureaucratic structures and research hierarchies with concentrated decision-making authority and resources in the hands of senior researchers and managers are a constraint on original scientific breakthroughs. Ultimately, if incentives for research efficiency overshadow those encouraging scientific curiosity,

---

[26] Schwab, *Global Competitiveness Report: 2019.*
[27] See Nature Index, https://www.natureindex.com/using-the-index, accessed 20 July 2021.
[28] The top ten institutions with Nature Index in 2020 included the Chinese Academy of Sciences (China), Harvard University (US), the Max Planck Society (Germany), the French National Centre for Scientific Research (France), Stanford University (US), the Helmholtz Association of German Research Centres (Germany), MIT (US), University of Oxford (UK), the University of Tokyo (Japan), and Peking University (China). See https://www.natureindex.com/institution-outputs/generate/All/global/All/score. Accessed 20 July 2021.

path-following research appears a much easier route in catching up according to simple indicators of performance.

Patents

In 2019, China applied for 58,990 patents under the Patent Cooperation Treaty (PCT),[29] —a 200 fold increase in twenty years—surpassing the 57,840 filed by the US, and became the country with the largest number of patent applications.[30] China started its first international patent application in 1993 and has experienced significant growth since 2000 (see Figure 2.3).

Among the world's top ten patent applicants (companies or individual), four were from China. Huawei, with 4,411 applications, led the top filings under the PCT in 2019, followed by Samsung Electric (South Korea), Mitsubishi Electronics (Japan), Qualcomm (US), Oppo Mobile (China), BOE Technology (China), Ericsson (Sweden), Pin'An Technology (China), Bosch (Germany), and LG Electronics (South Korea). Most top fifty applicants are in high-tech industries such as semiconductors, digital communications, computer technologies, software, electrical machinery, medical technology, audiovisual technology, and energy.

Though an imperfect indicator of innovation capability, many global innovation indices include patent applications in their measurement of innovation performance, and patent applications provide at least a partial indication of a patentee's (whether a company or a country) potential in innovation in certain technological fields.

Chinese government policies to encourage patenting have played a significant role in increasing the number of patents filed by Chinese firms domestically and internationally. Different layers of the government have set ambitious patenting targets

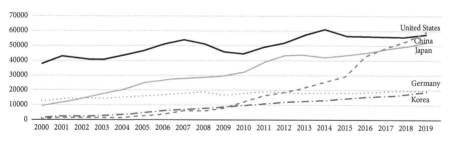

Figure 2.3 Number of patent applications filed under the PCT system, 2000–19
Source: WIPO Statistics Database

---

[29] The Patent Cooperation Treaty (PCT) is an international patent law treaty, concluded in 1970. It provides a unified procedure for filing patent applications to protect inventions in each of its contracting states. A patent application filed under the PCT is called an international application, or PCT application. See https://en.wikipedia.org/wiki/Patent_Cooperation_Treaty, accessed 20 July 2021.

[30] "China Becomes Top Filer of International Patents in 2019 Amid Robust Growth for WIPO's IP Services, Treaties and Finances." 7 April 2020. https://www.wipo.int/pressroom/en/articles/2020/article_0005.html, accessed 20 July 2021.

and rolled out intellectual property-conditioned state financial incentives. However, due to insufficient quality-related requirements for patents, these programmes may have contributed to the rising quantity of patents at the expense of quality, particularly for utility patents.[31] Many patents may not be economically, technologically, or commercially viable.

Another shortcoming of China's patents is that the country has a relatively short history of patent accumulation. Given that most high-tech industries are path dependent—the outcome of a process that depends on its past history[32]—'patent thickets'[33] held by incumbents are often barriers for Chinese firms' catch-up. China, for example, has become a global leader in the production of photovoltaic cells and modules, but the upstream sector of this industry is still protected by patent thickets which are mainly held by public research institutions in developed countries. To support companies that have the ability to develop patented indigenous technology, the government offers procurement opportunities, special tax incentives, and government grants.

Catch-Up Logic

From being a catch-up economy, China has grown into one of the world's major innovation leaders in a number of areas, as suggested by research and patent performance measures. Innovation policy has played an important role in its catch-up over the past four decades. Catch-up at the national level focuses on building innovation capabilities through various institutional instruments.[34] In practice this approach can emphasize holistic national interests that sacrifice the interests of individual organizations. The policy, for example, of 'concentrating strengths to do great things' has been used in catching up in strategic industries or technologies, often with political significance. This logic believes that national innovation capabilities, including absorptive capacity[35] and social capital, need high-level (i.e. national)

---

[31] China provides three types of patents: invention patents, utility model patents, and design patents. Unlike invention patents, utility model patents and design patents are granted rights after undergoing preliminary examination but not substantive examination, which makes them relatively cheap and fast to obtain, and they can be enforced as soon as they are granted: see https://english.cnipa.gov.cn//. Accessed 20 July 2021.

[32] In economics and the social sciences, path dependence can refer either to outcomes at a single moment in time or to long-run equilibria of a process. See more at https://en.wikipedia.org/wiki/Path_dependence, accessed 31 May 2021.

[33] A patent thicket is a concept with negative connotations that has been described as 'a dense web of overlapping intellectual property rights that a company must hack its way through in order to actually commercialize new technology', or, in other words, 'an overlapping set of patent rights' which requires innovators to reach licensing deals for multiple patents from multiple sources. (https://en.wikipedia.org/wiki/Patent_thicket). Accessed 20 July 2021.

[34] See R. R. Nelson (1993), *National Innovation Systems: A Comparative Study*, Oxford: Oxford University Press, and OECD (2002), National Innovation Systems. Paris: OECD. https://www.oecd.org/science/inno/2101733.pdf. Accessed 20 July 2021.

[35] The concept of absorptive capacity was first defined by W. M. Cohen and D. A. Levinthal (1990), 'Absorptive Capacity: A New Perspective on Learning and Innovation', *Administrative Science Quarterly*,

coordination and centralized resource mobilization. This model has some advantages under a central-planning economy, assuming that the 'great things' are known targets, and concentrated efforts can shorten the distance to those targets.

Catch-up with known targets can be achieved by knowledge acquisition, technology learning, and 're-innovation'. To catch up, for example, latecomers can reverse the direction of the product life cycle (PLC) in advanced firms.[36] The typical PLC in leading firms—research → development → manufacturing/assembly—can be reversed such that the process of capability building follows the pattern of manufacturing/ assembly → development → research. Learning that occurs in this process is cumulative during the movement from simple activities to more complex ones. At an industry level, latecomers do not necessarily have to rely on technology transfers from incumbents; instead, they can capitalize on windows of opportunity by creating their own trajectory.[37] Industry dynamics, including technological regimes,[38] market regimes,[39] and industrial policies, create the main windows of opportunity. However, latecomers are unable to seize opportunities unless they possess some degree of technological capability and absorptive capacity, which are critical in discerning opportunities and capitalizing on them. While windows of opportunity reflect external conditions, firms' strategies responding to these opportunities also matter in catching up.[40] Successful examples include the semiconductor industry in Japan and South Korea, the digital TV industry in South Korea, the IT service industry in India, and telecommunication industry in China. The experience of these industries shows that leapfrogging (or stage-skipping or path-creating) catch-ups are more likely to occur in those industries characterized by paradigm shifts in technological, market or policy regimes.

Using this approach, Chinese industry has achieved substantial innovation capability. Without considering technological paradigm shifts, catch-up at firm level is mainly a race along fixed trajectories, in which scale, speed, and cost advantages are critical. However, with the increasing pace of technological development, the real targets for catching up are often unknown or shifting. The development of mobile communications is an exemplar case of catch-up. When China rolled out the

---

35, 128–52. It describes a firm's 'ability to recognize the value of new information, assimilate it, and apply it to commercial ends (p. 128).'

[36] L. Kim (1997), *Imitation to Innovation: The Dynamics of Korea's Technological Learning*, Boston, MA: Harvard Business School Press.

[37] K. Lee and F. Malerba (2017), 'Catch-Up Cycles and Changes in Industrial Leadership: Windows of Opportunity and Responses of Firms and Countries in the Evolution of Sectoral Systems', *Research Policy*, 46(2), 338–51.

[38] A technological regime is defined by the particular combination of technological opportunities, appropriability of innovations, cumulativeness of technical advances, and properties of the knowledge base. See S. Breschi, F. Malerba, and L. Orsenigo (2000), 'Technological Regimes and Schumpeterian Pattern of Innovation', *Economic Journal, Royal Economic Society*, 110(463), 388–410,.

[39] Market regimes, in financial terms, refer to long-term, persistent states that can be utilized for making investments or trading decisions. In this context, the term means transactional logics and business models used in a specific market segment.

[40] L. Guo, M.Y. Zhang, M. Dodgson, D. Gann, and H. Cai (2018), 'Seizing Windows of Opportunity by Using Technology-Building and Market-Seeking Strategies in Tandem: Huawei's Sustained Catch-Up in the Global Market', *Asia Pacific Journal of Management*, 36: 849–79.

first- (1G) and the second-generation (2G) mobile networks, the country had hardly any of its own technology. Global firms such as Ericsson, Motorola, and Nokia occupied China's entire market. Meanwhile, a group of Chinese telecommunication firms, including Huawei and ZTE, started to develop their own telecommunication technologies largely based on the reverse PLC approach at the early stage. Initially, however, they were fenced off from the mainstream market because, first, they did not have advanced technologies and, second, incumbent firms held the technology standards and used aggressive pricing strategies to protect their market positions. This was a hard lesson for the Chinese government and firms: standard holders in mobile communications benefit significantly from network effects.[41] Early movers gain hundreds of billions of dollars over the next decade due to lock-in effects in infrastructure networks. China's lesson in this industry is one of lost opportunities in 1G and 2G, paying a high cost to learn from its failed attempt in its home-made 3G standard, and achieving substantial catch-up in 4G.[42] As a result of these experiences, China is determined to lead in 5G,[43] and Chinese companies collectively own the most 5G 'standard essential patents'.[44,45]

There have been continual debates about the extent to which China should rely on indigenous innovation or follow the paths of advanced countries. Different models work in different industries. In the car industry, for example, China adopted a strategy of 'trading market for technology';[46] however, after thirty years, China has lost

---

[41] The network effect is a phenomenon whereby increased numbers of people or participants improve the value of a good or service. The internet is an example of the network effect. See C. Shapiro and H. R. Varian (1998), *Information Rules: A Strategic Guide to the Network Economy*, Cambridge, MA: Harvard Business School Press.

[42] M. Y. Zhang (2016), 'Meso-Level Factors in Technological Transitions: The Development of TD-SCDMA in China', *Research Policy*, 45(2), 546–59.

[43] 5G standards, referred to as IMT-2020, are in line with the specification requirements for 5G by the International Telecommunications Union (ITU) and the 3rd Generation Partnership Project (3GPP). Currently, most 5G networks are built using NSA (non-stand-alone) mode (3GPP-R15-NSA), which can use the existing 4G core networks, complemented by 5G technologies. IMT-2020 is expected to continue to be developed from 2020 onwards, with 5G trials and pre-commercial activities already underway to assist in evaluating the candidate technologies and frequency bands that may be used for this purpose. The first full-scale commercial deployments for 5G are expected sometime after IMT-2020 specifications are finalized. https://www.itu.int/en/mediacentre/backgrounders/Pages/5G-fifth-generation-of-mobile-technologies.aspx. Accessed 20 July 2021.

[44] Standard Essential Patents (SEPs) are patents that are unavoidable for the implementation of a standardized technology. They represent core, pioneering innovation that entire industries will build upon. These patents protect innovation that has taken extraordinary effort to achieve. See J. Lerner and J. Tirole (2013), *Standard-Essential Patents*, Cambridge, MA: National Bureau of Economic Research, https://www.nber.org/system/files/working_papers/w19664/w19664.pdf, accessed 31 May 2021; T. Pohlmann, P. Neuhäusler, and K. Blind (2016), 'Standard Essential Patents to Boost Financial Returns', *R&D Management*, 46, 612–30.

[45] According to IPlytics (April 2019), a German company that tracks a huge patent database, 5G SEPs (standard essential patents) are shared by Huawei (15%), Nokia (13.8%), Samsung (12.7%), LG (12.3%), ZTE (11.7%), Qualcomm (8.2%), Ericsson (7.9%), Intel (5.3%), China Academy of Telecommunications Technology (5.2%), Sharp (4.5%), China's Oppo (2%), and others (1.4%). China, collectively, owns over one third of the SEPs for 5G. SEPs are those patents that any company will have to license when implementing 5G networks.

[46] An industry policy used during the early years of China's catch-up. The policy aimed to access foreign advanced technologies through joint ventures by allowing the foreign companies to enter China's market.

the market to global carmakers and is yet to develop its own technology. In the high-speed railway industry, China adopted a model of importing technology from which it absorbs and learns, which leads on to commercialization of imported technologies through re-innovation.[47] In the nuclear power industry, China adopted a hybrid strategy of using imported technology and developing its own innovation capability. In the last two cases, China's central budgeting, industrial policy, and huge market power helped the catch-up in a path-skipping or path-creating pattern.

After decades of development, most industries in China have developed a basic innovation capability and a strong system integration capability, the ability to combine modules and components of systems. A central problem facing China is that the country's self-sufficiency in technology is still constrained by bottlenecks— critical technologies in China's industrial value chain such as certain basic materials, high-end processing and production equipment, and core components and parts as intermediates. To break through these bottlenecks and develop self-sufficiency the country needs a long-term industry strategy aiming to strengthen its capability in basic science.

In China, both the invisible hand of the market and the visible hand of the government play important roles in promoting technological innovation. The government can use various policy instruments such as fiscal and tax policies to stimulate both the supply and the demand sides of innovation. Breakthroughs in innovation are often driven by entrepreneurs who aim to meet demand in the market. Potential demand provides initial incentives for entrepreneurs to innovate. The market is a fundamental driving force for enterprises to develop and upgrade their technological capabilities. In the absence of effective market mechanisms, technological innovations advocated by the government and policy can often be ineffective in competitive industries. To build an innovative country, China needs to cultivate a culture of respecting entrepreneurship, a core contributor to innovation.

Technological innovation, ultimately, is a market-driven activity. Companies that rely on government support often lack the motivation to innovate. The history of China's reforms in the past forty years has suggested that the market should be the primary driving force for innovation, as decentralized market decision-making has, so far, been the most effective way of supporting innovation, especially in unknown and unexplored areas. One task of institutional reforms in China is to separate the market and the government, that is, to distinguish what should and can be done by each. To achieve the goal of becoming an innovative nation, China must further reform its institutions. Effective policies, thus, should encourage rather than constrain market competition. Establishing a technological innovation system with

---

[47] Re-innovation or secondary innovation refers to the ability to make changes in something established, especially by introducing new methods, ideas, or products. See C. J. Cheng and E. C. C. Shiu (2008), 'Re-Innovation: The Construct, Measurement, and Validation', *Technovation*, 28, 658–66; X. Wu (1997), 'The Evolutionary Process of Secondary Innovation', in D. F. Kocaoglu (ed.), *Innovation in Technology Management: The Key to Global Leadership*, PICMET '97. 183. doi: 10.1109/PICMET.1997.653308.

in-depth integration of industry, university, and research institutes and building such a system in an open innovation ecosystem will be key to China's future.

China's catch-up policy in recent years has shifted from being science and technology-driven to an integrated policy framework covering all aspects of the innovation value chain. Its policy instruments range from providing financial support and tax incentives to 'special actors of innovation' to developing an innovation ecosystem to cultivate and support 'mass entrepreneurship and innovation'. This requires building an institutional environment that encourages innovation from the bottom up and guarantees innovators benefit from their innovations in fair market competition.

How Far Is China from Technological Frontiers?

A big part of China's development has been in technology, the result of which is shown in the growth of China's high-tech outputs. Since China joined the WTO in 2001, its global trade volume has increased rapidly, and its share of exports of high-tech products grew from 17 per cent in 2001 to 30 per cent in 2018 (see Figure 2.4).

There are marked differences in performance across technology sectors. From the comparisons of import and export volumes in different sectors (as shown in Table 2.1), we can see that, in computer and communication technologies, exports accounted for over 80 per cent of the balance in trade. In many other high-tech sectors, however, imports overweighed exports. This shows how in industries such as aviation and aerospace, biotechnology, computer-integrated manufacturing, and electronics, China relies heavily on imported technologies.

Despite these statistics and other indicators, China has not reached global technological frontiers in the manner of some of its international competitors.

To understand how far China is away from the technological frontier, we turn to the case of Huawei, one of China's most innovative firms. When in May 2020 the US announced further restrictions on using American technologies by Huawei and its affiliates, Huawei's CEO Xu Zhijun reacted by saying, 'This puts Huawei's survival at

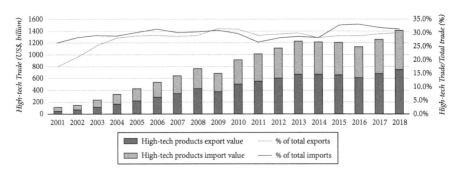

Figure 2.4 China's high-tech trade, 2001–18

Source: China Statistical Yearbook on Science and Technology (2019)

Table 2.1 China's high-tech trade by industry (2018)

	Total trade (billion US$)	Export (%)	Import (%)
Computer and Communication Technology	62,941	80. 2%	19.8%
Life Science and Technology	6,899	47.3%	52.7%
Electronics	49,895	28.4%	71.6%
Computer-Integrated Manufacturing Technology	7,467	21.9%	78.1%
Aviation and Aerospace	4,960	18.4%	81.6%
Photonics	6,931	41.8%	58.2%
Biotechnology	339	27.4%	72.6%
Material Science	1,228	60.8%	39.2%
Others	198	50.0%	50.0%

Source: China Statistical Yearbook on Science and Technology (2019)

stake.'[48] These new rules have a significant impact on the wider technology supply chains in China as a whole, as well as Huawei's. If Huawei's survival relies on imported technologies from the US, China can be seen to be far from global technological frontiers. Huawei's case allows us to examine the extent of technology dependency in China's industry supply chains.

Judged by market share, Huawei overtook Ericsson to become the largest telecom manufacturer in the world in 2012.[49] Before US sanctions were applied to Huawei in 2020, the company was the global leader in market share in all three of its major business areas. Its market share was largest in the carrier business, and the second largest in both enterprise and consumer businesses, after Cisco and Samsung respectively.[50] Huawei started its consumer business in 2012 and experienced rapid growth, with a compound annual growth rate (CAGR) of 35 per cent between 2013 and 2019. Its consumer business accounted for over 50 per cent of the company's revenue in 2019.[51] Huawei has recently established its fourth business area: Huawei's cloud, which is gaining market share rapidly.

Overall, as shown in Figure 2.5, Huawei gained a large proportion of its business in the global market, despite a decline between 2012 and 2019, largely due to strong growth of its consumer business, that is, smartphones, tablets, personal computers and other consumer products, in the domestic market. By the end of the first quarter

[48] Kathrin Hille (2020), 'US "Surgical" Attack on Huawei Will Reshape Tech Supply Chain', *Financial Times*, 19 May, https://www.ft.com/content/c614afc5-86f8-42b1-9b6c-90bffbd1be8b, accessed 1 June 2021.

[49] 'Huawei surpasses Ericsson as world's largest telecom equipment vendor', 25 July 2012. https://www.zdnet.com/article/huawei-surpasses-ericsson-as-worlds-largest-telecom-equipment-vendor/. Accessed 20 July 2021.

[50] According to a report on global telecom equipment market report by Dell'Oro Group, Huawei's market share (including China) in 2020 stayed on the top position of 31%, registered only 3% growth from 2019, despite taking over 60% market share in China. https://www.delloro.com/key-takeaways-total-telecom-equipment-market-2020/, accessed 20 July 2021.

[51] Huawei's 2019 Annual Report: https://www.huawei.com/au/press-events/annual-report/2019, accessed 1 June 2021.

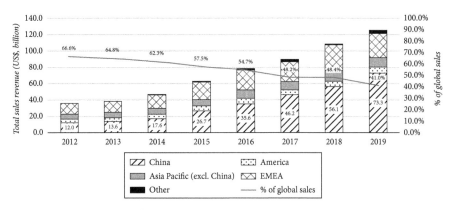

Figure 2.5 Huawei's global sales, 2012–19

Source: Huawei's annual reports[1]

[1] *The average exchange rates of USD/RMB used to calculate Huawei's sale revenue were*: USD/RMB=6.31, 6.15, 6.16, 6.28, 6.65, 6.76, 6.64, and 7.04 between 2012 and 2019 respectively.

of 2020, Huawei's market share in China's smartphone sector reached 40 per cent, compared to 17 per cent globally.[52]

Catch-up in market share and innovation often intertwine, but are not necessarily synchronized in pace. Innovation capability is essential for latecomers' catch-up, and building it is a cumulative process which entails both exploitation of existing knowledge and exploration of new knowledge. Approaching industrial frontiers, catching-up firms need to rely more on technological breakthroughs based on explorations of the unknown.

During Huawei's catch-up, the company developed different competitive advantages at different stages by building innovation capability and seeking market expansion in tandem. It did so in an upward spiral, responding to various windows of opportunity opened by changes in market conditions, policy frameworks, and technological regimes (from landline to wireless and generational changes from 1G to 5G) in communication networks.[53] As Huawei's founder Ren Zhengfei said: 'Searching for and grasping opportunities are the major tasks for latecomers; while creating opportunities and driving new consumption are for forerunners in the industry.'[54] He pointed out at the time that 'The telecommunication industry will face dramatic disruptions in the coming decades. For Huawei, we need to know where we will be when the revolution comes.' This philosophy explains Huawei's

---

[52] Due to the effects of the US trade ban against Huawei's access to high-end chips and Google's android system, Huawei's market share in smart phones fell out of the top five suppliers. https://www.statista.com/statistics/271496/global-market-share-held-by-smartphone-vendors-since-4th-quarter-2009/, accessed 20 July, 2021.

[53] Guo, Zhang, Dodgson, Gann, and Cai, 'Seizing Windows of Opportunity'.

[54] Ren Zhengfei periodically communicates his strategic thinking, his judgment on the company and the industry, his management philosophy, his values and expectations of employees with the company's stakeholders in Huawei's internal magazine *Huawei People*. Ren once claimed that he personally penned each piece. Given the strategic value of these talks and Huawei's leadership in China's telecommunication, these talks become available to Chinese public.

catching-up trajectory: from following paths of forerunners to exploring new ones, when approaching new frontiers.

As simply captured by Geoff Nicholson of 3M, the 'Father of Post-it Notes', 'research is the transformation of money into knowledge. Innovation is the transformation of knowledge into money.'[55] Huawei regularly invests over 10 per cent of its sales revenue in R&D, especially in 5G and future technologies.

In 2019 Huawei was the third largest R&D investor after Alphabet (the parent company of Google) and Microsoft.[56] Its R&D spending in 2019 was more than the total of its competitors in the mobile network business (including 5G), namely Ericsson, Cisco, and Qualcomm (see Figure 2.6). Huawei's R&D investment has paid off, especially in 5G. The US, on the other hand, has lost its leading position in 5G. This situation will be examined in greater depth in 'Why 5G' section.

However, another factor that matters is accumulation of technological capability over time. In areas where technological accumulation counts, Huawei has achieved catch-up in market share but still lags behind in technological leadership. During the early years of its catch-up, when incumbent firms dominated the market and controlled major technological knowledge stocks, Huawei entered the low-end market by capitalizing on government policy and market windows by building advantages such as low-cost production, customer-centric services, and integrative innovation capability. Using USPTO patent data to measure Huawei's catch-up during 2000 and 2012, Guo and colleagues confirmed the effectiveness of this strategy. In the established field of data communications (Huawei's enterprise business), where the technological trajectory was relatively stable and innovation was predictable, the strong patent protection of incumbents, such as Cisco, worked against latecomers and Huawei caught up mainly in market share and by innovation capability built on patent quantity rather than patent quality. In emerging mobile communications

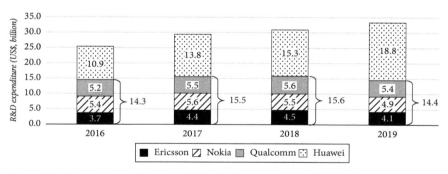

Figure 2.6 Comparison of Huawei's R&D with its competition, 2016–19
Source: Individual companies' annual reports

[55] See https://www.hardwarezone.com.sg/feature-dr-geoff-nicholson-father-post-it-notes-3m-innovation, accessed 1 June 2021.
[56] N. Grassano et al. (2020), 'The 2020 EU Industrial R&D Investment Scoreboard', 1 January, https://iri.jrc.ec.europa.eu/scoreboard/2020-eu-industrial-rd-investment-scoreboard, accessed 1 June 2021.

(Huawei's carrier business), where innovation is uncertain and frequent, incumbents such as Ericsson and Nokia did not hold such advantages in knowledge stock. Huawei managed to capitalize on the windows of opportunity of network generational changes and achieved catch-up in both market share and technology.[57]

The dilemma Huawei faces in its transition to technological leadership is its innovation capability. According to Guo and colleagues, a company's *overall* innovation capability is determined not only by the breadth of its knowledge accumulation, but by the depth of its *core* innovation capability.[58] Huawei's overall capability, underlined by its knowledge breadth, alone is insufficient for it to transition to leadership in industry-level innovations. To forge ahead and become an industry leader in innovation, Huawei needs to develop core innovation capability with a high level of technological value and industry influence, which is underlined by the depth of its knowledge stock and can only be achieved by accumulation of R&D in basic science and emerging technology.

Why 5G?

To understand the advantages of upgrading to 5G, envision a scene where 4G is inadequate. Imagine ten thousand people are sitting in a sports stadium watching a World Cup final game and they all want to text messages or send photos of the game at the same time. It will be very difficult to send the messages or photos through to each other, let alone to outsiders. The reason is that, in a concentrated area where only limited number of base stations are in proximity, the transmission capacity of the base stations quickly reaches their physical limits. In other words, messages will be jammed, waiting in a queue to be transmitted through base stations. The 4G network is designed in such a way that all traffic must go through its base stations, which means that direct device-to-device transmission is impossible.

This scene suggests that while 4G networks provide sufficient bandwidth for speed in daily life, they have a deficiency in network capacity. Theoretically, 4G networks can support about 100,000 devices per square kilometre. This capacity, however, is inadequate for concentrated traffic (e.g. in a stadium or a conference hall) or any future applications which require data transmission of a massive number of devices, data transmission in real time (e.g. remote surgery or driverless cars), or in a fast-moving environment (e.g. in high-speed vehicles or trains).

To judge whether demand for 5G is real or not, it is necessary to look beyond current knowledge or experience. Ultimately, the majority of applications for an innovation emerge and mature as the innovation is diffused in society over time: build it and they will come.

---

[57] L. Guo, M. Y. Zhang, M. Dodgson, and D. Gann (2019), 'Huawei's Catch-Up in the Global Telecommunication Industry: Innovation Capability and Transition to Leadership', *Technology Analysis & Strategic Management*, 31(12), 1–17.

[58] Guo, Zhang, Dodgson, and Gann 'Huawei's Catch-Up in the Global Telecommunication Industry'.

5G networks promise to provide fast, large-capacity, and enhanced real-time data transmission.[59] Compared to 4G, 5G's biggest advantage is its low latency data transmission. Latency is the time taken for devices to respond to each other over mobile networks. For instance, 3G networks have a typical response time of 100 milliseconds, 4G about 30 milliseconds and 5G as low as one millisecond. This low latency will enable real-time (virtually instantaneous) transmission between devices, which can be used in applications such as industry automation, driverless cars, machine-to-machine communications, and transport networks.

In mobile networks, radio spectrum is a critical resource. The allocation of spectrum is, therefore, at the heart of 5G competition. Currently, under the IMT 2020—the global standard and specifications for 5G by the International Telecommunciations Uniion (ITU)—two sets of relatively high-frequency spectrums (compared to those in 4G) can be used for 5G. The first is mid-band spectrums ('sub-6 GHz'), and the second is the high-band spectrum (millimetre Wave—'mmWave'). Most countries have sub-6 spectrums available for 5G networks, including China. Most sub-6 GHz bands in the US, however, are owned by the federal government and are extensively used by the defence forces.

5G using sub-6 GHz spectrums can better utilize current 4G base stations. The advantages of sub-6 GHz solutions are that data transmits over longer distances and penetrates more objects, compared to over mmWave spectrums. Sub-6 solutions are ideal for covering areas of up to ten square kilometres, such as large patches of city, residential areas, or rural expanses. However, mmWave spectrums have more bandwidth and the solutions for mmWave are ideal for small and targeted areas, such as sports stadiums. Huawei is a leader in sub-6 technology and has accumulated competitive capabilities in the engineering used for network constructions in 4G and 5G.

The US-led 5G solution using mmWave spectrum promises more dramatic changes in 5G. The technology is more complex, however, and will take more time to mature. This situation put the US in a difficult position: whether it should adopt the sub-6 solution but give up the leadership to Chinese firms or delay the deployment of 5G in the US by giving more time to its own mmWave solution. Another challenge is whether the country can free the sub-6 spectrum from military use. A short-term answer for the US is to push its allies, such as the UK and Australia, to also exclude Huawei from their 5G networks, on the one hand, limiting their ability to develop competitive advantages over the US, and to stop Huawei forging ahead with its 5G ambition, on the other.

In an infrastructure business such as 5G, scale is critical. The success of 5G networks relies on huge investments in R&D, as well as high capital costs in infrastructure. The larger a company's market share, the better it can afford these costs.

---

[59] The system architecture of 5G core networks uses network-slicing technology which allows separation of the major network functions, for example, the separation of computing and storage functions, to improve network efficiency. This system design, a service-based architecture, enables enhanced mobile broadband communications, ultra-reliable low latency communications, and massive machine-type communications.

Companies facing a shrinking market will find it harder to sustain the levels of investment required to stay competitive.

Unlike its predecessors, 5G is built more around a digital ecosystem. The growth of 5G is, therefore, more about an ecosystem in which multiple players (old and emerging) coexist and co-develop, supported by interconnected and interdependent IT networks (including AI, big data, and cloud computing) and global supply chain networks. The nature of 5G operating in an enlarged ecosystem means its development will not be driven by network operators or mobile network equipment manufacturers such as Huawei, Nokia, and Ericsson; rather, it will be driven by the proliferation of all kinds of complementary applications in the ecosystem.

According to a GSMA (Global System for Mobile Communications Association)[60] study, only 20 per cent of 5G traffic will be human-to-human communications. The rest will be between a massive number of devices. For example, the internet of things (IoT)—a system of interconnected computing devices, objects, animals, and humans, each embedded with a unique identifier (UID)—will make up the vast majority of 5G traffic. This study also suggests that the largest 5G applications will be in 2B (to business) sectors, and government will represent an important user for 5G applications. It suggests the number of devices, such as wearables on humans or animals, smart speakers at home, driverless cars, intelligent sensors and cameras in cities, automation equipment in factories, will increase exponentially, that is, growing at 10 to 100 times the current level.

Hence, 5G is a breakthrough technology; it extends the connections from human to human and human to computer to connections between devices without human interference. Potentially, applications powered by 5G can revolutionize modern practices and processes in manufacturing, agriculture, transport, medical and health care, education, entertainment, government, and many more.

All these depend upon a device: the integrated circuit (IC) chip.

Bottlenecks in China's Catch-Up in Innovation: The Case of Semiconductors

Despite China's impressive progress in innovation, there are still many bottlenecks in its innovation capability building. The IC chip is one of these bottlenecks.

For some core technologies, China still depends on supply from more advanced countries. Despite being the largest PC producer and market, for example, China relies on Intel and AMD for its high-end chips; despite running the largest high-speed railway networks, China relies on power systems and control systems supplied by Siemens and ABB; despite being the largest car market, China relies on imported

---

[60] The GSMA represents the interests of mobile operators worldwide, uniting more than 750 operators with almost 400 companies in the broader mobile ecosystem, including handset and device makers, software companies, equipment providers, and internet companies, as well as organizations in adjacent industry sectors.

car engines from global carmakers; despite being the largest steel producer, China needs to import special steel (300M alloy steel) from the US and Japan for special purposes such as aircraft landing gear and airframe parts; despite being the 'world factory' in manufacturing, China needs to import ultra-precision machine tools from Germany, Japan, and Switzerland.

Modern electronic devices are amongst the most complex things humans produce, and IC chips are the foundation of them all. The IC chip is an American invention, but chipmaking is a global business. High-tech innovation in semiconductors is a process of creating products through applying abstract knowledge in complex R&D activities along with precision production. This process is lengthy and risky, involves much trial and error, and requires huge investment. The brief history of the semiconductor industry in Silicon Valley illustrates this process, as shown in Figure 2.7.

The industry is built upon the discovery of semiconductors and the effect of transistors, which won Nobel Prize in physics in 1956. During the following two decades, huge efforts were put into applying this abstract knowledge through endless experiments into products with commercial value. This was followed by a period of building a global ecosystem of specialized suppliers embedded along a global value chain. It was an organic process, with no central planning; players found their niches and developed their specialties, and, eventually, formed an interdependent and interconnected ecosystem. This ecosystem has delivered efficiency and, collectively, has advanced the technological frontier of the industry. The value chain of semiconductor industry is illustrated in Figure 2.8.

EDA (electronic design automation) is a category of software tools for designing advanced IC chips containing billions of transistors. Compared to the size of the entire semiconductor sector, EDA's market is small, worth about $9.75 billion in 2018. It experienced stable growth with a CAGR of 6.8 per cent between 2014 and

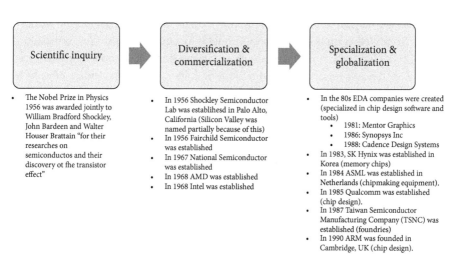

Figure 2.7 A brief history of the semiconductor industry

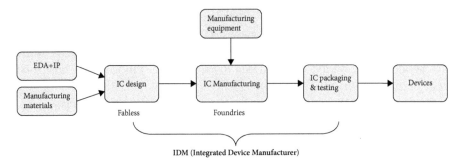

Figure 2.8 Value chain of the semiconductor industry

2018. IC chip design is so complex that only EDA tools can produce chip designs which can be manufactured in specific foundries: chipmaking factories. The global EDA sector is dominated by three American companies: Synopsis, Cadence, and Mentor Graphics (acquired by Siemens in 2016). Their market shares in 2018 were 32 per cent, 22 per cent, and 10 per cent, respectively. They provide software tools and intellectual property (IP) to major chip design companies such as Intel, AMD, and China's HiSilicon (Huawei's subsidiary). Their business model is not based on software licences. Rather, they collaboratively optimize the design and production of chips by linking fabless chip design companies (chip design houses without foundries) and chipmaking foundries. Through dynamic information flows enabled by PDK (process design kit)—a set of files between these players to model a fabrication process—this link co-designs specific IC chips for different purposes. Without EDA's help, chip design becomes almost impossible.

Manufacturing materials for IC chips include raw wafer and chemical materials. Both areas are dominated by American firms. A wafer is a thin slice of semiconductor, such as a crystalline silicon, used for the fabrication of IC chips. The wafer serves as the substrate for microelectronic devices built in and upon the wafer.

Wafers are fabricated by special equipment. There is only one firm in the world—ASML from Netherlands—that makes lithography equipment using extreme ultraviolet (EUV) light to enable the production of transistors small enough for advanced chips. ASML has spent decades, and billions of dollars, getting its cutting-edge technology to work. Its 180-tonne machines sell for $135 million per unit. Its customers include Intel, TSMC (the largest foundry owned by the Taiwanese), and Samsung. SMIC, a Chinese chipmaker, ordered one, but delivery becomes uncertain with the US sanctions against Chinese technology industry.[61]

Integrated device manufacturers (IDM) are semiconductor firms that design, manufacture, pack, and test, as well as sell their IC chips. A traditional IDM owns its

---

[61] A. Alper, T. Sterling, and S. Nellis (2020), 'Trump Administration Pressed Dutch Hard to Cancel China Chip-Equipment Sale, Reuters, 6 January, https://www.reuters.com/article/us-asml-holding-usa-china-insight/trump-administration-pressed-dutch-hard-to-cancel-china-chip-equipment-sale-sources-idUSKBN1Z50HN, accessed 1 June 2021.

own branded chips and does design in-house and has a fabrication plant where chips are manufactured. Intel (US), Texas Instrument (US), Samsung (South Korea), SK Hynix (South Korea), and Micron Technology (US) are examples of IDM. The advantage of keeping everything in-house is that they can optimize efficiency between chip design and production.

Specialized firms along the value chain of the IC industry have emerged and matured in the past three decades. Fabless companies such as Qualcomm (US), ARM (UK), MediaTek (Taiwan), and HiSilicon (China) are chip design companies that depend on foundries to turn their design powered by EDA into microchips. Compared to IDM, this type of firm takes a higher risk in their chip design, as they do not have information from production which could valuably connect to their chip design. One of the contributions of EDA is that it can help coordinate co-design between chip design and chipmaking companies.

Foundries are independent chipmaking plants that work for multiple design houses. The largest foundry is Taiwan Semiconductor Manufacturing Company (TSMC), which held 54 per cent of the global market share in 2019. It is one of only two firms capable of producing next-generation microprocessors (the other is Samsung, which holds a 20 per cent market share) such as 5nm and 7nm chips. TSMC supplies almost all Apple's and over 90 per cent of Huawei's smartphone chips before the US sanctions. Independent foundries are capital-intensive businesses, as they need to invest in R&D and expensive equipment such as ASML's EUV lithography machine. To survive, scale is key. China's SMIC has a 6 per cent market share. It can make chips as small as 14nm, which is at least two generations older than TSMC's or Samsung's chips.

Downstream of the value chain is IC packaging and testing, in which Chinese firms hold a substantial market share.

From the above value chain analysis, we can see that the semiconductor industry has become specialized and internationalized. The US, however, remains the strongest in this industry, with more than a 45 per cent global market share.[62] The semiconductor industry is critical to the global economic competitiveness and technology supremacy of the US. The healthy development of this industry, however, relies on continuous capital investment, which is grounded in a virtuous cycle connecting many stakeholders. To achieve such a virtuous cycle, firms need to rely on access to global markets to achieve the scale needed to fund very large R&D investments and purchases of expensive tools and equipment. The components of the supply chain of the semiconductor industry are deeply connected with one another: sometimes components are passed from one supplier to another across the globe several times. It can be very difficult for device companies that are often the end users of IC chips to track their entire supply chain.

---

[62] A.Varas and R. Varadarajan (2020), 'How Restricting Trade with China Could End US Semiconductor Leadership', Boston Consulting Group, 9 March, https://www.bcg.com/publications/2020/restricting-trade-with-china-could-end-united-states-semiconductor-leadership, accessed 1 June 2021.

Can China Break Those Bottlenecks of Core Technology?

Despite Huawei's leading position in 5G, its short-term survival is dependent upon the supply of several core technologies from the West, especially the US.

For seven consecutive years until 2019, semiconductor products accounted for the single largest imported item in terms of value into China. In 2019, its import value reached $445 billion (more than twice of the import value of unprocessed oil), about 35 per cent of the world total. On the other hand, semiconductor exports from China were $305 billion, only 7 per cent of the world total. The domestic production of semiconductors (excluding the production from manufacturing foundries of foreign semiconductor companies) covered only 14 per cent of China's domestic demand, and was mainly in low-end chips or services. Although Huawei has its own semiconductor subsidiary, HiSilicon, it still imported most of its chips and, in 2019, spent $11 billion on semiconductor components from the US alone, about 15 per cent of the total value of its supply chains.

Huawei's supply chains illustrate the reliance of China's technology industry on core technologies controlled by Western firms. Table 2.2 shows Huawei's supply chains in three product families before the US technology sanctions: electronic equipment, telecom equipment, and consumer electronics.

Huawei has ninety-two core suppliers in its supply chains, including thirty-three in the US, eleven in Japan, ten in Taiwan, four in Germany, two in Switzerland, South Korea, Hong Kong, and the Netherlands, one in France and Singapore, and twenty-five in mainland China.[63] Non-Chinese suppliers accounted for 72.8 per cent of Huawei's core supply chains. As shown in Table 2.2, Huawei relies heavily on imported components in the area of chip design and material supplies.

When in 2020 the US imposed further technology sanctions against Huawei and affiliates from using American technologies, SMIC, China's largest chipmaker, received $2 billion from the Chinese Government's IC Investment Fund, nicknamed as chip-focused 'Big Fund'.[64] In 2021, Chinese leading universities, including Tsinghua University, Peking University, Shanghai Jiaotong University, and Nanjing University, established IC schools, microelectronic colleges, and related programs to train the country's top students for the semiconductor industry. The question is whether China's investment can enable it to catch up in chips any time soon.

Even in the absence of American EDA tools and IP, China is catching up on chip design rapidly. Beijing-based Huada Empyrean Software, which are making good progress, are still perhaps ten years behind the forerunners in technology capability

---

[63] Huawei's core suppliers conference, December 2018.

[64] The China National Integrated Circuit Industry Investment Fund, nicknamed as chip-focused 'Big Fund', raised RMB 278 billion (around $29 billion) by the end of 2017, which triggered further investment of RMB 514 billion from the local governments. In October 2019, the second stage of 'Big Fund' raised RMB 204 billion from the Finance Ministry, state-owned firms, and local governments. The 'Big Fund' represents an effort to increase China's technological self-reliance and build a world-class semiconductor industry.

Table 2.2 Huawei's supply chain

	Design and material suppliers	Manufacturing and production service suppliers
Electronic equipment	• IC design: 17 suppliers all non-Chinese, 13 from the US • Storage: 9 suppliers all non-Chinese. Samsung (South Korea), SK Hynix (South Korea) and Micron Technology (US) accounted for 90% of the supply • Connector: 9 suppliers, 5 from China. Three Chinese suppliers are among the top 20 in the world • PCBs (printed circuit board): 8 suppliers, 5 from China	• Software and information services: 21 suppliers, 13 from China. US firms dominate EDA design tools and IP, open-source software, database, and operating systems. • Manufacturing contractors: 14 suppliers, 10 from China. TSMC for chips and Foxconn for smartphones. • Electronic equipment, including engine room, power supply, security, and camera sensors: 10 suppliers, 8 from China; top 2 from Japan (Mitsubishi and Panasonic)
Telecom equipment	• Optical fibre and cable: 9 suppliers, 6 from China • Optical module: 8 suppliers, 3 from China • Base station radio optical module: 7 suppliers, 5 from China	• Testing services and equipment: 5 suppliers, 1 from China. 2 from the US, 1 from Germany and 1 from Japan.
Consumer electronics	• Structural components: 100% from China • Optical modules (cameras): China (50%), Japan and Taiwan • Panel and glass cover: 100% from BOE[1], China • Battery and energy suppliers: 100% from China and Hong Kong	• Telecom engineering and services, including network construction and maintenance: all 6 suppliers from China

[1] BOE Technology is China's largest manufacturer of LCD screens and was ranked thirty-fourth on the Fortune 500 in 2000. In 2019, it surpassed South Korea's LG Display to become the world's largest FPD supplier: see https://technology.informa.com/614595/boe-becomes-worlds-largest-flat-panel-display-manufacturer-in-2019-as-china-continues-rise-to-global-market-dominance, accessed 1 June 2021.

Source: Huawei's annual reports, various industry analysis reports

and can only help design low-end chips at this stage. Since 2020, China has seen many startups in EDA. As EDA providers frequently upgrade their tools upon feedback from both fabless chip design companies and foundries using PDK,[65] it is very difficult for latecomers to find enough partners to create the economies of scale for survival, let alone compete with incumbents. This may change if a different technological trajectory emerges, such as carbon-based nanotube arrays which promise high performance in future chips.

If the US technology sanctions were not lifted, it would force China to develop a different ecosystem for semiconductors. China's market size could provide a natural experimental lab in which fast generational upgrades would eventually lead to products compatible in quality with the American-led ones. China could also sell its

[65] See further https://en.wikipedia.org/wiki/Process_design_kit, accessed 1 June 2021.

low-end products to developing countries. There are still more than three billion people in developing countries who are price-sensitive and would accept less optimal products if available. Such a strategy—using 'peripheries to enclose the core'—a wartime strategy used by Mao Zedong to defeat much more powerful enemies during the anti-Japanese war and the civil war with the National Party—could prove to be effective in developing an independent technology ecosystem.

Such a scenario would be disruptive of the current global order.

Innovation Capability and China's R&D Spending

Catch-up theories assume that, first, latecomers, at the national, industry or firm level, possess certain fundamental advantages, for example, fixed targets, technology transfer from technological leaders, low costs of production, and large-scale markets, which enable them to learn from the forerunners and rapidly develop their own overall innovation capability. Second, catch-up will slow down when the technological distance between the follower and the forerunner reaches a balanced point at which they stay for a long period, as the forerunners also advance their innovation, unless latecomers develop a certain core innovation capability which may change technological or market regimes radically. Apart from these apparent latecomer advantages, there are two significant latecomer disadvantages in their catch-up: technology and market. Technological disadvantages are often caused by the dislocation of latecomer firms from the central sources of science, technology, design, and R&D. Market disadvantages are caused by restricted access to more sophisticated users in the mainstream global market. These disadvantages explain why many catch-ups that occur are mainly in domestic markets and limited to catch-ups in market share rather than technological leadership.

Innovation capability building is a gradual and cumulative process by which latecomers expand their knowledge base in both scope and depth.[66] A large body of literature has confirmed that technology spillovers from technologically advanced countries are a critical source of technology building for latecomers during their early stages of catch-up.[67] When they move towards the technology frontier, knowledge from such channels becomes inadequate. Some Chinese firms in recent years have started to seek further technological capability building from global acquisitions. China's PC maker Lenovo, for example, acquired IBM's PC business, and the carmaker Geely acquired Volvo's brands and technology. Such technology acquisition strategies, however, are facing an increasingly hostile global environment.

Growth in total factor productivity (TFP), a broad measure of how productively an economy uses capital and labour, has declined in China in recent years despite an

---

[66] J. Cantwell (2017), 'Innovation and International Business', *Industry and Innovation*, 24, 41–60.

[67] M. Hobday (1995), 'East Asian Latecomer Firms: Learning the Technology of Electronics', *World Development*, 23, 1171–93, and K. Lee and C. S. Lim (2001), 'Technological Regimes, Catching-Up and Leapfrogging: Findings from the Korean Industries', *Research Policy*, 30, 459–83.

increase in R&D spending. China's R&D spending, however, is strongly skewed towards applied and experimental research—using existing knowledge to create materials or products—which may contribute to its overall innovation capability. More than 90 per cent of R&D spending was on applied and experimental research in 2019 (see Figure 2.9). In enterprise R&D spending, more than 96 per cent was channelled into experimental development, only 0.3 per cent into basic research— pure research or fundamental research aiming to improve scientific theories for improved understanding or prediction of natural or other phenomena (see Table 2.3). Basic research—underlying core innovation capability—in China accounts for only 6 per cent of research funding, compared to 17 per cent in the US, 18 per cent in the UK, 13.7 per cent in Japan, and an average of 15 per cent among thirty-six OECD countries.[68] Insufficient investment in basic research has been attributed as a key reason why China suffers from the bottleneck technologies controlled by overseas suppliers. At the People's Congress which concluded in March 2021, the central

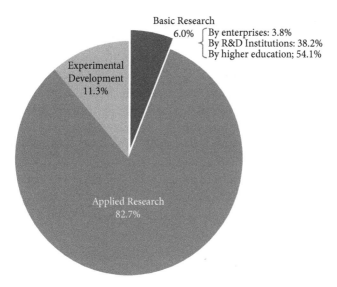

Figure 2.9 Breakdown of China's R&D expenditure by research type (2019)
Source: China Statistical Yearbook on Science and Technology (2019)

Table 2.3 Breakdown of China's R&D expenditure by research actor (2018)

Research Type	Enterprises	R&D Institutions	Higher education
Basic Research	0.3%	15.7%	40.5%
Applied Research	3.8%	29.6%	48.8%
Experimental Development	96.0%	54.7%	10.7%

Source: China Statistical Yearbook on Science and Technology (2019)

---

[68] See further https://www.natureindex.com/, accessed 1 June 2021.

government indicated that the country will increase its R&D spending in basic research, especially in pure mathematics and pure sciences, to 8 per cent during the Fourteenth Five-Year Plan period (2021–6).[69]

The skewness towards applied and experimental research is also shown in lower investments in basic research in higher education and research institutions, where R&D spending in basic research in 2019 was 40.5 per cent and 15.7 per cent, respectively. This bias can be seen in the country's Programme 863, the first large government-led science and technology project. Unlike similar state-driven projects in more developed countries, Programme 863 had very pragmatic goals. It aimed to learn the direction of progress in science and technology to inform catch-up. The programme tracked global developments on scientific and technological frontiers and concentrated its strengths to catch up with them. Essentially, Programme 863 provides a blueprint for China to learn, imitate, and achieve limited catch-up in science and technology, based on 'applied basic research'—which is path-following basic research that results in more certain returns in publications in contrast to pure basic research investments which may result in low or no returns in the short term.

The root reason for such a skewness can be traced back to the funding sources of China's R&D. Table 2.4 shows the breakdowns of China's R&D spending by funding source and by performing entity.

Over three-quarters of China's R&D spending in 2018 was self-raised funds. Government funding for R&D accounted for only 20 per cent and has been shrinking, from 26.6 per cent in 2004, 23.4 per cent in 2009, to 20.2 per cent in 2018.

The relative decline in government funding in R&D is related to increased investments by self-raised funds, especially from large enterprises. 85 per cent of R&D spending in enterprises is by large enterprises. The top five Chinese enterprises— all state-owned—accounted for almost 30 per cent of the total R&D spending in this category, a much higher proportion than among the top five companies in

Table 2.4 Breakdowns of China's R&D Spending by funding source and performing entity (2018)

R&D performers	Funding source			
	Government funds	Self-raised funds	Foreign funds	Other funds
National Total: $298.2 billion	20.2%	76.6%	0.4%	2.8%
Enterprises (77.4%)	3.2%	95.6%	0.4%	0.8%
R&D Institutions (13.7%)	84.9%	3.8%	0.2%	11.1%
Higher Education (7.4%)	66.7%	26.6%	0.4%	6.4%
Others (1.5%)	78.1%	9.9%	0.1%	11.9%

Source: *China Statistical Yearbook on Science and Technology* (2019)

---

[69] Interview transcript of Wang Zhigang, Minister of Science and Technology, at the People's Congress in Beijing, March 8, 2021.

the US and the EU, where large enterprises represented less than 20 per cent of total spending.

Chinese small and medium-sized enterprises (SMEs) especially aim to have quick returns on their R&D investment and focus their innovation and R&D activities mainly on applied and experimental research. Low-hanging fruit are more attractive in the short term. This type of effort does not generate technological breakthroughs. This situation is especially severe in the biotech/biopharmaceutics industry. Chinese firms innovate to produce medicine for the mass market, which brings quick returns. Spending on 'orphan precision medicine' that promises to cure rare diseases but with very high costs per patient is hardly an option for market-driven pharmaceutical firms in China before venture capital was introduced to the sector, which we will elaborate upon in Chapter 6.[70]

Other emerging technologies to attract policy attention include nanotechnology and quantum computing, where the government aims to increase national technological capabilities. Between 2001 and 2019, China created more than 170 innovation support policies at the central level alone, and many more at the local level. The 'visible hand' of the government may rectify the market when it fails to work, but it may also lead to opportunism or unfair competition. We will discuss China's industrial policy and its institutional logics in detail in Chapter 7.

Can China Forge Ahead to Become an Innovation Leader?

Analytically, a knowledge structure is an interrelated collection of schemes under which knowledge can be organized in relation to a domain. Core technology, such as semiconductors and advanced AI algorithms, can be foundational technology that has general and wide applications and influences the direction of development in an industry. But core technology can also be cutting-edge processing technology that enables the production of essential materials or products in an industry, such as lithographical technology in wafer fabrication.

Core technologies are those on the bottom of an inverted pyramid of a knowledge structure:[71] it is pivotal in this structure, as shown in Figure 2.10. In the knowledge structure of the semiconductor industry, for example, EDA is the core which is built upon deep knowledge; in the middle lie fabless IC designers and foundries which transform chip design into chips; downstream of IC packaging and testing, there are many players relying on broad knowledge.

Although they may catch up in some areas, the imbalance in latecomer firms' knowledge stocks often constrains their becoming true industry leaders. Latecomer

---

[70] Interviews with scientists in biopharmaceutical industries in China and the United States.

[71] A knowledge structure is an interrelated collection of schemes under which knowledge can be organized in relation to a domain. It is composed of mental constructions linked to other mental constructions by labelled relationships. See further https://www.igi-global.com/dictionary/experience-cognition-video-game-play/16464, accessed 1 June 2021.

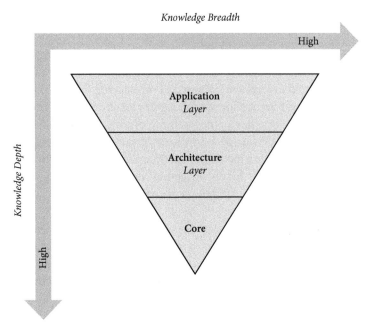

Figure 2.10 Knowledge structure

firms find it challenging to manage the transition to technology leadership due to narrow breadth or shallow depth, or both, in their knowledge structures. Substantive technological breakthroughs require breadth in firms' knowledge and, more importantly, depth. Chinese firms are not yet global leaders in any of the science-based industries which require deep knowledge structures. For complex products such as branded pharmaceutics or passenger jets, where China lacks knowledge stock in both breadth and depth, the dominant pattern of catching up is path-following of incumbents from advanced countries. In engineering-based industries such as high-speed railways, where breadth of knowledge can be very helpful, China excels.

In industries such as semiconductors and biotech/biopharmaceutics, two of the sectors with the highest R&D spending, more developed countries have accumulated experience and innovation capabilities over the past half-century. More critically, they have built the core in the knowledge structure of those industries, which is the foundational infrastructure for R&D and innovation at the higher layers. The advantage technological leaders in those countries possess compared to China is their deep and long-term capability accumulation in core technologies, which is more defensible in traditional fields than in emerging fields. In this light, the advantage Chinese firms built upon production capability through efficiency- and exploitation-oriented innovation cannot support its ambition to become a global leader (as will be discussed in detail in Chapters 3 and 4).

Radical innovations can provide better performance and involve unprecedented improvements or the non-continuous development of performance characteristics, based on a set of different processes or scientific principles. China's successes in 5G and EVs are good examples of latecomers' catching up using non-continuous technological innovation capabilities. As Huawei's founder Ren Zhengfei said, 'To compete in the uncharted zone, Huawei needs to invest in basic science.' In 1999, Huawei opened its first global research institute in mathematics in Russia, and it has over 700 mathematicians and over 800 scientists in physics and 120 in chemistry in its global R&D workforce today.

The short-term mentality in innovation is shown in China's investment community. China possesses the largest venture capital investors in the world. For them, however, investing in innovative business models at the application layer of the knowledge structure bears faster and more certain returns than investments in basic science that underlie breakthrough technologies. China has become an innovator in the field of internet applications based on its market size. It has a huge scale advantage of online traffic, which is a cash cow in internet-based business models. Innovation based on capitalizing on internet traffic, however, will not sustain China's ambition in catching up in core technology. The recent development of innovation in applications, especially in the digital sphere, such as mobile applications of WeChat, TikTok, Alipay, and so forth, though important in economic growth, emphasizes ephemeral market concerns, but lacks science-driven innovations in core technology.

China Has Caught Up in Many Areas, But Still Has Some Way to Go

After forty years' development, China's economy has entered a new stage of growth. Although China still lags behind the world's leading innovative nations in certain core technologies, it doubtlessly has become an innovative powerhouse with unmatchable capabilities in technological development and application, as suggested by global innovative indices. The government is determined to drive the country's future growth based on independent innovation. To do so, innovation capability needs to be upgraded from a quantity-driven to quality-driven policy, supported by innovation. China's catch-up policy should reflect the country's transformation in society, economy, and global influence. Future innovation policy should focus on systemic change induced by digital technology and the need for digital transformation. It should also focus on solving social, institutional, economic, and environmental problems brought about by technological innovation.

In the past forty years, the windows of opportunity opened by technological regime shifts in certain industries, emerging technologies, market conditions in both domestic and global environments, and changes in policy environment have played a crucial role in China's catching up in innovation. Successful firms, after a short period of path-following and capability accumulation, choose to create their own technological trajectory, which can be distinct from that of incumbents.

Benefiting from huge market demand, China's innovation machine in the past has been driven by obtaining quick returns. This advantage will become a disadvantage in China's innovation catch-up in the future. The advantages Chinese firms developed based on 'good enough' innovation to enter a market and seize non-mainstream customers by lower price and faster upgrades, however, will not work when Chinese firms approach the technological frontiers or enter unchartered zones.

Catch-up does not happen in isolation. Apart from firms' innovation capability and strategy, most cutting-edge industries encourage co-development and co-innovation in ecosystems. The traditional model of innovation by large companies independently innovating complex product development has now given way to a co-innovation model in innovation ecosystems, with many small firms developing their deep specialization. In such ecosystems, the rules of competition have changed, from between products/companies in an industry to between modules of value in a value system. The winning capabilities are those that are indispensable or irreplaceable in value networks.

As a result, a large number of technology enterprises have gradually come to the forefront of the global technology industry. As Ren Zhengfei wrote to Huawei's employees in an email at the beginning of 2021 after a very challenging time under the US sanctions and unfriendly global market:

> Chinese enterprises need to learn how to lead in such a transition [from a technology follower to a co-leader], the key is to build a larger ecosystem, to empower others and to develop indispensable or irreplaceable capability in the ecosystem. In this transition, enterprises need to develop a globalization strategy that is based on an open ecosystem model.[72]

Government policies and company strategies need to adjust to China's facing a hostile global environment. To acquire technologies either through technology transfer or through outward FDI from more developed countries is getting harder. To forge ahead, China needs to develop core innovation capability driven by basic science, which is built upon exploratory accumulation in previously unknown knowledge. This reinforces path dependency—the outcome of a process dependent on its past history—in innovation capability building and suggests that Chinese firms should build the depth of their own knowledge stocks as a longer-term strategy. It also suggests a need for greater investment in multidisciplinary research, in addition to research in fields that promise to transform entire industries and markets, such as biotechnology, nanotechnology, and high-performance computing, but produce little immediate return.

Demand-side policies have been emphasized more than supply-side policies, policies rewarding short-term returns have overshadowed long-term returns, and

---

[72] https://finance.sina.com.cn/chanjing/gsnews/2021-01-22/doc-ikftssan9635649.shtml, accessed 1 June 2021.

instruments aiding applied and experimental research have outnumbered those supporting basic research. As a consequence, with the resultant lack of attention to core technologies, short term-oriented policies will not allow China to forge ahead in the global innovation race. Further institutional reforms allowing the market to drive innovation, supported by an integrated system of research, industry, and policy, will be key.

In the end, to sustain China's catch-up in the global innovation race in the long run, China needs to strengthen its investment in basic science. To do so, it is not only the government that needs to increase its funding for basic science in higher education and research institutions, but also technology entrepreneurship. Policy instruments, including rewarding systems such as taxation and grant schemes, can help to make such a structural change. As China shifts from catch-up growth to the forefront of innovation, this need is getting more urgent.

The rapid rise of China's innovation in the global rankings in recent years shows, according to one source, that it was 'busy building up and readying for a prolonged trade war and thus urgently needed to do a lot of in-sourcing, and getting up the value chain of manufacturing.'[73] For example, China has made semiconductors a key area of its *Made in China 2025* plan, a government initiative that aims to boost the production of higher-value products. The government has also prioritized the development of digital innovation and aims for the country to become a global leader in key emerging digital technologies such as artificial intelligence, the internet of things, and Fintech. From the discussion in this chapter, we can see that China faces significant hurdles in becoming technologically independent in IC chips and other core technologies any time soon.

We turn in Chapter 3 to one of the most important features of China's innovation machine: its ability to manufacture to high specifications, quickly and cheaply.

---

[73] Francis Tan, investment strategist at UOB Private Bank CIO Office in Singapore, January 2020.

3

Effectiveness-Based Manufacturing as a Foundation of China's Innovation Machine

On 11 November 2019 a Chinese-made Tesla Model 3 electric saloon car emerged from the carmaker's Gigafactory in Shanghai, drawing applause from the workforce and the press. The car was the result of a $2 billion investment plan in China announced by Tesla CEO Elon Musk just one year previously. This investment is expected to produce Tesla Model 3 and Model Y electric vehicles, along with battery cells, for both China and global markets.

Referring to the investment, Elon Musk said: 'I've never seen anything built so fast in my life before, to be totally frank.' The project began in October 2018, when Tesla bid $140 million for a pocket of land (866,000 square metres) designated for industrial use near Shanghai Harbour. A building permit was granted in December 2018, and the land was prepared for construction with electricity installed onsite. In January 2019, Musk and Shanghai Mayor Ying Yong attended the Gigafactory's foundation ceremony. Construction of the steel architecture of the factory commenced in April and was completed the following month. Installation of industrial robotics and machine tools began in July, and by August the construction of the factory passed security and safety inspections.

At the same time, all eleven models of Tesla's cars from its Shanghai Gigafactory were approved to be listed as 'new energy vehicle catalogue exempted from vehicle purchase tax', by the Ministry of Industry and Information Technology (MIIT), the nation's policymaker for industry and IT. Tesla was the only wholly foreign-owned car maker on this list.

It took Tesla less than twelve months from getting approval to construct a factory to its first manufactured car being driven away. Tesla's success in China has contributed to the company's profits and market capitalization on Wall Street which made Elon Musk the world's richest man by the end of 2020.[1] Its production helped the company almost meet its 2020 production goal—the company shipped 499,647 vehicles, slightly under the target of 500,000 announced by Musk in 2014—and

---

[1] M Campbell et al. (2021), 'Elon Musk Loves China, and China Loves Him Back—for Now.' *Bloomberg Businessweek*, Jan 13, 2021. https://www.bloomberg.com/news/features/2021-01-13/china-loves-elon-musk-and-tesla-tsla-how-long-will-that-last, accessed 1 June 2021.

Demystifying China's Innovation Machine: Chaotic Order. Marina Yue Zhang, Mark Dodgson, and David M. Gann, Oxford University Press. © Marina Yue Zhang, Mark Dodgson, and David M. Gann 2022.
DOI: 10.1093/oso/9780198861171.003.0003

achieved profitability.[2] Between 2009 and 2019, the Chinese government provided a large sum of capital as subsidies for both EV makers and buyers. It did not, however, generate the desired competitiveness for local EV brands. (This market will be discussed in Chapter 7.)

As part of Tesla's deal in China, the Shanghai government guaranteed a discounted loan and subsidized land for its factory. However, the deal was conditional upon Tesla's investment of 14.08 billion RMB (about $ 2 billion at the exchange rate of the time of the negotiation) in capital expenditure in China in the coming five years, and a contribution of annual tax no less than 2.23 billion RMB (about $ 340 million at the exchange rate of 2021) from 2023 on. If Tesla fails to meet these conditions, the government retains the right to take back the land.[3] Another reason that the government welcomes Tesla to China on its terms (such as setting its factory as a wholly owned enterprise, the first in the car industry in the country) was that Tesla's entry would help China develop its own supply chains in the EV market. China has successfully used this model in the past in stimulating development and catch-up: Apple helped China develop its supply chains in smartphones, assisting, for example, China to develop many smartphone makers.

As expected, Tesla's entry stimulated EV supply chains, involving ten major parts/components, from power train system, charging, chassis, and central control to interior and exterior components. In 2020, Tesla's Shanghai plant contributed more than 26 per cent of its Model 3 production and sourced more than half of its components in supply chains domestically. The costs of tariffs, shipping, warehousing, and parts are 65 per cent lower compared to production in the US. Reduced costs have been reflected in Tesla's price drops in its Model 3 and Model Y in China. In response to Tesla's entry, acceptance of EVs has grown substantially in China, which has been reflected in the positive reactions to Chinese NEV makers (e.g. XPeng, Nio, and BYD) in the capital market.

Tesla's Gigafactory in Shanghai was built under Donald Trump's 'Putting America First' agenda and in the face of the growing tension of trade conflict between the US and China. It was also built in circumstances where Tesla had to sign a 'Valuation Adjustment Mechanism' with the Shanghai government, as well as facing competition from a group of Chinese EV makers that are catching up quickly in technology and market share domestically and internationally. Tesla's decision to invest in such a hostile environment and the speed of building the factory reveal the attractiveness of Chinese manufacturing to foreign investors.

The traditional view of an industry value chain is represented by a smiling 'U' curve of value-adding activities, with highest value-adding activities, R&D and design, on one end and marketing and sales on the other, and with manufacturing

---

[2] See https://www.theverge.com/2021/1/27/22252765/tesla-profit-q4-2020-earnings-elon-musk-record-sales, accessed 1 June 2021.

[3] According to an anonymous interviewee.

on the lowest point of the curve.[4] Yet manufacturing industry and the innovation that occurs within it play an active and critical role in productivity growth.[5]

China's performance in manufacturing, however, is often contrasted with the very high value-added elements of design and marketing found in other parts of global value chains. This is to underestimate the importance of innovation in manufacturing and its crucial role in the journey from research and design to production. China's manufacturing sector has been described as 'large but not strong'. As indicated by the World Bank, China has a strong manufacturing base and is the leading global exporter of manufactured goods. Its manufacturing 'fitness', a measure of manufacturing capability, is on a par with that of high-income economies.[6] According to '2020 China's Manufacturing Power Index Report',[7] China was ranked fourth after the US, Germany, and Japan in overall rank, and led in scale, but lagged behind on quality (seventh), structural optimization (fourth), and sustainability (seventh).

Companies such as Apple and Tesla that rapidly ramp up large-scale production of advanced technology products and quickly bring innovations to market have offered some insights into China's manufacturing strengths. But does innovation in China's manufacturing matter in global value chains, despite its ostensible low value-adding? This chapter explains the contribution made by China's manufacturing capability as the bridge between technological innovation and mass production seen in companies such as Apple and Tesla in global innovation value chains. The important contribution that China's manufacturing industry makes to the nation's innovation machine is also explained.

Building an Industrial Base

Prior to the foundation of the PRC, China was largely an agrarian society, with nearly 90 per cent of the population living in rural areas.[8] From dynasty to dynasty, China remained an agricultural economy for over two thousand years. One explanation for the maintenance of a relatively stable social structure, despite disruptive shifts

---

[4] The concept of smiling curve was first proposed around 1992 by Stan Shih, the founder of Acer Inc., an IT company headquartered in Taiwan. In the PC industry, the two ends of the value chain—conception and marketing—command higher values added to the product than the middle part of the value chain—manufacturing. If this phenomenon is presented in a graph with a Y-axis for value-added and an X-axis for value chain (stage of production), the resulting curve appears like a 'smile': see https://en.wikipedia.org/wiki/Smiling_curve, accessed 1 June 2021.

[5] J. Manyika et al. (2012), 'Manufacturing the Future: The Next Era of Global Growth and Innovation', McKinsey Global Institute, 1 November, https://www.mckinsey.com/business-functions/operations/our-insights/the-future-of-manufacturing, accessed 1 June 2021.

[6] World Bank Group (2019) *Innovative China: New Drivers of Growth*, Washington DC: World Bank. doi: 10.1596/978-1-4648-1335-1.

[7] Chinese Academy of Engineering, State Industrial Information Safety Research Institution and Nanjing University of Aeronautics and Astronautics (2020), '2020 China's Manufacturing Power Index.' See http://www.china.org.cn/business/2020-12/26/content_77052875.htm, accessed 21 July 2021. The study benchmarked the manufacturing power of nine countries (the United States, Germany, Japan, United Kingdom, France, South Korea, India, Brazil, and China), was using four dimensions: scale index, quality index, structural optimization index, and sustainability index.

[8] See http://www.xinhuanet.com/english/2019-09/03/c_138361758.htm, accessed 1 June 2021.

in ruling dynasties, is 'agricultural involution'.[9] Agricultural involution describes a phenomenon where, if the population exceeded the limit of what agrarian land could support, natural disasters, wars, or social unrest reduced it to bring it back to an equilibrium.[10] No real changes in social structure or living standards occurred as a consequence of dynasty shifts. Such stasis led to the dire situation where average life expectancy in China in 1949 was only forty years. As an indicator of how industrialization has overcome agricultural involution, by 1978 life expectancy in China increased to 67, and today is close to 80, on par with many developed countries. Industrialization in pharmaceuticals, specifically the production of antibiotics, which contributed to increased life expectancy, and chemicals, specifically the production of fertilizers, which increased farming productivity, avoided agricultural involution.

The PRC started to build an industry base during its first thirty years following its foundation in 1949. During China's initial 'five-year plan' (1953–7), with financial aid and technological support from the former Soviet Union and several Socialist countries in East Europe, China started close to a thousand industrial projects, some of which underpin today's industries.

The PRC adopted Soviet Union-type central planning, which has been criticized as the main cause of the country's economic backwardness at the time. However, the country was able to develop large-scale industrialization largely due to land released from agriculture by central planning. The Communist party imposed a dual residential system, separating the population into rural and urban residents, which enabled the party to reallocate land and labour from agrarian to industrial activities during this period. As a result, China's agrarian society of many thousands of years gave way to a mixed society that included industry. China's early industrialization focused on heavy industrial sectors that were considered critical to national development. Steelmaking and steel processing, for example, contributed to defence and construction, and the chemical industry laid the foundation for making basic drugs and fertilizers. Value added by industry and industry growth rate during this period are shown in Figure 3.1.

Top-down, centralized power, addressing land and social reforms, concentrated limited resources during the first thirty years of the PRC and laid the foundation for its further industrialization in the years that followed.

Accelerated Industrialization

China's industrialization rapidly accelerated following the economic reforms of 1978. Total industrial output has grown quickly since then, especially in light industry sectors that manufacture consumer goods. In the early days of the economic reforms,

---

[9] See C. Geertz (1969), *Agricultural Involution: The Processes of Ecological Change in Indonesia*, Berkeley, Califonia: University of California Press.

[10] See P. Huang (1985), *The peasant economy and social change in North China*, Stanford, CA: Stanford University Press and P. Huang (1990), *The peasant family and rural development in the Yangzi Delta, 1350-1988*, Stanford, CA: Stanford University Press.

Figure 3.1 China's total value added by industry, 1960–78

Note: Value added by industry, also referred to as gross domestic product (GDP) by industry, is the contribution of the primary sector (excluding the secondary sector of agriculture and the tertiary sector of services).

Sources: World Bank (https://data.worldbank.org/) and the Global Economy (https://www.theglobaleconomy.com/)

China's manufacturing capabilities and exports were greatly increased by the influx of foreign direct investment (FDI) from Taiwan and Hong Kong. These investments initially targeted the four coastal cities of Shenzhen, Zhuhai, Shantou, and Xiamen, which are designated as Special Economic Zones (SEZs) and offer particular incentives for inward investment. Investments focused on labour-intensive manufacturing, such as toys, shoemaking, textiles, and plastics. In the mid-1990s, manufacturing was extended into electrical appliances, electronic parts, personal computers, and watchmaking. The world-leading Taiwanese manufacturer Foxconn established its facility in Longhua, Shenzhen, in 1988, where the company still operates its largest factory in China.

China entered a stage of full-blown industrialization associated with globalization in the late 1990s. Along with the emergence of the internet and communication technologies, during this period a global division of labour emerged, with firms in more developed economies concentrating resources on R&D, design, brands, marketing, and sales, and outsourcing production to countries with low labour costs. By outsourcing production, firms in developed economies optimized their global allocation of resources. As the largest developing country, China attracted substantial amounts of FDI from multinational corporations (MNCs) in industrialized nations, including the US, Germany, and Japan. These MNCs set up subsidiaries as export platforms for Chinese-made products for the global market.

Beginning in 1998, China also embarked on dramatic economic reform of its SOEs. As a direct result, hundreds of millions of SOE employees became unemployed. Simultaneously, China introduced tax reforms which ruled local governments had to transfer a proportion of their tax income to central government. This forced local governments to replace lost income by attracting foreign investment. More land was offered to foreign investors to build modern factories, and hundreds of millions of farmers were forced to leave farmland to make their living in newly urbanized towns and cities. These events—the global outsourcing of production, reform of SOEs that provided abundant labour, and taxation changes that encouraged local governments to use land to attract MNCs to set up manufacturing plants—were the driving forces for China's modern industrialization in the 1990s. As shown in Figure 3.2, although the contribution by industry to the GDP declined, the total outputs in the industry sector witnessed rapid growth. China accelerated its industrialization further in the following twenty years. It possesses great breadth in its industry, covering all categories defined by the International Standard Industrial Classification of All Economic Activities (ISIC).

China's global competitiveness in labour-intensive manufacturing sectors has been developed on the basis of its heavy industrial strengths built during the first thirty years of the PRC. Two simple products illustrate these industrial strengths. China makes 90 per cent of the world's disposable cigarette lighters. Disposable lighters are a simple product with little technical sophistication. They include a flint, a steel wheel, and a plastic chamber containing liquid butane, all packed in a plastic shell. To produce such a simple product, however, materials from two major industries are required: the chemical industry, from which materials for plastic and liquid butane are sourced, and the steel (steelmaking and steel processing) industry, from which steel wheels are sourced. Both the chemical and steel industries are core elements of China's industrial base. Bicycles are slightly more complicated. China exports over one billion bicycles each year, including electrical bicycles, accounting for over 90 per cent of the world market. The competitiveness of the Chinese bicycle industry relies on access to abundant supplies of raw materials such as steel, rubber, plastic, and paint, as well as relatively low-cost, but highly skilled workers, all features of Chinese industry.

As shown in Figure 3.3, since China's entry to the World Trade Organization in 2001, its value-added manufacturing has grown substantially, though its contribution to the industry outputs maintained stable (except in 2011), which indicates a rapid increase in other industrial activities, especially construction, in recent decades. However, the share of value-added services as inputs to manufacturing is relatively

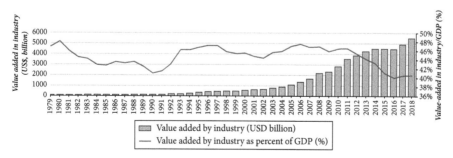

Figure 3.2 China's value added by industry, 1979–2018

Note: Value added by industry, also referred to as gross domestic product (GDP) by industry, is the contribution of the primary sector (excluding the secondary sector of agriculture and the tertiary sector of services).

Sources: World Bank (https://data.worldbank.org/) and the Global Economy (https://www.theglobaleconomy.com/)

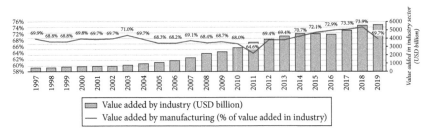

Figure 3.3 China's value added by manufacturing, 1997–2019

Sources: World Bank (https://data.worldbank.org/) and the Global Economy (https://www.theglobaleconomy.com/)

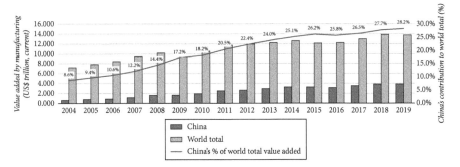

Figure 3.4 China's contribution to the world total of value-added manufacturing, 2004–19

Note: Value-added manufacturing refers the net output of a sector after adding up all outputs and subtracting intermediate inputs.

Source: World Bank and the Ministry of Commerce of PRC

small. As shown in Figure 3.4, China's contribution to the world's total in value-added manufacturing has grown rapidly from 8.6 per cent in 2004 to 28.2 per cent in 2019.

The global financial crisis in 2008, while disruptive, somewhat paradoxically also consolidated and strengthened Chinese manufacturing by forcing it to move up the global value chain. In 2010, China surpassed the US to become the largest manufacturer in the world, measured by China's share of global value added in manufacturing (as shown in Figure 3.5). In the course of one lifetime, China moved from an agrarian society to being the world's factory.

The nature of China's manufacturing capabilities and the challenges to be faced continue to evolve. There is a major trend towards producing more advanced products, but the sheer size of the sector sees great variation in levels of modernization and distinct differences between manufacturers at different levels of capability. According to a World Economic Forum report on future production readiness, China ranks in the top third for both technology and innovation and human capital.[11] But while China's manufacturing displays great strengths it also faces major

---

[11] See World Economic Forum in collaboration with A. T. Kearney (2018), 'Readiness for the Future of Production Report 2018', http://www3.weforum.org/docs/FOP_Readiness_Report_2018.pdf, accessed

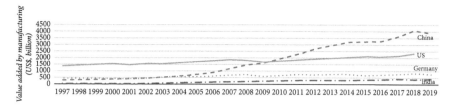

Figure 3.5 Country comparison of value added in manufacturing, 1997–2019
Source: World Bank and the Ministry of Commerce of PRC

challenges. The nation is the world's largest producer of carbon emissions. While the country is committed to becoming more energy-efficient, building an environmentally sustainable country is a monumental challenge. The results of China's efforts on sustainability in manufacturing remain to be seen.

The 'World's Factory': Effectively Using Resources to Efficiently Produce Standard Products

Western MNCs established manufacturing joint ventures in China, attracted to its booming markets, supportive policy, and cheap labour. Over time, with their help, China's manufacturing sector has developed a large pool of skilled workers and basic innovation capability. It has also developed a critical advantage that has made China's manufacturing globally competitive: its effectiveness-driven business models.

Business models can be conceptualized as a structural template of how a firm transacts with a large array of stakeholders, including suppliers and customers, forming a system of interdependent activities that transcends that firm and spans its boundaries.[12] Innovative business models allow a firm to organize its activities across boundaries in an ecosystem.

MNCs and companies operating in developed nations commonly search for novelty in business models that introduce new ways of conducting economic transactions. And they search for efficiency in business model innovation, which revises and improves existing economic transactions.[13] China's strength in innovation is not only led by novelty- or efficiency-driven ideas. Equally important, and a critical advantage, are innovations that provide the right solutions to the needs and demands of a specific user group at the right time. Chinese firms have learned that those innovations that deliver effective answers to pent-up or latent demand will have a

2 June 2021. The report assesses how well positioned global economies are to shape and benefit from changes in production being driven by the Fourth Industrial Revolution.
    [12] C. Zott and R. Amit (2007), 'Business Model Design and the Performance of Entrepreneurial Firms', *Organization Science*, 18, 181–99; C. Zott and R. Amit (2010), 'Business Model Design: An Activity System Perspective', *Long Range Planning*, 43(2–3), 216; D. J. Teece (2010), 'Business Models, Business Strategy and Innovation', *Long Range Planning*, 43(2–3), 172.
    [13] See Zott and Amit (2008), 'The fit between product market strategy and business model: Implications for firm performance', *Strategic Management Journal*, 29, 1-26.

better chance of being selected and diffused. China's effectiveness-centric business model in manufacturing provides an innovative way of connecting supply and demand. It is one of the secrets of China's rise in manufacturing power.

On the supply side, one factor that differentiates an emerging economy from a developed one is that in most industries multiple types of firms coexist.[14] In China, for example, there are industry incumbents (mainly MNCs) with sophisticated innovation capabilities, multitudes of newly founded local start-ups, and newly reformed former SOEs. There are also less successful global firms and relatively well-established local firms with R&D focused mainly on 'secondary' innovation or 'integrative capabilities'[15]—a capability that creatively recombines different modules in modularized and standardized production. This process will be discussed in detail in Chapter 4. Significant capability gaps, especially in technology and innovation, exist between these layers of firms.

On the demand side, given huge disparities in income between different consumer groups, market categorization in China is different from that often used in developed markets. Rather than segregating the market by consumers' purchasing power (such as mainstream vs fringe)[16] or innovativeness (such as innovators, early adopters, early majority, late majority, and laggards)[17] in adopting new products, the Chinese market can best be segregated by multiple macro- and micro-factors. These factors include consumers' socio-economic backgrounds, their educational levels, professions, *hukou* (residence permits), and geographical location. In countries as large as China and India any segment is simply too big to be considered a fringe and, therefore, cannot be ignored by incumbent firms because of the sheer size of the population living at the bottom of the pyramid.[18] Demand for certain products in emerging markets is also dynamic and changes as income levels increase. There are different temporal patterns in adopting a new technology/product or practice on the basis of these differentiated markets.

It is, therefore, not necessarily firms with the most novel or efficient business models that win; rather, it is those with the most *effective* business models—providing the right solutions to specific customer preferences at the right time—that stand a higher chance of winning. During the early days of China's catching-up, for example, local firms that had caught up with MNCs in fiercely competitive domestic markets, such as Lenovo in PCs and Huawei in telecoms, all used this strategy by providing the most suitable products for the right market segments at the right

---

[14] L. Lian and H. Ma (2010), 'Revaluation of FDI on the Economy Development of China—Is It an Entirely Unalloyed Benefit?', *International Journal of Business and Management*, 5, 184–90.

[15] X. Wu (1997), 'The Evolutionary Process of Secondary Innovation', in D. F. Kocaoglu (ed.), *Innovation in Technology Management—The Key to Global Leadership*. PICMET '97, 183. doi: 10.1109/PICMET.1997.653308.

[16] C. Loch and S. Stavadias (eds.) (2008), *Handbook of New Product Development Management*, Abingdon: Routledge.

[17] E. M. Rogers (1995), *Diffusion of Innovation*, 4th edn, New York: Free Press.

[18] C. Prahalad and H. Fruehauf (2004), *The Fortune at the Bottom of the Pyramid*, Philadephia, PA: Wharton School Press.

developmental stages. This strategy allowed these firms to develop secondary or integrative capabilities—integrating ready-to-go modular solutions with innovative modifications to cater for local customers—along the vertically integrated value chains controlled by incumbent MNCs. Firms that quickly developed these capabilities by partnering with the most suitable suppliers—global or local—and by integrating different resources more *effectively* were able to catch up with incumbents. The success of China's mobile handset manufacturers in the first decade of the twenty-first century illustrated the importance of effectiveness-centric business model innovation in latecomer firms' catch-up with incumbents in an environment where they lack technological advantages.[19]

Effectiveness-driven business models allow firms to source, allocate, and match dispersed resources, raw materials, talent, and technologies (sometimes suboptimal or even obsolete ones from other countries) and translate them into products for the market in the shortest time and at the lowest costs. This is seen in the case of Chinese wind turbine manufacturer Goldwind described in Chapter 1.[20] This case illustrates how effectiveness-driven models can allow latecomer firms with limited technological capabilities to catch up.

The success of effectiveness-centric business models is underpinned by innovation and production in manufacturing becoming highly modularized but integrated into global value chains, empowered by advances in ICT and network technologies. The future of China's manufacturing prowess lies in an ecosystem mediated by various platforms, connecting technology and material providers, manufacturers, suppliers, distributors, consumers and smart supply chains and logistics. We will develop this point later in this Chapter.

The 'World's Workshop': Turning Industrial Designs into Complex Products

At the beginning of the second decade of the twenty-first century, China entered a new stage of development in its manufacturing sector. Due to rising labour costs in China, especially in the eastern coastal cities where most manufacturing factories are clustered, and increasing tariffs on finished goods as trade tensions between the US and China intensified, many low-cost manufacturing facilities moved to countries such as Vietnam, India, and Mexico. The question is whether, as a result of these relocations, China will lose its status as the 'world's factory'. The answer lies in the way that China is already on the path of transitioning from the 'world's factory', manufacturing low-end goods, to the 'world's workshop', utilizing its advantages

---

[19] See H. Zhu, M. Y. Zhang, and W. Lin (2017), 'The Fit between Business Model Innovation and Demand-Side Dynamics: Catch-Up of China's Latecomer Mobile Handset Manufacturers', *Innovation: Organization & Management*, 19(2), 146–66.
[20] See https://en.wikipedia.org/wiki/Goldwind, accessed 2 June 2021.

where innovations are used to translate creative designs into complex products for the mass market.

Apple and Foxconn provide evidence of the nature of this transition. Apple's success with its iPhone is due primarily to its creative designs, branding and marketing. Without Chinese manufacturing, however, Apple's iPhone prices would be significantly higher. As seen in Chapter 1, in 2019, fifty-two of Apple's fifty-nine OEM factories were in China, sourcing 47.6 per cent of its supplies. The main factors restricting manufacturing of Apple's products are achieving mass production while maintaining engineering precision of their complex designs and controlling costs. Foxconn, Apple's largest OEM partner, uses its innovation to overcome these restraints. Foxconn operates the world's largest, yet most efficient and flexible factories and is one of the world's biggest users of advanced robotics. It has the capacity to manufacture complex products, sometimes composed of hundreds or thousands of modules, each of which contains from tens to hundreds of components, and has the engineering capability to mass-produce complex and advanced designs with precision and at low cost. In such processes, manufacturing is not simply assembly lines connecting together existing modules following pre-specified instructions; they are workshops that allow experimentation in production and process innovation. This type of innovation involves tacit knowledge-based skills and craftsmanship at a mass scale.

As Apple's CEO Tim Cook explained in an interview, Apple continues to favour China as its central base for manufacturing iPhones because China has a large number of mid-level engineers that can increase production at any time:

> The number one reason why we like to be in China is the people…The truth is, the process engineering and process development associated with our products require innovation in and of itself. Not only the product but the way that it's made, because we want to make things in the scale of hundreds of millions, and we want the quality level of zero defects…And the tooling skill is very deep here. In the US, you could have a meeting of tooling engineers and I'm not sure we could fill the room. In China, you could fill multiple football fields.[21]

As an expert in supply chains himself, Cook pointed out the essence of China's manufacturing today. China's rise as it moves from being the world's factory to being the world's workshop can be attributed to its capacity to make things better, cheaper, faster, and at mass scale. It excels in a type of process innovation with an exploitation orientation, empowered by a large pool of experienced engineers and workers. It is this which attracts foreign investors such as Apple and Tesla.

This aspect of China's manufacturing can be described as 'grey innovation'—an experiment-driven process, often in areas of ambiguity and covering multiple domains.

---

[21] An interview with Tim Cook at the Fortune Global Forum: https://www.inc.com/glenn-leibowitz/apple-ceo-tim-cook-this-is-number-1-reason-we-make-iphones-in-china-its-not-what-you-think.html, accessed 2 June 2021.

It is a process by which iteration between R&D and design with manufacturing creates a virtuous spiral to achieve scale, speed, precision, and cost efficiency in final products. It requires very effective two-way communication and learning between upstream and downstream actors, with Chinese engineers innovating by interpreting and acting upon market and technological opportunities. This connection between manufacturing and innovation is the most particular capability that Chinese manufacturing offers in the global industrial division of labour.

'Hidden Champions'

Benefiting from the advances in China's e-commerce and m-commerce platforms, which will be explored in Chapter 5, are a large group of 'hidden champions' in its manufacturing sector. 'Hidden champion' is a concept first introduced by Hermann Simon when explaining successful German manufacturers. According to Simon, hidden champions are export-oriented manufacturers specialized in a narrow niche but holding 50 per cent or more market share in the niche. They are rarely known by people outside their industries. In order to qualify as a hidden champion, a firm needs to be among the top three in market share globally in the niche area.[22]

According to Simon's research, in 2009 there were about 2,700 hidden champions in the world, roughly half of them German.

In the past twenty years, many hidden champions have emerged in China. For example:

- 50 per cent of the video cameras with 20x zoom functions, typically used in airports or other public spaces, are provided by Zhongshan United Optoelectronics Technology Company.
- 60 per cent of the magnetic plastic door seals used in refrigerators are manufactured by Anhui Wan Long Magnetic Plastic Company.
- 50 per cent of bottles used by global drinks brands such as Coca-Cola are manufactured on the precision moulds made by Guangdong Xing Lian Precision Machinery Company.

These companies share several characteristics: they are niche-focused, have customer-centric mindsets, a preference for self-financing with a long-term mindset, and are family-owned with paternalistic forms of employee relationships.

Unusually for China, each champion has a large group of complementary followers, and each individual champion evolves into a community-embedded enterprise system with a globalization strategy. More and more hidden champions have

---

[22] H, Simon (2009), *Hidden Champions of the Twenty-First Century: The Success Strategies of Unknown World Market Leaders*. Bonn: Springer.

emerged in lower-tier cities in recent years and have become integrated into global supply chains.

The manufacturing of violins offers a good example. Huang Qiao ('Yellow Bridge') is a small town in China's Jiangsu province and is the world's largest violin-making base, supplying 30 per cent of the world's market. Violin making in Huang Qiao began in 1968, towards the end the Cultural Revolution. A number of workers from a violin-making factory in Shanghai were sent to Huang Qiao to be 're-educated' by local farmers. In their spare time they started to make parts for violins for their Shanghai factory and taught locals to produce parts in their workshop. Over the years they expanded the workshop to make entire violins. The workshop became a branch for the Shanghai factory in 1985. In 1996, a joint venture was established with a US investor. The JV developed into Jiangsu Fengling Group, which now sells half of its products in the US market.

There are 197 procedures in making a violin, each done by hand. In addition to the Fengling Group, an entire value chain in violin making has emerged in Huang Qiao. There are over 220 musical instrument manufacturers and complementary component manufacturers employing over 40,000 skilled craftspeople in the town. The industry produces low-end to high-end products and makes instruments such as violins, cellos, and guitars for both the domestic and international markets.

It is not uncommon in China to see villages or towns such as Huang Qiao that dominate an entire industrial value chain in a finely defined space. For example:

- Song Xia, a small town in Zhejiang province, has over 1,500 manufacturers making umbrellas, including many OEMs for global brands. Output of umbrellas exceeds 500 million annually and generate revenues of over $1.5 billion.
- Guzhen, a small town near Zhongshan City in Guangdong, produces 60 per cent of the world's lighting and components.
- Heze, a small city in Shandong province, hosts thousands of coffin makers. Their products are exported to Japan, Italy, India, and South Korea. Exports from Heze account for 90 per cent of the Japanese coffin market. There are no notable coffin brands in Heze. The industry is composed of thousands of small workshops covering a long industry value chain, from timber preparation and carpentry to craftsmanship such as carving patterns on hardwood, painting, and shipping.

These types of regional clusters are especially concentrated in the Pearl River Delta and Yangtze River Delta.

Another type of hidden champion has emerged in recent years. Like the OEM manufacturer Foxconn, Shenzhou International Group Holdings Limited is an OEM partner for brands such as Uniqlo, Nike, and Adidas. Headquartered in Ningbo, Zhejiang province, Shenzhou was founded by Ma Jianrong and his father Ma Baoxing, both of whom began apprenticeships in garment making aged 13. They began their business as an OEM partner for foreign brands, and in 2005 the company was listed on the Hong Kong Stock Exchange. The father and son invested almost the entire amount of capital raised from the IPO (about $115 million) in upgrading machines and in new technologies. The company extended their business into Original Design Manufacturing (ODM), outsourcing design and manufacturing to partners. In 2019, the company employed 74,600 people and was ranked fortieth on the list of the largest non-SOE enterprises in China.[23] It was ranked 1282 on Forbes Global Enterprise List, 2020.[24]

A New Type of Smart Manufacturing

Since the global financial crisis in 2008/09, increasing numbers of Chinese factories manufacturing for global brands have chosen to leave their OEM partnerships, and since 2015 more OEM brands have moved bulk orders for consumer goods to lower-cost countries in South East Asia. Chinese factories leave their OEM partnerships so that they can engage in activities such as design, branding, channel building, and directly communicating with customers in ways previously undertaken by their OEM partners.

China's e-commerce platform firms such as Taobao/TMall and JD.com have helped these factories build channels with customers, largely in China. The domestic business environment, however, is very different from the export market. Domestic orders are often from fragmented markets, requiring short delivery cycles and more customized production. The challenge for Chinese factories is that when orders become smaller and more customized, it leads to reduced scale in production and profits.

Digital technologies are assisting with this challenge and becoming a new competitive advantage in manufacturing, reshaping production methods and business models. The new generation of information technology, the internet, big data analytics, and AI is accelerating the deep integration of online and offline businesses. To survive and thrive in the new environment Chinese factories are applying digital technology and big data for more flexible and agile manufacturing. Digital technologies can help companies manage customized production for small orders in each fragmented market. China's digital infrastructure and applications and highly skilled talent lie behind this transformation.

The key benefit of flexible production in a networked environment is the bigger the network, the greater its utility. China has such a network effect among its 900 million internet users, especially mobile internet users. The rise of Pinduoduo (PDD), a new platform in China's crowded e-commerce market, illustrates the power of this network effect.

---

[23] 2019 Hu Run China's 500 non-SOEs in China. https://www.hurun.net/en-us/info/detail?num=8D639CDB4FE1, accessed 21 July, 2010.
[24] See https://www.forbes.com/global2000/#45f1f402335d, accessed 3 June 2021.

PDD is a mobile-commerce platform for group-buying deals, established in 2015 by Colin Huang. At this time China's e-commerce market seemed well established and occupied by Alibaba and JD, among many specialized firms. Yet by 2018, PDD had attracted over 200 million users in the niche market of middle-aged consumers in smaller cities searching for deep discounts. This market in a niche that was fragmented, but large in scope led the company to be listed on NASDAQ in 2018, three years after its foundation. By 2019 there were 585 million users on its platform. In June 2020, PDD's market capitalization reached $100 billion and the 40-year-old Huang became the third richest man in China after Alibaba's founder Jack Ma and Tencent's founder Pony Ma.

To understand PDD's success it helps to compare it with traditional models of manufacturing. In the 1920s, Ford pioneered large-scale assembly line production in the car industry. This became the mainstream production model in many industries and was characterized by large-scale production, with few varieties of product, in centrally controlled and finely decomposed processes along assembly lines that improved efficiency and quality. The disadvantage of this model is the rigidity of assembly line production, which makes it difficult or costly to manufacture customized, small-batch products.

Flexible production of small-batch and customized production was assisted by the introduction of computers in the 1980s. The use of computer numerical control machines and flexible manufacturing systems improved responsiveness in manufacturing, although there were limits to this flexibility, which was costly and did not fully achieve the ultimate objective of responding to changes in demand with standardization in production. In recent years, with the development of AI, big data analytics, and cloud computing, the efficiency and speed of flexible production have improved. Many countries have adopted Industry 4.0 smart manufacturing, using digitalization, networking, and intelligence in production. Smart manufacturing includes various control, optimization, and management systems in design, R&D, production, logistics, and distribution, as well as equipment such as industrial robotics.

Due to its cost, many SMEs and micro factories are unable to adopt smart manufacturing as yet. Without investing huge amounts in digital technologies, some of these factories have found alternative ways to rearrange their production processes to achieve greater flexibility in production. The key lies in local clusters of large numbers of manufacturers, each developing a specialization in particular components, combining to flexibly produce in clusters. In a sense, flexible production is achieved by an extended assembly line across many factories organized in regional clusters or on digital platforms.

The value chain in the manufacturing industry is a system that includes design and development, raw material sourcing and procurement, warehousing and logistics, order processing, production, and distribution. In regional clusters or on digital platforms of flexible production, each of these functions is undertaken by specialized firms, including services firms supporting manufacturing. Another advantage of this flexible production model is that many of these functions, as well as management of knowledge, equipment, time, and personnel, can be shared. Increasing innovation efficiency and reducing transaction costs in a hugely diffused network involving millions of small and micro manufacturers on the one hand and hundreds of millions diverse consumers on the other is a real challenge, requiring efficient and low-cost coordination. Special service platforms are emerging which aim to address this challenge and help SMEs and micro manufacturers achieve smart manufacturing through smart networks for fragmented markets with high demand for customized products. PDD is one such platform.

PDD is actually more than a mobile-commerce (m-commerce) platform. From early on it embedded elements of games along with group discounts in its shopping experience, a model described by Colin Huang as 'Costco + Disney'. Users, for example, gain rewards (discounts) by winning embedded games, such as watering a virtual tree to receive free delivery of juice made from the fruit of the tree. Laterly, PDD's business model began facilitating flexible production by enabling a large number of SME and micro manufacturers to provide customized solutions to fragmented segments of consumers.

In this process, PDD functions as a middleman assembling collective needs, mobilizing manufacturing resources, and facilitating production. Each market niche segment is sufficiently large in China for manufacturers to achieve economies of scale, efficiency, and profits. In this model, the traditional value chain is reversed: production starts with customers' preferences and ends in production. PDD functions as a coordinator and organizer for manufacturers by collecting, analysing, and translating consumers' preferences for a product to manufacturers that can provide the highest ratio of value to price. Essentially, what PDD's model does is to decouple traditional industrial value chains, from raw materials and production to sales, using technology to replace physical supply chains with digital information flow.

Behind PDD's success is its technological strengths. A Fudan graduate with a computer science degree, Huang was subsequently trained in the US before working for Google. This experience encouraged him to instil strong 'technological DNA' in the firm he created. PDD is actually a technology company that uses AI and big data analytics to collect user data, translate it into business intelligence, and facilitate flexible production involving hundreds of thousand SMEs and micro manufacturers in finely specialized areas. PDD illustrates a different type of smart manufacturing by managing information flow through smart networking. It covers the entire value chain from product design to manufacturing, to marketing, to sales and services, but in a reverse order. While most m-commerce activities still use digital platforms such as Taobao/T-Mall and JD, the emergence of PDD's disruptive innovative business model enables a direct link between consumers and manufacturers. This model can be described as C2M (customer-to-manufacturer), enabled by advanced digital technologies. C2M production balances flexibility and standardization.

Flexible production extends assembly lines across many boundaries. Its success relies on collaboration between different actors in the supply chain and ecosystem, which in turn depends on mutual trust. Digital platforms facilitate such collaborations, and their role will be discussed in detail in Chapter 5.

Bottleneck Technologies in China's Manufacturing

Chinese manufacturing industry has made extraordinary progress since the 1980s. As well as world-leading manufacturers in China such as Foxconn, there are thousands of SMEs that are leaders in closely defined niche markets. Each of these SMEs, like a tiny cog in a huge machine, advances the nation's innovation capability in manufacturing. They are crucial elements of China's innovation machine. There are, however, many bottlenecks in China's manufacturing sector, such as Huawei's reliance on US technologies for its high-end chip design and production.

China's high-speed train exemplifies the country's high-end manufacturing power. Yet it relies on one bottleneck in its supply chain: the humble nut and bolt, which are made by Hardlock, a specialized Japanese manufacturer. Almost invisible in the supply chain, they connect all components by so-called 'never loose' products to secure against vibration in many high-end products such as high-speed trains and cars, as well as titanium nuts and bolts in aeroplanes. With all China's manufacturing power, it cannot compete with Japan's expertise in this specialized area of manufacturing.

Such high-end manufacturing sectors use highly advanced technology, produce high value-added components, and possess strong competitive positions.[25] They include precision processing of special components or devices, electronic components, semiconductors, new materials, and IT, and are built on knowledge- and technology-intensive production, and multidisciplinary and multi-field integration. This type of products is often the core of an industrial value chain, the level of development of which determines the overall competitiveness of the industry. This high end of global manufacturing value chains is primarily occupied by companies in the US, Germany, and Japan.

Although China has established a massive and broad-based industrial system, its high-end industrial capability remains comparatively weak. The fundamental reason for this is the manner in which industrial processing capability in manufacturing is accumulated over a long period of time. An enterprise specialized in making nuts and bolts accumulates deep knowledge underlying its high levels of precision, in Hardlock's case developed over 40 years. China has a short history of specialized and advanced industrial production. It also has a history of often pursuing speed over quality, limiting the development of professionalism in high-end manufacturing. The high-end manufacturing sector has, however, grown faster than traditional manufacturing in recent years.[26] According to the State Bureau of Statistics, between 2015 and 2018, high-end manufacturing witnessed strong growth in areas such as industrial robots, mobile communications base stations, IC chips, and fibre electronics. This is the result of intensive investment in the sector, as well as the accumulation of technological capability in certain core technologies. As shown in Table 3.1,

[25] Chinaventure Institute, 2020. 'White paper on investing in China's high-end manufacturing' (in Chinese). Beijing, China.

[26] Chinaventure Institute, 2020. 'White paper on investing in China's high-end manufacturing' [in Chinese]. Beijing, China.

Table 3.1 Number of high-tech enterprises in manufacturing by industry (2018)

	Number of enterprises	Share (%)
Manufacturing of medicines	4,134	15.5%
Manufacturing of aircraft and spacecraft and related equipment	683	2.6%
Manufacturing of electronic equipment and communications equipment	12,991	48.8%
Manufacturing of computers and office equipment	1,604	6.0%
Manufacturing of medical equipment and measuring instruments	7,148	26.9%
Manufacturing of information chemicals	49	0.2%
Total (high-tech enterprises in manufacturing)	26,609	100.0%

Source: China Statistical Yearbook on Torch Program (2019)

the number of high-end manufacturers is relatively small compared to the entire population of manufacturing enterprises in China. High-tech manufacturers in specialized areas such as aircraft and computers are still in short supply.

During the recent tensions between the US and China, the high-end manufacturing sector has clearly been a battlefield over future leadership. China may lead in manufacturing volume and flexibility in production, but it lags behind in high-end manufacturing. The advantages other leading manufacturing countries have over China include not only their leadership positions in technologies such as advanced chips and high-precision machine tools, but perhaps more importantly their deeply embedded scientific and R&D capabilities. China's manufacturing sector is large but does not have access to the accumulated scientific and managerial knowledge that underpins the advantages of advanced competitor nations. It takes time to develop the professionalism and accumulate the deep knowledge behind world-leading manufacturing. For China to compete, it needs to upgrade its independent innovation capability in its manufacturing sector. China's manufacturing sector is facing the challenge of transitioning growth based on high speed to high quality, adding being smart to being large and well connected.

'Made in China 2025'

Advances in IT and internet technologies, modularization, and standardization have transformed the assembly line-based, vertically integrated, production model into one that is network-based and flexible. China is making progress in this transformation, especially in using advanced AI and big data analytical technologies to achieve mass customization in production in sectors such as clothing, but has yet to make the full transition to smart manufacturing. Smart manufacturing is a complex process, including the entire life cycle of design, production, warehousing and storage, transportation and logistics, sales, and services. It requires integration of all actors in the supply chain in order to achieve 'automatic adaptation, automatic decision making and automatic execution' in production.[27] This is especially the case in sectors that involve complex and multiple raw materials and multilayered component suppliers. Compared to the linear model of production, the process of smart manufacturing involves a series of non-continuous steps, often iterative, in a risky and uncertain environment. Organizing this type of production is considered less transparent and less systematic.

Many industrialized countries, such as the US, Germany, the UK, France, Japan, and South Korea, have developed an Industry 4.0 type of strategic policies aiming to promote the transformation of manufacturing into smart manufacturing in their countries.[28] The evolution of industry is shown in Figure 3.6. The core of all these strategic policies is the use of cyber-physical systems (CPS) in manufacturing. According to the International Conference on Cyber-Physical Systems, CPS are physical and engineered systems whose operations are monitored, coordinated, and integrated by computing and communication technologies.[29] To an extent, the advances in CPS have paved the way for manufacturing transformation to Industry 4.0, within which all physical aspects of production are digitalized and synchronized with the cyber world.

China has a number of advantages upon which it can build to achieve smart manufacturing. The first step is the digitalization of the production process. China's advantages lie in areas that are closer to direct consumers, such as retail, media and entertainment, and payments, where China has achieved a high rate of digitalization. It has accumulated knowledge and experience in applications of the next generation of internet, 5G, and AI technologies, and has a natural advantage in big data, given its large user base. All this can help China transform into a smart manufacturing power.

Many enterprises in these areas are digital natives, the advantages of which are that they are not constrained by the legacy IT systems as in incumbent firms and have implemented digital strategies from their inception. The aim of smart manufacturing is to respond to the market in real time in a digital ecosystem, and China has made progress in this regard in consumer products such as cars, home appliances, clothes, pharmaceuticals, electronic and electrical appliances, and some industrial equipment. China has also made headway in applying CPS in other areas, such as smart grids and smart cities. In areas which rely on legacy infrastructures, such as public services and heavy industry manufacturing, however, the level of digitalization is relatively low. According to a study by Tsinghua University that used the

---

[27] iResearch, 2019. 'China's path to smart manufacturing' (in Chinese), Beijing, China.
[28] Industry 4.0-type of strategic policies include National Industry Strategy 2030 (Germany), US Leadership Strategy in Advanced Manufacturing Sector, New Industrial France, Japan is Back, Innovation in Manufacturing 3.0 Strategy (South Korea), and Industrial Strategy Building a Britain Fit for the Future (UK).
[29] 11th ACM/IEEE International Conference on Cyber-Physical Systems: see http://iccps.acm.org/2020/, accessed 3 June 2021.

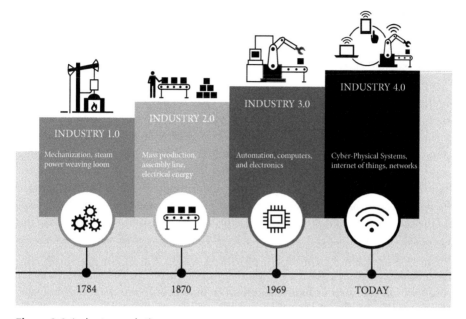

Figure 3.6 Industry evolution
Source: https://hammelscale.com/industry-4-0/ (accessed 3 June 2021)

World Economic Forum's typology, 80 per cent of China's industry is still in Industry 2.0, 50 per cent is in Industry 3.0, and only 25 per cent in Industry 4.0.[30]

In May 2015, China announced its *Made in China 2025* strategy, a ten-year, $300 billion, Industry 4.0-type plan for upgrading its manufacturing sector.[31] *Made in China 2025* aims to transform China from a large to a smart manufacturing country. This plan focuses on an 'innovation driven strategy to deepen institutional reforms, accelerate technology transfer and commercialization, build globally competitive manufacturing clusters, and move China's manufacturing sector up the global value chain'. The plan specified building smart manufacturing and green manufacturing capabilities as its strategic goals by developing technologies in ten technological areas:

- next-generation information technology
- numerical-control machine tools
- aerospace equipment
- advanced marine-engineering equipment and high-tech shipbuilding
- advanced rail and transport equipment
- energy saving

---

[30] Firms often use mixed production models between Industry 2.0, 3.0 and 4.0. So the total exceeds 100%.
[31] MIIT (Ministry of Industry and Information Technology), 2016. 'Implementation Guide of Building Manufacturing Innovation Centres' [in Chinese], Beijing, China.
MIIT (Ministry of Industry and Information Technology), 2018. 'Measures for Performance Assessment and Evaluation of the National State Manufacturing Innovation Centres' [in Chinese]. Beijing, China.

- smart-grid technology
- biomedical and advanced medical equipment
- agricultural machinery
- new materials

Under *Made in China 2025*, China has also created a series of manufacturing innovation centres. The purposes of these centres are to 'carry out R&D for common, generic-purpose technologies in a specific technological field, transfer and diffuse and commercialize innovation outputs, as well as provide public services such as testing and verification and standard setting for the industry, by building links between basic research and commercial applications'. These centres aim to create shared space for innovation by breaking down barriers between technology, industry, and capital. By the end of 2020, sixteen such manufacturing centres had been established at the national level, and more at the provincial level. To maximize their resource efficiency, the general principle is to have one national centre in each technological field and form alliances between research institutions and enterprises. The centres focus on core technologies such as basic materials (2), devices (6), processing technologies (3), and major equipment (4). The National Centres include:[32]

- Power Battery Innovation Centre
- Additive Materials Manufacturing Centre
- Printing and Flexible Display Innovation Centre
- Optoelectronics Innovation Centre
- Intelligent Robotic Innovation Centre
- Smart Sensor Innovation Centre
- IC Innovation Centre
- Digital Design and Manufacturing Innovation Centre
- Lightweight Material Forming Technology and Equipment Innovation Centre
- Advanced Rail Transit Equipment Innovation Centre
- Agricultural Machinery Equipment Innovation Centre
- Automobile Intelligent Network Innovation Centre
- Advanced Functional Fibre Innovation Centre
- Rare Earth Functional Materials Innovation Centre
- IC Processing, Packaging, and Testing Innovation Centre
- High-Performance Medical Device Innovation Centre

The government's approach to smart manufacturing builds on the country's digital strengths. In a 2019 State Government Report, it introduced the concept of 'Intelligent + Strategy', aiming to build internet platforms by adopting applications of big data and AI for smart manufacturing. The government plans to use 5G as a catalyst for

---

[32] 'White Paper for Manufacturing Industry Innovation centres' [in Chinese], China Electronics and Information Industry Development Institute (CCID), Beijing, China. May 2020.

this to happen, with the next generation of mobile networks extending beyond communications and evolving into the central nervous system of a smart manufacturing capability. China now has the world's largest 5G commercial network.

Although digital platforms and services have penetrated into Chinese manufacturing, led by the country's technology giants such as Alibaba, Tencent, PDD, and Huawei, unlocking their potential requires strengthening linkages with manufacturing. This is unlikely to be a smooth process, as investment in smart manufacturing is often substantial, and the return on investment is often slow and long-term, which poses challenges especially for SMEs.[33] And although Chinese companies are in strong positions in the provision of digital platforms, they are less advanced in some key technologies for smart manufacturing such as robotics and industrial software, including computer-aided design, computer-aided engineering, and enterprise resource planning.

Made in China 2025 is considered in the West, especially in the US, as a master plan for China to secure dominance in global technology, connected with the expansion of its global influence using the Belt and Road Initiative. It should, however, come as no surprise that China is no longer content to manufacture low-end products while sacrificing its environment. The real issues are whether the plan to transform China's manufacturing will succeed and what impact this will have on the global economy.

China's ambitions in smart manufacturing will not reshape the global economy. Given the difficult internal and external circumstances China is facing as a result of Covid-19, the country is dealing with a severe challenge in adjusting its economic structure from export- and investment-oriented growth to consumption- and services-oriented growth. Industrial value chains in smart manufacturing are longer and more complex, involve many more participants, and require greater cross-domain collaboration than Chinese industry is accustomed to. As argued in Chapters 6 and 7, to improve efficiency in resource allocation and utilization, it is critical to adjust boundaries between the government and the market, as well as building a market-oriented capital market that can finance the development of new technologies from SMEs. On this front, China has a long way to catch up.

Has the Role of China's Manufacturing in Global Value Chains Changed?

Since the 1990s there has been a global division of labour, with industrialized countries concentrating on innovation and emerging countries specializing in production and manufacturing.[34] This has led to a situation where hardly any country can claim

---

[33] A total of 84.2% of enterprise above the standard are small enterprises. Below the standard (annual revenue below 20 million RMB), there are over 2 million micro enterprises. These enterprises are the core of China's manufacturing sector. The level of intelligence of their manufacturing determines the implementation of China's goal in intelligence manufacturing.

[34] World Bank (2019), 'Global Value Chain Development Report 2019: Technological Innovation, Supply Chain Trade, and Workers in a Globalized World', https://documents.worldbank.org/en/

that it can be self-sufficient in supply chains. A World Trade Organization (WTO) study suggests that 70 per cent of global trade now involves global value chains (GVCs).[35] According to this report, the increase in the complexity of GVCs is illustrated by the growth in the share of foreign value added to a country's exports, which saw a jump from below 20 per cent in 1990 to nearly 30 per cent in 2011. In the global car industry, for example, 70 per cent of wheel hubs, and 30 per cent of tyres and engines are supplied by Chinese suppliers. Wuhan hosts a considerable proportion of the world's car supply chains, and when Covid-19 first hit the city in January 2020, it brought the production of the global car industry almost to a halt.[36]

Covid-19 has accelerated and amplified the challenges faced by global trade. Countries have become increasingly concerned about the positions of their manufacturing sector in GVCs and their self-sufficiency in the face of pandemics. Many countries have to make strategic decisions to reshore or nearshore the production of critical materials and supplies. They are rethinking global supply chains to achieve a balance between efficiency and resilience. The trend, however, of moving from global to regional or local value chains started before the pandemic. Since the beginning of this century competitive advantages of participating countries in GVCs have changed. As China's cost advantages diminished, many multinational manufacturers have moved part of their assembly lines to low-labour cost countries, such as Vietnam, India and Mexico.

The question is whether China has been replaced by lower labour cost countries in global value chains. On the surface, in recent years, some low-end production in China has been transferred to countries with lower costs. Foreign direct investment (FDI) is a good indicator of global industrial transfers. Figure 3.7 shows the net inflow of FDI into a country (measured by the percentage of the country's GDP) between 1980 and 2019.

Vietnam has consistently attracted a net inflow of FDI and experienced several peaks, including in 2008 and 2015. In 2019, Vietnam registered 7.2 per cent growth of its FDI inflow compared to the previous year. According to a McKinsey report, since 2010, Foxconn, Intel, Samsung, and other manufacturers have invested $15 billion in Vietnam's manufacturing facilities in electrical and electronic products. In 2019, South Korea was the top investor in Vietnam, followed by Hong Kong. Although China's investment ranked only fifth, investment through Hong Kong may not be included.[37] Most of this investment has been in manufacturing and can be attributed to two factors: lower costs of production and lower tariffs for exports.

It seems that Vietnam has siphoned manufacturing capacity from China. A closer examination of trade data between China and Vietnam, however, indicates that, in

---

publication/documents-reports/documentdetail/384161555079173489/global-value-chain-development-report-2019-technological-innovation-supply-chain-trade-and-workers-in-a-globalized-world, accessed 3 June 2021.

[35] World Bank (2019), 'Global Value Chain Development Report 2019'.

[36] A Few Thoughts on China's 14th Five-Year Plan', Deloitte, May 2020.

[37] See https://www.vietnam-briefing.com/news/fdi-in-vietnam-investment-by-sector.html/, accessed 3 June 2021.

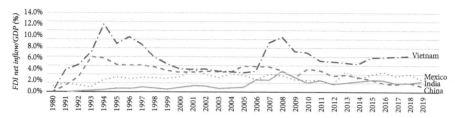

Figure 3.7 Country comparison of FDI to GDP ratio, 1980–2019
Source: World Bank

2018, China was Vietnam's largest trading partner: China accounted for 32.9 per cent of imports to Vietnam and 19.6 per cent of exports from Vietnam.[38]

Vietnamese production relies heavily on China's supplies of iron and steel, plastics, and fabric which are the outputs of China's heavy industries (see Table 3.2). Textile factories in Vietnam rely on imports of upstream intermediate products such as dye, a component from the higher value chain of China's chemical industrial base. Other examples include the production of generic drugs and low-end mobile phones, all of which have to rely on raw materials and intermediary components from China.

Firms shifted their investments from China to South East Asian countries such as Vietnam to benefit from lower labour costs, as well as to avoid the impacts caused by trade conflicts between the US and China. When Samsung closed its last factory in Huizhou, Guangdong, in 2019, moving its entire mobile handset manufacturing out of China, it was partly searching for cheaper labour, but more broadly reflected the company's strategic relocation of production to benefit from lower export tariffs in the countries where the final products are assembled. Samsung was also losing its market share in China to emerging domestic competitors such as Huawei, Xiaomi, OPPO, and Vivo.

On the other hand, in 2018, according to the Ministry of Commerce, the real FDI in China was $885.6 billion, representing a 0.9 per cent increase from the previous years. Of this investment, $41.3 billion was in the manufacturing sector alone, representing 23.1 per cent growth year on year. $13.7 billion was invested in high-end manufacturing, 38.1 per cent growth over one year earlier. Tesla, Ford, and BMW, for example, have all increased their investment in China since 2018.

The factors that attract foreign investment in China's manufacturing include the country's comprehensive industrial base, which supports the supply of raw materials, industrial products, and many intermediary components; infrastructure that is competitive in shipment costs and other logistic expenses; and local production facilities that are compatible with modern production standards. Additionally, MNCs continue to extend their business activities in China by increasing local R&D and high-end design capabilities, accessing Chinese resources and talent. In 2018,

---

[38] See https://oec.world/en/profile/country/vnm, accessed 3 June 2021.

Table 3.2 China's trades with Vietnam, 2019

Vietnam imports from China	Value ($ billion)	% of total imports	Exports from Vietnam to China	Value ($ billion)	% of total exports
Electrical and electronic equipment	21.44	32.7%	Electrical and electronic equipment	18.77	45.4%
Machinery, nuclear reactors, boilers	7.95	12.1%	Optical, photo, technical, medical apparatus	2.85	6.9%
Iron and steel	4.67	7.1%	Edible fruits, nuts, peel of citrus fruit, melons	2.85	6.9%
Plastics	3.32	5.1%	Cotton	2.12	5.1%
Knitted or crocheted fabric	2.72	4.2%	Footwear, gaiters and the like,	1.58	3.8%
Mineral fuels, oils, distillation products	1.83	2.8%	Rubbers	1.47	3.6%
Man-made staple fibres	1.78	2.7%	Machinery, nuclear reactors, boilers	1.16	2.8%
Articles of iron or steel	1.58	2.4%	Fish, crustaceans, molluscs, aquatic invertebrates	0.999	2.4%
Optical, photo, technical, medical apparatus	1.48	2.3%	Mineral fuels, oils, distillation products	0.942	2.3%
Man-made filaments	1.44	2.2%	Wood and articles of wood, wood charcoal	0.896	2.2%
Total imports	65.52	100%	**Total exports**	41.37	100%

Source: United Nations COMTRADE database

fifteen more foreign-funded R&D centres were established in Shanghai, adding the list to over 1,500 such R&D centres across China.[39] Multinational firms, such as Siemens, Schneider Electric, GE, and SAP, have established innovation or technology centres to support their smart manufacturing in China.

Siemens, for example, has actively invested in China's innovation ecosystem by building collaborative relationships with local governments, universities, research institutions, and enterprises. This serves the company's strategy of building a diverse global innovation network to benefit local customers. Siemens has established innovation centres in Qingdao, the first outside Germany, dedicated to intelligent manufacturing, robotics, modern logistics, big data, information security, and smart-city research and applications; an Industry 4.0-type of smart manufacturing innovation centre in Taiyuan; and another intelligent manufacturing centre

---

[39] See https://chinapower.csis.org/china-research-and-development-rnd/, accessed 3 June 2021.

dedicated to industry cloud computing, the industrial internet of things, and industrial big data in Chengdu.

BASF is an important foreign investor in China's chemical industry. Its total investment in China exceeds €6 billion, with extensive production, sales, marketing, and innovation networks in China. Its main FDI projects in China are in Nanjing, Shanghai, and Chongqing, and it has production bases all over the country. BASF's Innovation Park in Shanghai is its R&D hub. China is BASF's third largest market after Germany and the US. In 2017, BASF built two chemical factories in Shanghai, one for chemical catalysts and the other for car paints. The following year it announced an investment of $10 billion in an integrated plant in Guangdong, expected to be in production in 2030. This is BASF's largest investment project in China and will be BASF's third largest production base after Germany and Belgium.

The political impact of globalization on income distribution—widening the gap between the rich and the poor in each country—has also become more apparent. As a result, the established multilateral trading framework has been challenged by rising protectionism and populism. Trade conflicts have gradually extended to conflicts in technology, and even values and ideologies between China and the US. As well as the results of the pandemic, global trade faces other serious challenges. We will elaborate the implications of these challenges in Chapter 8.

In summary, a complete decoupling of China's manufacturing from GVCs would be extremely difficult. Building manufacturing capacity and proficiency in countries such as Vietnam, India, and Mexico will take a long time. The relocation of some low-end assembly activities in manufacturing value chains from China, especially to countries in South East Asia, reflects economic decisions by Chinese manufacturing firms (foreign-invested or domestically funded) that aim to internationalize their supply chain networks. Against the backdrop of the rapid rise in costs in labour and land internally and intensified trade conflicts which accelerate reshoring of the supply chains of its major trading partners, the role of China's manufacturing in global value chains still remains resilient. The agility and flexibility Chinese manufacturing firms have developed since the 1980s are still evident. In the six months from the outbreak of Covid-19, for example, 47,000 enterprises manufacturing face masks emerged to supply the global market, producing 200 million each day.

We now turn in Chapter 4 to the nature and importance of China's massive supply chains.

4
China's Mega Supply Chains

China's manufacturing power no longer derives from comparative advantages such as cheap labour or relaxed environmental protection requirements. Though China has a long way to catch up with the leading manufacturing countries such as the US, Germany, and Japan on the dimensions of manufacturing quality, structure, and sustainability, China's manufacturing capacity is the world leader. Its power is not only reflected in its scale, scope, and speed, but in the way it controls production costs in a smart way, as well as in the way it deals with unexpected events. China's mega supply chains underpin its manufacturing power. The reasons that multinational firms such as Tesla and BASF continually invest in production facilities in China is to benefit from all these supply chain advantages behind Chinese manufacturing capacity. For many businesses—particularly those in high-tech and consumer electronics—the speed of sourcing supplies and delivering products to market and the flexibility to combine different components and modules in production for mass customization are critical success factors. China's supply chains have formed an interconnected mega system. Efficiency at the firm level and resiliency at the system level have become a major source of competitive advantage for China's innovation machine.

China's supply chains have been built since the 1980s, and especially since the new millennium. They comprise a massive system that includes tens of millions of small and medium-sized enterprises (SMEs), micro firms, and individuals. In the early years of China's economic reforms, these firms clustered around regional manufacturing hubs in more developed regions such as the Pearl River Delta and Yangtze River Delta and supplied regional manufacturing. In recent years, with advances in ICT and the internet applications, these suppliers have joined larger supply chain networks, connected by the country's e-commerce platforms such as Alibaba, JD, Tencent, and Pinduoduo. These networks have become an ecosystem in which suppliers occupy different niches, form complementary relationships, and collectively produce at large scale. The ecosystems of diverse firms have open boundaries, but are integrated through interconnected value chains.

Contrary to the popular argument that China's economic growth results from the country's supportive industry policies and central planning, China's supply chains, in contrast, are the result of the organic, bottom-up evolution of many SMEs and micro enterprises, each striving to find and consolidate its own niche by building highly specialized capabilities within large ecosystems. The dynamism of the supply chain ecosystem is seen in the way it is growing at the macro level, but sees a high

Demystifying China's Innovation Machine: Chaotic Order. Marina Yue Zhang, Mark Dodgson, and David M. Gann, Oxford University Press. © Marina Yue Zhang, Mark Dodgson, and David M. Gann 2022.
DOI: 10.1093/oso/9780198861171.003.0004

rate of churn amongst firms at the micro level, with substantial business failures and the continuous injection of new entrants—new blood—into the system.

In an interconnected world of open borders, reduced barriers to trade, and cost-effective long-distance transportation, supply chains have become infinitely more complex, compounded by the widespread adoption of outsourcing and offshoring in manufacturing. Globalization has seen supply chains evolve and expand into complex international ecosystems, comprising many different organizations, featuring numerous multilayered interdependencies, spanning the borders of culture and languages, and crossing time zones. This chapter will analyse the development, strengths, and weaknesses of China's supply chains; explain its role in global value networks; and discuss their future in the light of current trade tensions, the pandemic, and other challenges to globalization.

Global Division of Labour

Modern supply chains are an advanced form of division of labour along industry value chains. They are physical and economic ties linking supplies of raw materials, technology, talent, and capital with market demand. Supply chain management includes 'the processes that plan and execute the acquisition of materials, transformation of materials into sellable products, delivery and return of products and services, in support of customer orders'.[1]

In the history of industrialization, supply chains were maintained with closely guarded boundaries to minimize transaction costs and to prevent spillovers of technology and production know-how to outsiders. For this reason, supply chains were often built following a hierarchical structure between enterprises and their close allies, mostly locally.

In the 1990s multinational corporations in developed countries started to concentrate on building an 'innovation economy'—focusing on design and innovation at one end of the value chain and sales and marketing at the other end—and outsourcing production to countries with lower labour costs such as China. China, at the same time, built vast numbers of factories to accommodate outsourcing demand from Western companies, utilizing the abundant supply of labour and land during the country's process of industrialization and urbanization.

Outsourcing has transformed supply chains from locally based, vertically integrated, structures to globally based, complex networks. In 2001, with China's entry to the WTO, many Chinese suppliers entered global value chains (GVCs).[2] Manufacturing

---

[1] According to the definition given by the Supply Chain Council (SCC).

[2] World Bank (2019), 'Global Value Chain Development Report 2019: Technological Innovation, Supply Chain Trade, and Workers in a Globalized World', https://documents.worldbank.org/en/publication/documents-reports/documentdetail/384161555079173489/global-value-chain-development-report-2019-technological-innovation-supply-chain-trade-and-workers-in-a-globalized-world, accessed 3 June 2021.

has transformed into 'a global enterprise',[3] with 'innovation economies' in developed countries combined with 'production economies' in developing countries. According to a report by the World Bank, 70 per cent of global trade involves global value chains. Even the countries best known for final products in key sectors such as cars, high-end machinery, and complex electronics rely heavily on inputs from global suppliers. Many of the iconic products in the world such as BMW's cars and Apple's iPhones have large amounts of imports that go into their final products.

Because of the global division of labour in manufacturing, the process of supply chain management has become modularized. A module refers to a composite or a set of components or parts grouped together by functionality. A chipset in smartphone production, for example, is a module composed of multiple chips to perform a certain function, such as image capture or voice recognition. Activities on traditional industrial value chains, such as procurement, production, distribution/sales, and services, have been broken down and modularized. Modularization in global supply has weakened the traditional dependence of part supplies from individual manufacturers. As a result, component and part suppliers become more independent and can achieve scale advantages by supplying multiple manufacturers. Production on a supply chain was segregated into smaller modules, and each module was produced by different suppliers following standard specifications of a product family.

Modularization in global supply chains that link raw materials, parts and components, and increasingly modules enables small and dispersed suppliers across national borders to be included in finished products. According to Martin Christopher, global supply chains have become 'the network of organizations that are involved, through upstream and downstream linkages, in the different processes and activities that produce value in the form of products and services in the hands of the ultimate consumer'.[4] Initially, specialized suppliers were coordinated by multinational firms. In recent years, such coordination has moved onto digital platforms, enabled by the internet, big data analytics, and AI. Global supply chains consist of end-to-end flows of goods, information, technology, and capital, enabled by technology. They are not simply linear chains or processes, as in the Industrial Age, characterized by automation along assembly lines organized by multinational enterprises.

Global production has, therefore, experienced a substantial reorganization around an interconnected and interdependent network of resources, skills, capital, and markets. In these circumstances it becomes increasingly challenging to constrain industry technology and production know-how within company, industry, and regional or national boundaries. In many industries with complex global supply chains, because the organization of production is highly distributed in networks or ecosystems

---

[3] R. Baldwin (2016), *The Great Convergence: Information Technology and the New Globalization*, Cambridge, MA: Harvard University Press.

[4] M. Christopher (2011), *Logistics & Supply Chain Management*, 5th edition, London: Financial Times Prentice Hall.

surrounding industry supply chains, it is difficult to see the locus of production within a company, a region, or a country.

Globally distributed supply chains are especially found in high-technology, knowledge- intensive sectors such as semiconductors and aeroplanes, where two phenomena are apparent. First, technology in such sectors is often sourced globally. Second, specialization has greatly extended the depth and scope of the global division of labour between stages of production.

The way that modern production is organized around global supply chains has also transformed global competition. The global supply chain network allows countries that specialize in particular activities to be included in and benefit from it. As developing countries move from exporting primary products to value-added manufacturing in parts and intermediary products or services via global supply chains, they also change the way they compete in the global market. As we saw in Chapter 3, China, for example, started out and continued for a long time at the lower end of value-adding in global supply chains, concentrating on labour-intensive assembly of parts produced elsewhere. In other words, in some products, the ratio of domestic value added to gross exports was small, despite significant Chinese gross exports. Since the late 1990s, China has engaged in reforms of its industrial structures, especially the supply side. As a result, the value-added contribution to the country's exports has improved. On global supply chains, however, much of the design and high value-added modules are still taking place in more developed countries such as the US, Germany, and Japan.

Modularity, Standardization, and Complementarity in Supply Chains

A modular design breaks a complex production system by dividing the process into different task modules that are connected via interfaces into the system.[5] In modular design, by following standard interfaces determined by system architecture, different modules can complement one another to form an expandable or evolutionary system. Each module can maintain a high degree of autonomy in a way that allows flexibility in combining different components and parts, as long as, at the module level, it follows predesigned interfaces. With the complexity and speed of manufacturing increasing, suppliers have considerable leeway in design and innovation and they can provide improvements and cost-saving solutions in production.

Some firms focus on developing general-purpose modules which can be used in multiple industries, and some on special-purpose modules which can be used in specific products. General-purpose modular components can be reused in a variety of models of similar products, which saves money and time. A group of platform

[5] C. Y. Baldwin and K. B. Clark (2000), *Design Rules*, i: *The Power of Modularity*, Cambridge, MA: MIT Press.

firms that predesign system architectures and interfaces in an industry have also emerged, facilitating the ability of different modules to interoperate and interconnect.

The car industry was among the earliest to adopt modularization and standardization in its supply chain management. In a traditional car supply chain, suppliers provided basic parts and components of, for example, car seats, to a specific car manufacturer. In a modular supply chain, the suppliers of car seat components can produce entire seats following standard interfaces specified by the chassis of the car manufacturer, which can be installed in other models that share the same chassis. Modularized supply chains create efficiency for both suppliers (such as car seat producers) and lead manufacturers (carmakers) in the value chain. This model of supply chain management has now become the norm in many industries with complex products, such as computers, aeroplanes, pharmaceuticals, and software.

Technology plays a crucial role in modularization and standardization in supply chains. Standardization and modularity reduce uncertainty in production. In so doing, best practices become codified, which enables the fast diffusion of complex technology. IT and internet technology has furthermore reduced firms' reliance on tacit knowledge. The last few decades have seen the emergence of platform business models. In industries such as carmaking, lead car manufacturers can function as platforms on which the match between supply and demand can be optimized using these technologies. Platform-based supply chain strategies, thus, change the way organizations conduct their business by becoming more open and by engaging external entities outside their immediate boundaries, allowing them to interact with a wide array of suppliers and consumers beyond their geographical boundaries.

Taking the role of an intermediary, platforms facilitate the interactions of different modules. Firms that provide a core platform within an ecosystem act as 'keystone' members[6] or 'hub' firms,[7] so that they become 'lead firms' within the ecosystem.[8] These lead firms not only lay out the architecture of an ecosystem but also set the rules, policies, and processes that maintain multilateral complementarity among different modules and actors. They therefore provide the foundations upon which all suppliers can join the supply chain ecosystem by developing complementary components, modules, technologies, products, or services based on certain standards.

The Development of China's Supply Chains

China has benefited enormously from being the outsourcing partner for overseas MNCs. Two factors have played an important role in the upgrading of China's supply

[6] M. Iansiti and R. Levien (2004), *The Keystone Advantage: What the New Dynamics of Business Ecosystems Mean for Strategy, Innovation, and Sustainability*, Cambridge, MA: Harvard Business Press.

[7] C. Dhanaraj and A. Parkhe (2006), 'Orchestrating Innovation Networks', *Academy of Management Review*, 31, 659–69.

[8] M. W. Peng, S. L. Sun, B. Pinkham, and H. Chen (2009), 'The Institution-Based View as a Third Leg for a Strategy Tripod', *Academy of Management Perspectives*, 23, 63–81.

chains. First, the spillover effects of foreign-invested joint venture OEM manufacturers on local suppliers. These OEM manufacturers dealt with their downstream customers, as well as developed their upstream suppliers locally. When Foxconn established its first OEM factory in mainland China, for example, it started to build and develop its own local supply chains. These local suppliers have to upgrade their technology and learn production know-how to be included into Foxconn's supply chains. The spillover effect is like seeds that spread technology and know-how into the upstream supplier community. Over time, regional clusters of suppliers in related industry supply chains emerged and developed. A successful example is the supply chains in consumer electronics in the Pearl River Delta, which supplies production not only for Apple and Samsung via Foxconn, but also for rapidly growing domestic producers of smartphones such as Huawei, Xiaomi, Vivo, and Oppo.

While questions were asked why the Shanghai government provided subsidized industrial land and discounted loans to Tesla and included its cars in the tax exemption list, the decisions make a lot of sense from the perspective of developing local supply chains for China's electric vehicle (EV) sector. As seen in Chapter 3, Tesla's China strategy is expected to play a similar role in developing local supply chains in the EV sector to that of Apple in smartphone supply chains.[9] Tesla has promised to increase local supply to 100 per cent by the end of 2021. That means that local suppliers have to upgrade their technology and improve their manufacturing capacity if they wish to work with Tesla. In the long run, this process will help Chinese supply chains in the EV sector to be more competitive. As a market stimulus, Tesla will create competition among Chinese EV makers, which will also benefit from the growth of the local supply chains. Industry policy for China's new and electric vehicle sector will be explored in Chapter 7.

The second success factor behind China's supply chains becoming a major hub in global supply networks is the large workforce and its pool of skilled engineers. China has the largest university-educated workforce in the world: the absolute number is larger than the population of many countries. It has the largest number of STEM graduates in the world.[10] More than half of China's university graduates are in STEM subjects and are competing in a job market that perhaps can absorb about 10 per cent of the graduates with relevant qualifications. Many university-educated people have entered the manufacturing workforce, which traditionally requires high-school or vocational education.

Employing seemingly overqualified workers is not a new phenomenon in China. Before the economic reforms in 1978, the university-educated mostly worked in SOEs, research institutes, or the public sector, where they enjoyed lifelong welfare but had little freedom or autonomy in what they could do in their jobs. During the

---

[9] M. Campbell et al. (2021), 'Elon Musk Loves China, and China Loves Him Back—for Now', Bloomberg Businessweek, 13 January, https://www.bloomberg.com/news/features/2021-01-13/china-loves-elon-musk-and-tesla-tsla-how-long-will-that-last, accessed 1 June 2021.

[10] See https://www.industryweek.com/talent/article/21998889/the-countries-with-the-most-stem-graduates, accessed 4 June 2021.

early years of China's industrialization in the 1990s, some university-educated personnel chose to leave the system of state-owned organizations. They left their white-collar jobs in inland cities to join the private sector, often as blue-collar workers, in joint venture factories in coastal cities, especially those in the Special Economic Zones. They gave up the social status associated with working in official organizations for a higher salary and more freedom. This group of pioneers often had an entrepreneurial spirit and were very pragmatic. Over time, many accumulated hands-on experience as shopfloor workers initially and then progressed into managerial roles in OEM factories. They became the carriers of industry knowledge and production know-how in manufacturing that was the foundation of supply chains in cities such as Shenzhen, Dongguan, Huizhou, or Xiamen, all of which became hubs of China's manufacturing clusters.[11]

The global financial crisis in 2008 accelerated the diffusion of the skilled workforce in China's manufacturing sector into more distributed supply chain networks. Many OEM factories that used to supply global customers were forced to de-integrate their assembly lines after the crisis. Experienced managers and skilled workers were forced to move to lower-tier factories or workshops specialized in smaller elements of assembly lines. This transformation from concentrated factories to small workshops explains why the number of large enterprises in the manufacturing industry has fallen but the total population of the workforce has increased in many manufacturing clusters.

In Da Lang County, for example, near Dongguan in Guangdong province, there are clusters of China's garment manufacturing plants. Instead of producing the whole product, each plant concentrates on one section of the value chain of garment making. These small factories develop high levels of efficiency by concentrating, for example, on cutting or sewing or attaching zips. The mutual trust that can be developed through geographical proximity allows coordination and collaboration.[12] Collectively, these clusters of small but specialized plants can be creative and innovative by recombining the vast array of their sections. In this process, a group of manufacturing services companies emerged that specialize in coordinating with upstream suppliers of raw materials and components and dealing with downstream customers. These services firms are the platforms on which suppliers of complementary modules and components collaborate in mass production. This type of firm manages production in networks of dispersed modularized suppliers for a specific product family in geographically embedded hubs and clusters. They are co-designers, logistic coordinators and, most importantly, connectors between the supply and the demand sides of markets.

Innovation capability in a manufacturing enterprise is not only determined by the innovation offered by machines and other hardware. The skills of the workforce, especially engineers and experienced workers, importantly translate complex designs into

---

[11] M. Y. Zhang, M. Dodgson, and D. Gann (2021), 'Entrepreneurship and Knowledge Flows in China's Supply Chains: The Roles of Platforms.' Academy of Management Conference (0nline).
[12] P. Cooke and K. Morgan (1998), *The Associational Economy*, Oxford: Oxford University Press.

products with precision and cost efficiency. The talent pool in China's supply chains is a form of the soft power behind China's innovation machine. Skilled engineers and workers possess the specific and often tacit knowledge to manage the production process while minimizing errors and maximizing precision and efficiency.

Supply Chain Efficiency

Supply chain efficiency is a measure of the ratio between a firm's input—be they raw materials, components, modules, or financial, human, technological, and physical resources–and output (intermediary or final products) through production. In other words, it measures the efficiency of value-adding in production processes. Supply chain management aims to improve productivity at the lowest cost and fastest speed, increasing cost- and time-efficiency.

Adam Smith's *Wealth of Nations* recognized the value of specialization for efficiency, as illustrated by the famous description of the division of labour in a pin factory. Efficiency derived from pin-making tasks being distributed amongst workers with specialized knowledge. In the case of supply chain management, the organization of specialized knowledge has been extended to an entire industry value chain. The global division of labour in supply chains helps firms absorb new technologies faster and more effectively by developing economies of scale in narrowly defined specialized areas.

Standardization and modularity in production have distributed even highly complex technologies across global value networks. This enables combinatorial innovation, because peripheral modules can be improved without altering the core of system architecture.[13] In other words, each module can be improved, adapted, and modified at the component level as long as it follows architectural standards without affecting the overall architecture of the product, which, in turn, increases the level of complexity and flexibility for mass customization. This, as a result, opens new opportunities for SMEs and micro suppliers to contribute their innovations to entire supply chains.

SMEs and micro enterprises are a major driving force for China's economic growth and an important element of China's innovation machine. According to the China State Council, SMEs and micro enterprises in the private sector account for 90 per cent of all businesses, employ over 80 per cent of the urban workforce, produce more than 70 per cent of technological innovations, and contribute over 60 per cent of GDP and 50 per cent of tax revenues in China.[14] From 2013 to 2018, the number of SMEs and micro enterprises grew by 115 per cent. At the end of 2018, over 18 million such enterprises employed over 230 million urban workers. This group of enterprises

---

[13] Y. Yoo, O. Henfridsson, and K. Lyytinen (2010), 'Research Commentary: The New Organizing Logic of Digital Innovation: An Agenda for Information Systems Research', *Information Systems Research*, 21(4), 724–35.
[14] See http://www.china.org.cn/business/2018-12/25/content_74310169.htm, accessed 4 June 2021.

are the main actors in China's supply chain networks. They are commonly entrepreneurially oriented, agile, and constantly search for new niches to survive.

Each of these SMEs and micro enterprises develops its speciality in narrowly sliced sections of production on each industry value chain. Such narrow specialty allows them to build efficiency in particular sections of production.

Supply Chain Resilience

Supply chain efficiencies can minimize costs and increase speed in manufacturing, from sourcing materials to production, packaging, and delivery. Unexpected events, however, such as pandemics, natural disasters, or changes in consumer demand, can undermine the most efficient supply chains.

Consider the following scenario: your company receives a sudden (and very large) order for one of its products, which relies on a critical component from another supplier. The latest shipment of this component has been delayed, and there are no alternative suppliers. Even worse, the supplier of this component is also dependent on other suppliers of critical raw materials, parts and modules, with which you have no direct contact. How fast and effectively can the company respond to this sudden and large order?

Supply chain efficiency in each module cannot guarantee supply chain resilience at the system level. Resilience is a measure that determines the efficacy and responsiveness of an entire supply chain which often have multiple layers under different circumstances. This requires supply chains to be flexible and agile.

Since the Second World War, modern supply chain management has adopted practices such as lean inventory management and just-in-time delivery that pursue efficiency while making little provision for flexibility and agility. These types of supply chain are vulnerable to unexpected events. Supply chain flexibility requires a large number of diverse and distributed suppliers in a value chain, which allows the system to respond quickly and adapt to new opportunities or challenges. Traditional approaches to building supply chain flexibility prepare for threats of natural disasters, but many firms do not have adequate contingency plans for unexpected events such as pandemics or quickly escalating trade wars.

Flexibility is essential for supply chain management. The greater the flexibility and adaptability in supply chains, the more resilient they are. As part of the move to the innovation economy, Western manufacturers gave up their capabilities in low-end production and focused much of their operational management in factories on procurement and supply chain management. The complexity and interdependency in deep-layered global supply chains, however, make it challenging for firms to deal with unexpected events. In some complicated products such as cars, supply chains may include up to ten layers. Firms may only know the first few layers of their suppliers, with lower layers largely invisible to supply chain managers. This has been starkly observed in 2020 in the failure of American carmakers to switch their production capacity to produce medical ventilators for Covid-19 patients. In the event, those car-makers were unable to identify, let alone contact, suppliers of some core components, including pressure sensors and valves controlled and made by professional suppliers supported by invisible overseas suppliers. Even the production of medical masks such as N95 needed to source materials and components from around the world.

In contrast, when Covid-19 hit countries in Europe and America in February 2020, China produced half the world's supply of face masks. Within one month, out-put increased to around 120 million every day, a twelve fold growth.[15] This increase of production capacity for face masks resulted from China's mega supply chains. *The Economist* explained the situation clearly:

a simple surgical mask consists of a woven layer fused to a non-woven layer, elastic loops that go around your ears and a thin metal band to fasten it to your nose. More sophisticated masks add a thin plastic filter and an activated carbon filter. Any country hoping to make masks on its own needs companies with expertise in textiles, chemicals, metallurgy and machining, along with sufficient supplies of raw materials, factory space, trained workers, engineers and capital. It cannot just be done from scratch, and a similar story plays out across thousands of products.[16]

China's distributed supply chain networks, backed by its comprehensive industrial base, allowed firms such as smartphone maker OPPO and carmaker BYD to quickly change their production lines to manufacture face masks and medical ventilators to combat the pandemic.

The challenges seen in Western firms when dealing with the Covid-19 pandemic extend beyond face masks. Many firms found that they rely on unknown suppliers for even the most essential products. A quarter of generic drugs sold in the US come from India. India's drug supply is heavily dependent on China for APIs (active pharmaceutical ingredients) and chemical intermediates.[17] Since 2000, the Chinese government has provided incentives to its pharmaceutical companies to build large API factories. There are currently more than 7,000 API manufacturers in China, compared with around 1,500 in India. This gives China's drug making supply chains scale and scope advantages over competitors. The Chinese government supports API production simply for the country to be self-sufficient in generic, low-cost drugs. The manufacture of APIs, supported by the WTO's special licences to its member countries to produce generic versions of patented medicines, have saved many lives and greatly improved public health around the world.

[15] See https://cn.nytimes.com/business/20200316/masks-china-coronavirus/, accessed 4 June 2021.

[16] Economist (2020), 'The Greatest (Trade) Show on Earth: China Is the World's Factory, More than Ever', *The Economist*, 29 June, https://www.economist.com/finance-and-economics/2020/06/23/china-is-the-worlds-factory-more-than-ever, accessed 4 June 2021.

[17] See https://glg.it/articles/chinas-role-in-global-generic-pharmaceutical-supply-chain/, accessed 4 June 2021.

At the system level, China's supply chains have resilience in two dimensions: first, operational resilience from vast numbers of small suppliers in value chains that are interconnected, mediated by regional or digital platforms, and second, the scale and scope of the firms in the supply chains that can innovatively configure so that they can serve the full spectrum of demand with variations in consumer tastes, regulatory requirements, and transport infrastructures with speed and agility. At the micro level, modular production in China's supply chains can achieve high efficiency by deep specialization. At the system level, they collectively have high levels of resilience when facing unexpected events.

China's Mega Supply Chains: Balancing Efficiency and Resiliency

Modern supply chain management requires firms to balance efficiency and resiliency: a challenging task. Firms achieving efficiencies through scale economies by producing standard and unified products sacrifice flexibility. By doing so they have to give up resilience in terms of flexibility and efficacy, as standardized products with little ability to modify technical features can lead to an excessive supply of homogeneous products and a lack of responsiveness to unexpected events. Likewise, if firms in supply chains pursue flexibility that meets customized and unexpected requirements, then they have to sacrifice efficiency in cost.

The division of labour in a market can only increase productivity if the market is open and large enough. In a closed market, the division of labour can improve efficiency in each player, but cannot increase systemic productivity. Closed manufacturing clusters, for example in regions, can increase efficiency through community-based knowledge sharing, empowered by mutual trust, but without connecting with external supply and demand, the introspective supply chain can become moribund when internal demand and supply reach an equilibrium.

Even in open markets, efficiency and resiliency are often independent. Three conditions promote their coexistence. First, there must be sufficient numbers of small firms, each specialized in narrow niche on the value chain. Second, the offerings of these firms form multilateral complementary relationships and combinations following standard interfaces that increase systemic productivity. Third, there are platform firms that coordinate these suppliers by maintaining and managing the flow of goods, services, capital, and information with minimum transaction costs. China meets all these three conditions in most supply chains.

Coase in his classic work *The Nature of the Firm* argued that the emergence and continued existence of firms results from efforts to minimize transaction costs involved in repeated negotiations and contracts when complete information is rare in the market.[18] For this reason, for a long time in the history of industrialization,

---

[18] See R. H. Coase (1937), *The Nature of the Firm*. doi: 10.1111/j.1468-0335.1937.tb00002.x.

firms maintained and managed their own vertical integrated supply chains to minimize transaction costs. In modern supply chains, a new form of organizational division of labour mediated by platforms is replacing traditional corporations by reducing transaction costs in open systems. In an open system, platforms emerge and facilitate knowledge sharing and information exchange, as well as coordinate collaboration, not only between supply and demand in the system, but also amongst multiple suppliers. Platforms in supply chains are intermediaries among independent but interdependent suppliers, as well as with downstream buyers, coordinating mass collaboration to create two- or multisided marketplaces for products or services.[19] In such organizations, multitudes of sellers, buyers, and complementors collaborate in R&D and innovation and share resources to achieve both efficiency and resiliency of supply chains. China has many leadership advantages on this front.

Another factor behind the shift in supply chains to a more distributed, open network in the division of labour is that innovations in emerging technological fields can penetrate traditional boundaries, whether technological, industrial, geographical, or national. Traditionally organized large corporates may not be effective in such boundary-spanning innovations. A distributed, network-based organization, on the other hand, can facilitate large-scale collaboration across traditional boundaries.

The Chinese government has adopted a highly pragmatic policy approach to support the growth of newly formed organizational forms in supply chains. It lets the market take the lead, using various policy instruments to encourage or constrain its development, and then uses regulation when the underlying technologies or innovations mature. We will illustrate this point in more detail in Chapter 7.

Clusters as Platforms

In the early days of China's supply chain development, developments in geographical proximity, such as high-tech parks, manufacturing parks, or industrial parks, functioned as platforms that facilitated shared resources and the exchange of information. Many of these developments started as government-driven initiatives, serving the main purposes of attracting foreign investment and hosting enterprises. This top-down approach, however, led them to serve mainly as landlords for enterprises that resided in their developments. Over time, they have evolved into regional clusters of firms in related industrial value chains.

In recent decades, although firms have benefited from a growing global circulation of information, knowledge, skills, and capital for innovation activities, the significance of industry clusters on firm performance has not diminished. In fact, firms in technology-intensive industries have relied even more on collaborations with their cluster partners to deal with increasing technological complexity and rapid

---

[19] A. Gawer and M. A. Cusumano (2013), 'Industry Platforms and Ecosystem Innovation', *Journal of Product Innovation Management*, 31(3), 417–33.

changes in product design and demand conditions.[20] Cluster networks are still one of the critical sources from which firms acquire ideas, information, and knowledge to improve innovation performance.

Shenzhen is the most successful example of a regional manufacturing cluster in China. It hosts complete supply chains for smartphones, for example, including suppliers of key modules such as communications, memories, gyroscopes, displays, cameras, and touchscreens. These suppliers interact, mediated by platform firms, to design, produce, and deliver products, with efficiency and flexibility, not only to large OEM firms such as Foxconn, but also to local brands such as Huawei and Xiaomi, as well as non-brand smartphone producers. OEMs and lead manufacturers are platforms that organize collaboration among multiple suppliers in this industry. There is also a type of professional platform firm that has emerged and serves as a hub in the mass collaboration of suppliers. For example, if a client wanted to have a customized smartphone, the platform firm will collect demand information, pass on the information to various module suppliers, encourage and moderate their competition, deliver the prototype to the client, then send the client's feedback to the winning suppliers for amendments and improvements, and, finally, deliver the product to the client. This process can be conducted in less than two days. Shenzhen has become a strong base for innovation in hardware, largely due to its advantages in these efficient and resilent supply chains mediated by platform firms.

DJI, the world leader in consumer unmanned aerial vehicles (UAVs, commonly known as 'drones'), is headquartered in Shenzhen. DJI's rapid growth is the result of its advanced design and engineering. Supply chains in related industries also contribute to DJI's success. The main material used in UAVs is carbon fibre, which comes, for example, from its supply for products such as fishing rods, and tennis and badminton rackets, in which China has accumulated experience and production capacity for decades. Another important component is the sensors used in UAVs. China has accumulated innovation and production capacity from its experience in manufacturing sensors for camera lenses and smartphones over decades.

Another successful regional cluster is Suzhou BioBay Park, an industrial park dedicated to biomedicine founded by Suzhou Industrial Park. It was one of the earliest industrial parks in China.

BioBay Park also began as a government-sponsored spatial development and has become one of the top biopharmaceutical clusters in China. Positioned as a bridge between enterprises and the government, BioBay built services platforms, including investing more than 100 million RMB (about $15 million at 2019 exchange rates) and encouraging start-ups in drug development, medical instruments, biotechnology, and nanotechnology. Close to Shanghai, Suzhou BioBay has attracted many research institutions and start-up firms.[21] It has a high concentration of talented researchers,

---

[20] See Z. Li, M. Y. Zhang, and H. Zhang (2020), 'Firm Growth Performance and Relative Innovation Orientation of Exploration vs Exploitation: Moderating Effects of Cluster Relationships', *Management and Organization Review*, 17(1), 1–30.

[21] See https://www.iotone.com/organization/suzhou-biobay/o398, accessed 4 June 2021.

with one founder in the park claiming in interview that seventy-two of the country's most talented workers in biopharmaceutical fields reside in Suzhou BioBay. In recent years, the rise of a group of biopharmaceutical firms in Suzhou shows how scientific progress in bioscience and biotechnology in China can be used in pharmaceuticals and drug making. It has developed a long industrial value chain in the biopharmaceutical industry, including drug R&D, screening, and production. The next step for BioBay is to develop clinical trials by building alliances with hospitals.

The role of the platforms in the regional biomedicine clusters, such as Suzhou BioBay Park and Shanghai Zhangjiang Pharmaceutical Valley, is significant. Many start-up founders are scientists educated at foreign universities, including several scientists who were trained at top US universities and gained extensive experience in the biopharmaceutical industry before returning to China. Sharing R&D resources and, sometimes, clients is common in these clusters. Human mobility is also high, which enables knowledge spillover. Since 2015, several start-ups have focused on drug R&D using frontier technologies such as gene editing or immunology. According to an interview with a scientist founder of a gene editing start-up, the talent pool and supply chains in biomedicine and biopharmaceutics in these parks are the greatest attraction for start-ups. Science-based entrepreneurship in biotechnology and biopharmaceutics will be discussed in Chapter 6.

Chengdu is a regional cluster of optoelectronic display manufacturing. In Chengdu's High-Tech Zone, Foxconn produces iPads and iPhones in its factory; Dell, Lenovo and Founders produce laptop PCs; and TCL and Changhong produce colour TVs. These firms are the downstream customers for optoelectronic display products. Together with upstream suppliers of raw materials and producers of intermediary display panels, a complete supply chain exists in this industry, including glass substrates, backlight modules, photomasks, displays, touchscreens for smartphones, and LCD displays for TVs. Chengdu's supply chain attracted BOE Technology, the country's largest LCD display manufacturer to build its manufacturing centre there. BOE supplies all types of screens from smartphone to laptop and TV, and is also a leader in flexible OLED screens—the type that can be used in foldable smartphones. LCD screens are composed of many components from multilayered suppliers. At their core, the screens are made of thin-film transistor liquid crystal display (TFT-LCD) panels, which are produced by a few factories in Taiwan, South Korea, and China. BOE also invested in Chengdu to access highly skilled engineers and workers in the cluster. There are high levels of worker mobility in the cluster.

From these three examples, we can see there are common features of these spatial platforms. Firms build direct or indirect links with others within the clusters to acquire relevant information, knowledge, and other resources, as well as talented people, to support innovation. Lead manufacturers such as Foxconn and BOE or platform firms in Shenzhen, and Suzhou can, due to their geographical proximity and industry-relatedness, facilitate large-scale collaboration and enable firms in supply chains to benefit from network relationships in those clusters. Close interactions between markets and the supplier networks through lead firms or platform firms enable mutual learning and, thus, promote intra-regional integration of supply chains.[22]

Digital Platforms

Since the global financial crisis in 2008, markets in China have become more fragmented, delivery cycles shorter, and production more customized. The complexity of deep-layered networks with many invisible suppliers in modern supply chains makes tracking the flow of goods, services, information, and capital a challenging task, even within geographical proximity. Digital platforms offer solutions to the problems these raise.

Through ICT and internet technology, digital platforms can connect firms across geographical boundaries to form a larger ecosystem in which more value can be created and exchanged. Digital platforms encourage more openness by including great diversity and complexity in production systems, without the constraints of traditional boundaries. Due to these advantages, digital platforms and their ecosystems have become central features in many industries and markets such as e-commerce, social media, and operating systems, as well as peer-to-peer sharing. Digital platforms such as Amazon, Airbnb, and Uber function as matchmakers and service providers which enable mass collaboration within open and complex networks.

SMEs and micro firms in general have low direct participation in international trade compared to large enterprises. This lack of participation is caused by the high fixed costs involved in transactions in export businesses. In theory, the spread of these costs among many firms should make it easier for small firms to participate in trade, as the segmentation of the production process makes it feasible for specialized firms to find niche markets globally. In reality, however, SMEs and micro firms cannot easily reach a large market beyond arm's reach, let alone a global one. The fundamental reason is that such small firms do not have sufficient credentials to enter supply chains.

On digital platforms, such credentials as who you are, where you live, and how big you are do not matter. On digital platforms, technology, not organization or geographical proximity, minimizes transaction costs.

On Alibaba's platform, for example, by the end of 2017, there were 316,000 distinct sellers who, collectively, achieved annual sales revenue of over 10 billion RMB (about $1.5 billion), and over 1,000 Taobao 'villages'—small clusters that produce and sell products in interrelated supply chains—each achieving annual sales revenue of 10 million RMB (about $1.5 million).[23] The platform-mediated open e-commerce

---

[22] See G. Herrigel, V. Wittke and U. Voskamp (2013). 'The process of Chinese manufacturing upgrading: Transitioning from unilateral to recursive mutual learning relations', *Global Strategy Journal*, 3, 109–125.

[23] AliResearch (2017), *Inclusive Growth and E-Commerce: China's Experience*, https://unctad.org/meetings/en/Contribution/dtl_eWeek2017c11-aliresearch_en.pdf, accessed 4 June 2021.

ecosystems, along with infrastructure such as mobile payment systems, the use of fintech, and logistic networks, have created an inclusive growth pattern, new opportunities, and accessible markets for countless SMEs and micro suppliers in China. E-commerce is an integral part of modern lifestyle and an important aspect of global supply chains.

In digital ecosystems, each firm is a contributor to the network and also a beneficiary of network effects. The matching between supply and demand on digital platforms can optimize operations in production and logistics. Entire supply chains are thus interconnected and form interdependent ecosystems, which increases both efficiency at the local level and resiliency at the system level.

Firms have traditionally used historical sales data in their production forecasts. Firms using more advanced technologies such as AI and big data analytics can assess the future from social-media trends and shifts in demand to inventory turnover and vendor behaviour. These technologies increase the predictability, transparency, and speed of delivery of supply chains. Advanced digital technologies enable platform firms to achieve visibility of all suppliers for complex products at all times, even in complex and multilayered networks of supply chains. Chinese digital platform firms lead in this transformation.

Digital platform firms are becoming larger and more powerful as they gradually diminish traditional boundaries in technology, business, region, profession, and industry. Cross-domain, large-scale collaboration is a strong feature of the digital economy. The super scale of such digital platforms has also blurred the distinction between normal competition and monopoly. Many such platform firms have built multiplatform ecosystems, achieving control of the entire supply chains in certain industries. Currently, most such platforms are in consumer goods and services. In the future, when platforms extend to other areas such as manufacturing services in the industrial internet age, how to manage the effects and risks of the digital economy and its key platform firms in the national and global economy remains a contentious question.

Moving to Smart Supply Chains

Digitalization will have more impact on productivity growth in supply chains in Industry 4.0 than steam, electricity, and ICT in the industrialization age and information age. The most essential feature of Industry 4.0 is Cyber-Physical System (CPS) integration enabled by technologies such as internet of things (IoT), AI and big data analytics.[24] Digitalization is key to this revolution, penetrating into all elements of industry value chains. Consequently, digitalization can empower limitless possibilities of combinations through CPS fusions in value chains, creating new

---

[24] See http://www.next-in.eu/2017/03/20/industry-4-0-the-fourth-industrial-revolution-of-cyber-physical-systems/, accessed 4 June 2021.

industries within and across industry boundaries. Especially influential will be the ways in which machines will replace humans in prediction and planning in supply chain management.

Industry 4.0 also requires the upgrading of organizations. In the ages of automation- and information-driven industrial revolutions, enterprises faced unilateral markets, that is to say, the transactions were largely one-to-one, trading products for products. The digitalization-driven revolution has transformed manufacturing towards multi-lateral transactions, that is, transactions can be among multiple players enabled by digital platforms such as Amazon and Alibaba.

Digitalization empowers countless Chinese SMEs and micro or individual sup-pliers to access global supply chains via technology, although access varies by firm size, as well as level of development across different regions. China's success in its digital economy illustrates the role of digital platforms, not just as a matchmaker and a digital infrastructure provider and system enabler, removing the constraints faced by SMEs and micro or individual suppliers in many developing countries and providing access to cloud computing power, electronic payments, and logistics. Public cloud computing provided by Alibaba, for example, helped reduce 70 per cent of the innovation costs of their sellers.[25] This exists alongside China's infrastructure providing access to a steady supply of electricity, high-speed internet connections, and nationwide delivery networks.

The digital economy comprises about one-third of China's GDP. It is seeing a smart supply chain being built by reorganizing the order of activities in industry value chains. Smart supply chains transform supply chain management from a linear model in which information flows from supplier to producer to distributor to consumer and back to a more integrated model in which information flows in all directions. The smart supply chains and logistic networks enabled by China's digital platforms offset the advantages of geographical proximity in production networks and function as the organizers and coordinators in production from consumers to manufacturers.

Some of these processes are being implemented through blockchain, the distrib-uted ledger technology that allows multiple parties to maintain copies of the same information in various locations, either in an open manner or by requiring individ-ual entities' permission to access the network. Its special feature is that historical entries cannot be altered.

Ant Financial Services platform, Alibaba's lending and mobile payments business, uses big data analytics for credit-profiling purposes based on scenario-driven ana-lyses of borrowers' behaviours and their relationships with others online. The loan approval and issuance processes are entirely digital and solely driven by credit scores based on borrowers' profiling. Using fintech (though Jack Ma calls it 'Tech Fin')— technology-driven financial services—this model has revolutionized the traditional loan business, which was previously almost closed to millions of SMEs and micro

---

[25] AliResearch, *Inclusive Growth and E-Commerce*.

enterprises in China. Ant Financial can provide almost real-time loan application assessment and approval, with the capacity to provide millisecond-level risk prevention. We will analyse Ant Group's strengths and weaknesses, responsibility, and liabilities in Chapters 6 and 7.

The Chinese government embraces digital technologies and has established goals for manufacturing moving up the global value chain. Building smart supply chains is key to achieving such goals, becoming in the process the foundation of entire economies, delivering huge benefits in inclusive patterns of growth, innovation, and entrepreneurial opportunities. In the complex network structure of interconnected and interdependent supply chains, the flows of goods, services, capital, and technology across firm, industrial, and national borders becomes multidirectional, which, from a perspective of global value networks, reflects the underlying technological and economic forces that are transforming the patterns of global trade. Global trade and investment can, however, be vulnerable in the absence of international agreements on the use (or prohibition of use) of digital data.

Can China's Supply Chains Be Replaced in the Global Value Network?

Global supply chains have become highly competitive, interconnected, fast-changing, and volatile. China's economic growth in the past thirty years is part of the changes in the global order and the system of governance of the division of global labor that have been build since the Second World War. In recent years, a growing backlash against globalization and the rise of protectionism are threatening this global order, with voices challenging current global and regional trade agreements. As we have seen, China has developed comprehensive supply chains with both efficiency (at the micro level) and resilience (at the macro level) since it joined the WTO. The question is, with the backdrop of opposition to globalization, whether China's supply chains will be sustained. In other words, will China's supply chains be decoupled from global value networks?

Trade conflicts between the US and China have accelerated since 2018. Global firms are under pressure to build alternatives to their supply chains in China. Firms are planning or considering reshoring (bringing offshore production home) or nearshoring (moving offshore production closer to home) to increase the security and self-sufficiency of their supply chains. Western multinational firms have actually been reassessing their supply chain strategies for a number of years, and in certain industries some firms started diversifying their supply chains or even expanding operations reshore or nearshore. Technological advances such as 3D printing technology, industrial robotics, and other technologies of Industry 4.0 have encouraged these firms to move some production home and to other developed countries.

In theory, these measures of replacing offshore production facilities to mitigate risks of relying too much on Chinese supply chains make sense. Industry 4.0 type of production based on automation equipment and advanced digital technologies in the developed countries can, on the surface, offset cost advantages of those offshore production facilities in the developing countries, including China. However, China has become the largest global market for automation equipment since 2013.[26]

The argument that supports reshoring or nearshoring options underestimates the time involved in building efficient and flexible supply chains at or near home and improving automation and cost efficiency in production in offshore facilities. For these reasons, China's advantages in global value networks are not easily replaced. The power of supply chains in an industry is the aggregate capacity of all its elements, from energy and raw materials to goods, services, and labour. It also depends on the mechanisms provided by platforms to minimize transaction costs in mass collaboration amongst multitudes of suppliers. It has taken China two decades to create such efficient and resilient supply chains in many industries. Contrary to a popular opinion that China's industry policy has helped the country to grow into the 'world's factory', the reality is that the mega supply chain network in China is not the result of the design of any genius mind or the central planning of any government policy. It is the result of the organic evolution of bottom-up experiments by countless organizations and individuals over decades.

Numbers of firms have relocated their production to low-cost countries such as Vietnam, India, and Mexico. As we discussed in Chapter 3, this move does not reflect the transfer of China's manufacturing capacity; it is more an extension of Chinese supply chains in those countries for materials, as well as for labour and tariff advantages. Manufacturing capacity in those countries still relies on China's supply chain networks.

Ultimately, relocation of long-established supply chains reflects firms' strategic purposes. The proportion of trade that has moved out of China represents elements in which Chinese firms have lost advantages, such as the labour-intensive assembly of final products. Foxconn's production facilities in Vietnam and India, for example, still rely on suppliers from China, as there are long-term embedded relationships between Chinese suppliers and Foxconn's overseas assembly lines. It is costly and time-consuming to rebuild supply chains, especially in some heavy industrial sectors, in other countries. It does not make economic sense for multinational firms to develop their own comprehensive supply chains if they can import materials, components, and intermediaries from China so easily and cheaply.

Comparison between exports to ASEAN countries and the US in 2018 and 2019 from China (as shown in Figure 4.1) suggests that production in ASEAN countries relies on China's imports of components and intermediaries for final assembly tasks. As shown in Figure 4.1, China's exports to ASEAN countries in 2018 and 2019 increased but decreased to the US. According to China's Customs Statistics, the majority of the country's exports to the US are consumer products (final products),

---

[26] See https://ifr.org/img/worldrobotics/Executive_Summary_WR_2020_Industrial_Robots_1.pdf, accessed 23 July 2021.

Figure 4.1 China's exports by country (month by month, 2018–19)
Source: China's Customs Statistics

but the majority to ASEAN countries are industrial machine tools and intermediary products.

By way of example, the textile industry involves relatively low value-adding manufacturing. Since 2015, many Chinese and multinational textile factories have relocated to India, Vietnam, Sri Lanka, and low-labour cost countries in South East Asia. Production facilities in those countries, however, rely heavily on imports of the specialized machinery needed to make seamless fabrics and other higher value-adding textiles. China's export share into Vietnam, for example, doubled from 2005 to 2017.

This trend can also be seen in net foreign direct investment (FDI) in China. Inbound FDI has played an important role in China's economic development and export success. As shown in Figure 4.2, between 2017 and 2019, China's net FDI flow was positive, which indicates that there was more inbound than outbound FDI.

The net FDI figure suggests that the relocation of global supply chains may help China upgrade its industrial structure. The situation in China's manufacturing clusters, such as in the Pearl River Delta and Yangtze River Delta, is that low value-added modules have moved offshore, and the remaining part has been upgraded for higher value-adding production.

China has invested heavily to accelerate its indigenous innovation in the past decade. It is promoting home-grown, industry-critical technologies such as operating systems, industrial software, and technical standards, and directing vast resources and the country's highly educated workforce to advance technologies in these areas. These efforts will produce results in decades to come and are likely to be seen soon in the case of advanced semiconductors.

At the same time, to maintain social stability and employment levels, the country has developed its domestic market. The ratio of a country's total trade (import and export) to its GDP reflects the country's dependence on international markets. In 1978, China's dependence on foreign trade was only 9 per cent, growing to 38 per cent in 2001, when China joined the WTO, and reaching a historical high level of 64 per cent in 2006. As shown in Figure 4.3, this trend has slowed and was around 35 per cent in 2019. This trend suggests that China's economy has indeed relied on

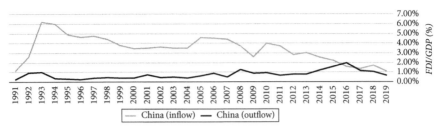

Figure 4.2 China's FDI/GDP, 1991–2019

Source: World Bank

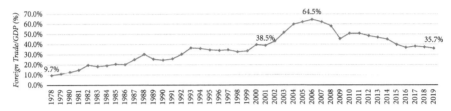

Figure 4.3 China's foreign trade to GDP, 1978–2019

Source: World Bank

the international market to drive the rapid growth since its opening-up and the economic reforms in late 1970s. In recent years, however, demand in the domestic market has become an important driving force for China's supply chains.

So, Are Firms Leaving China?

A survey conducted by the American Chamber of Commerce in China in February 2020 shows that companies were not leaving China despite the China-US trade war and Covid-19. A total of 83 per cent of respondents in the survey indicated that they had no plans to relocate production and supply chain operations or source outside China in the near future.[27] Similar results from a survey of German companies conducted by the European Union Chamber of Commerce in China in March 2020 suggested that, despite the negative impact of Covid-19 on their businesses, they were not changing their overall strategy in China. Many of them delayed or cancelled investment decisions, but only 4 per cent were considering relocating part of their production away from China.[28]

---

[27] American Chamber of Commerce in China (2020), '2020 Business Climate Survey', https://www.amchamchina.org/press/2020-business-climate-survey-released/, accessed 4 June 2021.

[28] European Union Chamber of Commerce in China (2020), 'Business Confidence Survey 2020: Navigating in the Dark', https://www.europeanchamber.com.cn/en/publications-business-confidence-survey, accessed 4 June 2021.

Firms make decisions based around economic fundamentals. Most of the reasons that attracted firms to invest in China in the first place, including market size, a skilled workforce, comprehensive industrial value chains, and infrastructure, remain unchanged. As a contingency plan, many firms have, however, started to adopt a 'China plus one' strategy to diversify their supply chains and operations by adding one new location, mostly in Asia, to be close to China's supply chain networks.

The cost of leaving China to reshore or nearshore production to replace Chinese supply chain networks is more costly than policymakers in Western countries may have hoped. Assembly factories in Vietnam and India not only still rely on imported materials and components from China to support their production, but have the disadvantage of having to stockpile surplus supplies, which costs money and limits flexibility in production. These costs will eventually be assumed by consumers and shareholders. Policymakers may help stimulate demand for long-term growth, but they may be helpless in fixing supply interruptions.

Firms also stay close to China to access skills and innovation capability in its supply chains. The tacit knowledge that underlies the efficiency and effectiveness in China's supply chains requires continual experimentation by skilled designers and operators through a long-term trial-and-error practice, which cannot be obtained through codified narratives or handbooks in setting up new factories. Chinese experienced managers and skilful workers who are hired by some factories in Vietnam to bridge the gap between their local assembly lines and China's supply chain network provide a good example of the importance of tacit knowledge.

On the other hand, with the help of advanced technologies such as industrial robotics, Western companies can reshore their production by building smart factories. The smart part can often be captured in technology alone, in explicit knowledge. The production part cannot be easily replaced by machines, and the tacit knowledge that lies in craftsmanship and engineering capability is hard to transfer. There is still a great deal of tacit knowledge embedded in the skilled workforce distributed along China's supply chains.

From the point of view of the global production network, China plays an increasingly important role as both a supply and a demand hub in global trade. While the US, Germany, and Japan remain the most important hubs in complex global value networks, China has emerged as a new hub connecting the suppliers of raw materials and production facilities in developing countries and consumer markets and technology in developed countries.

The Future for China's Supply Chains

We are entering a new stage of globalization. Competition between the world superpowers has extended into their controls of industry standards such as 5G, core technologies such as semiconductors, and access to critical infrastructure such as oil pipelines and cross-ocean cables and tunnels. These technologies and infrastructure support global supply chains, allowing the flow of materials, information, goods and services, and capital around the world with minimum transaction costs. The essence of this competition is to build more connections with suppliers, physically and economically. The most connected will win in this competition.

Recent policies have suggested that China is working in the following areas to improve its supply chains:

- building self-sufficiency in R&D, especially in basic sciences and breakthroughs in bottleneck technologies;
- integrating resources by building alliances and clusters in China and beyond, especially through One Road One Belt Initiative;
- extending its 'Internet Plus' policy by encouraging investment in the 'new infrastructure', including platforms, industry software, industry internet, and industry cloud computing power;
- investing in ecosystems of co-evolution and interdependence in industry value chains, along with capital and talent;
- leapfrogging in emerging industries empowered by advances in AI, big data analytics. and fintech.

These issues will be addressed further in subsequent chapters. In should be noted, however, that developing independent technologies and infrastructure could hold some dangers for China in the long run. China's domestic market is large enough to support a technology standard or an indigenous industry. However, if China were cut off from the global value network and needed to maintain an isolated ecosystem, the country could fall into the trap of involution. In a world of high interdependence in open ecosystems, the impact of a complete decoupling is likely to be profound. We will discuss the implications of China's decoupling in different scenarios in Chapter 8.

We now turn in Chapter 5 to the nature and consequences of China's digital economy.

5

China's Digital Economy

Survival of the Most Connected

The internet and advances in digital platforms have allowed China to make great progress in its digital economy. Its success has been built upon ubiquitous digital infrastructure such as 4G and 5G coverage, widespread and far-reaching logistics networks, and its well-developed digital ecosystems supported by the country's internet giants, such as Alibaba in e-commerce, Tencent in social media, and ByteDance in online media and entertainment. China's leading internet players have adopted an ecosystem mentality, which in biological terms refers to a community of interactive and interdependent actors each occupying unique ecological niches and interacting among themselves as well as with their environment. In China's digital ecosystems, the most connected survive. The architecture of China's digital ecosystems enables system-level evolution and thus accommodates emerging activities amongst its actors. In ecological terms, the evolution of Chinese digital ecosystems enables the population to generate, select, and amplify variations ('genetic mutation') to develop into higher-level features for the benefit of the ecosystem. In these ecosystems, which are similar to natural ones, certain mechanisms such as standards, regulatory controls, or capital support may constrain phenotype variations, which play a hand in their development.

Since the turn of the century, China has seen the growth of several massive internet firms such as Baidu, Alibaba, Tencent, JD, Meituan Dianping, ByteDance, and Ant (Financial) Group. Together, these firms are the top echelon in the digital economy and founders of tightly woven innovation, transaction, and investment ecosystems. These ecosystems connect online and offline applications and cover retail, transport, sharing, crowdfunding/sourcing, education, healthcare, media, entertainment, and sport, as well as industry services and tools. They are also active venture investors in innovative ideas in China, investing, for example, in over 70 per cent of China's 'unicorns': firms that are younger than ten years old but have achieved over one billion USD in revenue. These massive internet firms are the power behind China's innovative applications such as mobile payments and short-video platforms; and they are fomenting the growth of the next global ventures in emerging industries, such as self-driving vehicles and other applications of artificial intelligence.

This group of digital firms presents a distinctive approach to innovation in China. Once copycats of established business models in developed countries, especially the US, these firms emerged and thrived via technological innovation, capital support

Demystifying China's Innovation Machine: Chaotic Order. Marina Yue Zhang, Mark Dodgson, and David M. Gann, Oxford University Press. © Marina Yue Zhang, Mark Dodgson, and David M. Gann 2022. DOI: 10.1093/oso/9780198861171.003.0005

from both global and domestic sources, and access to the largest market with many enthusiastic users for innovation connected via their mobile phones. These firms are not just innovators in technology and business models; their interdependent ecosystems have changed many industrial structures and consumers' behaviour, as well as precipitating institutional reforms. The questions to be explored in this chapter include how these ecosystems emerge and develop, and how firms in the ecosystem manage cooperative and competitive interactions alongside the inevitable influence of government. The chapter will also question whether the rise in power of these giants will enable or constrain further innovation in China.

There is an expression used by China's digital innovators and entrepreneurs when talking about their value propositions: 'The future is in the present. It is just invisible to most people and hidden in undefined corners.' This displays an awareness that those hidden corners may be nurturing the next giants that may emerge one day to disrupt the entire ecosystem. As seen in the rise and fall of China's short-video application TikTok in the US and India, such disruption can be especially turbulent. Chinese internet firms can lead in technological and business model innovations, yet lag behind in corporate governance, especially in areas such as data security and privacy protection. China's digital ecosystems will not become sustainable until concerns over the ethical use of their astronomical amounts of data and platform governance are addressed.

In this chapter, we explain how China's digital world operates and how it differs from the rest of the world, and predict what the future holds for China's digital economy.

The Rise of China's Digital Economy

At the turn of the century, today's digital world was simply a science fiction film scene for many Chinese. The internet had only reached urban elites and leading universities. Even by 2015, China's digital economy was a long distance behind that of the more developed world, especially the US. By 2020, however, China was challenging global leaders with its own innovation.

According to China's National Statistics, in 2019 the digital economy accounted for 36.2 per cent of China's GDP, up from 34.8 per cent in 2018, and contributed 67.7 per cent of the GDP growth of 2019. These numbers reveal how the digital economy has become a new engine for China's economic growth. As shown in Figure 5.1, by the end of 2019, most of China's digital economy was focused on consumption rather than the industrial sector, with over 44 per cent in e-commerce and location-based lifestyle services, close to 20 per cent in internet financing, and the remainder in media, entertainment, education, transport services, and healthcare and other services. China's vast population and rapid economic development have enabled the country to become the largest market for the consumption of internet services. The number of internet users in China exploded from 59 million in 2002 to 989 million

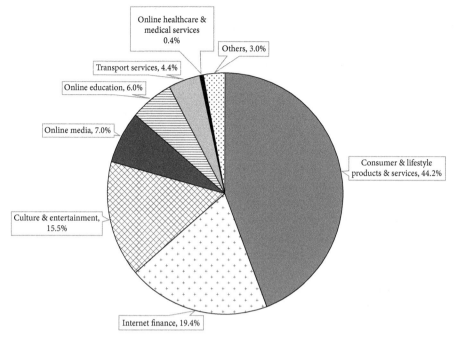

Figure 5.1 Composition of China's digital economy
Source: IMF (2019)

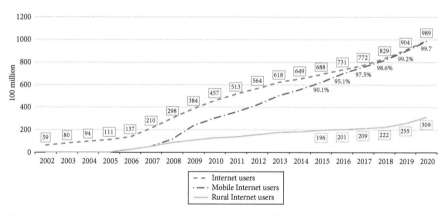

Figure 5.2 China's internet, mobile internet, and rural internet users
Source: CNNIC (2002–20)[1]

[1] China Internet Network Information Centre (CNNIC) (2020), The 45th China's Internet Development Report. http://www.cac.gov.cn/2019-08/30/c_1124938750.htm, accessed 30 May 2021.

in 2020, or a compound annual growth rate (CAGR) of nearly 17 per cent. From 2006 to 2020, mobile-phone users grew almost twice as fast, at a CAGR of nearly 30 per cent, jumping from 27 million to reach 986 million (Figure 5.2).

China's population not only caught up on the internet, but has transformed into a mobile technology society. Over 99.7 per cent of users accessed the internet using their mobile devices in 2020. The wide adoption of smartphones in the mobile internet has allowed China's rural population to benefit from the development of the digital economy. A total of 309 million rural residents had access to the internet in 2020; this is attributed to the availability of broadband and 4G networks which cover 98 per cent of China's villages and wide-reaching logistic networks which cover 96 per cent of Chinese villages, as well as cost-effective smartphones made by a host of Chinese manufacturers such as Oppo, Xiaomi, Vivo, and Huawei. China also offers relatively competitive prices for both fixed broadband and mobile networks compared with other Asia-Pacific countries and some higher-income economies. Enabled by e-commerce and logistic networks, the rural population embraces the convenience of e-commerce, not just as consumers, but also as suppliers.

The development of e-commerce in China has seen rapid and consistent growth since 2008. China had less than 1 per cent of the global value in e-commerce transaction at that time, and a decade later reached more than 40 per cent, exceeding that of France, Germany, Japan, the UK, and the US combined.[1] China is also one of the fastest-growing markets. E-commerce contributes to economic growth by extending market reach in both supply and demand sides and by improving transaction efficiency. The annual value of e-commerce transactions (B2B—business-to-business and B2C—business-to-consumer) grew over thirty-fold from 2004 to 2018, reaching 34 trillion RMB (about $5.13 trillion).[2]

The expansion of mobile commerce built on the rapid adoption of smartphones (e.g. Taobao and Pinduoduo), social networks (e.g. Weibo and WeChat), and many emerging mobile-based applications, including location-based lifestyle services (e.g. Didi Chuxing and Meituan Dianping), real-time user-generated content applications (e.g. Douyin/TikTok and Kuaishou), and sharing businesses (e.g. Tujia and HelloBike). However, e-commerce varies across different regions in China. More developed areas such as Guangdong, Zhejiang, Beijing, and Shanghai account for over half of the transaction value. Income disparity explains such an imbalance, despite overall well-laid digital infrastructures across the country.

Many digital successes can be attributed to the levels of capital investment in the field. In 2020 there were 450 'unicorns' in the world, 112 of which are from China, second in the world after the US.[3] According to CB Insight, the world's top three most highly valued private non-US unicorn companies were Chinese: ByteDance, valued at $75 billion, Didi Chuxing, at $56 billion, and Kuaishou (Douyin/TikTok's competitor in China), at $18 billion. All three grew from mobile applications. This is hardly surprising, as on average the Chinese spend nearly five hours on the mobile internet every day. More investment has been injected in technology hardware,

---

[1] World Bank Group (2019), *Innovative China: New Drivers of Growth*, Washington, DC: World Bank. doi: 10.1596/978-1-4648-1335-1.

[2] China's Ministry of Commerce (2019), *China E-commerce Report 2019*, http://www.199it.com/archives/1076562.html, accessed 5 June 2021.

[3] 'The Complete List of Unicorn Companies', CB Insights, March 2020. https://www.cbinsights.com/research-unicorn-companies, accessed 26 July 2021.

new-energy cars, healthcare, and fintech, and an increasing number of unicorns are expected to come from these sectors in the future.

While venture capital investment has contributed to the rise of China's internet businesses, corporate venture capital, for example from China's giant firms such as Alibaba and Tencent, has played a more significant role in China's digital ecosystems. In some instances, these two firms expand their own strategic investment portfolios by co-investing in emerging technologies to further the development of an ecosystem.

The digital economy represents a paradigm shift in industrialization and a notable success of one of the Chinese government's national strategies. The paradigm shift opened windows of opportunity for latecomers such as China to catch up with forerunners. The country still faces many obstacles, however, in its industrial internet businesses. Expanding into industry services, especially in manufacturing, through the internet is a common vision for both the Chinese government and many internet enterprises. Developing advanced 5G networks and constructing 5G-related infrastructure (named 'new infrastructures') are considered one opportunity that China must capitalize on to develop its future competitive advantages. Policies on the 'new infrastructure' initiatives will be elaborated upon in Chapter 8. Industries that have progressed in this area include the aircraft, new-energy cars, rail transport, and chemical industries.[4] 5G and industry internet based on the aggregation of new technologies such as cloud computing, edge computing, big data, AI, VR/AR (virtual reality/augmented reality), security technology, and numeric control systems will be the next areas for China's technological catch-up. These are considered new engines for manufacturing to transform into a digital, networked, and intelligent system. In this transformation, data will become extremely valuable. Later in this chapter, the development of AI in China will be used to illustrate China's ambition in its 'new infrastructure'.

'Being Digital'

In 1995, Nicholas Negroponte, a MIT Media Lab professor, published a book titled *Being Digital*[5] in which he described digital technology and its impact on the future. He could not have predicted the enthusiasm for being digital in China. Internet start-ups such as Sina, Sohu, Alibaba, and Tencent, backed by venture capital investors such as IDG and Sequoia, quickly emerged to catch the wave of 'being digital'.

Being digital is not just about acquiring digital technology in traditional economic activities in the physical world, as described by Negroponte. It is also about digital transformation from inside out, including developing a digital mentality and

---

[4] China Academy of Information and Communications Technology (CAICT) (2020), 'China's Digital Economy Whitepaper', July 2020. Beijing China.
[5] N. Negroponte (1995), *Being Digital*, New York: Vintage Publishing.

building digital practice and capability into the fabric of everyday economic activities. Being digital brings value-adding activities into the consumer sector and applying digital skills, equipment, and technology into the production of goods and services. Being digital means the digital transformation of business models and processes.[6]

Data is a crucial factor in productivity in the digital economy, just as land, labour, and capital are in the industrial economy. Everybody is interconnected in the digital economy in an interdependent ecosystem: every participant is not just the consumer, but also the generator, of data. Everyone makes a contribution to the ecosystem by fulfilling his or her self-interested economic activities. We use Google Maps for our own interests, for example, but the data generated from our use feeds back and makes the Google map more accurate and predictable. In a digitally interconnected world, even the way we use air conditioners at home can generate valuable data and feedback to the ecosystem of air conditioners and improve their efficient use in a community.

China's sheer size, together with the country's aggressive plans to roll out the 5G networks and build an 'Intelligent + X' economy, enables the connections of humans and devices, generating astronomical amounts of data, which will become a new competitive advantage for China.

Digital Transformation

Enterprises that are digital natives lead in the digital economy. Digital transformation still faces enormous hurdles in traditional industries. In the healthcare sector, for example, particularly in hospitals, digitalization has been slow to transform traditional paper-based systems of care to digital-based systems. The challenges are not just around digitizing content, but about implementing a digitalization strategy for the whole system. According to the OECD definition, digital transformation refers to the use of digital technologies as an integrated part of the modernization of businesses to create value and support the production of and access to data.[7] Essentially, it relies on a digital ecosystem, which could include all stakeholders in society, enterprises, governments, non-governmental agencies, and individuals.

Digital transformation is not only a technological revolution, but also a cognitive revolution. It requires a systematic change that involves corporate strategy, organization, operations, and people management. Digital transformation is not a top-down command by leaders in an organizaiton; it must be driven by bottom-up change

---

[6] According to the Gartner Glossary, 'Digitization is the process of changing from analog to digital form' and 'Digitalization is the use of digital technologies to change a business model and provide new revenue and value-producing opportunities; it is the process of moving to a digital business' (https://www.gartner.com/en/information-technology/glossary?glossaryletter=D, accessed 5 June 2021).

[7] OECD (2014), Recommendation of the Council on Digital Government Strategies, https://www.oecd.org/gov/digital-government/Recommendation-digital-government-strategies.pdf, accessed 26 July 2021.

agents in business thinking and processing. At its most profound, digital transform-ation is a revolution that is the co-evolution between humans and technology, and the co-development of digital and physical worlds.

Digital technology is an enabler of digital transformation, as it transforms busi-ness models and customer experiences. On this front, China's internet firms are pioneers. The booming of new forms of economic activities in China's digital econ-omy, such as O2O (online-to-offline)[8], sharing, and online education, and health-care, provide good examples.

The most successfully transformed firms are those that use the internet as a foun-dation to expand their business scope beyond their immediate boundaries. In this model, they build new partnerships, leveraging resources and talented people beyond their immediate reach, and deliver products to customers who would be invisible under previous circumstances. Firms need to adjust their organizational mentality from keeping control to empowering others to share control, from operat-ing in isolation to forming interdependencies with partners, from linear thinking to complex thinking, from emphasizing central power to distributed power, and from operating in a closed system to operating in an open ecosystem. It is an unsurpris-ingly challenging task for many traditional firms to manage these changes.

Most traditional firms, constrained by their legacy business systems and organiza-tional mentality, simply adopt a model of 'X plus Internet', in which they merely digitize their activities and build presence on the internet. This model is not trans-formative. For example, few traditional retailers have successfully transformed their businesses into online businesses. The most successful retailers, such as Walmart, have tried and failed in many attempts at digital transformation, and there are many similar examples in China. In contrast, the most successful e-retailers are those 'born digital'. They began with the internet and built their e-commerce platforms as core to their businesses. Traditional firms treat the internet as a tool and a means to an end, but not as the foundation of their businesses.[9]

To promote digital transformation in traditional industries, in 2015 the Chinese government first introduced the 'Internet plus X' initiative, seen, for example, in internet + finance, internet + healthcare, and internet + logistics as a core strategy for digital transformation, aiming to use digital technology for industrial upgrading and productivity improvement. This model has been widely used in areas such as education, healthcare, public services, and manufacturing. The industries closest to direct consumers (such as retail, media and entertainment, and finance) have achieved the highest rate of digitalization. Despite the successes we have described in Chapters 3 and 4 in China's supply chains and manufacturing sector, according to an industry report more than 50 per cent of China's manufacturing sector is still at

---

[8] The rise of platform-based businesses expanded to the physical world on a large scale in China. In fact, the term 'O2O' (online-to-offline—the spread from the online to the offline world of network effects) was coined by China's AI 'Rockstar' Andrew Ng of Baidu.

[9] This is seen in by comparing the success of online retail stores with the closure of high street shops during the Covid-19 crisis.

the stage of exploring strategies for digitalization. This is lower than the global average of 67 per cent of large manufacturers that have already adopted digital transformation as their core strategy.[10] China still has a long way to go in its digital transformation of traditional industries.

One of the consequences of Covid-19 in China is that businesses accelerated the pace of digital transformation, from media consumption to online education and healthcare, as well as using digital technologies and applications to combat the virus itself.

Digital Platforms

The digital economy has been developed along with the revolution in digital platforms.[11] There are multitudes of digital platforms in terms of activity, business model, and functionality. Examples include social media/communication platforms (e.g. Facebook, WeChat), media/entertainment platforms (e.g. YouTube, TikTok), online marketplaces (e.g. Amazon, Alibaba), collaborative platforms (e.g. iTunes, Google APIs), and information/matching platforms (e.g. LinkedIn, Match). Although they serve different purposes, it is possible to distinguish commonalities amongst innovation platforms, transaction platforms, and hybrid platforms.[12]

It is challenging to offer a unified definition that includes the diversity of digital platforms. However, there are some common features that arise in all types of digital platforms. Digital platforms can be defined as intermediaries supported by digital technology, facilitating interactions of multisided actors (i.e. users and suppliers, and complementors—those businesses whose products or services are complementary to the products or services of others on the same platform) in interdependent relationships. From an economic perspective, digital platforms can mitigate distance barriers, reduce information asymmetries, streamline information exchanges and business processes, and thus improve productivity in innovation and transactions.

Platform businesses have surged in China. According to a government policy document, 'The platform economy, as a new growth engine and way of organizing production, has contributed to the optimization of resources, upgrading of industries, expansion of consumption, and the creation of jobs.'[13] Alibaba's ecosystem, for example, includes around 110,000 direct employees, but its platforms indirectly create more than 10 million jobs as complementors to its core products/services.

[10] IDC (2020) Asia Pacific SME Digital Readiness Report. Beijing, China.

[11] G. Parker, M. Van Alstyne, and S. P. Choudary (2016), *Platform Revolution: How Networked Markets Are Transforming the Economy and How to Make Them Work for You*, New York: W. W. Norton.

[12] M. A. Cusumano, A. Gawer, and D. B. Yoffie (2019), *The Business of Platforms: Strategy in the Age of Digital Competition, Innovation, and Power*, New York: Harper Business.

[13] State Council (2019), 'Platform Economy to Be Promoted', 8 August, http://english.www.gov.cn/policies/latestreleases/201908/08/content_WS5d4bdd9bc6d0c6695ff7e685.html, accessed 5 June 2021.

Platform businesses, however, raise many ethical issues. On the one hand, digital platforms break barriers of time and space and create flexibility and autonomy in the job market. On the other, digital platforms often use the most stringent algorithms to calculate the productivity of their workers and provide opportunities to exploit their indirect workforce. Chinese media has reported multiple cases of delivery workers and platform companies abused by customers for failing to deliver goods or services according to the time estimated by algorithms without taking into consideration any contingencies in the physical world.

Data as New Factor Productivity

Digital platforms allow information to be exchanged, transactions to be completed, and collective intelligence to be created, online. Essentially, digital platforms have elevated competition from the firm to the system level.[14] As a part of this transformation, companies that own and operate digital platforms can monetize internet traffic (i.e. data) arising from the digitalization of flows of information and transactions, as well as the interactions of platform actors. Digital platforms intermediate collaboration and transaction beyond traditional boundaries, digitalizing the interactions (internet traffic) of multitudes of actors, which are sources of data. The more data a platform can generate and access, the more valuable the platform.

In 1999, when Alibaba started as a B2B e-commerce platform connecting Chinese suppliers with buyers in the West, its value was to match SME sellers with buyers who were locked out of traditional international trade systems. When Alibaba launched its Taobao platform for C2C e-commerce in 2003 and TMall for B2C e-commerce in 2008, linking individuals and SME sellers on Taobao and corporate sellers on Tmall with individual buyers in China's domestic market, it massively expanded the extent and scope of the data it can generate and access. On the surface, Alibaba is a digital platform company. However, behind the scenes, it is a data company. Alibaba helped the sellers on its platforms not only digitize their products/services but also digitalize their business processes. In the early days of building its B2B platform, the company had to send out a large salesforce to convince and help millions of suppliers to 'be digital'. Details included verifying suppliers' identities, credentials, and financial circumstances, as well as digitalizing processes for customs clearance, credit issuing, tax returns of exports, and logistics in foreign trades. Data collection at this stage was found to be far more complicated and time-consuming than expected.

On the buyer side, with the rapid development of internet businesses, China quickly had a large number of buyers willing to try e-commerce. However, until AI and big data technologies became widely used in platform businesses, as demonstrated, for example, in 'intelligent services' on the user side provided by Ant

---

[14] A. Gawer and M. A. Cusumano (2014), 'Industry Platforms and Ecosystem Innovation', *Journal of Product Innovation Management*, 31(3), 417–33.

Financial Services and ByteDance, digitalization was not easy to achieve. ByteDance uses advanced algorithms to push personalized content based on new tags the company allocates to each customer. In this tagging system, fragmented and distributed customers are segmented by common attributes rather than their typical market categories. If segmented by category, customers in fragmented and remote areas will not be reached and understood. In this new intelligent tagging system, however, each customer can be tagged into different groups on the basis of common features. One person can, therefore, be tagged into many different groups. This algorithm-based method enables ByteDance to digitalize user-side data. WeChat has done this as well, but adds the relationships of the users in the social networks in the algorithms to improve the efficiency of information distribution on the basis of personal and social attributes.

Another example is in location-based lifestyle services. Meituan Dianping, the merger of Meituan and Dazhong Dianpin, provides an example of data consolidation at both the seller and the buyer sides in platform business. Meituan was founded in 2010 as a platform that provides group purchases for buyers. It had, over time, built a large user database, especially of users of location-based lifestyle services, such as those who ordered Groupon-type deals in local restaurants and shops. Dazhong Dianping, in contrast, started as a platform that collected rankings and ratings of suppliers, especially location-based service providers such as restaurants and shops. While both firms were successful, they could not become a super platform. The merger of the two in 2015 (facilitated by their investors, Alibaba and Tencent, respectively) allowed Meituan Dianping to create an entire loop of data connecting both the demand and the supply sides, optimizing the match between the two sides. After the merger, in 2017, the transaction volume of Meituan Dianping exceeded 360 billion RMB (about $53 billion), accounting for over 85 per cent of the market share in location-based lifestyle services. The company's food delivery transactions reached 488 billion RMB (around $75 billion) in 2020, generating 114.7 billion RMB (around $17.6 billion) in revenue.[15] Meituan Dianpin illustrates the power of large-scale digitalization and the value of data in platform businesses.

Advanced digital technologies such as AI, big data, blockchain, and cloud computing, as well as automation technologies such as robots and drones, have penetrated platform businesses. As a result, these businesses have extended from online to offline, as O2O business models. Broadly speaking, O2O covers online information exchange and transaction processing (including payments), but offline consumption (i.e. goods and services are delivered and consumed offline). Examples include AirBnB and Uber types of services. Although O2O business models originated in the US, they have developed to a much higher level in China. O2O businesses on digital platforms have touched almost every aspect of Chinese lives. O2O services include ride sharing, pet caring, food ordering and delivery, location-based

---

[15] Meituan's Annual report, 2020. The company also changed its name from Meituan Dianping to Meituan. http://media-meituan.todayir.com/20210326170104177 3929787_en.pdf, accessed 26 July 2020.

services such as dry cleaning pickup and drop-off and car cleaning, grocery procurement and delivery, housekeeping, estate agencies, and tutorial services.

O2O businesses generate large amounts of data. With the increasing popularity of GPS applications in smartphones, Didi Chuxing (China's Uber equivalent), allows passengers and drivers to interact through their GPS locations. A passenger's location at a certain time (including information about their destination) is valuable for drivers; a driver's location (distance from pickup location and arrival time) is important information for passengers. For platform companies, such data is extremely valuable in allowing them to optimize the match between the two.

Sharing is another business model arising from data-driven platforms. A narrow definition of sharing business is the short-term transfer of property rights of individual goods between consumers. A broader definition is such that C2C sharing activity is enabled by digital platforms: short-term property rights of physical goods can be digitalized, and the transfer of such rights can also be digitalized. Examples include sharing rides, sharing accommodation, and sharing kitchen facilities. Again, the large amount of data generated through sharing businesses makes those sharing platforms valuable. Sharing businesses accounted for a large proportion of China's top unicorns.

Big data analytics are an important enabler for data-driven platforms. The term big data refers to the capability to extract information and insights at large scale, where previously it was economically and technically unfeasible. This is achieved through the use of computerized systems that can analyse extremely large databases to identify patterns and predict trends by building correlations of different variables at different layers. Rapid developments in computing power, sensing technologies, robotics, AI, the internet of things, and cloud computing are making this possible and profitable. In platform businesses, in addition to multisidedness, intermediation, and interdependence, the most critical success factor is data. The more data a platform can generate from any side and the more sides of data it can have access to, the more valuable the platform. The adage is true that in the information age data has become the oil of the industrial age.

Data Labelling Has Become a New Profession

Data labelling refers to activities that label objects not just by their broad category, but also by their nuanced features. For example, when labelling eyes, attributes such as colour, shape, size, position, similarity, and difference between species are used. These nuanced attributes can be used as learning materials to train AI. Data labelling is important in deep learning and machine learning. Currently, data quantified for modelling only captures a small fraction of the real world. In the application of AI, the larger the data set, the more intelligent AI will become. The visuals for computers and comprehension of natural languages that are so important in AI applications such as video surveillance, facial recognition, self-driving vehicles, smart cities, and disease diagnosis all rely on computer vision technologies. This means that large amounts of data must be treated with the contextual information that computers can recognize and intelligently understand in their meaningful contexts.

With the continuous development of data technology, the demand for standardized data increases. Therefore, data labelling—a labour-intensive activity—has emerged as a key task. While many internet companies in the more developed countries focus on algorithms, software, computing, and other hardcore technologies in AI, China has developed a new profession of data labelling. China has a natural advantage in data labelling, and thousands of small enterprises and workshops have entered this market. Low entry barriers and high demand have led to a large number of rural and small-town employees in this new profession. Data labelling is concentrated in areas with low labour costs, with the emergence of many data-labelling villages in inland provinces such as Shanxi, Henan, and Inner Mongolia. Data labellers in those villages tag a stream of faces, medical images, and cityscapes.

Underpinning the success of China's AI firms such as Megvii and SenseTime, both of which are world leaders in facial recognition, is a sprawling digital infrastructure through which data is collected, cleaned and labelled before being processed into machine-learning algorithms. Without this data-labelling infrastructure, China's AI services would not have progressed. It remains uncertain whether China will share this infrastructure with the rest of the world.

Digitalization of the Demand Side

So far, much of China's digitalization has occurred at the supply side, although a new trend is emerging of digitalization of demand side factors, which is particularly challenging. China's consumers are scattered in hundreds of cities, tens of thousands of towns, and hundreds of thousands of villages. They are not a unified market or a segmented market divided by mainstream and peripheral consumers, as is common in products and services in more developed countries. Consumers form a gradiented multilayered structure in China, segmented not just by age, gender, and income, but more by socio-economic status, educational background, geographical location, urban or rural residential status, among other dimensions. Most importantly, each layer is large and, therefore, commercially attractive. How to reach each layer and provide its consumers with what they want at prices they can afford presents a significant challenge.

China has four first-tier cities (Beijing, Shanghai, Guangzhou, and Shenzhen), fifteen quasi first-tier cities (Chengdu, Chongqing, Hangzhou, Wuhan, Xi'an, Tianjin, Suzhou, Nanjing, Zhengzhou, Changsha, Dongguan, Shenyang, Qingdao, Hefei, and Foshan), and thirty second-tier cities. But a significant proportion of Chinese society lives beyond these cities, including the third- and fourth-tier cities and the vast countryside, which have a total population of close to one billion. People in these parts of China still follow many 'hidden rules' such that bloodlines and tightly woven social relationships are still dominant elements of the social fabric. This can be thought of as the bottom of pyramid in China. Although living standards have improved overall throughout China, people earn much less in these areas than those in the large cities.[16] Their consumption behaviours and power are vastly different from those in the upper layers of Chinese consumers, and they will be attracted to low prices. A young waitress in a restaurant in a third-tier city, for example, might only earn 3000 RMB (about $450) per month, but her consumption power is such that she could comfortably buy a lipstick for 5 RMB (about 75 cents) from Pinduoduo.

In such a complex, multilayered, and diverse market, innovative companies using advanced digital technologies have built channels to reach their targeted customers. Companies that have reached each segment and built digital links with their con-sumers win the market. Most consumers cannot afford a Tesla electric car (costing about 300,000 RMB, or $45,000, before government subsidy), even though they are made in China with many Chinese components. For them, electric scooters are the first choice for transport. The top selling brand of electric scooters (costing 2,000 to 5,000 RMB each, about $300 to 750) is a Chinese brand named Yadea. Its manufac-turer was listed on Hong Kong Stock Exchange in 2015 and the company had sold more than 36 million electric scooters by 2020.[17] Yadea was an official sponsor of the 2018 FIFA World Cup in Russia, to promote its brand in the targeted customers among youths in China's small cities, towns, and villages, who are invariably football fans and watch the games.

In the digital age, consumers' footprints online can be recorded, labelled, and tagged, which becomes valuable data. Companies with access to such data profit from intelligently pushing targeted and personalized information, goods, services, news, or entertainment to their targeted consumer groups. The data protection and privacy issues and potential involution of such feeds of information will be explored in Chapter 8. The point here is that platform firms that make the effort to reach deep and far in the market and build emotional connections with each customer can sell lipsticks for 5 RMB and electric scooters for 5,000 RMB to hundreds of millions of customers.

Xiaomi is an emerging manufacturer with a very diverse product line, from smartphones to PCs and flat panel TVs, from rice cookers to microwave ovens, from robotic vacuum cleaners to Segway scooters, that has built a broad and deep sales network reaching third- and fourth-tiered cities and beyond. This explains why Xiaomi could reach the benchmark of $10 billion in revenue in less than ten years, half the time it took Alibaba.

With huge value in the digitalized demand side, Chinese platform firms are pushing the digitalization of consumer data. 'Data-driven marketing' has become a buzzword among the investors in Chinese internet businesses. Two types of

---

[16] According to China's National Statistics Bureau, in 2019, Chinese urban residents earned 42,359 RMB per annum, but rural residents earned only 16,021 RMB. http://www.stats.gov.cn/english/PressRelease/202001/t20200119_1723719.html, accessed 26 July 2021.

[17] See https://www.yadea.com.cn/home/about/course.html, accessed 5 June 2021.

innovative data-driven businesses have emerged recently: social e-commerce and interactive commerce.

Social e-commerce platforms, such as Weibo and WeChat, which are based on interpersonal networks, connect sellers and buyers through social media. Essentially, they are a fusion of e-commerce and social media in which social networks provide the means by which transactions are completed. Communications through trusted social relationships can be effective on these platforms, and the transaction conversion rate is high. If e-commerce leverages supply side data, social e-commerce leverages demand side data. WeChat's mini programs, for example, which are app-like light programs embedded in WeChat's social networks, have proven to be an important social e-commerce platform for many individuals and micro sellers targeting their social connections for e-commerce transactions.

WeChat's social e-commerce is built upon the QR code-based ecosystem, supported by a range of digital infrastructure, such as WeChat Pay owned by its parent company, Tencent. There are not only traditional micro-e-commerce enterprises in Tencent's ecosystem, but also mini programs for services such as DiDi ride hailing, Meituan food delivery, and Ctrip travel management. These services are all supported by WeChat Pay.

Another example of a social e-commerce platform is Xiaohongshu, in which Alibaba is an investor. Xiaohongshu operates like a combination of Instagram, Pinterest, and Amazon. Its users can post photos or short videos of themselves and tag clothes, accessories, or make-up products they use to corresponding e-commerce listings within the platform.

Interactive commerce, a concept coined by Pinduoduo, is an integration of supply side and demand side data based on its 'Costco+Disney' business model. Through gaming, entertainment, and community-based social connections, PDD engages with different customers and builds user loyalty at the demand side (the Disney model). Through direct contacts with the suppliers, PDD achieves economies of scale at the supply side (the Costco model). In a way, interactive e-commerce humanizes the online shopping experience. A common comment made by PDD's users is, 'We look for inspiration for products through window shopping, but we order and complete the transactions through online shopping from PDD, as it provides value for money.'

PDD is different from traditional e-commerce platforms such as Alibaba and JD.com, which focus on efficiency, diversity, and convenience in their transactions, as it emphasizes rich user experience through gaming and community building to deliver value for money. PDD's core capabilities include both gaming and algorithms, which underpin its achievements as an interactive commerce platform.

China's demography has seen the rise of digital natives, those born in the 1990s and 2000s, who have become key influencers in China's consumer market. They have not experienced the hardship faced by their parents and grandparents, and they do not have strong brand loyalty. For them, products carrying cultural or emotional value are more important than product quality and functionality, the attributes treasured by older generations.

Furthermore, communications have changed in the era of the mobile internet. Consumers inhabit online communities formed by similar values, backgrounds, interests, and even a common appreciation of film or sport stars. Opinions of peers in those communities, especially those of key influencers, matter in their purchase decisions. Douyin and its competitor Kuaishou, both short-video platforms for people to create and share their user generated content, are hugely popular in these markets. Douyin and Kuaishou are both important media for Chinese brands to reach their targeted customers through live-stream broadcasting. One of the top internet celebrities, Li Jiaqi, is a young man who is a key opinion leader online. He used to be a sales representative for an international cosmetics brand, and once sold 1,000 bottles of sunscreen in eighteen seconds through his live stream broadcast. His record is achieving 3.5 million RMB (about $500,000) in sales revenue in cosmetics products in five hours.

In the digital age, marketers need to understand such changes to reach customers in the hidden markets at the bottom of the pyramid in China. They also need to develop emotional links with their customers; closing a deal is not the end of the transaction, but the beginning of a long-term relationship, not just with the individual buyer, but with the entire community to which the buyer belongs.

The Power of Connectivity

There are several characteristics in being digital. First, digital technology accelerates the pace of innovation and the rate of innovation diffusion. Second, being digital means demolishing traditional boundaries and enabling multitudes of collaborations, including with upstream and downstream actors in any industry value chain. Third, because of the speed of change and the legions of partnerships in collaboration, being digital also means managing complexity in the recursive feedback loops and interdependency of multiple stakeholders in the system. Digital transformation starting in individual firms results in aggregated and systemic changes in industry and society.[18] In the digital economy, competitive advantages move from being different, unique, or rare to being connected with as many as possible in an ecosystem.

Digital Ecosystems

An ecosystem can be defined as an interdependent network of self-interested actors jointly creating value.[19] This definition highlights three important characteristics of

---

[18] R. Adner (2017), 'Ecosystem as Structure: An Actionable Construct for Strategy', *Journal of Management*, 43, 39–58; R. Adner and R. Kapoor (2010), 'Value Creation in Innovation Ecosystems: How the Structure of Technological Interdependence Affects Firm Performance in New Technology Generations', *Strategic Management Journal*, 31, 306–33; E. Autio and L. Thomas (2014), 'Innovation Ecosystems', in M. Dodgson, D. M. Gann, and N. Phillips (eds.), *The Oxford Handbook of Innovation Management*, 204–88.

[19] M. Bogers, J. Sims, and J. West (2019), 'What Is an Ecosystem? Incorporating 25 Years of Ecosystem Research', Academy of Management Conference, August, Boston. .

an ecosystem: interdependence, network, and self-interested actors. The implication is that joint value creation in an ecosystem is accomplished by its actors working together to achieve outcomes that none of them may be able to do on their own.[20] This definition of business ecosystems reflects an origin in and similarity to natural ecosystems, which are biological communities of interacting organisms and their interdependencies (not necessarily direct but through food chains) and their interactions with the physical environment.[21] Hence, business ecosystems are not just about the multilateral interdependencies of ecosystem actors, but also interactions of ecosystem actors with their environment—a broader societal, technological, economic, and institutional context. Essentially, digital ecosystems are systems built upon digital platforms on which multisided marketplaces can be created to achieve information exchange and resource sharing through co-development and co-evolution.

In the interplays with contextual factors, digitalization creates potent 'digital affordances' that are likely to have a transformative effect upon ecosystem actors.[22] Affordance is what the environment offers individuals in an ecosystem which carries the potentiality of an application for a focal innovation. This term was first coined by the American psychologist James Gibson[23] to explain how visualization is influential in our perceptions. According to this theory, affordances in environments provide potential which can conduce certain courses of action of ecosystem actors.

In complexity economics,[24] the interplays of individuals in a system have compounded impacts on the system, and vice versa. Because of the complexity of such interplays, the system rarely reaches and stays in a state of equilibrium. Innovations in products and business models are constantly disrupting the status quo and existing business orders, and creating new ones. If one local shop responds to the emergence of e-commence in a community and moves online, for example, it is not a simple individual action. Such action will have ripple effects on other shops in both its physical and online communities. It may lead to more and more shops moving online, which may lead to increased competition online. To stay competitive, innovators will find new ways to reach more customers and mobilize resources in a more efficient way. This is how e-commerce, social e-commerce, and interactive commerce have emerged and developed in China. In an interconnected world, the economic system is like a natural ecosystem which evolves and self-upgrades.

---

[20] R. Adner (2006), 'Match Your Innovation Strategy to Your Innovation Ecosystem', *Harvard Business Review*, 84, 98; Bogers, Sims, and West 'What Is an Ecosystem?'; M. Iansiti and R. Levien (2004), *The Keystone Advantage: What the New Dynamics of Business Ecosystems Mean for Strategy, Innovation, and Sustainability*, Cambridge, MA: Harvard Business School Press.

[21] See *Oxford English Dictionary*, s.v. ecosystem.

[22] E. Autio, S. Nambisan, L. D. W. Thomas, and M. Wright (2018), Digital Affordances, Spatial Affordances, and the Genesis of Entrepreneurial Ecosystems', *Strategic Entrepreneurship Journal*, 12, 72–95; S. Nambisan, K. Lyytinen, A. Majchrzak, and M. Song (2017), 'Digital Innovation Management: Reinventing Innovation Management Research in a Digital World', *MIS Quarterly*, 41, 223–38.

[23] J. J. Gibson (1979), The Ecological Approach to Visual Perception. East Susses, UK: Psychological Press.

[24] W. B. Arthur (2009), *The Nature of Technology: What It Is and How It Evolves*, London: Penguin Books.

In such a complex ecosystem, however, being innovative is insufficient. To stay ahead of the competition, firms need to build connections with other actors in the ecosystem. An ecosystem enabled by digital platforms is a multi-actor system. If there is only one type of actor, there is no ecosystem. The more diverse the actors in an ecosystem (like species in a natural ecosystem), the greater its power, in which lies the core competitiveness of ecosystems enabled by platforms. This requires platform firms to create and maintain an open system to encourage interactions among diverse actors, protect multiple innovative ideas, and allow the system to select the winners amongst them. This is similar to the mutation-isolation-selection process in natural evolution.

Interdependence

Sharing and collaboration are not new in innovation and the global innovation system has characteristics of an open innovation model which enables multi-stakeholder collaboration. The use of open-source technology and increasing decentralization in organizations have accelerated knowledge diffusion and reduced innovation costs. In the digital age, resource allocation and the mechanisms for innovation have moved onto digital platforms. Cross-region, cross-industry, and cross-organization platforms can empower collective intelligence and facilitate crowdsourcing. In this new system, stakeholders' relationships in an ecosystem are entirely interdependent.

Sharing via platforms is a reciprocal behaviour that creates value for interactive parties. If there are no mutual-benefiting outcomes in such interactions, platforms will be unsustainable. This requires that traditional linear thinking in innovation based on siloed mentalities has to give way to open innovation ecosystems. Enterprises, large and small, need to work together across organizational, industry, regional, and even national boundaries. Standards and rules are needed for ecosystem actors to work together, as are governance mechanisms to maintain the development and sustainability of platforms. In ecosystems, the borders between supply and demand, and the distinctions between physical and digital worlds, become blurry, as everybody is interdependent on one another. In interdependent and multicentric ecosystems, platform firms need to let go of the desire to control and amass power; instead, their focus is on learning how to empower others for collective, systemic benefits. It is a strategy of sharing control in order to retain it.

Multiplatforms

Digital ecosystems are different from traditional business models in which firms tend to control through a hierarchical structure to organize not just their internal resources such as personnel and capital, but also external resources such as partners and channels to market. In digital ecosystems, all ecosystem actors are theoretically supposed to be equal. In other words, power is distributed, and the ecosystem has multicentral nodes or platforms. Maintaining equality on a platform means that every actor follows the same standards and rules for cooperation and competition, whether it is product development, marketing, or customer service. A good platform can influence its own user base and also can expand its influence over the ecosystem it builds by redefining industry architectures and setting industry rules. The higher the degree of openness of the platform, the more connections and value can be built. Within Alibaba's ecosystem, for example, data can flow not just within its transaction platforms, such as Taobao, TMall, and Ali Express; it can also flow across these platforms, supported by its utility platforms such as Alipay, Cainiao Logistics, and Ali Cloud. In other words, Alibaba maintains an ecosystem based on complementary multiplatforms. This strategy is an extension of multisided platforms in which it is not individual complementor firms, but complementary platforms, that are interconnected.

Successful business models in this area are those that have adopted an open mindset in their platforms. Douying (and its English version TikTok) is the first non-utility application to have attracted over 800 million users worldwide. ByteDance, its parent company, has created an open entertainment platform on which ordinary people (and pets) can be the main characters of their own show. Using advanced algorithms, these platforms organize like-minded audiences together and generate value from such interactions. Founded in 2012, ByteDance began by launching its mobile-based news portal Today's Headlines ('jin ri tou tiao'), which pushes news to individuals on the basis of their search history and personal preferences. 'Jin ri tou tiao' quickly disrupted the dominance of Baidu, a PC-based search engine and news portal. In 2016, ByteDance launched its short-video platform Douyin in China, and in 2017, introduced TikTok globally. In 2019, ByteDance launched an enterprise product, Lark. In 2020, ByteDance's value was estimated as high as $100 billion. The significance of ByteDance's success is not the direct value it creates; it is the connections it manages through its complementary multiplatforms.

Super Platform Firms

The above-mentioned examples of Alibaba and ByteDance own and run complementary multiplatforms, or super platforms, where different platforms complement one another. Such super platforms can nurture emerging platforms at their early stage by sharing and transferring their user bases and other resources within their ecosystems. Entrepreneurial start-ups with innovative business models or technologies can transform the entire ecosystem by leveraging their connections with other actors on other complementary platforms in the ecosystem. Platforms and digital infrastructures make sharing a new norm in the digital economy. With more people and more devices connected into the ecosystems, the costs of platforms and infrastructure reduce substantially. For some firms, they can expand the scope of their businesses to reach extreme ends on the value chains and thus reduce transaction costs. The power of connectivity has enabled the growth of super-platform firms, those that sponsor and operate complementary multiplatforms in their ecosystems, including Google, Facebook, and Amazon in the US, and Alibaba, Tencent, and ByteDance in China. The difference between the US and China is that, in the US, those super-platform firms mostly dominate in one related area; but in China, through corporate venture capital investment, these super platform firms build an interconnected network covering many domains.

China's super-platform firms have played an important role in empowering entrepreneurship and innovation and in creating economic growth and employment opportunities. During the Covid-19 pandemic, for example, a large number of traditional enterprises digitally transformed with the help of the country's super-platform firms. According to a survey by China's restaurant chain association, at least 50 per cent of restaurants started food delivery mini programs on WeChat platform during Covid-19. These super-platform firms also functioned as digital infrastructure providers during the pandemic. The government provided consumption coupons to its citizens through Alipay and WeChat Pay, which resulted in the growth of domestic consumption (as the coupons cannot be cashed out).

With the help of new generations of digital technology, interconnection of all links of business activities and industrial operations can be achieved in the digital ecosystems which are increasingly controlled by the super-platform firms. Having initially been a stimulus to innovation, whether the size of these firms is an enabler or a constraint on sustainable innovation still remains to be seen.

The Case of Mobile Payments

How China developed the world's largest mobile payments on the basis of a backward technology and in a rigid institutional environment has attracted considerable attention from both academics and practitioners. China's mobile payments illustrate the emergence and development of super-platform digital ecosystems in China and explain the roles played by super-platform firms such as Alibaba and Tencent in this process.

Mobile payments have played a significant role in China's transformation in applications such as e-commerce, sharing economy, and social networking, and the advances in the O2O model, connecting online and offline transactions, which have greatly transformed Chinese people's lives. The popularity of mobile payments in offline transactions has also driven behavioural changes amongst consumers and institutional adjustments in payment reforms in particular, and technology in the financial services sector in general.

China's Mobile payment market is a world leader in user adoption and transaction volume. Mobile payments are replacing cash in China. As shown in Figures 5.3

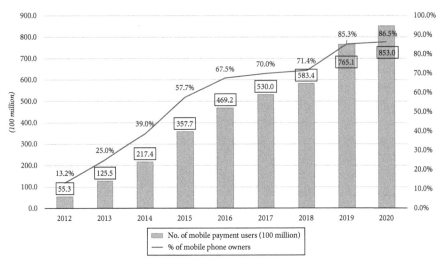

Figure 5.3 China's mobile payment users

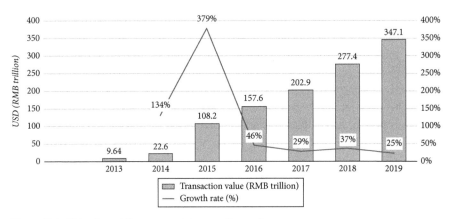

Figure 5.4 China's mobile payment transaction value
Source: CNNIC (2012–20)

and 5.4, the number of mobile payment users reached 853 million by the end of 2020, accounting for 86.5 per cent of mobile phone users. Total transaction value in 2019 reached over RMB 347 trillion (around $51 trillion). Alipay and WeChat Pay are the duopoly players in this market, with a market share of 53.9 per cent and 39.5 per cent respectively in 2019. WeChat Pay is dominant in offline payments, and Alipay in online e-commerce.

A Brief History of Mobile Payments

In the late 1990s, mobile payment technology evolved from SMS-based and WAP-based payments to contactless (proximity) payments via various short-distance transmission technologies (such as RFID and infrared). In 1997 Coca Cola in Helsinki, Finland, introduced the world's first mobile payments in beverage vending machines, where users could pay with just an SMS authorization. Around the same time, the oil company Exxon Mobil introduced an RFID device, SpeedPass, which could be attached to a keyring and allowed users to pay for petrol simply by putting the keyring near a sensor placed on the petrol pump. In 2002, Starbucks customers in South Korea could pay for their coffee by flashing their mobile phones, which embedded their bank account information through infrared readers.

Since then, hundreds of mobile payment services have been introduced all over the world. Strikingly, many of these efforts have failed. Most, if not all, of the dozens of mobile payment services available in EU countries in 2002 were discontinued in 2008.[25]

As mobile handsets continued to develop and mature into multifunctional devices, so did secure and convenient short-distance transmission technology. In 2005, Nokia launched the world's first NFC- enabled phone.[26] In 2007, NFC technology became a de facto industry standard for proximity mobile payments. In 2011, Apple and Google both announced NFC-based mobile payment solutions. Due to the delayed development of NFC-enabled smartphones, Apple launched Apple Pay in 2014 when it released the iPhone 6. In 2015, Google introduced Google Pay and Samsung announced Samsung Pay on Android mobile phones using NFC technology. Despite the fact that firms such as Apple and Google all have a large user base and marketing capability, their NFC-based payment schemes did not become a mainstream method for instore mobile payments in many countries. Two bottlenecks can be identified as key reasons for the delayed diffusion of NFC-based proximity payments. Changing customer's payment behaviour was one obvious reason; convincing merchants to invest in the extra hardware of NFC-enabled point of sale (POS) terminals was another.

Third-Party Payments for Online Transactions

In 2003 Alibaba launched its e-commerce platform Taobao, an online marketplace facilitating C2C transactions. A bottleneck constraining e-commerce was that the country did not have a user credit system that could guarantee the safety of payments for online transactions between strangers. In December 2004, Alipay was created, aimed at solving this problem. As Jack Ma, the founder of Alibaba, said in a media interview:

---

[25] T. Dahlberg, N. Mallat, J. Ondrus, and A. Zmijewska (2008), 'Past, Present and Future of Mobile Payments Research: A Literature Review', *Electronic Commerce Research and Applications*, 7, 165–81.
[26] Near Field Communication (NFC) is a subset of radio frequency identification (RFID). It is regarded as one of the most popular means of short-distance contactless communication between two devices. Transactions through NFC-enabled devices do not require multiple levels of authentication, which thus offer convenience, security, and speed in mobile payments. However, one of the major disadvantages is that the transmission requires special hardware in both smartphones and POS terminals. Apple Pay and Google Pay both use NFC.

The lack of development in Chinese e-commerce was due to one missing piece—a mechanism that could facilitate trust between people. I believe that Alipay is the mechanism that can fill this gap. If Alipay wants to have value in China, it must establish a trust system.... Only with this system would it be possible for users to send strangers money and merchandise solely based on a picture and a few sentences posted online.[27]

Alipay's business model was simple: a guarantee platform that is an intermediary between buyers and sellers online. As a third-party payment platform, Alipay receives payments from a buyer for their online purchases, verifies the funds' availability with the buyer's bank, debits the payment to the seller's account, and only forwards the payment to the seller when the buyer confirms receipt of the purchased goods/services. PayPal pioneered this business model. Unlike PayPal, however, Alipay was not a profit-maker at the time. It was a longer game of being a trust-builder facilitating the growth of e-commerce. It was not, however, without risk. As commented upon by both Alibaba's internal personnel and industry observers, Alipay was operating in a grey area of institutional void for years. In a self-recorded video, Jack Ma said 'I understand the regulatory risks associated with creating Alipay in China. If I have to go to jail for doing so, I will.'[28]

On the institutional side, the policy environment was largely an institutional void where third-party payment solutions were ahead of institutional arrangements for payment services by non-financial institutions. Overall, the policy framework was such that it did not intervene in the development of third-party payments, and, as a consequence, there emerged over 1,000 third-party non-financial payment operators. These were mainly in two categories: non-independent providers such as Alipay which operated as a payment platform for its own e-commerce transactions and Tencent's TenPay for online games; and independent providers that facilitate online payments in niche markets such as purchases of insurance policies and plane tickets and paying utility bills.

The emergence of third-party payments streamlined payment processes in online transactions such that sellers and buyers did not need to deal with their banks every time they engaged in an e-commerce transaction. As a consequence, e-commerce took off in China.

Peer-to-Peer (P2P) Money Transfer

In 2012, Alipay launched its Quick Pay application based on NFC technology aiming at connecting online and offline transactions. Although the app gained more

---

[27] F. Zhu, Y. Zhang, K. Palepu, A. Woo, and N. Dai (2019), 'Ant Financial (A)', Harvard Business School Case 617-060, https://www.hbs.edu/faculty/Pages/item.aspx?num=52493, accessed 6 June 2021.

[28] See https://mp.weixin.qq.com/s/rUlsZweOyP8wRwnaAcu-ww, accessed 14 February 2020.

than 100 million users, it did not generate many transactions due to the lack of NFC-based POS terminals in merchants, despite the fact that Alibaba subsidized them to install NFC readers.

In 2013, Tencent launched WeChat Pay using its TenPay third-party payment licence. WeChat Pay introduced a QR-based[29] mobile payment solution which enabled P2P (peer-to-peer) money transfer. Essentially, these allow payments through users' smartphones scanning the QR code of a merchant, or having the users' payment QR scanned by the merchant online or offline, without downloading and installing any mobile banking apps.

Tencent launched several marketing campaigns to promote QR-based mobile payments. During the 2014 Chinese New Year, WeChat Pay introduced virtual *hong bao*: red envelopes with money inside given by parents and grandparents to their children and grandchildren or by seniors to juniors in organizations during the Chinese New Year celebrations. WeChat Pay even created a virtual bidding game which allowed senders of *hong bao* to create a lucky draw of the money embedded in WeChat groups. In such games, each member could get a random amount of money decided by his or her responding speed to the *hong bao* and, of course, by luck. WeChat Pay's virtual *hong bao* revolutionized a centuries-old tradition of person-to-person (P2P) money transfer among family and friends during these festivities. By leveraging its social networks, through this scenario, the number of WeChat Pay's users grew from 30 million to 100 million in one month. By the end of 2014, WeChat Pay had been adopted by 400 million users, challenging Alipay's dominant position in third-party payments. During the Chinese New Year in 2015, even more Chinese users adopted WeChat Pay as a virtual *hong bao*, and Alipay joined the *hong bao* game. Unlike WeChat Pay, Alipay sent out a large amount of bonuses (sponsored by merchants) for users to compete for, determined by their responding speed to open the *hong bao* and by luck.

Hong bao was a digital affordance: it triggered users' adoption of WeChat Pay for money transfer. To participate in *hong bao* games, users needed to bundle their bank accounts to their WeChat account. 'Hong *bao* was such a sensational app which locked millions of Chinese on their smartphones to bid for just a few RMB, or less.' 'Money transfer among family and friends goes viral on WeChat pay.' For users, 'It's not about money; it's about winning among friends and family.' 'I added my bank account on my WeChat Pay to join the *hong bao* competition. It's so natural. I didn't need to think a second time. It turns out it has changed my life.' These are comments from our interviews with WeChat Pay users.

As one investor we interviewed commented, 'WeChat Pay created payment scenarios that triggered Chinese users to adopt mobile payments naturally and rapidly.'

---

[29] QR (quick response) code is an advanced form of the older version of the two-dimensional barcode. QR code can be used in bill payments, mobile top-ups, and peer-to-peer or peer-to-merchants money transfers. It enables customers to complete secure and speedy payments. WeChat Pay and Alipay use QR code in their mobile payments.

Online-to-Offline (O2O) Ubiquitous Payments

To translate these mobile payment accounts into offline transactions, WeChat Pay created a payment scenario in ride-hailing services, that is, an O2O transaction that uses online booking and offline consumption. Teamed with DiDi (China's equivalent of Uber; it means 'taxi' in Chinese), Tencent started a campaign to subsidize DiDi drivers and passengers. Alibaba and its partner KuaiDi (DiDi's competitor; it means 'fast taxi' in Chinese) joined the campaign, and quickly the competition between the two became a price war, with competition on rebates to both drivers and passengers for those who settle payments via their mobile payment accounts. Between January and May, there were five rounds of price war between DiDi/ WeChat Pay and KuaiDi/Alipay. According to Pony Ma, the CEO of Tencent, his company lost 20 million RMB a day on average and as much as 40 million a day during the price war. In 2015, Jack Ma of Alibaba and Pony Ma of Tencent agreed to end the price war, and they facilitated the merger of DiDi and KuaiDi, which became DiDi Chuxing, one of the unicorns in China.

In 2016, WeChat Pay aggressively rolled out its mobile payment application in coffee shops, convenience stores, restaurants, gyms, hospitals, supermarkets, shopping centres, and even the wet markets that are commonly Chinese people's retail outlets for daily groceries. By the end of 2016, WeChat Pay was available in over 10 million such retail outlets, and Alipay was available in over 2 million retail outlets.

Another battlefield for offline payments occurs in location-based lifestyle services. There were two such large service providers: Meituan (in which Alibaba was an investor) and Dazhong Dianping (in which Tencent was an investor). Both payment companies competed to acquire users by subsidization (e.g. those who chose to pay their orders by Alipay or WeChat Pay for food takeaways and suppliers such as restaurants and food delivery services that accepted payments using either Alipay or WeChat Pay). After several rounds of a fierce price war, in 2017 Meituan and Dazhong Dianping merged to become Meituan Dianping, and users can use either Alipay or WeChat Pay interchangeably.

There was great enthusiasm for the service on the user side. One interviewee said, 'My 80-year-old mother uses WeChat Pay to buy vegetables in the local wet market every day.' Another said, 'You can use your QR code on your WeChat Pay or Alipay to unlock the storage box in which your e-commerce goods are delivered and stored.' An industry observer said, 'A mobile payment app is now a must-have app for Chinese now.' A foreigner travelling to China commented, 'Without WeChat Pay or Alipay, it is so difficult to even buy fast train tickets, let alone order your favourite dishes at one station and get them delivered to your seat at the next.' All these quotations suggest that mobile payments have become backbone applications for China's digital ecosystem.

Together, Alipay and WeChat Pay have transformed the payment industry in China. Numbers of interviewees explained their experiences of integrated mobile payments for China's digital ecosystem: 'Doesn't matter you use WeChat Pay or

Alipay; they are largely the same, and available in all kinds of payment scenarios.' 'You don't need to install any online banking apps on your phone. You only need to have a WeChat Pay or Alipay account with a bundled bank account from any Chinese bank, and you can live and travel in China without carrying cash.' 'The payment scenarios are pervasive. You can pay your ride-hailing services, hire a bike, have your car cleaned, pay your house cleaning and drying cleaning, or your child's school fees or hospital bills by your mobile phone.' The ability to pay utility bills through mobile payments is a massive incentive when in the past this involved queueing for hours in government offices or bank branches.

An Adaptive and Responsive Policy Approach

As shown in this case, and unlike a common (mis)perception that China's top-down approach played an instrumental role in the emergence and development of new technologies, China's policy framework in mobile payments followed an adaptive and responsive approach. China's fast-changing markets see bottom-up innovation and entrepreneurship followed by top-down institutional arrangements. Fast change in business practices in a nascent market where entrepreneurs search and pursue opportunities may cause disruptions in policymaking or create institutional voids[30] where no existing laws or regulations exist. Innovations in entrepreneurial activities commonly develop ahead of institutional arrangements, such as third-party payment in e-commerce. These innovations can disrupt incumbent practices, circumvent existing institutional constraints, and sometimes challenge existing institutional frameworks.

The emergence and development of China's mobile payments saw several major policy changes. Each time the government reacted to market developments by policy adjustments. These policies were essentially very liberal when a plethora of third-party non-financial payment services emerged, following Alipay's lead in 2004. An industry observer commented, 'Regulators were trying to balance innovation and progress with potential risk, when things were very unclear.'

The government took more focused action when a de facto standard emerged for third-party payments in 2010. Relevant government regulators issued a series of policies targeted at regulating non-financial payment institutions for third-party payment services. After appraisals and evaluations, in 2011, 101 third-party payment licences were granted by People's bank of China (PBOC, the central bank), 96 in 2012, 53 in 2013, 19 in 2014, with the last one granted in 2015. Altogether, 270 (out of over 1,000 applications) third-party payment licences were granted. Many third-party payment operators did not get a third-party payment licence and were forced out of business. Both Alibaba's Alipay and Tencent's TenPay were among the first

---

[30] T. Khanna and K. G. Palepu (2010), *Winning in Emerging Markets: A Road Map for Strategy and Execution*, Cambridge, MA: Harvard Business School Press.

batch of non-financial institutions to obtain a licence in 2011. These licences were critical and carried significant meaning for this new type of payment method: they legitimated a practice which had been operating in an institutional void.

In 2016, when QR-based payments had become an enabling technology for China's mobile payment platforms, PBOC officially approved QR as a standard for mobile payments. This endorsement encouraged many complementary apps or mini programs on mobile payment platforms, which finally enabled mobile payments operators to profit from the huge volume of transactions, mainly through a large amount of user deposits between transactions. In 2017, policymakers started to impose rectifications on third-party payments. During 2017 and 2018, several policies were introduced. The most significant one was establishment of NetsUnion Clearance Co. in August 2017, which sits between the third-party payment platforms and the banking clearance platform of UnionPay, operating a central reserve account for user deposits. This policy ended the profits earned by non-bank payment institutions (such as Alipay and WeChat Pay) from user deposits. 'We can't make profits by arbitrating on different interest rates any more, as we are cut off from the direct links with any banks. All transactions have to go through NetsUnion now,' commented one of the mobile payment operators.

In the course of China's development of mobile payments, while facing potential risks and uncertainties, China's regulators did not take a one-size-fits-all approach to constrain the emerging technology. Instead, policymakers adopted a pragmatic policy, maintaining an open attitude towards new trends in technologies and business models, especially conscious of market reactions to such trends. Once an emerging technology or business model is accepted by the market, policymakers aim subsequently to guide its development with detailed implementation policies. For example, in financial services provided by non-financial institutions, such as Ant Financial Group, which runs Alipay, policy encouraged inclusive financial services to complement the state-owned financial sector. As the market matured, policy became more regulated in issues such as payment security and fraud prevention.

As shown in the case of China's mobile payments, institutional intervention followed a zigzag pattern. Policymakers tried to encourage innovation and economic development but minimize potential risks. As one government official commented on the development of mobile payments, 'A regulatory framework to balance technological innovation and social stability is our top priority.' The central role of the mobile payments regulatory body was to provide balanced supervision to promote technology/business model innovation and to ensure the safety and efficient operation of the system.

Entrepreneurial firms in China, even those as influential as Alibaba and Tencent, are never as powerful as policymakers. Instead of using political and social influence and skills to persuade policymakers of the virtues of their innovation, platform firms such as Alipay and WeChat Pay championed the development of their innovation ecosystems. Once user behaviours and market structures changed in the ecosystems, policymakers reacted with institutional interventions. In a sense, the maturity of the market in the ecosystem of mobile payments legitimized the innovations championed by these platform firms. The emergence and development of China's mobile payment industry is, therefore, not the result of central planning from top-down institutions or a result of bottom-up business model innovations. Instead, a dynamic interplay between the two followed an iterative and evolutionary rhythm at the ecosystem level. Overall, the interplay of the two is a dialectic and recursive process by which emergent technologies and business models and adaptive policy instruments drove the advance of digital ecosystems in China.

Scenarization and Digital Ecosystems

Scenarization emerged as a critical factor in China's mobile payments. According to *Collins English Dictionary*, scenarization is the process of turning a story or idea into a scenario for a play or film.[31] As mentioned by a venture capital investor in China's mobile businesses during our interviews, 'Scenarization of payments played a significant role in the success of mobile payments in China.' Mobile payments were located in different scenarios, in which potential users were triggered and encouraged to use the payment method.

Alipay and WeChat Pay started by working independently as third-party payment providers for China's e-commerce. During this stage, e-commerce provided a payment scenario in which users were triggered to adopt third-party payments to complete online transactions. During the move to P2P and O2O transactions, Alipay and WeChat Pay created several payment scenarios in which they competed to acquire users for their payment methods.

Once the third-party payment business model become a de facto standard and was endorsed by the government (i.e. licences were granted), companies competed to acquire users through different payment scenarios. At this stage, competition was directed to user numbers (i.e. how many users bundled their bank account information with their mobile payment accounts and how many such accounts could be translated into transactions), the frequency of payments, and transaction value.

When mobile payments penetrated the majority of Chinese people's lives, competition in mobile payments shifted from acquiring users to improving user experience. The key to improving user experience in mobile payments is interplatform compatibility and availability in all payment scenarios, covering daily living, transport, medical care, education, and public services. The two dominant platform firms invested in each other's territories. Tencent acquired shares in JD.com, an e-commerce competitor to Alibaba. Alibaba acquired shares in Sina Weibo, a social media competitor to Tencent. These cross-investment activities suggest that both companies were expanding their original platforms to form a super-platform ecosystem based on complementary multiplatforms. As one industry observer commented,

---

[31] See https://www.collinsdictionary.com/dictionary/english/scenarization, accessed 5 June 2021.

'From the ecosystem perspective, such cross-investment activities made a lot of sense.' Through cross investments and partnership portfolios, both companies run multiplatform ecosystems covering information, social networking, e-commerce, and O2O platforms. The battle for market share between mobile payments is less to do with profits—charges barely cover costs especially during price wars—and more to do with expanding their business ecosystems, in which mobile payments are a platform of platforms that enables such super-platform firms to share user bases and other resources, including user data generated in customer spending habits and financial transactions, across other platforms in their respective ecosystems. This process was an effective way to direct online traffic—customer flows—from one platform to another, and from online to offline environments.

Neither Alipay nor WeChat Pay, for example, focus on generating profits from their payments, but use their mobile payment platforms to enable the development of other businesses in their ecosystems. The more actors their mobile payments can attract, the greater value in their ecosystems. This point can be seen in a comparison of Alipay and its global counterpart, PayPal. Alipay's core business is to enable e-commerce and facilitate the development of a large ecosystem. PayPal in contrast is a company whose core business is based on charging commission on transactions. In a sense, the key to the success of platform firms such as Alipay and WeChat Pay is whether they create value for other platforms in the ecosystem.

The development of the entire digital ecosystem was critical to the success of a nascent industry. Mobile payments supported the overarching network of the digital ecosystem. The role of the digital ecosystem in the development of mobile payments was that it signalled the market acceptance of mobile payments, which, in turn, forced policymakers to endorse innovative payments at different stages, and adjust the institutional arrangements for the payment industry.

Lessons from China's Mobile Payments

There are several reasons behind the success of China's mobile payments. First, they developed due to a lack of legacy payment systems. From the consumers' perspective, the switching costs involved in adopting mobile payments are a critical success factor. In Western society where credit cards have long been accepted as a mainstream payment instrument, for customers to change their payment behaviour carries high switching costs. Thus mobile payments often encounter greater resistance, requiring a longer period of adaptation. China developed its mobile payments from a relatively immature base of modern payments methods. Before third-party mobile payments, many Chinese consumers, especially those in less developed cities and rural areas, had little or no access to banking services, let alone credit card-based payments. Mobile payments enabled China to bypass card-based payments and go straight to mobile phone-based payments. The emergence of third-party payments, as a trust-builder, solved the bottleneck issue of a lack of trust in e-commerce transactions.

Second, China's mobile payments developed from QR technology thanks to its easy applications without extra costs for both the demand and the supply sides. For NFC payments such as Apply Pay, consumers have to use NFC-enabled smartphones, and merchants have to update their POS terminals to include an NFC reader, which greatly delayed its diffusion. QR codes, although an inferior technology to NFC, provided a simple and low-cost payment solution which solved the bottleneck issue of merchants' investing in extra hardware. QR-code based payment has subsequently moved on to be biometrics-based. In 2018, there were 61 million users using facial recognition for mobile payments, and this number almost doubled in 2019.

Third, mobile payments benefited from the rapid development of mobile networks and the adoption of smartphones. In 2015, mobile internet users were almost 90 per cent of China's total internet population. As a lifestyle enabler, QR-based mobile payments quickly covered most high-frequency and small-amount transaction scenarios in the consumer market in China.

Last, but not least, mobile payments developed as they became a core element of the infrastructure of China's digital ecosystem. The digital ecosystem has formed a positive feedback loop for the development of mobile payments, but, more importantly, it signalled the legitimacy of mobile payments, which enabled dialogues between payment operators and policymakers.

Similar cases of less developed technology becoming a de facto market standard are found in other less developed markets. In Kenya, where the coverage of modern banking services is very low (i.e. 1.5 banks and 1 ATM per 100,000 population), when M-Pesa, a type of mobile payments, was launched, it quickly diffused in the country. Using a functional mobile phone (non smart phone), a user can use M-Pesa to pay bills and transfer money between peers and to pay merchants. It expanded to cover payments in shopping, healthcare, and education. Low or no legacy in existing payments, as well as low or no requirements for extra hardware, contributed to the rapid adoption of M-Pesa. As a consequence, it has benefited the poor in the country. M-Pesa has become one of the most successful mobile payment cases in the world and has expanded to Tanzania, Afghanistan, India and other low-income countries.[32]

Both Alibaba's e-commerce ecosystem and Tencent's social networking ecosystem are highly distributed systems composed of multiple platforms. Such ecosystems are based on co-specialized and complementary multiplatforms, but organized around one or more keystone or platform of platforms, such as mobile payments. Data sharing across their multiplatforms (such as the payment and fintech platforms,

---

[32] M. Dodgson, D. Gann, I. Wladawsky-Berger, and G. George (2013), 'From the Digital Divide to Inclusive Innovation: The Case of Digital Money', Royal Society of Arts, https://www.thersa.org/globalassets/pdfs/reports/rsa-digital-money-report-june_2013.pdf, accessed 5 June 2021.

e-commerce and logistic platforms, cloud computing and storage platforms) drives the efficiency of the entire ecosystem. Such super ecosystems are a result of the evolutionary growth of complementary platforms built upon one another over time. The lessons of China's case are that super-platform firms, by adopting an open network architecture, drive the mass collaboration of ecosystem members and improve system efficiency and sustainability.

Mobile payments are not a stand-alone application, and the directions of their evolution cannot be determined by a single actor or policy. For policymakers to encourage and nurture the growth of emerging technologies and business models it is necessary to have an open-minded and adaptive approach. During this process, building a dynamic interplay with industry innovators following an evolutionary rhythm at the ecosystem level is key.[33]

What's Different in China?

There are certain commonalities in the way firms thrive using different strategies in the digital age from those in the industrial age. First, as opposed to the industrial age where firms operate within their organizational boundaries, traditional boundaries are less critical, and they need to engage in boundary-spanning activities. Second, in a digital ecosystem, the mentalities and practices of competition give way to the practices and mentalities of collaboration. The number and quality of relationships a firm has with other ecosystem members can be more critical than its own resources or capability. Third, in the digital age, system-level goals are as important as firm-level goals. Firms that empower others through partnerships gain more from system-level growth. Both Western and Chinese firms adopt these business strategies and approaches in their digital platform businesses. The question is what is different in China.

China has the advantage of the largest internet population. Although the penetration of the internet in its entire population is less than 65 per cent, its sheer scale means there are about three times the number of smartphone users and eleven times the number of mobile payment users in China than in the US. In China, intensive investment in telecommunications networks, a rapidly growing national economy, a large market, and the availability of low-cost smartphones from local manufacturers led to the booming of the internet-using population, including many from lower-tier cities and rural areas as first-time internet and mobile users.

Chinese technology firms such as Alibaba, Baidu, and Huawei support China's advanced technological infrastructure, including broadband and 4G networks, extensive logistics networks, mobile payment networks, and cloud computing power. China has perhaps some of the world's most extensive digital infrastructures, which are the foundation of the country's consumer internet (2C) businesses. These

---

[33] M. Dodgson, D. Gann, I. Wladawsky-Berger, S. Sultan, and G. George (2015), 'Managing Digital Money', *Academy of Management Journal*, 58(2), 325–33.

technology firms, unlike their counterparts in the West, provide comprehensive consumer services in many distinct but related areas.

The political and institutional environment is such that the Chinese government can mobilize the necessary resources to achieve ambitious goals with supportive industrial policies. For example, China approved a plan—the so called 'new infrastructure investment'—at the National People's Congress after the outbreak of Covid-19 pandemic. It plans to invest $1.4 trillion from 2020 to 2025 to deploy 5G networks, install intelligent cameras and sensors, and automate its manufacturing sector. In implementing these plans, China aims to lead in global standardization efforts, which are known as the 'China Standard 2035 Project'.

Two factors that have played different but instrumental roles in China's development of its digital economy are the policy framework and capital investment.

The First Visible Hand in China's Digital Ecosystem: Policy Intervention

As shown in the case of mobile payments, the Chinese government adopts a highly pragmatic approach in consumer areas. To encourage innovation, policymakers use general and often ambiguous policy guidance towards an emerging field by allowing sufficient room for the market to experiment and test different options, before issuing detailed plans aiming to direct market development. This approach, however, may shape much of the country's R&D efforts, especially those undertaken in industry, seeking projects with quick returns on investment, with wide and immediate applications.

For infrastructure projects, top policymakers have been aware of the need for China to develop its own technological advantages in next-generation digital ecosystems such as computing power, network infrastructures, big data, and AI, which are the foundations of Industry 4.0. AI technology and applications are a particularly strong focus in China's national policy priorities. China's policymakers are determined to lead in the shift from information-driven industry to intelligence-driven industry. The government is using a 'visible hand' in the development of applications, including computer visual images, intelligent translation, biometrics, natural language comprehension, driverless vehicles, intelligent controlling systems, and human-machine interfaces.

China first released its blueprint for developing the next-generation AI technology and detailed three-year implementation plans, after announcing its *Made in China 2025* policy in May 2015. From the top down, with its 'Intelligent plus X' initiative launched in 2019, China aims to promote the convergence of the next generation of advanced digital technologies, including AI, blockchain, cloud computing, and big data (nicknamed 'ABCD' technologies), instilling intelligence in products, equipment, and production in manufacturing. These initiatives set the tone for the discussion about the development of AI technology in China, providing guidance on skills and education, basic research, industrial economics, and institutional arrangements. AI-related policy frameworks are listed in Table 5.1.

AI policy in China followed a path aiming at building a national strategy involving multilevel collaborations in which the government plays an active role. As seen in multiple documents issued by key government agencies such as the Ministry of Industry and Information Technology, these efforts target the integration and convergence of state-guided and private-run investments and activities. Specifically, a great deal of attention has been directed at the implementation of large-scale state

Table 5.1 Policy initiatives related to China's next-generation digital ecosystem

Time	Policy	Purposes
2015	• *Made in China 2025* • A blueprint for developing next-generation AI technology and detailed three-year implementation plans.	• Setting the tone for discussion, involving multiple players in academia, industry and government.
2016	• Intelligent manufacturing and industrial robotics listed as the top Scientific Innovation Projects 2030 in the 13th national Five-Year Plan. • 'Internet plus X' initiative.	• Providing policy guidance in six areas to support AI development, including capital, standards, IP protection, human talent development, as well as building infrastructures of innovation platforms, industrial systems, and AI standardization.
2017	• A developmental plan for the next-generation AI. • AI was listed in the Government Report by Premier Li Keqiang. • AI was included in the report of the 19th National Congress of the CPC, specifying the convergence of AI-related technologies with the physical world.	• Setting the goal that AI is China's new engine for future growth. • Setting 2030 as the deadline for China's ambitious AI goal. • Laying out milestones for AI development until 2030.
2018	• AI was listed a second time in the Government Report by Premier Li Keqiang. • Developing AI curriculum for undergraduate and graduate education.	• Emphasizing the functionalities of AI in supply side reforms. • Promoting AI applications into specific scenarios, such as intelligent healthcare, education, city management, etc.
2019	• AI was listed a third time in the Government Report by Premier Li Keqiang. • 'Intelligent plus X' initiative based on AI. • Guidance of deep convergence between AI technology and the physical economy. • Governance principles in AI—building a responsible AI ecosystem.	• Accelerating AI basic research and commercialization. • Building industrial internet. • Moving towards a platform-enabled ecosystem. • Policy guidance of AI applications in mass entrepreneurship.

Source: Compiled by the authors from various government sources

and private collaborations in R&D labs and open innovation clusters. The thrust of these policies is seen in the 'New Infrastructure' blueprint aiming to accelerate China's economic recovery after the Covid-19 pandemic.

Digital RMB

The world is moving towards a transformation in digital currencies. Facebook's announcement of a digital currency, Libra, in June 2019, attracted significant attention.

Unlike Bitcoin or Ether, which are encrypted currencies (or assets) whose transactions are supported by blockchain technology, Libra aimed to become a global digital currency backed by reserve assets such as a basket of sovereign currencies and government bonds. A key question was the role of Libra's 'central bank', which needed to provide global governance (like the role of IMF) to maintain the stability of the Libra currency. Libra's stability can be influenced by fluctuations of exchange rates in reserve asset currencies and by the market's confidence in and expectations of each currency or bond in the basket. Without effective global governance mechanisms, it remains challenging to have both currency stability and asset profitability in future digital currencies such as Libra.[34]

China's central bank, the People's Bank of China, in response to the global movement in digital money, announced a trial of its own digital currency—digital RMB (known as DC/EP—digital currency and electronic payment)—in Shenzhen, Suzhou, Chengdu, and Xiong'an New District near Beijing. China aims to become the first major economy to adopt a digital currency. The advent of digital currency is an evolutionary result of digital payments, which accommodate the increasing digitalization of goods, services, and assets, and ubiquitous transactions through digital or mobile devices.

The issuing and exchange of digital RMB will follow a dual structure, that is, both the Central Bank and commercial banks will issue digital RMB or exchange banknotes to digital RMB free of charge for their users. Commercial banks need to open reserve accounts at the central bank and pay 100 per cent of the reserve assets for digital RMB they intend to issue or exchange. In other words, digital RMB is a digital equivalent to banknotes, taking the form of encrypted strings of digital numbers. Users do not have to have a bank account to possess digital RMB, needing only to have a smartphone with a digital RMB wallet app. Such users can use the smartphone to keep currency, engage in P2P transactions, and make digital payments at any outlet (online or offline) with a digital RMB reader. These transactions can be done even without an internet connection. For example, two users with digital RMB wallet apps can transfer money by touching their smartphones via NFC.

---

[34] Opinion on digital currency by Mu Changchun, the director of Digital Currency Research Institute, the People's Bank of China. See C. Mu (2021), 'China's Digital Wallet Designed to Meet Everyone's Needs', Caixin Magzine, June 16, 2021, https://www.caixinglobal.com/2021-06-16/opinion-chinas-digital-yuan-wallet-designed-to-meet-everyones-needs-101727437.html, accessed 26 July 2021.

While the claims for digital RMB include improving payment efficiency, increasing the liquidity of RMB, and providing more inclusive mobile payments to those who do not have access to the internet or a bank account, with the convenience, reliability, and safety of digital payments, it is criticized as a tool of the CPC in implementing a form of virtual control over its people.[35]

China began its research on digital currency as early as 2014, intending to strengthen its digital payments' safety and security and to prevent fraud in money transactions from corruption, gambling, and money laundering. As Fan Yifei, the Vice Governor of the central bank, pointed out, 'Digital RMB is not for profit. Its purposes are to maximize the social benefits and social welfare for its people.'[36] The People's Bank of China will establish a value transfer system for digital RMB and install a payment infrastructure. In other words, digital RMB will be a sovereign currency in China. The issuing, exchange and circulation of digital RMB is based on M0, which means that the central bank digital currency held by the public is still a central bank liability, and the central bank provides a credit guarantee with legal compensation.

Digital RMB is thus considered a threat to China's ubiquitous mobile payment institutions such as Alipay and WeChat Pay, which are commercially run payment platforms where users' payment accounts must be backed by their bank accounts or credit accounts. In industries close to consumers, bottom-up innovators such as Alipay and WeChat Pay have advantages in their ability to cover more emerging payment opportunities. Digital currency, however, may play an instrumental role in stimulating more competition in digital payments and rectify some misconduct, such as the forced bundling of services by payment platforms, but it is less likely to form a direct threat to market-driven digital payments.

Digital RMB carries more strategic purposes for the government. It intends to increase its discourse power in the standardization of digital currencies and global clearance systems by adopting digital currency. Although the government has not specified the technological architecture of digital RMB, blockchain technology is believed to play a central role. Blockchain technology serves as a decentralized ledger of transactions. While the advantages of decentralization in transactions are apparent, decentralization, in fact, also means that all transactions have to go through all nodes in a network, which will substantially slow down the speed of digital payments. It can potentially, however, be used in global transactions, which can challenge the current dominance of the SWIFT system, the current standard that enables financial institutions worldwide to securely send and receive information about financial transactions.

---

[35] J. Kynge, and S. Yu (2021), 'Virtual control: The Agenda behind China's New Digital Currency', *Financial Times*, 17 February, https://www.ft.com/content/7511809e-827e-4526-81ad-ae83f405f623, accessed 5 June 2021.

[36] Fan Yifei, 'Analysis on the Policy Implications of the Positioning of Digital RMB M0', September 2020, https://blockcast.cc/news/fan-yifei-deputy-governor-of-the-central-bank-policy-perspective-analysis-of-digital-rmb-m0-positioning/, accessed 26 July 2021.

The Second Visible Hand in China's Digital Ecosystem: Capital Investment

The top-down policy frameworks in next-generation digital technology have strong spillover effects on local governments and state-owned enterprises. Since 2016, a large amount of capital investment driven by both local governments and the venture capital community, including corporate investments from China's technology firms, has been poured into the development of next-generation digital technologies.

Institutional capital investment in the US is largely composed of pension funds (30 per cent), market-based funds (21 per cent), high net-worth investors, sovereign funds, insurance companies, and banks. In China, in contrast, about half of the institutional investors are government-backed guiding funds from central and local governments, and SOEs at both central and local levels. This structural difference in capital investment means that China's investment strategies and priorities are different from those in the US. Whereas in the US the power of institutional funds is relatively distributed, and professional fund managers play an important role in investment, in China government-guided funds generally look for low-risk infrastructure projects. However, government-backed funds have flow-on effects, often attracting follow-up investments from SOEs. These types of funds have played an important role in long-term industry transformation and upgrade.

To compensate for the deficiency of investment in high-risk and high-growth technologies and ventures, China's venture capital (VC) and private equity (PE) investment is investing more aggressively and making better returns than their counterparts in the US. Between 2010 and 2020, for example, the average time it takes for a VC-backed start-up to become a unicorn is four years in China, compared to seven in the US. China has maintained an attractive market for VC and PE investors due to its sheer size and the growth rate of the internet market, especially its mobile internet market, as well as the growing consumer market.

Corporate venture capital (CVC), investment by the country's super-platform firms, especially Alibaba and Tencent, has become an important contributor to China's new economy. CVC invests in start-ups and high-growth firms, and in mergers and acquisitions (M&A). Firms such as Alibaba and Tencent have accumulated rich industry data and abundant cash and have access to low-cost capital. One critical factor in decisions about CVC investment, especially from Alibaba and Tencent, is the way it plays a critical strategic role in their entire business ecosystems. In other words, missing an opportunity to expand in a certain area of technology is a much bigger concern than investing in the wrong company or technology. CVC investment from Alibaba and Tencent has strong trickle-down effects: their investment is likely to attract follow-up investments from independent VC and other technology firms. When Alibaba or Tencent leads investment in a project, it sends a strong signal to the market of its high potential. Alibaba's accumulated investment between 2105 and 2018 amounted to 505 billion RMB (about $76 billion), and its accumulated return reached 138.7 billion RMB. During the same period, Tencent's four-year accumulated investment amounted to 406 billion RMB, with an accumulated return of 47.6 billion RMB. Between 2010 and 2020, Tencent invested in about 700 start-ups at different stages, of which 63 have been listed on stock exchanges, and 122 have achieved a market valuation of more than $1 billion. In 2018 alone, Alibaba's investment reached around 180 billion RMB, and Tencent's around 90 billion RMB.[37]

These two companies, although adopting different investment philosophies and strategies, each invest with the purpose of building and expanding their digital ecosystems. Alibaba's investment strategy is such that it aims to maintain controlling shares, especially in those ventures that are critical complementors to its core business, that is, e-commerce. According to Cai Chongxin, the founder of Alibaba's investment arm, 'Venture investment is like playing the game of go—every piece should have a purpose on the chessboard, and it's up to the player to determine where it should go to maximize the return at the aggregate level.'[38] Alibaba helps its invested ventures grow by empowering them with shared resources, including its user bases and online traffic generated through its Taobao and TMall e-commerce platforms. Whether its investments produce capital returns is a secondary concern to achieving complementarity of the invested ventures in its ecosystem. Alibaba's successful investments include Weibo, China's Twitter-type social media platform, Momo, a social networking platform connecting strangers, and the bike-sharing company HelloBike. These firms are important actors in Alibaba's digital ecosystem.

Tencent, on the other hand, adopts a more hands-off investment strategy: it does not seek controlling shares; rather, it allows the invested ventures to grow on their own and obtain independent IPOs if possible. Successful cases include JD.com, Meituan, and Pinduoduo, each of which has contributed over 10 billion RMB (about $1.5 billion) to Tencent's profits. Liu Chiping, an executive director of Tencent, commented at the company's 2019 annual investment conference, 'Tencent focuses on what we are good at. That means we will not seek controlling power in our invested ventures. We expand our ecosystem through building partnerships with our invested firms.' This strategy allows Tencent to enter into new areas through its investments. As a social networking platform, Tencent is at the centre, surrounded by many small clusters, each operating on its own. Collectively, they form its ecosystem. The closer a cluster is to Tencent's core businesses of social networking and gaming, the more influence Tencent has over the firms in that cluster. In such an interrelated system, Tencent empowers the invested ventures by sharing its infrastructure resources, such as WeChat Pay.

While Alibaba and Tencent are making major contributions to the growth of China's digital economy, the concern that they may have become too big has drawn a lot of attention. CVC investment serves two strategic purposes: first, to identify and develop new technological trends as complementors to core businesses; second, to defend

---

[37] The VC/CVC database from ITJuzi.com.
[38] Cai's speech on Alibaba's Investors' Day, September 2018.

market positions by not allowing threatening technologies to grow independently. The first functions in a manner of developing social goods in an innovation ecosystem. The second may constrain the growth of future innovations. One of the interviewees, a venture capital investor in the technology, media, and telecommunications area, commented, 'It is very hard for a new venture to grow big without Alibaba or Tencent.'

Since 2015, both Alibaba and Tencent have started to invest in South East Asia, including in India and Indonesia. The two giants are exploring new investment opportunities, especially in the 2B market in internet businesses. Unlike the 2C market, where winners take all or most, and investment pursues the top players, in the 2B market, there are still many uncertainties and many investment opportunities. Table 5.2 summarizes the areas invest in by Alibaba (including Ant Financial Group) and Tencent in 2018, which illustrate new trends of growth.

Future Digital Technologies

China's digital economy has largely been built upon the advantages of a rapidly growing internet-using population and increasing consumer online traffic. During its rapid growth period, firms have tended to focus on short-term gains through swift actions. For example, a popular motto adopted by Chinese technology firms, is 'moving fast and breaking barriers'. However, as China is facing an economic slowdown in the domestic market and an increasingly complex and hostile global

Table 5.2 Investment portfolios (Tencent vs Alibaba + Ant Financial) in 2018

Investment area	Tencent: number of investments	Alibaba + Ant Group:[1] number of investments
2B services	19	11 + 7
Car & transport services	9	7 + 7
Healthcare & medical services	4	6 + 2
Education	9	0 + 1
Hardware	3	5 + 3
E-commerce	13	11 + 3
Culture & entertainment	49	7 + 0
Finance	10	2 + 8
Logistics	5	
Sports	5	1 + 0
Location-based lifestyles services	4	6 + 5
Games	12	0
Software tools	4	0 + 3
Real estate	2	3 + 0
Advertising	1	1 + 1
Agriculture	0	1 + 0
Social media	0	0 + 1

[1] Ant Group (known as Ant Financial Group until 2020) is the financial arm of Alibaba, which spun off from Alipay in 2011, but runs Alipay and other technological financial services.

Source: itjuzi.com and CB Insights (2019)

market, the question is whether growth based on these advantages has come to an end.

As shown in previous chapters, although China has made impressive progress in economic growth, especially industry development, it still relies on imports for some critical technologies, including industry software such as operating systems and design tools, high-end chips, and tools to make chips, such as lithography machines and design software, and some critical raw materials such as high-purity semiconductor silicon wafers and bearing steel, all of which are essential to China's industry. Without its own technologies in these critical areas, China faces a challenging future.

China has learned a hard lesson from relying on imported technologies in the past. For future growth, the government is determined to develop its own technological innovations which would enable the country to develop a sustainable digital future. To achieve this ambition, AI, the internet of things, and industry internet are the core.

Artificial Intelligence

Basic research in artificial intelligence (AI) is still largely dominated by the US, but China is catching up rapidly. While it is still a distant future for humans to fully understand and apply artificial general intelligence, there have been some significant breakthroughs in specific AI applications in recent years. These are based on three conditions: large amounts of data, enormous computing power, and sufficient numbers of skilled workers. China has accumulated certain advantages in all three conditions, although it still faces major challenges.

In contrast to its approach to many emerging internet technologies, AI research and applications have been identified by the Chinese government as a priority for its digital future and have been driven by a top-down policy approach. Policies have supported the attraction of top AI scientific talent, developed the AI educational curriculum, and encouraged public-private collaborations. Alongside the *Made in China 2025* initiative from central government, local governments have actively responded to the national call for strengthening the AI industry. Many provincial and city governments have produced policies and invested capital to attract people with AI skills and to develop AI applications at the local level. Of all the local efforts, the city governments of Beijing, Shanghai, and Shenzhen have made the most progress in terms of detailed implementation plans for AI applications. How effective these seemingly overlapping investments will be too early to judge.

AI research in China remains largely academic-driven. According to research at Tsinghua University, by the end of 2017, China was home to the second largest pool of AI scientists and engineers after the US.[39] Chinese authors have the highest number of AI publications,[40] although the US still leads the world in citations of publications and the number of PCT patents.

China has attracted many returnees, although the most talented people in their fields may still choose to stay in the West, especially after gaining an education at leading universities or research institutes. There are signs, however, that this situation is changing. China has offered top researchers, especially those with industry experience, high salaries and other incentives, including research autonomy and capital support for establishing research labs in the top Chinese universities. Besides these benefits, large data sets, dedicated and hardworking students, and supercomputing power are all attractions for China-born computer scientists. The increasingly hostile working environment in the US will perhaps push more Chinese scholars to return. In order to attract AI talent, Chinese enterprises have also established reward systems to join them in China or abroad. Alibaba, for example, has set up its Damo Academy to recruit top international AI researchers and engineers. iFlytek, an AI-based linguistics company, established AI labs and offices in the US, Canada, and elsewhere to recruit talented staff.

The government also promotes the development of human capital in AI through education. By 2020, the Ministry of Education had approved thirty-five AI-related curricula for undergraduate, graduate, and professional education. Enrolments in such programmes are growing rapidly. As in every other area of science and innovation in China, progress varies across different regions in the country. In the top technology universities such as Tsinghua University, Nankai University, and Xi'an Jiaotong University, there are established AI research institutes headed by leading AI scientists.

Increasing efforts from industry have been directed to AI development, especially AI applications. The number of AI-related enterprises and the investment in AI development in China rank second in the world after the US.[41] China's technology firms, such as Baidu, Alibaba, Tencent, and Huawei, have all invested heavily in AI R&D and applications, including technologies in computer vision, natural language, voice recognition, and self-driving vehicles.

As in so many areas, China's advantage in AI is its sheer size. The interconnectedness in its digital economy has generated massive amounts of data which can be used to train AI systems. The country has huge advantages in data collection and labelling, not just because it has less stringent data protection policies, but also due to a large workforce dedicated to data treatment. Massive amounts of data are essential for

---

[39] China's AI Development Report. China Institute for Science and Technology Policy, Tsinghua University, July 2018, Beijing China.

[40] Ministry of Science and Technology of China released 'China's New Generation Artificial Intelligence Development Report 2019' on 24 May 2020, http://chinainnovationfunding.eu/china-new-generation-artificial-intelligence-development-report-2019/, accessed 26 July 2021.

[41] China's New Generation Artificial Intelligence Development Plan, Department of International Cooperation, Ministry of Science and Technology, China, July 2017, https://super-ai.diascreative.net/new-generation-of-artificial-intelligence-development-plan, accessed 26 July 2021.

machine learning for AI, especially in artificial general intelligence: training machines to think like humans.

China has several world-leading companies in computer vision, speech recognition and natural language processing, and facial recognition. For example, Face++, a facial recognition company, uses biometrics in many situations, such as entry into high-speed trains, office buildings and campuses. Robots are also used in automated warehousing. JD.com, for example, uses automated robots in its Shanghai distribution centre for organizing, selecting, and shipping 200,000 orders a day, with only four workers on duty. Hikvision, the world's leader in security cameras and sensors, uses an innovative method in human body recognition which has been used in airports, surveillance cameras, traffic lights and many security checkpoints. The privacy and political control aspects of these technologies will be addressed in Chapter 8.

The central government has announced policies to promote state-corporate collaborations in open innovation platforms for AI. These include self-driving vehicles in collaboration with Baidu, smart cities with Alibaba, software design with Huawei, intelligent sensors with Hikvision, medical imaging with Tencent, intelligent language processing with iFlyteck, and smart homes with Xiaomi. Altogether, fifteen such AI open innovation platforms have been established in Beijing, Zhejiang, Anhui, Guangdong, and Shanghai.

The Internet of Things

The internet of things (IoT) is a system of interrelated computing devices connected by unique identifiers (UIDs). IoT enables interactions of human to human, human to device, and device to device. China is actively promoting the development of IoT, especially in its manufacturing sector. IoT is being developed alongside the penetration among Chinese manufacturers of digitalization in production equipment, key numeric control systems, and production processes. The adoption of industry software in CAD (computer-aided design), MES (manufacturing executive system), PLM (product lifecycle management), and design software has also increased, which has led to digital transformation in manufacturing.

Examples of IoT applications in China include:

- Intelligent medicine is becoming human-centric. IoT technology can effectively help the management of hospital patients and treatments intelligently. Virtual reality (VR) technology has been applied in various ways in medical and healthcare services.
- Intelligent security has progressed quickly. An intelligent security system includes access to control systems, anti-theft alarm systems, and video surveillance systems. Mobile phone-controlled, QR code-controlled, remote, and cloud data-enabled entrance and facial recognition-enabled access control systems are becoming common in China.

- Logistics companies have developed AI and IoT technologies that have transformed logistics into an intelligent industry. Accuracy and efficiency in logistics management have improved as a result, and logistics costs have been reduced.

Industry Internet

We have seen how China's consumer internet, such as e-commerce, mobile payments, and online entertainment and education, has developed rapidly. In the industrial internet, however, China lags behind the longer-industrialized countries, such as the US, Germany, and Japan. In recent years, AI-related applications have been growing fastest in 2B services such as enterprise services, industrial robotics, healthcare, intelligent securities, internet services, and fintech. The convergence of 5G, cloud computing, and AI technology will significantly advance the development of the industry internet.

The industry internet fully reflects the value creation of data in the digital economy. Each enterprise in the industrial ecosystem can digitally process data by using advanced technologies to make data a part of product value and, thus, change value creation in the entire industry. Traditional manufacturing industry will move towards a new development mode that emphasizes digitalization in product design and production, and integrates manufacturing and services. Progress in B2B digital transformation enabled by industry internet, however, is slow, due to a lack of open industrial platforms that can empower SMEs.

Companies such as Alibaba and Huawei have enhanced their cloud computing services, making them more agile, flexible, and cost-efficient for industrial clients. Such cloud providers have adopted an ecosystem mentality, empowering others in the ecosystem and benefiting the ecosystem-level growth.

China's Digital Future

China has made impressive progress in its digital economy and has shown determination to catch up and lead internationally in next-generation digital technology, including AI, IoT, and industry internet. However, the nation is facing an increasingly complex environment both domestically and globally, and if China wants to integrate its digital economy into the world's digital ecosystem, it faces many challenges.

China's 1980s reforms aimed to introduce the market economy in the short term and democratic politics and the rule of law in the long term. The progress China has made in economic reforms has not been matched by political reforms. To achieve its long-term goals, China has relied on high degrees of centralized political control. Because of this, China is facing opposition from some trading partners. Trust is difficult to establish and maintain, especially with those who are different. China will be different for the foreseeable future. The question is, for countries with different political and cultural values, how to collaborate harmoniously while maintaining differences. How do they address Confucius's view that '*jun zi he er bu tong*' ('Superior people seek harmony with diversity')?

Data flows globally in the digital economy. When data flows, so do the political ideals and cultural values embedded within and around it. Facebook, Google, and Twitter are all banned in China. The nation is facing an increasingly hostile global environment for exports from its technology firms, such as Huawei, Tencent, and ByteDance. The nature of the internet is its super network effects, but political and cultural differences are segregating the internet, especially between China and the US. This decoupling will force China to develop an isolated digital ecosystem from the rest of the world.

For decades, China's growing prosperity has been built upon policies of opening up to the outside world. Ironically, however, in the digital age this trend is reversing. For an efficient and sustainable digital ecosystem, the world needs the US and China to work together: US firms have huge advantages in science and technological innovation, and China has huge advantages in market size and data. The recent retreat to a closed system in both countries is detrimental to the global digital ecosystem.

The internet's infrastructure has been dominated by a small number of powerful technology companies: Google, Apple, Facebook, and Amazon in the US, and Tencent, Alibaba, Baidu, and ByteDance in China. While these firms have contributed a great deal to building digital platforms which facilitate collective innovation and mass transactions, they increasingly control the way information is distributed. Algorithm-enabled news feeds, for example, are no longer simply competing with established news providers but are used systematically to spread personalized information and news to users based on their preferences collected by AI through their online footprints. This feeds the tendency of people to hear what they want to hear and the selection bias that accentuates division in polarized societies. The 2016 elections in the US and the Brexit referendum in the UK provide stark evidence of this.

Given the censorship in China, such selection bias leads in a different and equally divisive direction. As China's economic power increases, so does the sentiment of national pride among its people. As part of this sentiment, two collective complexes have emerged: a 'great power complex' of China again becoming a world great power and a 'rejuvenation complex' of China rising to restore its historic glory in science and technology. These have been reinforced and amplified through social media and have become a common misperception. This sentiment can be very dangerous, as it can easily develop into nationalism and further isolate China from the global economic and political system. As China gains economic power, it needs not only to share its market and data with the world, but also to participate in the establishment of rules and laws for them in a constructive way.

Another concern about the powerful technology companies is their growing power in influencing future directions of innovation. Whether these firms, due to their sheer size in both user base and capitalization, will be enablers or constrainers of further innovation and entrepreneurship remains unclear. By acquiring (and sometimes killing) potential challengers before they become a real threat, spending millions lobbying governments to ensure their core businesses stay intact, and benefiting from leveraging their large user base across different platforms and applications for their own advantage, these firms' dominant positions are increasingly perceived as threats to industry competitiveness, ecosystem sustainability, personal privacy, and sometimes social stability. Data privacy, for example, has become a vital issue facing the development of the digital economy. Challenging questions arise as to how governments and these firms can work together across national borders to mitigate such threats, especially in data usage in commonly agreed legal and ethical frameworks.

There is still much work to be done in China, both by the government and firms, to develop regulations for data safety and data protection issues, and align China's practices with the rest of the world. The rule of law to ensure the large-scale application of data needs to be under appropriate governance and supervision. Otherwise, unless it complies with these laws, China's digital ecosystem will always operate in isolation from the rest of the world.

6

Technology Entrepreneurship

The pressures of the economic slowdown that China has faced since the global financial crisis in 2008, especially its result of increasing unemployment among university graduates, have led the government to promote entrepreneurial activity, largely by providing financing and policy support. Numerous regional hubs of entrepreneurship, often in conjunction with university science parks, have been established, and subsidies have been provided for technology ventures in newly created 'mass-makers' space'. Multiple sources of funds have been allowed to enter China's primary capital market for venture financing, and a series of reforms in the secondary capital market for entrepreneurial listings and facilitating the business registration process have since been introduced. Other policies have aimed at attracting overseas scientists, technologists, and entrepreneurs back to China and encouraging domestic scientists, technologists, and university students to become entrepreneurs. Many of these policies aiming to promote entrepreneurship have focused specifically on technological innovation.

China's efforts to build its National Innovation System accelerated in the late 1980s.[1] Since then, the government has recognized the close connections between innovation and entrepreneurship, as well as their impact on the economy and employment. Innovation-driven entrepreneurship creates more employment, and innovation undertaken by entrepreneurs boosts economic growth. This realization was a self-correction of the views that 'entrepreneurial activity was capitalism' during the era of China's central planning economy, which overlooked the creative power of entrepreneurs, especially innovation-based new ventures. This appreciation has been strengthened since the late 1990s, when China embraced the digital economy. Since then, in industries such as communication technologies, internet businesses, medical devices, and pharmaceuticals, entrepreneurial firms that were either newly created or reformed from their state-owned parenting entities have been China's leaders of innovation.

The pattern of new ventures playing a key role in stimulating innovation has been pronounced in the twenty-first century. Firms such as Alibaba and Tencent in the internet business, Huawei and ZTE in communications manufacturing, MindRay and BeiGene in medical and healthcare, and BYD and Geely in electric vehicles are

---

[1] See M. Dodgson and L. Xue (2009), 'Innovation in China', *Innovation: Management, Policy and Practice*, 11(1), 2–5; and S. Gu and M. Dodgson (eds.) (2006), 'Innovation in China: Harmonious Transformation?', Special Issue, *Innovation: Management, Policy and Practice*, 8(1–2).

Demystifying China's Innovation Machine: Chaotic Order. Marina Yue Zhang, Mark Dodgson, and David M. Gann, Oxford University Press. © Marina Yue Zhang, Mark Dodgson, and David M. Gann 2022. DOI: 10.1093/oso/9780198861171.003.0006

at the frontiers of technological innovation in their fields. Two areas, consumer internet and biotechnology/biopharmaceuticals, have experienced the most revolutionary innovation driven by entrepreneurship. We have analysed the development of China's digital ventures in previous chapters. In this chapter, we will use China's biotechnology/biopharmaceuticals sector as a case study to examine the role of technology entrepreneurship.

Historically, entrepreneurship was not considered a 'noble' career choice in Chinese culture, in contrast to those of scholars and government officials, and it was banned in the Mao era. It has since become recognized as an engine for economic growth and employment opportunities. The earliest entrepreneurs were those who were dissatisfied with the constraints of the status quo and, following the advice attributed to Deng Xiaoping that 'To get rich is glorious,' wanted to 'get rich first'. These pioneers initially created their ventures in manufacturing, property, and commerce, largely by leveraging on information asymmetry and price disparities across regions. In the late 1980s, entrepreneurs such as Huawei's Ren Zhengfei, Lenovo's Liu Chuanzhi, and Haier's Zhang Ruiming created entrepreneurial ventures in technology sectors that have grown into China's modern industrial backbone.

Internet-based entrepreneurship has laid the foundation for China's digital economy. Entrepreneurs such as Alibaba's Jack Ma, Sohu's Charles Zhang, and Tencent's Pony Ma started their ventures by introducing internet business models into China. As the world was recovering from the global financial crisis of 2008/2009, a new generation of internet entrepreneurs emerged who grew up in a more open and prosperous China and includes ByteDance's Zhang Yiming, Pinduoduo's Huang Zheng, and DJI's Wang Tao. They started their ventures by creating brand new business models catering to both China's supply and demand conditions and actively using their innovations to expand globally. In today's China, entrepreneurship has never been so 'noble'; talented young people embrace it to chase their Chinese dreams.

China is facing unprecedented challenges, domestically, with issues such as an ageing population and an economic downturn, and globally, with the trade conflicts and increasing suspicion of Chinese technological inroads into the global market. More importantly, it shares the existential threats to the planet such as climate change and unknown viruses that can cause pandemics and halt the global circulation of goods, capital, and people. To overcome these challenges, technological innovation and entrepreneurship should play an important role: China needs the world, and the world also needs China. China's successes and failures in innovation-driven entrepreneurship should hold critical lessons for other countries in similar straits. In these circumstances Chinese entrepreneurship should be seen not just as a threat but as a sophisticated contributor to solving confronting problems. Ultimately, the benefits of science and technology should belong to the entire human race.

China's National Innovation System (NIS) and Technology Entrepreneurship

As it recovered from the economic meltdown of the Cultural Revolution, China's economy in the 1980s relied on its SOEs, including for the bulk of innovations that underpinned its industries. This was manifested in a model of concentrated capital injection into the country's strategically critical projects led by its SOEs, the so-called 'eldest sons' who have inheritance rights to the estate of their parents. This model produced some successes. However, China overlooked the creative power of entrepreneurial firms until the late 1990s, when a series of SOE reforms changed China's economic structures and released the 'creative destruction' of new ventures. These ventures have arisen to take central positions in innovation, employment opportunities, and economic growth in many industries.[2]

The emergence and development of technology entrepreneurship is one of the most significant aspects in China's national innovation system. Before the twenty-first century, despite the awareness of and the attention to the need for technology transfer and innovation commercialization, technology entrepreneurship had not yet become an integral part of China's national innovation system.[3] The top-down design of a framework for technology entrepreneurship consisted of five components: the sources of technology entrepreneurship (origin), incubators (incubation), high-tech industrial development zones and science parks (growth), exit routes (harvest), and a supporting system.[4] Under this design, technology entrepreneurship mushroomed in China, and resulted in the improvement in the service sector supporting entrepreneurship. A substantial amount of this effort, however, did not generate desirable technological outcomes, but made contributions to property projects.

In the 1980s and 1990s, technology entrepreneurship began to emerge from universities, research institutes, and incumbent enterprises. There were two distinct patterns. The first was an individual model such that people with entrepreneurial spirit started their technology-based ventures either independently or by reforming their parent SOE enterprises. Huawei, Geely, and Fusun are examples of this category. The second is an organization model such that universities, research institutes, or enterprises formed their own technology-based entrepreneurial spin-offs. Examples of this category included Founder Group from Peking University, Unigroup from Tsinghua University, and Lenovo Group from the Chinese Academy of Sciences.

The success of China's early technology entrepreneurship can be attributed to an institutional reform which endorsed a mechanism of trading technology for commercial value. This allowed technological innovations by private enterprises to be

---

[2] J. Gao, X. Liu, and M. Y. Zhang (2011), 'China's NIS: The Interplay between S&T Policy Framework and Technology Entrepreneurship', in S. Mian (ed.), *Science and Technology Based Regional Entrepreneurship: Global Experience in Policy & Program Development*, Cheltenham: Edward Elgar.

[3] M. Y. Zhang (2014), 'Innovation Management in China', in M. Dodgson, D. M. Gann, and N. Phillips (eds.), *The Oxford Handbook of Innovation Management*, Oxford: Oxford University Press, 355–74.

[4] Gao, Liu, and Zhang 'China's NIS'.

commercialized. This change marked the shift of innovation actors in China's NIS from research institutions and SOEs to include enterprises, especially technology ventures. It brought about China's two-pronged approach to innovation: top-down policies that determine challenges with strategic significance and bottom-up entrepreneurship, especially in the consumer sector. China's innovation machine has been driven by the interplays of these two approaches since the turn of the century.

Especially early in this development, high-tech entrepreneurial start-ups often emerged and developed outside the framework of the existing institutional environment, which provides another case of institutional reforms to match the development of market-driven technological innovations, creating a virtuous cycle.[5] Technology entrepreneurship naturally moves ahead of institutional reforms; and institutional actors reacted to such entrepreneurial activities by rectifying policies and governance regimes. This is not to say that there have been no mistakes in China's institutional regime. On the contrary, there can be higher growth in industries where there is little proactive institutional intervention. For example, Shenzhen's success in transforming from a provincial region of small towns and fishing villages in the 1980s into a key manufacturing centre in China and a technology and innovation hub in the world can be attributed to the power of the market, in which entrepreneurs/enterprises are the main actors, supported by, but not led by, the government. Nevertheless, it is fair to claim that China's current national innovation system has been driven by technology-driven entrepreneurship step by step and developed gradually from bottom-up initiatives to top-down endorsement. Shenzhen's successful economic transformation is discussed in Chapter 7 in more detail; it holds valuable lessons for other regions considering spatial and economic transformation through technology entrepreneurship.

In the early years of the economic reforms, the majority of enterprises chose to acquire technology to build their innovative capacity rather than developing their own endogenously. The cases of Huawei and Lenovo, both of which exemplify Chinese technology-based entrepreneurship successes, illustrate differences in innovation strategies. Huawei, as China's flagship technological innovator, has adopted a tandem approach in its growth. The company developed its own technological capacity as one wheel driving its growth and expanded into the global market using its unique innovative approach as the other, the result of which is that Huawei has become a leading player in the communication industry.[6] This can be described as an 'innovation-industrialization-trading' model. On the other hand, Lenovo adopted a 'trading-industrialization-innovation' approach to benefit from China's rapidly growing market for personal computers, but did not pay sufficient attention to its own innovation capabilities. While the company won market share, it did not build its

---

[5] Zhang, 'Innovation Management in China'.

[6] L. Guo, M. Y. Zhang, M. Dodgson, D. Gann, and H. Cai (2018), 'Seizing Windows of Opportunity by Using Technology-Building and Market-Seeking Strategies in Tandem: Huawei's Sustained Catch-Up in the Global Market', *Asia Pacific Journal of Management*, 36: 849–79.

leadership in the computing industry, despite the acquisition of IBM's PC business in 2005.[7]

Mass Entrepreneurship and Innovation

Despite the development of technology entrepreneurship and its contribution to the national economy, it was not until February 2012 in the 'Notice of the State Council on Approving the Employment Promotion Plan (2011–2015)'[8] that the term 'entrepreneurship' was first linked with employment in an official document in China. It was not until 2014 in the 'Notice of the General Office of the State Council on Doing a Good Job in Organizing Entrepreneurship as an Employment Option for Graduates from Regular Colleges and Universities in the Country'[9] that the term entrepreneurship was promoted at the central government level as an engine for creating employment opportunities for university graduates.

Premier Li Keqiang first proposed 'mass entrepreneurship and mass innovation' as an engine for China's growth at the World Economic Forum's Summer Davos Forum in September 2014. In March 2015 the State Council officially embraced the concept of 'mass entrepreneurship and mass innovation' in the document 'Guiding Opinions of the General Office of the State Council on the Development of Makerspace to Promote Mass Entrepreneurship and Innovation'.[10] Between 2015 and 2018, the term 'entrepreneurship' was closely linked with innovation in thirty-three State Council documents. In 2015, for example, the State Council issued several policies and measures to promote 'mass entrepreneurship and mass innovation' which clearly aimed to stimulate creativity and develop innovation-driven entrepreneurship as a new national strategy for growth.

In 2018, the State Council reiterated the importance of promoting high-quality development based on innovation and entrepreneurship by emphasizing the leading role of innovative entrepreneurs in the country's growth, emphasizing the challenges China faced in trade conflicts with the US and the technology sanctions on China's technology industry by the US.

While innovative entrepreneurial start-ups are recognized as one of the driving forces behind technological changes in the modern economy, limited by liabilities of newness and smallness, they often face enormous challenges in becoming viable in the long term.[11] They are, however, crucial elements of the new growth driven by the internet and the new generation of IT technology, the popularization of internet applications, and the overwhelming process of digitalization and knowledge

---

[7]   360doc, 2018, 'Who is Winning? Huawei's "Innovation-Industrialization-Trading" vs Lenovo's "Trading-Industrialization-Innovation"', http://www.360doc.com/content/18/0418/20/37113458_746730862.shtml, accessed 28 July 2021 [Chinese online library].

[8]   See http://www.gov.cn/jrzg/2012-02/08/content_2061241.htm, accessed 29 July 2021.

[9]   See http://www.gov.cn/xinwen/2014-05/13/content_2678979.htm, accessed 29 July 2021.

[10]   See http://www.lawinfochina.com/display.aspx?id=21057&lib=law, accessed 28 July 2021.

[11]   M. Y. Zhang and M. Dodgson (2007), *High-Tech Entrepreneurship in Asia: Innovation, Industry and Institutional Dynamics in Mobile Payments*, Cheltenham: Edward Elgar.

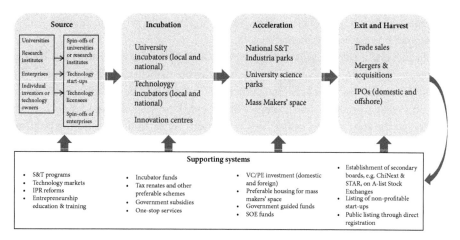

Figure 6.1 Technology-oriented entrepreneurship

accumulation which is the new normal in the digital age. The creative destruction of Schumpeterian growth through innovation has replaced economic growth driven by the capital and labour productivity factors of the industrialization age. China has embraced this change well. In this process, innovation-driven enterprises use emerging technologies and leverage their business model and institutional innovations to create new value for their customers and for society and the environment.

The model shown in Figure 6.1 summarizes China's efforts in enhancing technology entrepreneurship in its National Innovation System.

Sources of Technology

In the 1980s and 1990s, the 'last mile' of the commercial journey from research and knowledge to technology was one of the biggest barriers in China's NIS. A lack of an effective technology transfer system was the main reason for this deficiency. Of all policy frameworks, the legitimization of technology markets is the most critical in enhancing China's technology-oriented entrepreneurship. Technology markets refer to mechanisms in which technology transfer and commercialization are driven by market rules. Technology markets bridge technology supply and demand.

The establishment of technology markets in the late 1980s provided a channel for technology transfer and innovation commercialization from research institutes to those enterprises willing to pay for advanced technologies to boost productivity. As an intermediate arrangement, these technology markets were a unique Chinese institution which connected research institutes and enterprises during the country's economic transition from central planning to a market economy. These arrangements are still in place; however, there are many bottlenecks in this setting.

Policy ambiguity over the ownership of intellectual property is one of the most significant constraints faced by universities and research institutes in technology commercialization. An official at a university in Zhejiang, where technology entrepreneurship is active, commented:

If a successful enterprise is willing to pay 100,000 yuan for a scientific result from a university, but the relevant government departments believe that the value of the result should be worth at least 500,000 yuan. There would be a strong suspicion of the university's practice. For example, the relevant personnel could be accused of 'letting go the state-owned assets'. This is a serious accusation, often having political implications for individuals who are involved in the deal. Nobody is willing to take such a risk.[12]

Without a complete market mechanism in technology transfer, especially including technology valuations, scientific and technological achievements remain on paper.

Scientific and technological achievements are often intangible assets, and their value is commonly difficult to quantify. Their real value can only be realized after they are commercialized. According to the Science and Technology Evaluation Centre of the Ministry of Science and Technology, 688 of China's 3,200 universities and research institutes have established technology transfer centres. Only 307 of them are considered to play an important role in the transformation of science and technology into commercial products.

A scientific researcher at a university in Beijing made similar comments to his colleague at Zhejiang University. He said, 'China has a law to promote the transfer of scientific and technological achievements, but relevant documents clearly state that the profits from such transfers should be appropriated by the research institutions, rather than by the individual researchers.' To promote technology transfer and the commercialization of innovation, China needs to have new laws and regulations, especially on with whom and how to share the profits of technology transfer and commercialization. Reward systems in Chinese universities and research institutes are such that the quantity of publications weighs more for career promotion. In these circumstances it is pragmatic for researchers to pursue rapid promotion based on the quantity of publications, even if few contribute to science, as higher positions in the academic system mean greater prestige, more monetary awards and more resources. This practice, however, has long-term and often negative impacts on the country's innovation-oriented entrepreneurship. A reward system based on quality and long-term potential rather than on quantity would bring many benefits. Individual researchers should be encouraged and rewarded for pursuing research interests that carry risks but have long-term potential for technology transfer and commercialization. To achieve this, as Premier Li Keqiang said, China should establish its own Bayh-Dole Act to promote innovation-driven entrepreneurship.[13]

---

[12] According to our interview with the official, whose identity remains confidential.
[13] See http://www.gov.cn/xinwen/2016-02/18/content_5043447.htm, accessed 29 July 2021 [in Chinese].

Incubators and Accelerators for Technology Entrepreneurship

To boost technology entrepreneurship, the government provides financial and policy support to build incubators in different forms.

In the early years, most policies were opportunity-driven, aiming at creating a more favourable environment for technology entrepreneurship, including building information flows, capital, and technical support. Many technology incubators were created as a result. These incubators are often closely linked with university science parks, overseas returnee pioneer parks, national innovation centres, or specialized industrial incubators (e.g. in biotech, software, or new materials) and have attracted many innovation-oriented entrepreneurial start-ups. Zhongguancun Science Park in the university district of Beijing, for example, has received policy and capital support to improve its entrepreneurial environment and has become one of the most active innovation hubs in China.

University science parks are both the incubators for technology-based new ventures and centres around which many research institutes cluster. The intensity of science and technology talent is much higher than in other incubators. Some overseas returnee pioneer parks and university incubators have become national innovation centres authorized by the Ministry of Science and Technology. In 2018, there were 114 national-level university parks: 15 in Beijing, 13 in Shanghai, 15 in Jiangsu province, 6 in Zhejiang province, and 2 in Guangdong province. In 2019 the central government spent over $190 million on these national-level university parks, with over 57 per cent going to these five regions.[14]

China has also established a large number of technology incubators apart from science parks, mostly at local levels. As shown in Figure 6.2, the number of such incubators and the number of enterprises incubated grew rapidly after 2014.

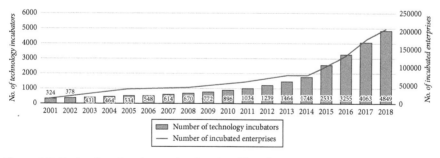

Figure 6.2 Technology incubators (national and local), 2001–18

Source: Compiled by the authors from the *Chinese Torch Program Statistical Yearbook* (2019)

---

[14] *Chinese Torch Program Statistical Yearbook* (2019), Beijing: China Statistic Press.

National-level technology incubators (about 20 per cent of the total in 2018) received the most incubator funds and their incubated enterprises obtained the most venture capital (VC) or other investments. The five most active regions in innovation-oriented entrepreneurship received the greatest amount of support, as shown in Table 6.1. These five regions accounted for 46 per cent of the total number of national incubators, and received 62 per cent of total incubator funds from the government, incubated 45 per cent of the total number of enterprises, employed 44 per cent of total employees, and generated 59 per cent of total income. In the five regions, 47 per cent of the incubated enterprises received VC or other investments, which accounted for three-quarters of the total VC or other investments. Jiangsu is the most active province among the five regions.

According to China's Torch Programme[15] under the administration of the Ministry of Science and Technology, at the national level, there were 52 Science and Technology Industrial Parks with 12,980 enterprises and 991,000 employees in 1995. In 2018, there were 169 such parks with over 120,000 enterprises and nearly 21 million employees (see Figure 6.3).

Incubators have proved to be the cradles of technology entrepreneurship, where entrepreneurs like to cluster. High-tech enterprises residing in incubators are also more likely to receive government financial and other support, and it is relatively easier for them to hire technologists, engineers and managers and access related professional services. The distribution of such resources is highly correlated to a region's economic development, number of educational institutions, and other complementary infrastructures. The rising prices of property in these regions will however be a constraint in the future.

Since 2015, China has established 'massmakers' space' as accelerators for technology entrepreneurship. By the end of 2018, there were nearly 7,000 such spaces countrywide, with the majority run by local governments, accommodating over 20 million (accumulated) tenant start-ups.[16] Table 6.2 summarizes basic statistics of China's massmakers' space.

Entrepreneurship Education

Compared to the development of the incubation and growth components of China's technology entrepreneurship framework, other supporting systems that link science and technology with industry such as IP enforcement, capital markets, and entrepreneurship education and training are relatively weak. The experience of developed countries such as the US, UK, and Israel suggests that the more comprehensive the

---

[15] The Torch Programme is China's most important programme of promoting high-tech industries. Launched in 1988, the programme provides an environment favorable to the development of new and high-tech industries, managing science and technology industrial parks and technology business incubators.

[16] *China's Science and Technology Statistics Yearbook,* 2019. Beijing: China Statistics Press.

Table 6.1 National-level technology incubators in five regions (2018)

	Number of incubators	Number of incubators (% by region)	Total incubator funds (billion yuan)	Total incubator funds (% by region)	Number of incubatees	Number of incubatees (% by region)	Number of employees of incubatees	Number of employees of incubatees (% by region)	Total income of incubatees (billion yuan)	Total income of incubatees (% by region)	Number of incubatees obtained investment	Number of incubatees obtained VC or other investment (% by region)	Total amount of VC investment for incubatees (billion yuan)	Total amount of VC or other investment for incubatees (% by region)
Total	967	100.0%	49.93	100.0%	86,632	100.0%	1,346,893	100.0%	362.93	100.0%	6,396	100.0%	34.51	100.0%
Beijing	55	5.7%	16.58	33.2%	5,211	6.0%	105,107	7.8%	64.37	17.7%	421	6.6%	7.22	20.9%
Shanghai	47	4.9%	1.60	3.2%	3,446	4.0%	41,766	3.1%	12.09	3.3%	360	5.6%	5.17	15.0%
Jiangsu	175	18.1%	6.57	13.2%	15,916	18.4%	242,383	18.0%	70.00	19.3%	1,001	15.7%	6.01	17.4%
Zhejiang	68	7.0%	3.04	6.1%	6,271	7.2%	83,354	6.2%	17.14	4.7%	611	9.6%	2.68	7.8%
Guangdong	108	11.2%	3.26	6.5%	8,539	9.9%	130,322	9.7%	52.73	14.5%	642	10.0%	4.74	13.7%
Subtotal of the entrepreneurial active regions		46.8%		62.2%		45.5%		44.8%		59.6%		47.5%		74.8%

Source: Compiled by the authors from the *Chinese Torch Program Statistical Yearbook* (2019)

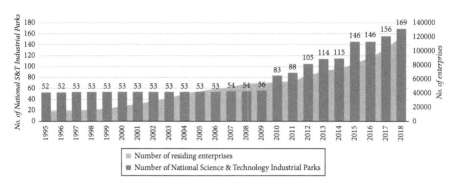

Figure 6.3 National Science and Technology Industrial Parks, 1995–2018
Source: Compiled by the authors from the *Chinese Torch Program Statistical Yearbook* (2019)

supportive technology-oriented entrepreneurship system is, the better the outcomes for technology-oriented entrepreneurship.

China's IP policy and enforcement will be discussed in Chapter 7, and China's reforms in the capital market in the next section of this chapter. Here we will briefly discuss China's entrepreneurship education and training. Traditionally, China's higher education emphasizes rote learning. Pedagogy and classroom teaching are limited to teachers imparting information to students. Graduates from such a system often have a solutions-oriented mentality that centres around what they have learned and what they know. Such a mentality militates against solving unknown problems; a workforce with such a mentality is unprepared for the demands of 'mass entrepreneurship and mass innovation'.

The practice of entrepreneurship in the digital age has changed, which calls for changes in the way it is taught and learnt. One of the most significant changes is that future employment is shifting to smaller firms with more specialized makers, innovators, and entrepreneurs who can often work and learn from anywhere. To survive and thrive in the digital age, graduates need to develop practical problem-solving skills, be able to collaborate with others, be resilient and flexible, and have an interdisciplinary approach. Central to these skill sets are creativity and the ability to confront and define emerging and uncertain problems. This requires new teaching methods and means. Around 2010, Chinese universities and training organizations started their own experiments in entrepreneurship education, which centred on the debate whether entrepreneurship education is for educational or entrepreneurial purposes?

Experiential learning with a focus on improving practical ability based on real-life projects has been introduced into China's entrepreneurship education curriculum, requiring students to move beyond pre-existing learning traditions, boundaries, and frameworks. This method is very different from learning in traditional Chinese classrooms. Universities, especially those in the five entrepreneurially active regions, have embraced this method. Tsinghua University's X-Lab provides a case in point. The 'X' in 'X-Lab' has a double meaning: it represents an unknown variable in

Table 6.2 China's massmakers' space, 2017–18

Statistics of Massmakers' Space	2017	2018
Number of Massmakers' Spaces with Data (unit)	5,739	6,959
National Massmakers' space	1,976	1,889
Non-National Massmakers' space	3,763	5,070
Space Area (sq. m)	25,226,824	33,837,046
Number of Service Personnel	105,218	145,412
Number of Serviced Entrepreneurial Groups or Start-Ups	237,126	238,969
Number of Tenant Groups	115,010	126,498
Number of Serviced Start-Ups	182,462	169,541
Government Funds Received (million USD)	470	480
Number of Groups and Start-Up s That Received VC or Other Investment	18,410	19,045
Amount of Investment Received by Groups and Start-Ups (million USD)	101	113
Accumulated Amount of Investment Received by Groups and Start-Ups (billion yuan)	169.15	380.26
Number of Employees by Groups and Start-Ups (million person)	1.73	1.60
Number of Recruited University Graduates	466,654	287,627
Number of Valid IPRs Held by Tenants	152,286	227,799
Number of Invention Patents by Tenants	33,449	41,798

Source: Compiled by the authors from *China's Science and Technology Statistical Yearbook* (2019)

mathematics; it also means 'crossing' in English. So, X-Lab means 'exploring the unknown in an interdisciplinary laboratory'. The word 'laboratory' means 'action-oriented learning and teamwork'.[17]

X-Lab relies on practical and experiential learning taught by teachers from various colleges and departments, as well as entrepreneurs and investors. 'The educational platform of Tsinghua X-Lab is positioned at the discovery and training of creative, innovative, and entrepreneurial talents.'[18] Its value derives from three aspects: first, the integration of multiple disciplines across fifteen schools and colleges on campus covering science, engineering, medicine, liberal arts, art, and other subjects; second, the combination of various external resources, including professional institutions, the investment community, and entrepreneurs; third, the provision of business opportunities for student-led projects to find ways and paths to realize their commercial and social value. The X-Lab is run by Tsinghua School of Economics and Management, which has unique disciplinary advantages and connections with a wide array of external resources. Venture capital investors and entrepreneurs from Silicon Valley in the US and China's equivalent—Zhongguancun Science Park—have been invited to teach courses such as 'Innovation and Entrepreneurship: China-US New Observations', 'Innovation and Entrepreneurship: Silicon Valley Insights', and 'Innovation and Entrepreneurship: China's Insights'.

---

[17] One of the authors participated in the preparation of X-Lab and worked as a mentor on the platform at an early stage of its operations.
[18] http://www.x-lab.tsinghua.edu.cn/, accessed 6 June 2021.

To encourage students engaging in innovation-oriented entrepreneurship, universities also help students participate in competitions at national and provincial levels in entrepreneurship and innovation, such as business model contests, international innovation contests, and innovation and entrepreneurship for the internet contests. The winners of these competitions receive seed funds or VC investments and other forms of support for their technology ventures.

According to a judge in the 'University Students Competition for China's Internet Plus Innovation and Entrepreneurship', which began in 2015 and is led by the Ministry of Education, the competitions attracted over 2.65 million participants in 2018 (out of nearly 30 million students in the university system). Contests start at the university level, with the winners moving up to participate in city-, then provincial-, and, finally, national-level competitions. The majority of students are in sciences and engineering and receive special entrepreneurship training in addition to the regular entrepreneurship education they receive from their universities. Most prizes are provided by successful entrepreneurs and enterprises. Successful student groups have received VC investments and generate millions of RMB in revenue.[19]

Through these competitions, students develop a problem-oriented mentality in their entrepreneurial approach; they understand that a technology venture starts from solving a problem faced by targeted customers rather than from what they have in their toolbox of existing knowledge or experiences. 'The competition awards those with such mentality,' an interviewee commented.

Entrepreneurship education in China is clearly for entrepreneurial purposes and has become an integral part of China's technology entrepreneurship framework.

The Capital Market for Technology Entrepreneurship

Many of China's policies aiming to drive innovation through entrepreneurship would have become a simple slogan without the support of the capital market. One lesson that China has learned from the US is the 'marriage between technology and capital' model in which technology start-ups are funded by angel investors and venture capital for rapid growth.[20] Well-intentioned top-down policies for technology entrepreneurship could not achieve their goals without a market-oriented capital market. Hence the government has made a major commitment to reforming China's capital market to address a previous lack of effective mechanisms to match capital with innovative ideas and talent. Figure 6.4 summarizes the evolution of China's capital market, including critical milestones and key events in the primary market and the secondary market.

[19] The author's interview with the competition judge in Beijing in December 2019.
[20] Interview with a senior government official in policy research at China's Securities Regulatory Commission.

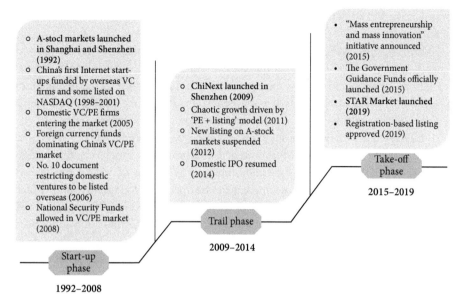

○ A-stocl markets launched in Shanghai and Shenzhen (1992)
○ China's first Internet start-ups funded by overseas VC firms and some listed on NASDAQ (1998–2001)
○ Domestic VC/PE firms entering the market (2005)
○ Foreign currency funds dominating China's VC/PE market
○ No. 10 document restricting domestic ventures to be listed overseas (2006)
○ National Security Funds allowed in VC/PE market (2008)

○ ChiNext launched in Shenzhen (2009)
○ Chaotic growth driven by 'PE + listing' model (2011)
○ New listing on A-stock markets suspended (2012)
○ Domestic IPO resumed (2014)

• "Mass entrepreneurship and mass innovation" initiative announced (2015)
• The Government Guidance Funds officially launched (2015)
• STAR Market launched (2019)
• Registration-based listing approved (2019)

Take-off phase

2015–2019

Trail phase

2009–2014

Start-up phase

1992–2008

Figure 6.4 The evolution of China's capital market

Source: Compiled by the authors from secondary sources such as government documents and critical events reported in the media

Public Capital Market

There are three critical milestones in the development of China's capital market: the establishment of its A-share markets in both Shanghai and Shenzhen in 1992, the launch of Nasdaq-style ChiNext in Shenzhen in 2009, and the launch of STAR Market in Shanghai in 2019.

ChiNext is an important component of China's multi-tier capital market system. As an independent secondary board, ChiNext offers a new capital platform for ventures engaged in independent innovation and other growing ventures. It provides different mechanisms in financing, investment, and risk management from the main boards of A-share stock exchanges. Most importantly, ChiNext provides a new exit route for venture capital investment in China's technology entrepreneurs. In contrast to the US Nasdaq, however, ChiNext requires profits before a venture can be listed, which is a high barrier to entrepreneurial exit.

In July 2019, the Shanghai Stock Exchange Science and Technology Innovation Board (known as STAR Board) was established, aiming to finance China's most promising technology ventures. The STAR Market prioritizes 'hard technology' firms and has promised a fast route for listing for ventures in six sectors: next-generation infotech, the internet of things, artificial intelligence, big data, biotech, and new energy. It competes with the Hong Kong Stock Exchange, and its launch was designed to attract Chinese tech unicorns (billion-dollar start-ups) to list on the mainland.[21]

Both ChiNext and STAR markets have also introduced market-friendly reforms encouraging so-called 'red chip' companies[22]—enterprises that have their businesses based on the mainland but are incorporated offshore—to relist in the mainland or Hong Kong.[23] Registration-based public offering rules which enable faster Initial Public Offering vetting on these new boards are expected to be implemented.

Building capital markets has a long learning curve and can take many years until tangible effects are realized. Most watershed reforms in Chinese capital markets began in 2019/2020. Although the establishment of STAR was a critical equity market reform, it remains unknown how much it can be opened to foreign investors, which would improve pricing and liquidity on the exchange and bring best-in-class risk management practices. The China Securities and Regulatory Commission announced that, from 1 November 2020, international investors would be allowed to trade in China's public capital markets. This rule is seen as a new liberalization of China's tightly controlled financial system.

Venture Capital and Private Equity Funds

While the secondary capital market provides an open marketplace for the public to participate in the growth of entrepreneurial ventures, innovation also needs capital from the primary markets such as investments from VC and private equity (PE) funds to share the visions and the risks of innovative entrepreneurs with breakthrough technologies and business models. The primary capital market, VC in particular, has played a vital role in entrepreneurship and innovation.

Unlike the US and other more developed countries where VC has been small component in technological breakthroughs relative to corporate expenditures in R&D, China has developed its own VC/PE market, which has become an integral part of China's technology entrepreneurship.

As shown in Figure 6.4, China experienced a long start-up phase for its VC/PE development. Before 2009, this market was dominated by foreign currency funds.

[21] J. Fioretti (2020), 'China's Star Board among the World's Top Three IPO Venues', *Bloomberg*, 3 August, https://www.bloomberg.com/news/articles/2020-08-03/china-s-star-board-among-world-s-top-three-ipo-venues-ecm-watch, accessed 6 June 2021.

[22] China's national telecommunications operations, China Mobile, China Telecom and China Unicom, are among the earliest such 'red chip' companies that were listed on New York Stock Exchange. In May 2021, these three companies announced that they would be delisted from NYSE upon the results of appeal. If unsuccessful, they would consider relisting on either A-Stock on Hong Kong Stock Exchange. See https://www.reuters.com/business/media-telecom/three-chinese-telecom-companies-be-delisted-by-nyse-2021-05-07/, accessed 29 July 2021.

[23] G. Lee (2020), 'ChiNext, Star Market, China's Rival Tech Boards, Target Hong Kong "Red Chip" Secondary Listings as Competition Heats Up', *South China Morning Post*, 15 August, https://www.scmp.com/business/banking-finance/article/3097449/chinext-star-market-chinas-rival-tech-boards-target-hong, accessed 6 June 2021.

IDG Capital from the US, SoftBank from Japan, and several institutional investors from Hong Kong and Taiwan were the first VC firms to enter China.

The year 2005 marked a turning point in China's VC market. Local VC firms were formed and began to invest in China's technology ventures. It was not easy, however, for local VC funds to harvest from their non-tradable shares in their invested ventures. On 29 April 2005, the Chinese Securities Regulatory Commission issued a 'Notice on Issues Related to the Pilot Share-Trading Reform of Listed Companies', which provided local VC investors with an exit route on the secondary capital markets in China. Since then, the local VC market has become a major player in China's venture financing.

On 8 August 2006, led by the Ministry of Commerce, six ministries jointly published the 'Regulations on the Acquisitions of Domestic Enterprises by Foreign Investors' (known as the 'No. 10 Document'), which imposed constraints on domestic ventures backed by foreign currency funds to be listed on overseas stock exchanges and restricted what was deemed to be malicious mergers and acquisitions of leading domestic firms by foreign investors. The impact of the 'No. 10 Document' was profound, with indirect listing on overseas stock exchanges becoming difficult. Despite these constraints, China's internet boom attracted international investment giants such as Blackstone and KKR. The total VC/PE investment in China reached $1.778 billion by 2006, a 52 per cent increase on the previous year, and foreign currency funds managed to have their invested ventures listed overseas, largely through offshore shareholding arrangements.[24]

In April 2008, the National Development and Reform Commission approved the National Social Security Fund participating in China's lucrative VC/PE market, by investing independently in industrial funds and market-oriented equity investment funds. This fund had nearly $7.2 billion to invest. In 2010, several regulations liberalized the restrictions on insurance funds participating in equity investments, allowing 3 per cent of total insurance assets (roughly $30 billion) into the VC/PE market. The participation of the National Social Security Fund and the insurance funds in China's VC/PE markets ended the dominance of US funds in China.

The consequence of such relaxation in policy led to a turbulent period between 2009 and 2014. The industry moved back to regulated growth in 2014, when the government issued a series of measures to restrict the participation of mergers and acquisitions funds, property funds, and other private equity funds in the VC/PE market.

Between 2015 and 2019, China's VC/PE market was dominated by domestic funds. The second largest market in the world, China's VC/PE fundraising nearly tripled between 2015 and 2017, in large part driven by government-led funds.

Figure 6.5 shows the changes in the composition and amounts in China's VC/PE market from 2007 to 2018.

[24] D. Ahlstrom, G. Bruton and K. Yeh (2007). 'Venture Capital in China: Past, Present, and Future', Asia Pacific Journal of Management, 24: 247-68. DOI: 10.1007/s10490-006-9032-1.

(a)

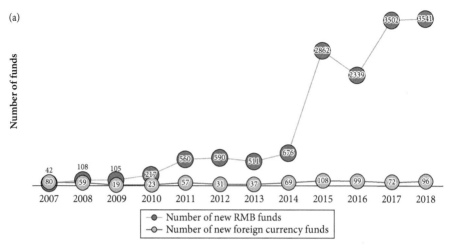

Figure 6.5a RMB vs foreign currency funds (number of funds), 2007–18

(b)

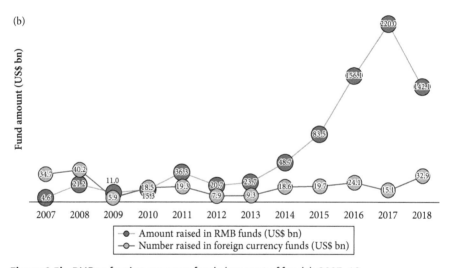

Figure 6.5b RMB vs foreign currency funds (amount of funds), 2007–18

Note: The average exchange rates of USD/RMB from the List of World Bank nominal exchange rates were used. From 2007 to 2018 they were 7.61, 6.95, 6.83, 6.71, 6.46, 6.31, 6.15, 6.16, 6.28, 6.65, 6.89, and 6.98.

Source: Adapted from Zero2IPO Research (2019); data from Pitchbook and PEdata

Government-Led Funds

Government funds in China include national fiscal funds, credit-guaranteed bank loans, VC, and other market-driven financing channels aiming to initiate and nurture the growth of technology entrepreneurship. Government investment funds, so-called 'Funds of Funds' and 'Government Guidance Funds', have been a major source for VC/PE since 2019. In first-tier cities, the government funds are often matched with capital from other investors such as SOEs and private enterprise investors.

The Government Guidance Fund was first used in 2002 to finance Zhongguancun Science Park in the form of an industrial investment fund established by the central government to upgrade the country's industrial structure and accelerate the development of its industries with strategic significance. Such funds officially became the Government Guidance Fund approved by the National Development and Reform Commission in 2005.[25]

The Government Guidance Fund, comprised of 1,686 such funds set up by governments and state-owned enterprises at all levels, had invested over $670 billion in government-sponsored venture funds by the end of 2018.[26] These 'guidance funds' use state money to guide private VC/PE firms to invest in industries with national significance by non-controlling stakes. Between 2015 and 2018, China's VC/PE market experienced a boom, with one effect being overpriced ventures. Despite a looming trade war and Chinese government restrictions on capital outflow, China-based VC/PE funds and corporate investments continue to pump a vast amount into technology entrepreneurship into areas such as biotech start-ups and AI-equipped robotics.

As government investment funds are required to minimize financial risks, they are less effective in supporting innovative but risky ventures. These funds tend to avoid projects with high risk in the short term but high potential in the long term. Government investors, nearly half of which are government departments or investment arms of SOEs, are risk-averse, preferring to invest in late-stage projects which have proven successful:

> For example, some government investors believe that it is safe to lend to state-owned enterprises, but lending to private enterprises, especially entrepreneurial start-ups, is politically risky. Their investment philosophy is to do nothing rather than avoid making political mistakes. This perception and practice can be detrimental to technology entrepreneurship.[27]

As a consequence, this investment strategy often leads to an abundance of money for those that do not need financing, but little or none for those that need seeding or growth funds. While generous investment can create the slack that stimulates creativity, it can also lead to wasteful duplication as multiple companies pursue the same limited opportunity in the same manner.

The government has accepted that markets should play a decisive role in allocating resources and that the government's role should be limited to supporting the market.

[25] T Ziyi and X. Xiaoli (2020), 'Four Things to Know about China's $670 Billion Government Guidance Funds', Caixin, 25 February, https://www.caixinglobal.com/2020-02-25/four-things-to-know-about-chinas-670-billion-government-guidance-funds-101520348.html, accessed 6 June 2021.

[26] *China VC/PE Market Review 2018*. Zero2IPO Research, February 2019. https://report.pedata.cn/1550832271140000.html, accessed 28 July 2021.

[27] Interview with a former IBM executive who was in charge of the firm's government relations in Beijing in June 2019.

After-school private education is a good case in point. Over 12,700 organizations were created in this field in the decade from 2010, with over 4,000 backed by VC/PE funds and many successfully listed in New York.[28] As a result, a private secondary education system is challenging the formal education system. The government's restrictions barring private education providers from making profits led to drops in value of those listed overseas.[29] While the policy is adaptive and pragmatic at the infancy of new business models, intervening and rectifying measures are often taken when the market start to challenge the formal institutions.

As the former head of China's Securities Regulatory Commission, Xiao Gang, pointed out in a speech on institutional reforms in China's finance, 'The role of the capital market is to build a bridge between technology and industry.' He emphasized that 'the Chinese stock exchange markets must embrace the mission of serving entrepreneurship and innovation. This is the ultimate goal of institutional reforms in the capital market…The development of an industry must have technological innovation behind it. Capital is behind the R&D and technological innovation.'[30]

However, how to interpret what the government says requires political and cultural judgement by Chinese entrepreneurs. While China seems to be partially liberalizing its financial system and letting the market choose the winners in innovation and entrepreneurship, policymakers are also adjusting their policy instruments to ensure the safety and stability of the financial system. Two days before Ant Group's dual listing in both Shanghai and Hongkong, which was expected to raise over $37 billion for the world largest fintech venture, the IPO was suspended. A spin-off of Alibaba, Ant Group runs China's mobile payment platform Alipay and a host of innovative financial services for SMEs/micro enterprises and consumers in loans, insurance, user credits, etc. Weeks before this, Alibaba's and Ant Group's founder Jack Ma openly criticized China's state-owned banks for operating with a 'pawnshop mentality' at Bund Financial Summit in Shanghai [31]. Judging by the dates of the events, one could easily conclude that Ma's speech might have led to the suspension of the lucrative IPO. However, it would have taken more than one day to deliberate and draft a document as significant as this one. So Ma's speech was more likely responding to this imminent regulation, which could have significant and profound impact on the firm's IPO. In fact, Ma's innovative business models often challenged the status quo of the existing institutional settings, and, once the business models were accepted by the market, they would trigger institutional reforms which would make the innovative practices legitimate. Whether Ma has the same luck this time remains to be seen.[32] This will be explained in further detail in Chapter 7 in the discussion about China's institutional logics.

---

[28] See https://www.itjuzi.com/edu/atlas/597, accessed 29 July 2021.
[29] Financial Times. 2021. 'China's education sector crackdown hits foreign investors', https://www.ft.com/content/dfae3282-e14e-4fea-aa5f-c2e914444fb8, accessed 29 July 2021.
[30] See https://finance.sina.com.cn/stock/zqgd/2020-07-08/doc-iirczymm1187749.shtml, accessed 6 June 2021.
[31] See https://www.youtube.com/watch?v=dGYL3nTRv6w, accessed 6 June 2021.
[32] Major media outlets including *People's Daily* have reported and commented on this event.

Unicorns

The concept of a unicorn venture was first introduced by the American venture investor Aileen Lee in 2013.[33] Unicorn, a fictional creature in myths and legends, resembles a white horse with a spiral horn on its head. The appearance of the unicorn signifies the arrival of fortune and glory in both Eastern and Western legends. According to Lee's definition, unicorn ventures are typically less than 10 years old, but have reached a market value of $1 billion or more. The number of unicorns in a country is one measure of its activities in new and high-technology industry. The US and China have the largest numbers of unicorns in the world. According to Hurun Global Unicorn Index 2020, the total number of unicorns in the world reached 586, an increase of 92 from the year before. These start-ups are based in 29 countries in 145 cities, with 80 per cent selling software and services, 60 per cent consumer products/services, and 5 per cent in traditional sectors. The US had 233 unicorns, just ahead of China's 227, and the 2 countries made up 79 per cent of the world's total. The EU, India, and South Korea followed the US and China in unicorn numbers.[34]

If a unicorn's market value is more than $10 billion, it is considered a super unicorn. According to Hurun Global Unicorn Index, China and the US also dominate the super unicorn club. The top ten are Ant Group (China), ByteDance (China), Didi Chuxing (China), Lufax (China), SpaceX (US), Stripe (US), Airbnb (US), Kuaishou (China), Cainiao (China), and Palantir (US), in descending order of estimated valuation.[35] The US venture capital firm Sequoia Capital is the world's biggest investor in unicorns with stakes in ninety-two, followed by China's Tencent Holdings and Japan's Softbank as the second and third largest investors in unicorns, with forty-six and forty-two respectively. Ten cities, Beijing (93), San Francisco (68), Shanghai (47), New York City (33), Hangzhou (20), Shenzhen (20), London (16), Palo Alto (12), Nanjing (11), and Redwood (10) host the most unicorns.[36]

Compared to those in other countries, Chinese unicorns have several characteristics. First, almost 60 per cent of Chinese unicorns are less than 6 years old and 35 per cent are less than 4 years old. It takes four years, on average, for Chinese unicorns to reach this status; while American ones normally take seven years.[37] Second, about

---

[33] A. Lee (2013), 'Welcome to the Unicorn Club: Learning From Billion-Dollar Startups', 3 November, *TechCrunch*, https://techcrunch.com/2013/11/02/welcome-to-the-unicorn-club/?guccounter=1&guce_referrer=aHR0cHM6Ly93d3cuZ29vZ2xlLmNvbS88&guce_referrer_sig=AQAAAMMzs85Ay-jXRbq9SnTHL_nJycN6RjT61LEPOaGSnFDWwCdxUETnlGPZs37uFpBEUuOGzI5VNshtcKXO-eB7oxn-aeAA9Plm2Ahin7qTtJizcUhHcowsxC-jeHoy5yU_mJKGnafLhgWfQgFqfTKFFaCqWiX-YqQavuwoCA5m6raQV, accessed 6 June 2021.
[34] Hurun (2020), 'Hurun Global Unicorn Index', https://www.hurun.co.uk/hurun-global-unicorn-index-2020-full-report.php, accessed 6 June 2021.
[35] Since the publication of this list, Didi (DiDi), Lufax (LU), Airbnb (ABNB) and Kuaishou (1024.HK) have been listed either in New York or Hong Kong.
[36] See https://www.statista.com/statistics/1062457/cities-highest-number-of-unicorns/, accessed 29 July 2021.
[37] Credit Suisse (2020), 'China Unicorns: Emerging from the Stables', *APAC Equity Research Reports*, 4 May 2020, https://www.credit-suisse.com/cn/en/content-hub/equity-research.html, accessed 6 June 2021.

40 per cent of Chinese unicorns were founded by the generation born in the 1980s or later. Third, Chinese unicorns concentrate in the following five industries: entertainment and media, new energy vehicles and transport services, e-commerce, financial technology, and medical and healthcare. Fourth, Chinese unicorns are concentrated in Beijing, Shanghai, Hangzhou and Shenzhen. Fifth, most of the unicorns are located in national high-tech parks.

Unicorns thrive in a breeding ground of entrepreneurship ecosystems (such as geographical clusters, discussed in Chapter 4) and innovation ecosystems (such as digital platforms, discussed in Chapter 5) to access complete industry value chains and supportive infrastructure, especially complementary assets and partners. This explains why the majority of Chinese unicorns are concentrated in the national high-tech parks in the cities that are economically more developed and have more mature manufacturing industry value chains, a higher concentration of universities, more preferential policies to attract talent and capital, and better public infrastructures. Apart from these basic conditions, another critical condition is the co-location of leading enterprises such as Alibaba in Hangzhou, Tencent in Shenzhen, ByteDance and Baidu in Beijing, and Meituan Dianpin in Shanghai, which form centres of gravity of technology entrepreneurship in those cities. This can be seen in the industry focuses of the unicorns. For example, unicorns in Hangzhou concentrate on e-commerce or internet finance, surrounding Alibaba's digital ecosystem; in Beijing they concentrate on culture, big data, and AI, surrounding Baidu and ByteDance; unicorns in Shanghai cluster on in Internet+ and consumer markets, surrounding Meituan; and in Shenzhen they are in media, surrounding Tencent.

Policy support plays an important role in a city's breeding ground for unicorns. In Nanjing, for example, in order to enhance the city's innovation capacity and cultivate more unicorns, in April 2018 the city government issued its own definition of unicorns: annual income should be no less than 5.5 million RMB (about $830,000) and the growth rate no less than 50 per cent for three consecutive years in areas related to new-generation IT, new energy vehicles, high-end intelligent equipment, biopharmaceuticals, and new materials for energy conservation and environmental protection. In contrast to other cities, the Nanjing government does not offer cash rewards; rather, it provides support to the unicorns, according to its own definition, through platforms—regional clusters or hubs—on which resources can be mobilized and shared. As a result, Nanjing is catching up rapidly in its number of unicorns.

These super-platform firms are also active venture capital investors in China's unicorns. At the early stage of China's internet boom, the nation's top three internet players, namely Baidu, Alibaba, and Tencent, were critically important investors in China's corporate VC for tech start-ups. Founded in the late 1990s, these big three companies successfully built their empires in search engines, e-commerce, and social networks, but expanded their ecosystems covering payments, cloud computing, and digital entertainment through cross investments. Importantly, they seized the opportunity in the mobile internet age and invested in the rise of new ventures in big data, AI, O2O, and the sharing economy through their corporate venture capital investment. JD.com has also joined this corporate VC club.

Spin-offs from the super-platform firms discussed in Chapter 5 have become a new way of generating unicorns in China. In 2018, about 50 per cent of unicorns were related to super-platform firms. Among them, twenty-seven were related to Alibaba, thirty-seven to Tencent, and sixteen to Baidu.[38] Relying on the platform companies' capital, user bases, online traffic, complementary assets, and other resources, the unicorn companies have a born advantage in cross-platform network effects and are more likely to enjoy rapid growth. Just as platform firms are breeding grounds for unicorns in China, the unicorns spun off from the super platforms have become important complementary platforms/components to their parent's ecosystems, as discussed in Chapter 5.

The number of unicorn companies shows the improvement in China's overall innovation strength, which is the result of China's policy initiatives that promote technology entrepreneurship. In summary, the formula that enables young technology entrepreneurs to grow billion-dollar ventures in a short space of time is 'technological innovation + platform ecosystem + high-tech parks + capital and policy support'. In contrast to the tech ventures in the early days of China's internet boom that developed their markets in China by being copycats of business models in the US and other more developed countries, the younger generation of technology entrepreneurs create their own business models and deliver sustainable profitability for their investors.

Most of these unicorns affect their industries in a profound way, as these companies often represent new trends in their industries which have spillover effects in upstream and downstream industries and internationally.

AI represents a new growth engine for China's unicorns in the future. Table 6.3 profiles some potential Chinese unicorns. They concentrate in technology-oriented high-end manufacturing and AI applications, such as AI chips, robotics, big data, computer visuals, biotech, and cloud computing.

Technology, Talent, and Capital: The Emergence of the Biotechnology/Biopharmaceutical Industry

The case of biotechnology/biopharmaceuticals illustrates how new industries have emerged and developed from technology entrepreneurship in China.

China has a deep capacity for manufacturing basic pharmaceuticals built upon international exchange and cooperation in the development and modification of relatively mature drugs. Since 2016, China's policy framework for developing its biotechnology/pharmaceutical industry has emphasized indigenous innovation. Apart

---

[38] IT Juzi, 2019: see https://www.itjuzi.com/, accessed 6 June 2021.

Table 6.3 AI unicorns

Company Name	Company Profile
DJI Innovations	Founded by Wang Tao in 2006 in Shenzhen, DJI is a global leader by market share in civilian drones and aerial imaging technology. DJI's unmanned aerial vehicles (UAVs), commonly known as drones, are used by individual consumers as well as professionals in film-making, agriculture, conservation, construction, search and rescue, energy infrastructure, and so on. DJI's success can be attributed to the related industry value chains in Shenzhen. For example, the main material of UAV carbon fibre comes from the supply of carbon fibre that has been used in products such as fishing rods, tennis rackets, and badminton rackets, in the production of which China has accumulated expertise and capacity for decades. Another important component is sensors used in UAVs. China has accumulated innovation and production capacity from its experience in manufacturing sensors for camera lenses and smartphones over decades.
	Founding team: Wang Tao (founder and CEO) founded DJI in 2006 while pursuing his Master's degree at Hong Kong University of Science & Technology. Roger Luo (president) joined DJI in 2015 as operation vice president and was named as DJI's president in 2017. Previously, he has served in many hardware and software companies, including Apple, Foxconn, and Siemens. Focus: Hardware and AI in UAV https://www.dji.com/
Intellifusion	Founded by Dr Cheng Ning in Shenzhen in 2014, Intellifusion is an AI company focusing on 'non-cooperative' visual intelligence. Its products are used in public security, city governance, and new retail. Its public security solutions have been used in over 100 cities in mainland China and ASEAN countries. The company has over 30,000 networked front-end cameras deployed in over 20 cities, which have assisted in solving over 10,000 cases involving missing elderly people and children. Functionalities include entry controls with facial recognition, centralized equipment management, car number plate recognition, and centralized management systems using IoT and biometrics technology to increase the level of security and reduce costs.
	Founding team: Dr Chen Ning (founder, chairman, and CEO) earned a PhD in electrical engineering from the Georgia Institute of Technology. Dr Wang Xiaoyu (co-founder and chief scientist) obtained his Bachelor's degree from the University of Science and Technology of China, and his PhD and MS in electrical and computer engineering and statistics from the University of Missouri. He is a renowned specialist in facial recognition. He was a founding member of the Snap AI Lab and served as the chair of Computer Vision. Prior to joining Snapchat, he was a research staff member at the NEC Labs America. Focus: AI/Big Data/Robotics/Software https://www.intellif.com/

Linklogis	Founded in Shenzhen in 2016, Linklogis specializes in supply chain finance, helping SMEs gain access to timely and low-cost funding. It leverages technologies such as big data, AI, blockchain, and cloud computing to solve financing difficulties in lending to SMEs and micro suppliers. As of December 2019, Linklogis had helped arrange more than RMB10 bn to more than 10,000 SMEs and micro firms. Linklogis has engaged in collaboration with Tencent's fintech team, which launched the blockchain platform TrustSQL in April 2017.

Founding team:
Qun Song (founder and CEO) served as a finance strategy adviser for Tencent, prior founding Linklogis. Mr Song obtained an MBA from University of Melbourne in Australia and a Bachelor's degree in engineering from Huazhong University of Science and Technology of the PRC. He also served as the president and CEO of China Resources Bank in Zhuhai and as the global head of trust and agency services at HSBC.
Focus: Fintech
https://www.linklogis.com/#/

YITU Technology	Founded in Shanghai in 2012, YITU Technology is a leading AI research company that integrates advanced AI technology business applications to build a safer, faster, and healthier world. YITU now works in sectors such as security, finance, transportation, and medical and healthcare. YITU's visual intelligence algorithm covers facial recognition, vehicle identification, text recognition, target tracking, and feature-based image retrieval. Leveraging rich experience in computer vision and deep insights into urban transportation systems, YITU Tech has worked on the application of the City Data Hub. Using models built upon massive traffic data and urban transportation analysis, it manages to improve road utility and efficiency and help optimize urban traffic management in multiple levels and dimensions. YITU seeks breakthroughs in healthcare using AI technologies. It helps doctors to give accurate diagnoses, stipulate suitable treatment plans, and improve overall patient experience.

Founding team:
Dr Long Zhu (co-founder) received his PhD in statistics from the University of California, Los Angeles (UCLA). Dr Zhu specializes in statistical modelling of computer vision and AI. He was a postdoctoral fellow at MIT AI Laboratory, studying brain science and computational photography, and a research fellow in the Courant Mathematics Research Institute run by Yann Lecun, the founder of Deep Learning, at New York University.
Chenxi Lin (co-founder, CEO), a former senior expert at Ali Cloud of Alibaba, received his Master's degree from Shanghai Jiao Tong University in 2005. In 2002, Lin was selected as a member representing Shanghai Jiao Tong University to participate in the ACM-ICPC (Association for Computing Machinery International Collegiate Programming Contest). Before joining Alibaba Group, Lin worked with Microsoft Research Asia (MSRA) in the field of machine learning, computer vision, information retrieval, and distributed systems.
Focus: AI/big data/robotics/software
https://www.yitutech.com/en

Continued

Table 6.3 *Continued*

Company Name	Company Profile
Cambricon Technology	Cambricon started as an AI project in a computer laboratory at the Chinese Academy of Sciences (CAS). In 2016, Cambricon was co-founded by brothers Drs Chen Tianshi and Chen Yunji as a spin-off from CAS. It quickly became a leading AI chip designer, including for the supply chains of Huawei for its AI chip-powered smartphones. The company also designs core processor chips for various types of cloud servers, smart terminals, and intelligent robots. The company is expected to be listed on China's STAR Market with an estimate valuation of 2.8 billion RMB (about 400 million USD). *Founding team:* Dr Chen Tianshi (co-founder and CEO) and Dr Chen Yunji (co-founder) are both graduates of the University of Science and Technology of China (USTC). Dr Chen Tianshi, the younger brother, obtained his PhD in computer science from USTC, and the elder brother, Chen Yinji, received his doctoral training at the Chinese Academy of Science (CAS). Before co-founding Cambricon, the pair were AI researchers at CAS, where the elder brother still holds a faculty position. Focus: AI chips http://www.cambricon.com/
UBTech	UBTech is a leading global AI and humanoid robotics company founded by Mr Zhou Jian in Shenzhen in 2012. UBTech is the only unicorn start-up in the field of AI service robotics in China. Cooperating with Disney, UBTech launched AR interactive robot for the film *Star Wars: The Force Awakens*—the First Order Stormtrooper robot. It manufactures consumer humanoid robots, enterprise service robots, and STEM skill-building robots for children at home and in the classroom. Tencent is one of UBTech's early investors. Founding team: Mr Zhou Jian (founder and CEO) is considered the founding father of humanoid robots in China. Focus: service robots https://www.ubtrobot.com/?ls=en

Source: The information is from publicly available sources including the subject companies' websites, the founders' LinkedIn pages, media reports, and interviews

from policy support, a huge amount of capital has flowed into the biotechnology and biopharmaceutical industry since 2016. The major sources of financing in this industry are government guidance funds, VC/PE capital, and R&D expenditure by pharmaceutical firms. The government has utilized talent recruitment schemes such as the Thousand Talents Programme to recruit top scientists from overseas, especially those with a Chinese background, to join China's leading universities and research institutions, and technology start-ups. The combination of technology, capital, and talent is turning China into an innovative drug maker. As the European drug maker AstraZeneca recently commented, 'Much of [China's] innovation in the last three to four years has been "me too", but now on the horizon we can see first-in-class innovation.'[39] The Chinese government has determined that the next strategic area where the country should strengthen its position is as both a large-scale pharmaceutical manufacturer and an innovative drug developer/maker.

China's Advantages

Just as China has worked its way from largely being a copycat of Western technology and business models to the world's super-platform ecosystems in the internet, it aims to do the same in the medical and healthcare sectors. China has advantages to allow it to do so.

First, China's population means that, even for rare diseases, it has a large number of patients. From an investment perspective, China's market is attractive, even though the average treatment revenue per capita will remain low. This is very different from Western countries, especially the US, where the vast majority of investment is directed at drug R&D for a few diseases with large market potential. This situation is determined by its medical insurance system. As a result, there is a lack of incentive to develop new drugs for rare diseases, as their market potential is small, or the prospect is uncertain for them to be approved by the US Food and Drug Administration as treatable diseases, which means such drugs are unlikely to be covered by commercial insurance. Instead, investors are more interested in drugs for diseases that include age-related cancers and cardiovascular and metabolic diseases, which are more likely to affect people who can afford insurance. China may seize the opportunity and become a global leader in the development of new drugs and innovative therapies for rare diseases. One of our interviewees commented:

> We work on the applications in the treatment of rare diseases, and we have achieved effective results in animal (mice) models. However, these tools are invented by foreign scientists, and we do not own core patents. It is easier to experiment in animal models. However, it is challenging to apply gene editing technology in clinical trials and treatments on real patients. China's population certainly is a plus. Currently, the area is still unclear, in terms of policy.

So whereas the scale of the population provides advantages, unresolved regulatory issues remain.

Second, China's government-led security net for medical insurance, especially its payment mechanisms for medical services, means that the country's healthcare system is structured to pay for disease prevention. China has an ageing population, which means more people will need medical and healthcare services. Chronic

[39] T. Hancock (2019), 'AstraZeneca Backs $1bn China Biotech Fund for Smaller Ventures,' *Financial Times*, 5 November, https://www.ft.com/content/5727e4fc-ffe1-11e9-be59-e49b2a136b8d, accessed 6 June 2021.

diseases, such as diabetes, and cardiovascular and neurological disorders are common conditions in elderly populations, and investments in building on China's strengths in diagnostic platforms as contributors to preventive medicine will help the ageing population.

Third, China's advantages in digital technologies, especially AI and big data analytics, mean that Chinese firms are moving towards the forefront in areas such as precision medicine (treatments tailored to an individual's genes, environment, and lifestyle) using AI and other digital technologies. Tencent and Baidu, for example, have jointly invested in the deep learning-based drug discovery start-up Atomwise. Baidu also invested in Engine Bioscience, an AI-based healthcare start-up. Such investment projects complement these internet firms' digital ecosystems, as well as leveraging their digital and AI advantages to advance pharmaceutical development. Digital technology is vital in new drug development and precision medicine. A respondent who is a bioinformatics expert summarized its advantages:

> Digital technology can reduce the time required to develop a new drug from ten years to two to three years;...it can quickly screen the population that is most suitable for a certain drug, which provides a basis for personalized treatment. Without the aid of digital technology, a cancer patient may need three or four attempts to find the most effective treatment plan. Relying on digital technology can accurately match the patient's genetic attributes with the most suitable drugs, which can achieve the best treatment efficacy with the lowest possible side effects and at the lowest possible costs. This is also the most exciting part of digital technology.

Fourth, China's relatively more relaxed institutional environment in biotechnology, bioengineering, and biopharmaceuticals can attract large numbers of researchers and investments for cutting-edge innovations. Chinese universities and research institutions and businesses, including incumbent pharmaceutical manufacturers and new ventures in biotechnology and biopharmaceuticals, are all actively recruiting talent, especially Chinese returnees. One of the world's leading immunologists, Dr Liu Yongjun, for example, who has a rich experience in both academia (including as a professor at the University of Texas MD Anderson Cancer Centre) and industry (including leading Sanifo's global R&D), recently joined Innovent Biologics, a Hong Kong listed venture in new drug development. Dr Liu commented:

> We are at a golden age of biopharmaceutical development. China is among the innovative forces of this age. I am touched by Innovent's mission of 'developing high-quality medicines that are affordable by ordinary patients'. I am very happy to be a member of this pragmatic and innovative company. I hope to work with everyone to contribute to the development of more innovative drugs that can benefit patients around the world.[40]

---

[40] See Innovent (http://innoventbio.com/en/#/, accessed 15 October 2020).

Fifth, China's technological innovation is contingent upon its self-regenerating capability in ancillary innovation, which, in some areas, is more important than technology itself. In the past, for example, China had to send samples to the US or Europe for DNA testing. China now leads in the speed and efficiency of DNA sequencing and testing. During the Covid-19 pandemic, for example, DNA and RNA tests were conducted on the entire population in cities such as Wuhan, Beijing, and Qingdao at a rate of 10 million tests per week. Its scientific competence is also seen in the case of Covid-19. According to the World Health Organization, the local government in Wuhan reported a cluster of pneumonia on 31 December 2019, which it eventually identified as a novel coronavirus. Other respiratory pathogens having been ruled out, Covid-19 was isolated on 7 January. China shared the generic sequence of Covid-19 on 12 January, which was crucial in the global search for a vaccine.[41]

China's Bottlenecks

China still faces enormous challenges to achieving its goal of becoming an innovative drug maker, especially in R&D and innovation in biotechnology. An official statement from the Ministry of Science and Technology admitted that 'China lacks original scientific discoveries and disruptive technologies, has a weak research base in areas like biological big data, and lacks independent intellectual property rights.' As discussed in Chapter 2, from 2018 to 2020, China's scientific outputs in life sciences caught up rapidly, ranking second after the US (the same as in earth and environmental science and physics, and it leads in chemistry).

The biopharmaceutical industry has distinct characteristics that make it a complex and volatile area for R&D and innovation, including its high-risk, high-investment, uncertain technology and long cycle of development. Many start-up firms in the Chinese biopharmaceutical industry are founded by scientists who have achieved certain scientific results, but will need to overcome many challenges to commercialize their scientific achievements. There is a long distance from laboratory to hospital and pharmacy. Supportive policy, capital, and experienced managers are needed to make such transitions, which also rely on mature ecosystems that China does not possess. The US, on the other hand, has a sophisticated biopharmaceutical ecosystem, not only in life science R&D but also in the commercialization of biotechnology and bioengineering breakthroughs, and in strong IP protection. There are three tiers of funding that support the biopharmaceutical industry in the US: national funding, such as National Institutes of Health grants, which have played a vital role in basic research in life science; VC/PE funds and the secondary market in Wall Street, which have helped absorb risks and nurtured new ventures with

---

[41] See https://www.who.int/news/item/27-04-2020-who-timeline---covid-19, accessed 6 June 2021.

promising but unprofitable start-ups; and large pharmaceutical firms, which have funded R&D for new drug development and clinical trials.[42]

One interviewee commented:

> For a long time, domestic VC investment has adopted an approach that is risk-averse of unproven biological concepts or technologies. How to meet the challenge is not just a matter of a scientist or a company, but the entire ecosystem, including VC, governments, hospitals, doctors, patients, and scientific research workers. There must be a consensus on the new challenges.

While availability of capital provides one 'wheel' in new drug development, many actors are needed in the journey from laboratories to clinical trials to hospitals and pharmacies. 'It takes over ten years and perhaps over one billion US$ in R&D to develop a new drug,' commented by an interviewee who leads immunotherapy research in one of the largest US pharmaceutical companies. He said, 'This process is a market-oriented one, but the risk is very high. China's IP law and patenting systems should be reformed to truly serve the drug development.'

Regardless of whether a technology is transformed into clinical treatments or products, commercial transformation ability is completely different from scientific research ability. An interviewee who joined a Chinese gene-editing start-up commented that 'Talented people who are competent in the management of innovative biotechnology companies and have rich experience in technology transformation are still rare in China.' He continued, 'For example, in the area of gene editing techniques, there is little difference in China and in the US. However, in terms of technology transformation, no place in the world can be compared with the Cambridge in Boston, where a complete ecosystem supports R&D and commercialization of biotechnology.'

The US is a beacon model for China. Both the central government and local governments in China have invested heavily in life sciences R&D. Between 2010 and 2017, for example, the central government allocated about 10 billion RMB (about $1.6 billion) to six National Major Scientific Research Programmes, in nano studies, quantum regulation studies, protein studies, growth and reproduction studies, stem cell studies and global change studies. Over 48 per cent of this investment went to three life sciences: 18 per cent to protein studies, 15 per cent to growth and reproduction studies, and 9 per cent to stem cell studies.[43]

Biotechnology and biopharmaceuticals have also attracted VC investment in recent years. In Q1 of 2019 alone, China-based VC funds invested $1.4 billion in biotech firms, mainly concentrated in innovative drugs, biotechnology, medical devices, medical information, and health management. During the same period in

---

[42] S. Moore (2020), 'China's Role in the Global Biotechnology Sector and Implications for US Policy', Brookings Institute, April, https://www.brookings.edu/research/chinas-role-in-the-global-biotechnology-sector-and-implications-for-us-policy/, accessed 6 June 2021.

[43] *China's Science and Technology Statistic Yearbook* (2019).

2018, investment was only $125 million. This huge jump represents a major shift in China's VC focus, and was seen in May 2019, when JD Health received a capital injection of more than $1 billion, the largest in the sector's Series A preferred stock financing. JD.com remains the controlling shareholder of JD Health.

The shift of VC investment from internet/mobile internet to biotechnology was assisted by the relaxation of listing on the Hong Kong Stock Exchange in 2018 such that unprofitable biopharmaceutical companies are allowed to obtain public listing. Since then, several companies such as Ascletis Pharmaceutical (an antiviral platform), BeiGene (a biopharmaceutical company focusing on developing molecular and immuno-oncology drug candidates for the treatment of cancer), Innovent Bio (focusing on innovative drug development in immunotherapy), and HuaMedicine (focusing on original drugs for diabetics) all listed in Hong Kong.

This policy change has profound implications for China's biotechnology and biopharmaceutical start-ups, as public capital provides a financing channel for as yet unprofitable new drug makers to continue their development and commercialization. As one interviewee who heads R&D in one of the new drug development ventures listed in Hong Kong commented:

> This change is a huge progress. Given the long cycle of new drug development, if an unprofitable start-up's R&D is strong enough, and it has entered the clinical trial stage, it has a good chance to have a new drug in five to ten years. An IPO will provide not just capital for further research, but also incentives to attract more talent, to push forward the development. Luckily, so far, the investors have shown considerable interest in us and are willing to accept the risks.

The bottleneck of lack of capital investment is being addressed. Innovative drugs in areas such as regenerative medicine, genetic testing, gene therapy, and cell therapy, as well as medical services, dentistry, ophthalmology, medical aesthetics, Chinese medicine, assisted reproduction, rehabilitation, pain, and day surgery centres, have all become investment hotspots.

New Drug Development

The ability to develop innovative new drugs is still in its infancy in China. The new drugs marketed in China are still largely in the 'me-too' or 'me-better' category, that is, they are copycats of imported drugs without IP protection. However, respondents in the biotechnology/biopharmaceutical industry indicated that Chinese firms are improving in innovation. Pharmaceutical start-ups used to rely on the business model of importing a foreign technology or drug and then marketing it in China. Once the drug or technology got approved by China's National Medical Products Administration, they searched for VC/PE investment to scale up their Chinese operations. Once the product was sold to a large enough market, they aimed for an IPO on the Hong Kong Stock Exchange. This model has lost its attraction. An interviewee who is an executive in a pharmaceutical company commented:

As well as the Chinese government encouraging new drug development for diseases, including many for cancers and autoimmune, infectious, and rare diseases, where no effective treatments are available, it is also streamlining the new drug registration review system. As a result, the time difference between a new drug's registration in China and in foreign markets has been shortened from ten to fifteen years (the typical time for small-molecule drugs) to four years (the typical time for immunotherapy drugs).

Given the risks involved and the large amount of investment required in drug R&D, many start-ups firms cannot afford to build their own facilities for new drug development. To break this bottleneck, a new type of business model in Chinese biopharmaceuticals has emerged: the contract research organization (CRO). This is a type of company that provides research services to pharmaceutical, biotechnology, and medical device industries as outsourced contractors. Their services include drug R&D, route process development, and clinical trials. Examples include WuXi AppTec and Tigermed.

From the perspective of innovation, the services provided by a CRO have changed from a 'technology transfer + customized production' to a 'cooperative R&D + customized production' model. While Chinese firms are still weak at identifying innovation targets in new drug development, they are good at the execution in R&D and the transformation from ideas to research outputs once the targets are discovered. In 2019, China's CRO market size was estimated to be $9.47 billion, due mainly to increased R&D spending by multinational pharmaceutical companies in China.[44]

> If large pharmaceutical firms do not have original drugs or innovation in making drugs, they face a lot of pressure in the market. They cannot rely on the profits from making and marketing generic drugs to subsidize new drug R&D. In the future innovative pharmaceutical companies need to focus on R&D and innovation for new drug development. Finding niche markets is key for high profits; but making generic drugs on production innovation for mass market is still for survival.

In the long run, it appears pharmaceutical companies will continue to increase the proportion of CRO services in their overall R&D expenditure. As an executive of Wuxi AppTec commented, 'Innovation itself is not only about technology, but also about creating synergies in the innovation value chain. This is not something that can be achieved by one person or one company. Execution is key in this process.' About 12 per cent of the world's biological drugs are developed on Wuxi AppTec's new

---

[44]   BEROE (2020). 'China CRO Market Intelligence', https://www.beroeinc.com/category-intelligence/cro-china-market/, accessed July 28 2021.

drug development platform. According to its CEO, there are about ten 'first-in-class' new drugs have been 'born' from the platform.[45]

Such CRO platforms enable sharing R&D resources. This type of service is particularly important for small and start-up firms, as they are less likely to have their own laboratories and other clinical research facilities. This will bring more innovation to Chinese new drug discovery. As the Wuxi AppTec interviewee commented, 'In the future, biopharmaceutical companies can integrate two or even four drugs into one molecule. New drugs are concentrated in areas such as oncology, Alzheimer's, and infectious diseases.'

Curing the Poor with 'God's Hands'

From cell therapy to the treatment of genetic diseases, the powerful functions of CRISPR, the gene editing scissors, sometimes referred to as 'God's hands', offer the hope of curing many genetic diseases once considered incurable.

Thalassaemia is a single-gene genetic disease. There is no effective treatment at present other than blood transfusion and allogeneic haematopoietic stem cell transplantation, which is used infrequently, as it is difficult to matching donors and receptors. For patients with thalassaemia, editing the gene of their autologous haematopoietic stem cells and then transfusing the gene-modified cells back to them has proven an effective treatment. It can minimize immune rejections caused by stem cell transplantation. Treatments for thalassaemia include gene therapy and gene editing therapy. From an economic point of view, gene therapy needs to use viruses as vectors, the cost of which is very high and the production process very complicated. So, the price for treatment with gene therapy can be very high, with the cost of a one-time cure around $2 million, which is obviously beyond the reach of most patients. A gene-editing therapy with considerable efficacy has recently been developed by an American company and has been approved for use in Europe and the US.

Thalassaemia is a disease that is distributed among the population along the Equator, but is largely concentrated in Europe and North Africa. There are, however, a large number of patients in southern China. In Guangdong around 17 per cent of the population and in Guangxi around 20 per cent of the population are gene carriers. If two carriers of thalassaemia have a child, the probability of the child having thalassaemia is one-quarter.

EdiGene (Inc.) is a biomedical company dedicated to accelerating drug R&D for innovative therapies for a variety of genetic diseases including thalassaemia. The company was founded in 2015 by Professor Wei Wensheng, using scientific results from Wei's Laboratory in the School of Life Science at Peking University. His findings were published in *Nature* in 2014 in an article about CRISPR as a high-throughput

---

[45] See Wuxi Apptec (https://www.wuxiapptec.com/, accessed 6 June 2021).

genome editing and screening platform for new drug R&D.[46] Subsequently, the biotech start-up established an *in vitro* cell gene editing therapy platform for haematopoietic stem cells and T-cells, an *in vivo* gene therapy platform based on RNA single-base editing technology, and a high-throughput genome editing screening platform. The firm owns the independent intellectual property rights of these platforms. Since Dr Wei Dong joined the firm as the CEO in 2018, it has received multiple rounds of VC/PE investments.[47]

Unlike many biotech start-ups, EdiGene's advantage is it owns its own original technology for gene editing. The combination of gene-editing and cell therapy represents a brand new direction in innovative treatments for cancers and other genetic diseases such as thalassaemia. Technologies at the level of haematopoietic stem cells for thalassaemia have achieved good results, but they are not yet available to Chinese patients. As Dr Wei Dong explains:

> Gene-editing therapy for thalassaemia has changed the lives of the severe patients in the US and Europe, but is not available for Chinese patients. It won't make any sense for those American drug makers to enter China, given the price system and the investment required to get approval for production in China.

As a result, according to Dr Wei:

> When little options are available for Chinese patients, especially those who are poor, we have to do it ourselves. We have technologies in gene editing and screening technologies. Using these advantages, we work with multinational pharmaceutical companies in the screening of certain diseases and develop therapies for some rare diseases including thalassaemia. I hope 'Gods hands' will also help Chinese patients.

AI-Enabled Healthcare

China has developed applications in medicine and healthcare using digital platforms, AI, and big data analytics. Ping An Good Doctor, for example, an AI-enabled healthcare platform, is a spin-off of Ping An Insurance Group. Good Doctor offers more than 500,000 online consultations a day to customers who are looking for health-related advice. Since 55 per cent of health expenditures are government-covered

[46] Y. Zhou, S. Zhu, C. Cai, P. Yuan, C. Li, Y. Huang, and W. Wei (2014), 'High-Throughput Screening of a CRISPR/Cas9 Library for Functional Genomics in Human Cells', *Nature*, 509, 487–91. doi: 10.1038/nature13166.

[47] Both Professor Wei and Dr Wei were classmates of one of the authors at the Biology Department of Peking University. The author visited Wei's Lab and interviewed them multiple times.

items in China, Good Doctor operates in 258 cities, helping local governments process medical claims and improve their work efficiency.[48]

One challenge medical institutions everywhere have faced is to share patient data safely across platforms. Data sharing generates more data. Once technical and privacy issues are resolved, there are potentially massive benefits from digital technologies. Big data analytics in medical services can lead to higher accuracy in disease diagnosis and more effective treatment. Blockchain technology can allow hospitals, patients, and all parties in medical services to share data without worrying about data security and integrity. Using blockchain technology, DXY.com is a 'medical connector' through its three networks: medical, medicine, and information. This platform claims to provide a one-stop solution to health management for users, by integrating online and offline patient data. Invested in by Tencent, DXY.com is a professional and authoritative content sharing platform, and a hub that connects hospitals, doctors, scientific researchers, biomedical companies, and insurance companies with patients. DXY's platform has the largest doctor community in China, sharing information across the country.

Challenges Ahead

China's biotechnology sector is still in its infancy and does not have any companies comparable with Huawei in communications or Alibaba in e-commerce. There are a few areas in which Chinese biotechnology firms are globally competitive, including gene sequencing, gene editing, and immunotherapy. In the technology in these innovative treatments China is on par with or even more advanced than some Western countries. Such advantages derive from China's lower-cost engineering capability, discussed in other chapters, and less strict regulations, which allow such technologies to be used as a medical device rather than a drug in innovative treatments. To catch up, however, China needs to build its institutional environment, such as enforcement of IPR protection, ethical use of advanced technologies such as gene editing, and technology transfer from research to industry. To do so, building comprehensive ecosystems is key.

Given China's population and massive number of medical institutions, predictive analytics and personalized medicine using AI and big data analytics can unleash valuable treatment data and create social and economic value. It should be noted, however, that while data quantity is important, so is data quality. Inconsistent record-keeping in Chinese hospitals across the country and a population with limited racial diversity may diminish the value of biomedical data from China.

---

[48] J. Tan and J. Ngai (2018), 'Building a Tech-Enabled Ecosystem: An Interview with Ping An's Jessica Tan', *McKinsey Quarterly*, 4 December, https://www.mckinsey.com/featured-insights/china/building-a-tech-enabled-ecosystem-an-interview-with-ping-ans-jessica-tan, accessed 6 June 2021.

Innovative technology entrepreneurship has become a core driving force of China's national development. China's practice in technology entrepreneurship carries significant implications for both entrepreneurship research and policy for other countries. It shows the value of appreciating the processes that connect bottom-up and top-down action. Particular insight can be gained from the performance of start-ups in the digital platform economy and the speed of adjustment at industry and government levels, mechanisms of resource allocation, and governance and other rule making.

7
Institutional Logics in Innovation

The critical issues about China's innovation machine are not how much innovation it has produced, but rather how it has developed its innovation capability, especially its systemic power in innovation, and the future of that capability.

China started its industrialization at the foundation of PRC, and for almost half of the time since it was a central-planning economy. During the first decade of the PRC (1949–58), central planning supported the development of heavy industries, following the Soviet model. During the second two decades (1959–78), China was ideologically opposed to technological innovation, which led the country to the brink of economic bankruptcy.

As innovation is often unpredictable, central planning finds it hard to countenance. Economic and institutional reforms in the forty years from 1979 to 2019 have been the main driving force for China's economic success, and the encouragement of innovation through the introduction of market forces has been a key platform of its policies. China's market economy today is, however, still very different from a typical free market economy in the West. The differences are most prominent in its economic structure and state presence. The proportion of state-owned enterprises (SOEs) in the economy, for example, is still high, and government intervention remains very powerful in industry and innovation policies compared to free market economy countries.

Economic development has been subject to two hands or 'logics': the visible hand of strong government intervention and the emerging invisible hand of the market. Understanding the dual logics in China's economic development and their dynamic interactions helps explain how China's innovation machine developed and points to its future potential.

The debate about which logic is more important in China's economic success continues.[1] Chinese liberal economists believe that market logic is key to its success. Chinese conservatives, on the other hand, believe that government intervention plays a vital role in directing limited resources to strategically critical industries and technologies and has been the foundation of China's industrial development and economic growth. A market logic emphasizes improving competitiveness and productivity, using fewer resources for more and better outputs. Innovation capability

---

[1] See, for example, the debate between two prominent economists: Z. Weiying and L. Yifu (2016), 'Do We Need Industrial Policy', 9 November, http://www.xinhuanet.com/fortune/caiyan/ksh/193.htm, accessed 6 June 2021.

Demystifying China's Innovation Machine: Chaotic Order. Marina Yue Zhang, Mark Dodgson, and David M. Gann, Oxford University Press. © Marina Yue Zhang, Mark Dodgson, and David M. Gann 2022. DOI: 10.1093/oso/9780198861171.003.0007

around advanced technologies, especially that possessed by entrepreneurs, is critical to these goals, as has been found in the US and other Anglo-Saxon countries. The statist interventionist logic has been seen to play a vital role in the catching-up of latecomer countries such as Japan, South Korea, and Taiwan.[2] Innovation and industrial policies were the driving force for their catch-up. Despite differences between these two schools of thought, a form of consensus emerged in China, where the market is seen as important for China's economic development, but government intervention is also necessary, especially when the market fails, which can happen quite often in a transitioning economy.

The trajectory of China's economic and institutional reforms has been towards establishing a market and managing its integration with its central planning. These reforms have sought a balance between the influences of the visible and the invisible hands, the logic of the market and that of government intervention. The country has made substantial progress in this regard, seen for example, in two major institutional reforms: the dual-track pricing system[3] and improved property rights and ownership.[4] Policymaking has generally followed a highly pragmatic and adaptive framework dependent upon the stages of the country's socio-economic development and its internal and external environments.

Government intervention tends to set directions, allocate resources, and establish protected markets for industries and technological innovation with national strategic significance. The entrepreneurial spirits of private enterprises compete to apply technologies, often imported, to improve product innovativeness and engineering efficiency in production. This model has enabled China to move up on the industrial value chain on the basis of its huge scale advantage. But in many industries, bottlenecks in industrial development have occurred due to deficiencies in core technology. Chapter 3 showed, for example, how China still relies on imports of critical components or tools in high-end manufacturing industry.

While China's market economy has been criticized as 'national capitalism', some analysis suggests that the positive impact of policy intervention, particularly financial policy intervention, overweighed its negative impact.[5] However, as Huang

---

[2] R. Wade (2004), *Governing the Market: Economic Theory and the Role of Government in East Asian Industrialization*, Princeton, NJ: Princeton University Press.

[3] The dual-track pricing reform was introduced in 1984 to balance the interests between the vested state-owned sector and the emerging private sector. The system is an institutional arrangement for a smooth transition from central planning to market-driven in production. However, the policy was considered a hotbed for rent-seeking behaviour and corruption, as people could make profits by buying low from one track and selling high on the other track, largely leveraging their positioning power to access information and products. On 9 November 1989, the dual-track system merged into one.

[4] In 1992, the law makers started discussions on establishing limited liability shareholding companies, or limited liability companies, and in 1993 China's first 'Company Law' was passed. These changes were a watershed moment, as, until then, there were no property rights of entrepreneurship and private enterprise protected by law. See http://english.mofcom.gov.cn/aarticle/lawsdata/chineselaw/200211/20021100053543.html, accessed 27 July 2021.'

[5] Y. Huang (2019), 'China 2049: What Has Been the Reason for China's Economic Success over the Past 40 Years?', https://ishare.ifeng.com/c/s/v0020X4-_DZacfQYcVcNC6O8H6mry28zoWh14zT--IgNZo6DQ__?from=timeline&isappinstalled=0, accessed 28 July 2021.

Yiping, a professor of economics at Peking University, also pointed it out, less intervention has been more beneficial for economic development. The successes of China's mobile communication equipment manufacturing, mobile phones, the internet, and e-commerce, which received less government support, are good examples of market forces working.

Cases such as the Ant Group, whose IPO in Shanghai and Hong Kong was suspended by the government in November 2020, as we discussed in Chapter 6, and DiDi Chuxing (the country's largest ride-hailing company), which was investigated for potential violation of data privacy and national security law two days after its IPO on New York Stock Exchange in June 2021,[6] show the continuing power of the visible hand. China's antitrust regulator, the State Administration of Market Regulators, and its cybersecurity watchdog, the Cyberspace Administration of China, are behind a larger movement to regulate the country's technology giants, including Alibaba, Tencent, Meituan and DiDi, as well as introduce tighter controls over overseas listings of Chinese technology companies.

The rapid development of China's internet industry has been largely due to China's relatively relaxed regulatory environment, but relaxation does not mean no regulation. For the government, the long-term stability and security in the finance sector, and national security over data are far more important than teconomic returns of technology giants.

The government's pushback on Ant's IPO and investigation of Didi after its IPO triggered worries that tightened control of private business might suppress China's further innovation.[7] The balance between the visible and invisible hand is still being negotiated. Building self-sufficiency in China's science and technology has been identified as a key task for the country's Fourteenth Five-Year Plan (2021–6). However, according to Xu Kuangdi, the former mayor of Shanghai and a fellow of the Chinese Academy of Engineering, 'Original and disruptive technological innovation is difficult to achieve under the current approval and evaluation system.'[8] Indeed, whether China can forge ahead in its innovation catch-up and become a true global leader in innovation is hinged upon how China is going to reform its innovation institutions, and how it does this will depend on the relationship between the state and the market.

Cultural Roots

Scholars emphasize the importance of context in policy and management research. Context refers to the general conditions of the natural, institutional, and cultural

---

[6] See https://www.reuters.com/technology/china-cyberspace-administration-launches-security-investigation-into-didi-2021-07-02/, accessed 28 July 2021.

[7] Economist (2020), 'China Takes Aim at Its Entrepreneurs: Private Enterprise Faces Formidable New Obstacles', *The Economist*, 12 November, https://www.economist.com/business/2020/11/12/china-takes-aim-at-its-entrepreneurs, accessed 7 June 2021.

[8] See http://caifuhao.eastmoney.com/news/20201031192947476226000, accessed 7 June 2021.

environment in which specific economic activities occur.[9] In China's case, contextual factors include unique factors in its history, culture, and emerging status. These contextual factors deeply influence its institutional logics.

Politically, China is a nation state. Most ethnic Chinese, however, think of it as a civilization with thousands of years of history and culture centred on Han nationality. Chinese civilization originated in and developed around the central plains of China comprising the middle and lower reaches of the Yellow River. It was complemented through many 'outside in ripples'—outsiders invading and conquering China who eventually became Chinese.[10] The central plains are considered the cradle of Chinese civilization and the melting pot for other nationalities becoming Chinese.

Unity has been the single most important political value in defining and maintaining Chinese civilization. The need for unity has been used by China's rulers (including those who conquered the central plains and became China's emperors) for generations to defend against any threat from internal rebellions or outside invasions. Chinese people are proud of being part of a grand and historic civilization. History plays a key role in Chinese society and is in some ways its religion. Sentimentality towards Chinese history is shared by those who live away from the country and has been a protective fortress for any rulers in China, whether emperors or political parties, maintaining their ruling legitimacy.

As seen in Chapter 1, the Chinese language has been a bond maintaining unity. Chinese is a high-context language in which rich contextual information is embedded and it seeming ambiguity leaves room for interpretation depending upon contexts.[11]

Order in Chinese society is maintained through a top-down chain of command: the hierarchical power structure. Throughout Chinese history, each emperor came to the throne through leading mass riots, and they were entitled to pass on the throne to their sons until overturned by new mass riots led by the next emperor. To avoid social unrest and prevent mass riots, emperors tried to maintain social harmony through economic development. However, in this system, emperors' heaven-given absolute power most commonly led to corruption and economic downturns that were the main reasons for social unrest.

There were never any significant forces in Chinese history, such as church, science, or even independent thinking, that could challenge the emperors' power. To maintain social order, 'shi da fu', social elites including government officials at different levels and influential intellectuals, especially those who were close to the emperors, were a kind of counterpower to central authoritarian power. However, the power of the shi da fu was granted by their emperors as long as they maintained their loyalty.

---

[9] S. A. Zahra (2007), 'Contextualizing Theory Building in Entrepreneurship Research', *Journal of Business Venturing*, 22(3), 443–52.

[10] T. Y. Zhao (2016), The Making and Becoming of China: Its Way of Historicity [in Chinese], Beijing: CITIC Press.

[11] H. Nakamura (1964), *Ways of Thinking of Eastern People*, Honolulu: University of Hawaii Press.

In other words, emperors could grant power to *shi da fu*, and they could also take away that power. The rule of law was weak in this power structure. On the other hand, *shi da fu* saw themselves not only as government officials but also as educators and the moral fortress of Chinese society. Therefore, rule by morals was a critical part of Chinese society. The best *shi da fu* could do was to influence their emperors, hoping that through him authority would stay in their safe hands.[12] From the top down, Confucian cultural values were used by *shi da fu* as a moral fortress to strengthen their power and to rule the people by influencing their emperors.[13]

The state, to an extent, guards Chinese civilization by maintaining unity. For this reason, the government in China has more authority than in anywhere else in the world. The government, representing its people, has the mission of maintaining unity in the country. As long as there is a grand collective goal or an enemy, and the realization of that goal or the defeat of that enemy relies on the power of the state, the legitimacy of the government remains unshaken.

Using Hofstede's national cultural indices, Table 7.1 examines the influence of Chinese culture on innovation.[14]

These measures of Chinese culture represent an overview of average attributes. There are divergences in every society between 'who can see a target no one else can see' and 'who can hit a target no one else can hit'.[15] China has a large enough pool from which such odds drive innovation through their entrepreneurial endeavours. Institutional reforms, especially the introduction of a market economy, have provided a fertile ground for those odds to divert from cultural mores.

China's Institutional Logics

To understand China's policy, it is important to make sense of what it is doing, rather than listening to what it is saying, even though top-down policies typically reveal the biggest concerns and priorities for the Chinese leadership. This is because China has complex and multifaceted institutional logics behind how policies are made at the central level and how they are implemented at the ministerial and local levels.

From the foundation of the PRC, the country started to build a new power structure and a new model of state governance. Looking back at China's institutions over seven decades reveals that many of China's institutional practices have strong connections with its history. The challenges and difficulties facing China's governance such as a large population, vast geographic coverage, resource constraints, unbalanced development between regions, and threats of social unrest have persisted for

---

[12] J. T. C. Liu (1989), *China Turning Inward: Intellectual-Political Changes in the Early Twelfth Century*, Cambridge, MA: Harvard East Asia Center, Harvard University.

[13] See more in G. Redding (1990), *The Spirit of Chinese Capitalism*, Berlin: de Gruyter.

[14] See https://www.hofstede-insights.com/country/china/, accessed 7 June 2021.

[15] The quotation is adapted from the philosopher Arthur Schopenhauer, cited in G. Satell (2014), 'How a Genius Thinks', *Forbes*, 1 June, https://www.forbes.com/sites/gregsatell/2014/06/01/how-a-genius-thinks/?sh=340132f40619, accessed 7 June 2021.

Table 7.1   Cultural influence in China's innovation

Hofstede's Cultural Dimension	Meaning	China's Index	Implications for Innovation
Power distance	The power distance index considers the extent to which inequality and power are tolerated. In this dimension, inequality and power are viewed from the viewpoint of the followers—the lower level.	80	China has high power distance, i.e. is a society that believes that inequalities amongst people are acceptable. People in lower power positions are less likely to express their opinions, which constrains creativity and innovation.
Individualism vs collectivism	The individualism vs. collectivism dimension considers the degree to which societies are integrated into groups and their perceived obligations and dependence on groups.	20	China is a highly collectivist society where people act in the interests of the group and not necessarily of themselves. Collective thinking can be a constraint on innovation.
Uncertainty avoidance	The uncertainty avoidance index considers the extent to which uncertainty and ambiguity are tolerated. This dimension considers how unknown situations and unexpected events are dealt with.	30	China has a low score on uncertainty avoidance, which means that Chinese are comfortable with uncertainty and ambiguity, which is also shown in the Chinese language. While it is rich in context, a lack of precision is a constraint in scientific inquiries.
Masculinity vs femininity	The masculinity vs femininity dimension is also referred to as 'tough vs tender,' and considers the preference of society for achievement and its attitude towards sexuality equality, behaviour, etc.	66	China is a masculine society in which success, measured by career advancement, academic achievement, and economic power is valued. Taking risks in innovation through trial and error is not encouraged as they may not bring immediate success.
Long-term orientation	Long-term orientation shows a focus on the future and involves delaying short-term success or gratification in order to achieve long-term success. Long-term orientation emphasizes persistence, perseverance, and long-term growth.	87	China is a society with a very long-term orientation, which means that links with the past are important while dealing with the challenges of the present and future. This dimension also means that Chinese people value saving and investing, thriftiness, and perseverance in achieving long-term results. This is important for long-term plans in policy and strategy in innovation.

| Indulgence vs restrain | The indulgence vs restraint dimension considers the extent and tendency for a society to fulfil its desires. In other words, this dimension revolves around how societies can control their impulses and desires. | 24 | China is a restrained society with a low index in indulgence. People with this orientation have the perception that their actions are restrained by norms and the status quo, which is a constraint on innovation. |

Note: A nation's cultural dimensional is indexed from 0 to 100. The higher the index, the more the national is positioned on that dimension.

Source: Summarized by the authors from various sources on cultural dimensions including Hofstede Insights and Wikipedia

thousands of years. China's institutional environment, therefore, follows multiple logics influenced by China's cultural traditions and bureaucratic system for thousands of years.[16] Traditionally, the society is ruled from top to bottom. However, the system design of China's governance emphasizes political centralization at the central level, but economic decentralization at the local level.

The top-down approach in governance assumes that top-level policymakers are rational, intelligent, moral, and operate beyond self-interest, which leads to a series of institutional arrangements. As humans have bounded rationality, however, decision-making, including the top-down approach in governance, can be influenced by a variety of factors. Thus, policymaking is often a result of a compromise of different political interests. China's policymaking, including that directed at science and technology, innovation, and industry, arises from holistic understandings of past experience, reflections on current challenges, and perceptions of future possibilities.

This institutional design is believed to be more effective in mobilizing resources and, thus, achieving the country's ambitious goals. During catch-up, China's centralized system was effective when the target was clear, as it is conducive to making full use of the latecomers' advantages and concentrating resources. Under this regime, once a target is confirmed, implementation can be fast and effective. For example, once China determined to develop its new infrastructures for the digital economy, it undertook to invest $1.4 trillion in the kind of technologies discussed in Chapter 6 such as 5G wireless networks and artificial intelligence in which the country is highly advanced. Public policymaking is a lengthy and recursive process, with many rounds of internal consultations with relevant interest groups. This reveals how unlikely it was that the government rushed a new rule to regulate the country's technology giants as shown by Ant Group and Didi. Once a policy is established, it is expected to cause minimal disruption.

From a social learning perspective, China's policymaking is a deliberate attempt to adjust the goals and techniques of policy in response to history, past experience, and new information. Policymaking in China often responds less directly to current

---

[16] X. G. Zhou (2017), *Institutional Logics of Chinese Governance: An Organizational Perspective* [in Chinese], Beijing: Sanlian Press.

social and economic conditions than it does to the consequences of past policy.[17] In other words, the interests and ideals that policymakers pursue at any moment in time are shaped by policy legacies or reactions to previous policies. As a single-party state, policymaking in China is less influenced by factors such as election cycles, opposition parties, and international influences. Rather, it often has a long-term orientation considering three variables: the overarching goals that guide policy in a particular field, the techniques or policy instruments used to attain those goals, and the precise settings of these instruments.[18] Essentially, the policymaking framework underlines the fundamental institutional logics and the balance between formal and informal governance, as well as between central and local governments.

One aspect of China's policymaking is that it often leaves room for self-correction. Expansive and ambiguous language is commonly used in major policy announcements, which leaves sufficient room for interpretation. As one government official interviewed explained, major policies are often implemented in smaller and less critical areas to test the water, providing room for correction and adjustment, before a full-blown implementation is carried out nationwide,

This system design can, however, suppress difference in opinions and constrain the creativity that is required to identify emerging problems.

The Balance within China's Bureaucratic Hierarchy

China's bureaucracy has high expectations of the quality and morality of the officials who run the system. This system has been criticized for being a hotbed of rent-seeking behaviour and corruption, and despite facing severe sanctions it has witnessed many such examples. However, bureaucratic problems should not be simply seen as resulting from low moral standards. Specific governance structures and management mechanisms can often shape the behaviour of officials.

In this system, lower-ranking officials are obliged to obey and demonstrate loyalty to their superiors. On the other hand, higher-ranking officials also need to rely on their subordinates for policy implementation and reactions to it, which also provides the basis for how to reward or punish subordinates. In other words, subordinates are accountable to their superiors rather than to the people they administer. This system creates a dilemma: subordinates have high incentives to choose less innovative ways of implementing policies to avoid mistakes, and to misinform or, in the worst case, even to deceive their superiors. In this system, the worst scenario is that it puts officials' loyalty above competence and is filled with mediocre cadres who have little motivation to perform well.

---

[17] Interview with a senior diplomat in Canberra, Australia.
[18] Y. F. Zhao and S. L. Lin (2015), 'National Institutions and National Governance: China's Logics', *Chinese Public Administration*, 359(5) [Chinese journal].

When Xi Jinping took the reins of the CPC in 2012, he launched a countrywide anticorruption campaign, aiming to rectify this flaw in China's governance structure. However, as one anonymous interviewee commented, 'Under the high-pressure environment of an anticorruption campaign, most people, including senior government officials, only care about self-protection,' and 'They don't want to be the first to speak up. They wait for their superiors to make decisions and are only accountable to their superiors instead of the people.'

At the beginning of the coronavirus pandemic in Wuhan, for example, for local government officials it was easier to hide the truth from those higher up the hierarchy than to deal with potential mistakes by revealing what happened to the public before the whole picture became clear. The delayed decision about the pandemic was catastrophic. In situations such as a pandemic, even the best-meaning attempts to sugar-coat the truth are self-defeating, because, apart from the costs to health, they spread mistrust, rumours, and, ultimately, fear. However, once the decision was made at the central level to stop the disease at any cost, the virus was forcefully controlled.

In this sense, how to maintain the balance within China's bureaucratic hierarchy will determine the direction of China's political future.

The Balance between Central and Local Governments

The governance system in China is hierarchical and power cascades from central to local officials. The central government designates quantified targets such as GDP growth, unemployment levels, or innovation performance for each province. Provincial government decomposes its targets for next-level government, and they cascade all the way down to the lowest-level governments. This practice from the central-planning era still dominates China's governance.

In policy implementation, however, local governments have certain degrees of autonomy in economic activities.[19] As the Chinese expression goes, 'The mountains are high and the emperor is far away.' Local governments have become the main economic actors and direct operators in their administrative regions, from provincial to city, county, and village levels. The central government has introduced a mechanism for selecting local champions through competition between local governments. The competition between local governments refers to cross-regional competition typically at the same bureaucratic level for policy, investment, talent, and technology, as well as legal environment and government efficiency. This mechanism, again, cascades down the hierarchy. Local governments have been competing for capital and projects for some time, and now they are moving to compete for talent and skilled labour.

---

[19] Li Daokui, 'China is economically decentralized for competition among local governments [in Chinese]'. See http://www.bjnews.com.cn/finance/2020/08/06/756083.html, accessed 27 July 2021.

This mechanism has stimulated local governments to pursue a balance between economic and political interests. Ultimately, to enhance the legitimacy of their governance, maintaining economic growth is key. Although this mechanism is widely considered to be a fundamental driving force for China's rapid economic growth, it also laid the foundation for rent-seeking behaviours at the local level.

The balance between central government (which holds policymaking power) and local governments (which hold policy implementation power) is fluid and dynamic. The central government sometimes chooses to retain its nominal and symbolic power and hand over the real power of governance to local or ministerial governments, but, when needed, the central government can recall the real power back, typically through political campaigns.[20] This is to show lower-level officials who holds the real power in governance.

The Balance between Formal and Informal Governance

Historical studies on the relationship between central and local governments have placed emphasis on their formal relationships, such as centralism and decentralization, that determine how the central government distributes its power to the local governments, and the mechanism by which the central government controls the power distribution to local governments. However, even in periods of high centralism in the formal system, there is room for local governments to operate with discreet power, maintaining a great deal of flexibility in governance and policy implementation. Such an arrangement can temporarily solve one of the challenges of China's governance, namely the contradiction between centralization and effective flexibility in governance. This method, on the one hand, allows the central government to govern with a uniform policy but be flexible in dealing with local conditions. On the other hand, local governments use informal systems to deal with specific conditions when implementing central policies. In this system, the 'unchangeable' of the formal system and the 'changeable' of the informal system resolve the contradiction between centralization and the complexity of local conditions. If detailed implementation governance were used, many policies might not be implemented at the local levels at all. This institutional logic maintains the authoritative power of the unified formal system and the effectiveness of the informal system.

Informal power is at the heart of Chinese governance logic, and it is interdependent with the formal system. In China's national governance, the formal system can only function with the support of its complex informal system, often in 'unwritten codes'[21] such as the government-enterprise relationship networks that are common and widespread in Chinese society. The better the political relationship an enterprise

---

[20] X. G. Zhou (2012), 'Rethinking about China's Institutional Logics: Political Campaigns' *Open Times*, 9, 105–125. [Chinese journal]

[21] S. Wu (2009), *Unwritten Rules* [in Chinese], Shanghai: Fudan University Press.

has with the government, the more likely it is that it will receive political resources which are beneficial for its economic activities. The implication for those who invest in innovation is that without a good political relationship they may not have a fair chance of competing in the market.

In summary, the formal system embodies the institutional arrangement of the central government's authority from the top down, while the informal system embodies the flexibility and adaptation of local governments in policy implementation. Sometimes local implementation can deviate from central policy guidance with central government acquiescence and is the pragmatic institutional arrangement that maintains flexibility within the unified system.[22]

The Balance between the Visible and Invisible Hands: Government Intervention vs Market Forces

A prominent feature of modern China since its opening-up policy is its increasing pluralism and diversity in values. Modern communication technology and the internet have enabled people to access more diverse opinion and to have more channels to express their ideas and thoughts. The combination of the two has imposed a great challenge for China's governance, with the government using the visible hand more than the invisible hand for the sake of maintaining social stability.

The emergence and growth of Alipay and then Ant Group are a good example of the balance between government interventions and market forces. When Alipay was created, it was an intermediary between buyers and sellers on Alibaba's e-commerce platforms. A non-banking private company serving as a payment operator was obviously beyond China's existing institutional frameworks. However, the regulatory bodies 'kept one eye open and one shut' when dealing with such innovations in the market, which provided room for such a disruptive innovation to grow. In this game, instead of using political and social influence and skills to persuade policymakers of the virtues of their innovation, firms such as Alibaba and Tencent used the market based on the lever of creating digital ecosystems. Leveraging their large user bases across platforms through cross-investment, such firms entered many areas, including financial services, in the digital sphere. As seen in Chapter 5, they became super platforms controlling China's digital economy.

The financial industry is an important element of 'public good' infrastructure in China, and the government is highly aware of the lessons from history that instability in the financial market can lead to economic crisis. The Basel Accords, which was criticized as an 'old men's club' in a speech by Alibaba's founder Jack Ma in an influential financial summit,[23] and which was a suspected reason behind the suspension

---

[22] X. G. Zhou (2010), 'The Institutional Logic of Collusion among Local Governments in China', *Modern China*, 36(1), 47–78.

[23] See https://economictimes.indiatimes.com/news/international/business/jack-ma-blasts-global-financial-regulators-curbs-on-innovation/articleshow/78862649.cms, accessed 28 July, 2021.

of Ant's IPO, is, in fact, an important safeguard for modern financial systems. It is unsurprising that the government started to intervene in the fintech market, as was seen particularly in its introduction of the e-yuan, after a period of market-driven growth.

Two issues to emerge in the discourse on China's regulation of internet are platform neutrality and data privacy. Ant Group makes about 36 per cent of its revenue from Alipay, about 40 per cent from 'microlending technology' in which customer credits to 500 million consumers contribute 80 per cent, and the rest from supply lending to 20 million SMEs and micro enterprises.[24] To put these figures in perspective, the consumer loans of all of China's consumer financial institutions including credit cards were one-third of Ant's consumer lending, in which Ant leveraged only 2 per cent of its own capital. As in the case of Didi, the government concern was on data. With nearly 500 million annual users and 15 million drivers in 15 countries, 90 per cent in China,[25] Didi's GPS based traffic data can be politically sensitive, for example in being used to track who goes where and predict traffic patterns in real time. In this context, the government decided that online technology companies in financial services should abide by financial regulations to avoid any systemic risks and maintain the stability of China's financial sector.

Questions thus arise such as whether these super platforms are neutral to allow open and fair competition in the market. This raises numerous issues, such as: Who owns user data? While platform firms profit by pushing targeted products/services to users, or even sell such data to a third party, are users aware of such behaviour? Are they entitled to share the profits? More serious concerns arise as some data can be of critical importance to national security, and the kinds of laws or regulations to protect such data.

When such firms became too big to fail, regulators began to take action. Their argument was that, for example, fintech had not changed the nature of finance; hence fintech firms should be subject to financial regulations. The government also released a draft of anti-monopoly measures aiming to control these super platforms. The draft plan argued that while consumers enjoyed the convenience of such platforms, they gradually lost their choices in products and services.

China's national governance has been relatively introspective for a long time, and it has not been subjected to international pressure. Today, globalization, whether it is economic interaction, movement of people, or transfer of ideas, means that China's governance needs to develop an open and internationalist mentality. For example, when China exports its products, especially intangible products, it competes with others not just on technology but also on values. TikTok's difficulties in the US and India is a good example. Values, civil rights, and the very governance system are all under scrutiny when China exports its technology. Looking forward, we can see

---

[24] See Ant's IPO prospectus (2020), https://www1.hkexnews.hk/listedco/listconews/sehk/2020/1026/2020102600165.pdf, accessed 28 July 2021.

[25] See Didi's IPO prospectus (2021), https://www.sec.gov/Archives/edgar/data/1764757/000104746921001194/a2243272zf-1.htm; 28 July 2021.

that China is facing an increasingly hostile international environment, and the question is the extent to which its bureaucracy and policymaking adjust to this new environment.

Policy Framework

Science and Technology Policy

China's science and technology system, which was built upon a central-planning model, uses policy intervention in research activities in government-funded universities and research institutes, as well as in SOEs. This model has been criticized for constraining autonomy and freedom in science. During the early years of China's catch-up, research on basic science was challenged by policymakers on whether enough social and economic usefulness could be created. As a result, for a long time China's research in science and technology was driven by the search for immediate results.

China adopted a centralized S&T policy to serve its purposes of catching up with more advanced countries. In such a system, policy intervention aims to strengthen the role of the central power in core technology areas that are of strategic importance to China's national strategy. Consequently, China's science and technology planning system does not offer much freedom in research, which leads researchers to avoid highly risky and speculative experiments with less controllable results, which, if successful, mighty have far-reaching impact.

Government-led funding, mainly in research institutes and universities, accounts for about 20 per cent of China's total R&D expenditure. The remaining 80 per cent is contributed by industry. However, the levels of investment are low compared to more developed nations, and SOEs, in particular, have limited ambition and capacity to invest in basic science. As we discussed in Chapter 2, Huawei provides one example of such an industry leader committed to basic science. Table 7.2 shows the R&D expenditures by leading Chinese vs US technology firms in 2019.

Table 7.2 Comparison of R&D expenditure by top digital technology firms (2019)

No.	Chinese Company	Annual R&D expenditure (US$ billion)	US Company	Annual R&D expenditure (US$ billion)
1	Huawei	20.0	Amazon	35.9
2	Alibaba	6.6	Alphabet	26.0
3	China Mobile	3.6	Apple	16.2
4	Baidu	2.8	Facebook	13.6
5	JD.com	2.7	Cisco	6.6

Source: Data from the subject companies

The most challenging task in research is to frame the problem and to find research directions. When catching up on existing trajectories, it is easier to understand the problems and find the research directions by following the signposts of the forerunners.

Since the foundation of the PRC, S&T has been one of the core areas for the country's economic development. China's S&T policy has been through four phases:

- First phase (1949–59): S&T policy supported the development of heavy industries along Soviet lines.
- Second phase (1959–76): S&T policy witnessed economic stagnation and ideological domination of technology projects.
- Third phase (1977–2001): S&T policy focused on market-oriented and product-driven research.
- Fourth phase (2002–19): S&T policy aimed to develop high-technology industries, including the internet, communications, and clean-energy technologies.

For China, these S&T reforms reflect a country transitioning from a centrally planned economy to a mixed market economy with strong state presence. S&T investments have successfully improved productivity and efficiency in production. However, bureaucratic structures and discipline-based governance with central-planning attributes have constrained the effectiveness of China's S&T policy as the nation moves towards positions of international leadership.

To solve this problem, the government's blueprint for the Fourteenth Five-Year Plan (2021–6), aims to adjust its S&T policy to encourage interdisciplinary and issue-driven scientific research. For example, industry leaders are encouraged to organize innovation alliances with universities and research institutes to undertake major scientific projects. This policy shift reflects the fact that a group of Chinese firms have appeared that have been aware of and willing to engage in basic science to search for future-orientated problems and solutions. Another significance of this policy is that such an approach allows innovation actors to pursue issue-driven research where there are real problems, especially where China lags behind.

Technology policy, as part of the S&T system, is a policy instrument that supports science-based technologies such as nuclear power, space technology, new-generation computers, genetic engineering, and nanotechnology which are seen as being at the very forefront of future economic growth and sustainability. In some of these technological areas, China has moved from being a follower, absorbing and using existing knowledge, to a leader, building capacity in producing science-based technologies and applying them in practice.

Fusion energy is an area of science in which China is determined to be an international leader. The nation has three experimental tokamak fusion machines, and has invested $700 million in an ambitious programme to construct the Chinese Fusion Engineering Test Reactor (CFETR). This is being built alongside the world's largest scientific project, the fusion reactor ITER (International

Thermonuclear Experimental Reactor) in France. China is a member of the international consortium building ITER, which is due to begin operations in 2025, and is estimated eventually to cost around $40 billion. CFETR is based on ITER technology, but aims to produce more energy. Fusion energy is considered to be a potentially important contribution to the energy mix in future decades, most probably from the 2040s. It provides an example of China investing in long-term science with extensive international collaboration, especially with Europe and the US.

Innovation Policy

Innovation policy is concerned not just about how innovative ideas are generated, but also about how the application of those ideas is diffused and used to create economic and social value such as productivity growth, increased employment, national competitiveness, and reduced poverty and inequality. The objectives of China's national innovation policy are aligned with its political agenda. Most of the time since the foundation of the PRC, China's innovation policy has been centred on catching up. As the country approaches the frontier of innovation, many constraints—such as bottleneck technologies—have been exposed. Facing technology sanctions from the US, the government is advocating building China's technology self-sufficiency. It is also increasing its commitment to international technology agencies, determining, for example, to join global standard-setting organizations, as shown in its 'China Standard 2035' Plan.

There are two types of innovation policy in China. The first type aims to promote innovation within the institutional context, and overlaps with policy instruments used in S&T policy. The second aims to change the institutional context in order to promote innovation in that context and involves reforms of R&D, education, IP, labour markets, and capital markets, among others.

Indigenous Innovation

In 2006, the government released its 'Medium and Long-Term Plan for Technological Development (2006–20)' in which 'indigenous innovation' was recognized for the first time as a national innovation strategy. China's technological catch-up in many industries, especially in manufacturing, has been built on imported technologies that are generally one or two generations behind the forefront of innovation, which is itself a moving target, China's catch-up in this regard has not been effective, revealing the disadvantages faced by latecomers. For this reason, China's policymakers were adamant that the nation needs to develop independent innovation capability and build an innovation-driven industry producing high-quality growth. Information technology, robotic manufacturing equipment, aerospace parts and manufacturing equipment, renewable energy vehicles, raw material extraction technology, pharmaceutical manufacturing and medical equipment, high-tech ship components, agricultural equipment, and mobile phones were identified as pillar industries.

This policy was followed by many implementation plans at ministerial and local levels. Using policy instruments such as government procurement, intellectual property rights, technical standards, and anti-monopoly policies, the policy framework of indigenous innovation aimed to turn large SOEs into multinational enterprises with core technologies and global competitiveness.[26]

This policy has also attracted criticism from the West, especially in the way government procurement to support products from indigenous innovation was considered protectionism. For this reason, in 2010, relevant plans to promote indigenous innovation through government procurement were suspended. The policy thrust remains, however.

From the perspective of an ideal-type innovation policy, as espoused by the OECD and other organizations, China's innovation policy faces three problems. It is subject to a political agenda; the power balance between different ministries and local governments in policy implementation is variable; and there is inefficiency in its current governance and organizational structures, especially in universities and research institutions. Addressing these issues will require further institutional reforms. On 29 October 2020, at the concluding session of the Fifth Plenary Meeting of the Nineteenth Central Committee of the CPC, 'building scientific and technological self-sufficiency' was again emphasized as a strategic goal for national development. This strategy is a further iteration of China's indigenous innovation.

IP policy and Enforcement

Intellectual property (IP) can provide an incentive for innovation by protecting new knowledge creation, giving inventors confidence that they will be able to benefit from their investments. Intellectual property rights (IPR) protection can motivate technological innovation, especially in some sectors.

Patent applications are an indicator of emerging technological prowess. China became the top international patent filing country under the Patent Cooperation Treaty (PCT)[27] for the first time in 2019, and maintained this position, achieving 16.1 per cent growth in 2020, despite Covid-19.[28] In 2018, the value added in patent-intensive industries reached $1,508 billion in China, contributing to 11.6 per cent of national GDP in that year. Total deficit of imports and exports of IPR royalties increased nearly fivefold from $8.5 billion in 2007 to $41 billion in 2019. China's

[26] B. Naughton, (2011), 'China's Economic Policy Today: The New State Activism', *Eurasian Geography and Economics*, 52(3), 313–29.

[27] World Intellectual Property Organization (2020), 'China Becomes Top Filer of International Patents in 2019 amid Robust Growth for WIPO's IP Services, Treaties and Finances.' 7 April, https://www.wipo.int/pressroom/en/articles/2020/article_0005.html, accessed 28 July 2021.

[28] See https://www.wipo.int/pressroom/en/articles/2021/article_0002.html, accessed 28 July 2021.

high and rising IP payment deficit is a reflection of two factors: (1) the growing integration of Chinese firms into global value chains, which requires the use of globally sourced inputs; and (2) China's increasing adherence to strong IP protection.[29]

China's entry to the WTO in 2001 marked a milestone in China's attempts at integrating into the global IP regime. Not only did China become a party to TRIPS (Trade-Related Aspects of Intellectual Property Rights), but it also began to modernize its legal system to protect intangible assets. In 2008 China released its National Intellectual Property Strategy, which outlined specific goals, benchmarks, and a guiding strategy for an intellectual property system that was part of its national innovation policy.

China National Intellectual Property Administration (known as the Sino IP Office before August 2018) grants three types of patents: invention, utility model, and design patents.[30] Of these three types, invention patents are the most substantive and rigorously examined, as they face the highest scrutiny and the strictest screening for quality and novelty in the approval process. The utility model and design patents generally cover more incremental inventions (with no substantive examination required) and product designs, respectively.[31] One consequence of China's innovation policy was that local governments initiated a major change to reward domestic firms for indigenous innovation. The policy had particularly strong implications for SOEs. New performance metrics of patents were introduced that incentivized SOEs to make trade-offs between quality and novelty in patents for quantity.[32] This point can be seen by the fact that many SOEs obtained non-invention patents.

Maintenance of patents requires continuous investments, and SMEs generally cannot afford this cost. One interviewee, a private business owner whose company competes on cutting-edge technological innovation in high-end manufacturing in Dongguan, Guangdong, commented:

> We stopped applying for patents, not just because of the high fees involved, but also because we were concerned about the disclosure of our inventions through patent documents. It is very easy for firms in the same industry to imitate our technology by the keywords disclosed in patents. The only way to maintain competitiveness is through continuous and rapid innovation.

Recognizing the issue, the government has introduced a series of policy instruments to address the problem.[33] As a result, more patents have been granted to private businesses in recent years.

---

[29] See http://english.cnipa.gov.cn/, accessed 7 June 2021.
[30] See http://english.cnipa.gov.cn/, accessed 7 June 2021.
[31] A. G. Hu, and G. H. Jefferson (2009), 'A Great Wall of Patents: What is behind China's Recent Patent Explosion?', *Journal of Development Economics*, 90(1), 57–68.
[32] N. Jia, K. G. Huang, and C. M. Zhang (2019), 'Public Governance, Corporate Governance, and Firm Innovation: An Examination of State-Owned Enterprises', *Academy of Management Journal*, 62(1), 220–47.
[33] National Intellectual Property Administration (2015). White Paper on the Intellectual Property Development. http://sipa.sh.gov.cn/annualreport/20191130/0005-28464.html, accessed 27 July 2021.

Since around 2015, progress has been made on enforcing IP rights, although it is far from optimal. Efforts have been made to generate public awareness of the importance of respecting intellectual property. The key challenge in IP protection is the lengthy and non-transparent law enforcement process, as suggested by a survey of AmCham (American Chamber of Commerce in China) member companies. In the technology and other R&D-intensive sectors, inadequate IP protection limits their investments in China, according to the AmCham survey. 'Difficulty prosecuting IP infringements in court or via administrative measures' was cited as the top IP challenge by 26 per cent of the firms, although this did fall from 39 per cent the year before.[34] Among the enterprises interviewed by the European Chamber of Commerce in China, the proportion that think that China's laws and regulations on IPR protection are appropriate or very effective has increased annually, and now exceeds 60 per cent.[35]

The standards of law enforcement are not always consistent. China uses an IPR protection system called the 'two-track system', or 'dual system', which goes through both administrative law enforcement and civil litigation to adjudicate infringements. The main bodies of administrative law enforcement are the State Intellectual Property Rights Office and local IPR bureaus, as well as a number of administrative groups with IPR law enforcement functions. Additionally, in 2017, the National Intellectual Property Administration established a number of intellectual property protection centres nationwide, and the efficiency of administrative law enforcement was further improved. Normally, civil litigation is less efficient but has more uniform trial standards. After the establishment of the intellectual property court, it is argued that the rulings are more impartial.

SMEs in China with foreign investment have been particularly affected by insufficient legal enforcement of IP protection. These problems are mainly attributed to local protectionism, inconsistent law enforcement standards, and a lack of experience in the judicial departments that handle litigation and infringement cases, as well as weak laws and regulations. A patent lawyer interviewed suggested, 'Typically it takes a long time to win litigations of IP infringement cases for foreign firms. The compensation for the infringed IP was small and the legal cases were largely a matter of principle.' A major deterrent to the effectiveness of judicial IP enforcement is the low amount of damages awarded in IP cases, which can be attributed to the fact that judges tend to rely on statutory damages rather than the full damages afforded by the law.

As Chinese private firms move towards the frontier of technological innovation, demand for protecting digital and other intangible assets grows. As a result, on 31 August 2018, the Standing Committee of the National People's Congress of the PRC published the long-awaited PRC E-Commerce Law ('E-Commerce Law'). The law is

---

[34] American Chamber of Commerce in China (2020), '2020 Business Climate Survey', https://www.amchamchina.org/press/2020-business-climate-survey-released/, accessed 4 June 2021.
[35] European Chamber of Commerce in China (2020), 'Business Confidence Survey 2020: Navigating in the Dark', http://www.europeanchamber.com.cn/en/publications-business-confidence-survey, accessed 4 June 2021.

set to 'protect legal rights and interests of all parties' and 'maintain the market order' in e-commerce.

IP-related businesses—those that contribute to knowledge-intensive sectors such as biopharmaceuticals, IT and the internet, and semiconductors—are industries where core competitive advantages of firms are embedded in intangible assets which underlie firms' overall profitability and share of capital that flows into globalized equity markets. Thus, Chinese technology firms increasingly demand better protection for their patents, copyrights, and trademarks, domestically and globally.

In the course of building new infrastructure supporting the practical applications of a large number of digital technologies, policymakers are paying more attention to judicial interpretations to make relevant laws and regulations more enforceable. One change includes the utilization of blockchain technology, which has become a new phenomenon in the protection of IPR. The Supreme People's Court has issued technical guidelines which recognized blockchain as a technical means to underpin the authenticity of electronic data in civil law enforcement.

Talent Policy

The education, recruitment, and retention of talent such as scientists, engineers, researchers, innovators, and entrepreneurs have been an important policy instrument in China's innovation policy. Competence-building through the provision of education and training and the production and reproduction of skills through learning in the labour force have been used to enhance China's innovation and R&D activities.

'Brain circulation' through attracting overseas returnees from more developed countries acted as an important channel for absorbing international knowledge spillovers and plays a crucial role in latecomer countries' catch-up.[36] Experience from Taiwan confirms this approach. The returnees educated in the US contributed to technology transfer and subsequent industrial upgrading in Taiwan in the 1980s.[37] Based on the Silicon Valley-Hsinchu (Taiwan) experience, the effective technology transfer between Silicon Valley and Hsinchu via Taiwanese returnees enabled the latecomer to achieve technological catch-up. In fact, 'brain circulation' has resulted in a reciprocal knowledge transfer between the host and home countries.[38]

Chinese returnees are those who were born in China but educated (as students, visiting scholars, or visiting researchers) in OECD countries for at least one year and

[36] A. Saxenian and J. Y. Hsu (2001), 'The Silicon Valley–Hsinchu Connection: Technical Communities and Industrial Upgrading', *Industrial and Corporate Change*, 10, 893–920.

[37] M-C. Hu, T. Kastelle, and M. Dodgson (eds.) (2013), Innovation in Taiwan, *Innovation: Management, Policy and Practice*, 15, 4; M. Dodgson, J. Mathews, T. Kastelle, and M. C. Hu (2008), 'The Evolving Nature of Taiwan's National Innovation System: The Case of Biotechnology Innovation Networks', *Research Policy*, 37, 430–45.

[38] A. Saxenian (2002), 'Transnational Communities and the Evolution of Global Production Networks: The Cases of Taiwan, China and India', *Industry and Innovation*, 9, 183–202.

who returned to China for career development.[39] According to China's Ministry of Education, between 1978 and the end of 2019 over 4.23 million had returned home, accounting for more than 86 per cent of the total students who completed their higher education or research overseas and 65 per cent of the total went abroad to conduct research.[40] Although they account for a small proportion of the entire returnee population, overseas returnee entrepreneurs have become a striking phenomenon in China. They play a critical role not only in stimulating innovation through entrepreneurial ventures, but also in attracting venture capital investment and bringing advanced business models and management experiences to their ventures.

Following the Hsinchu model, technocrats in Beijing promote China's own 'brain circulation' scheme, aiming to speed up industrial upgrading.[41] This policy of recruiting from its global knowledge diaspora was first initiated by former President Jiang Zemin to reverse the brain drain of the 1980s and 1990s.[42]

China's Thousand Talents Programme, a public plan to fast-track the country's science and innovation, identifies and rewards foreign scientists, focusing mostly on those with Chinese roots, and then recruits them to work in China's universities. These foreign-educated Chinese have had a significant impact on the translation of the culture and practices of Western models of organizing science and conducting research into Chinese universities. They also provide much of the leadership of innovation in high-tech industry.

Beijing's Zhongguancun Science Park, for example, was established as a major hub for highly skilled talent, especially returnees.[43] Within it there are thirty-seven tailor-made 'Overseas Student Pioneer Parks', bundled with attractive incentive packages. These incubators have attracted a large number of returnees, many of whom have founded or incubated ventures since 2010.

Current geopolitics, especially the trade conflicts between the US and China, has been another trigger point which has caused an influx of overseas returnees.

Education Reforms

China's first modern university, Beiyang University (today's Tianjin University), was established in 1895, followed by Qiushi Academy (today's Zhejiang University) in 1897, and Jingshi University (today's Peking University) in 1898. By the time the

---

[39] H. Wang (2012), *Globalizing China: The Influence, Strategies and Successes of Chinese Returnees*, Bingley: Emerald Group Publishing.
[40] See http://www.moe.gov.cn/jyb_xwfb/gzdt_gzdt/s5987/202012/t20201214_505447.html, accessed 28 July 2021.
[41] M. Y. Zhang (2014), 'Innovation Management in China', in M. Dodgson, D. M. Gann, and N. Phillips (eds.), *The Oxford Handbook of Innovation Management*, Oxford: Oxford University Press, 355–74.
[42] D. Zweig (2008), 'A Limited Engagement: Mainland Returnees from Canada', Asia Pacific Foundation of Canada Research Reports, https://www.asiapacific.ca/sites/default/files/filefield/ChinaReturnees.pdf, accessed 7 June 2021.
[43] Y.-C. Chen (2008), The limits of brain circulation: Chinese returnees and technological development in Beijing. *Pacific Affairs*, 81, 195–215.

PRC was founded, there were 227 higher education institutions in China.[44] Under Mao's regime, China's higher education developed following the former Soviet style under which only a small number of universities were under the administration of the central education ministry and the rest were governed by ministries of specific industries. This created a fragmented but occasionally overlapping administrative structure. The formal university entrance examination system was abolished during the Cultural Revolution, only to be reinstated by Deng Xiaoping in 1977.

Today, those who wish to enter China's higher education as undergraduate students undertake the national university entrance examinations, commonly known as *gaokao*. It is held annually, and its results determine a student's fate of being accepted by different levels of university. According to the Ministry of Education, in 1990, less than 5 per cent of the students who undertook *gaokao* were admitted to China's higher education institutions. In 1999, the government launched higher education reforms to expand university admissions, and the ratio of students admitted to universities reached 56 per cent that year, and the ratio has seen a steady growth ever since, reaching over 80 per cent in recent years.[45] The total number of students undertaking *gaokao* reached the historical high of 10.5 million in 2008 and then declined for over a decade, until the number reached a new high of 10.71 million in 2020 and 10.78 in 2021.

The growth of recruitment scale through *Gaokao* was the result of China's higher-education reforms since 1998. The reforms also include consolidating administrative systems such that all public universities are all under the administration of the Ministry of Education.[46] Since 2010, higher education reforms have shifted to enhance the quality rather than quantity of students, as stated in the 'State Outline for Medium-to-Long-Term Education Reform and Development Plan (2010–2020)'.[47] While some goals of this plan, such as cultivating a group of internationally recognized universities, including a number of top-ranking ones, have largely been achieved, measured by university rankings, some critical goals such as granting more autonomy to university administrators and academic freedom to researchers have been slow. According to a senior academic administrator in a leading university, 'Though relevant laws have given considerable autonomy to Chinese universities, their rights and responsibilities are vaguely defined.' In areas where rights and responsibilities are not clearly defined, multiple government administrative powers can intervene, which leaves little autonomy. As for academic freedom, for example, creative initiatives by young researchers to pursue fresh research ideas can be hampered not only by the bureaucratic structure but also by research hierarchies in

---

[44] R. Hayhoe (1996), *China's Universities 1895–1995: A Century of Cultural Conflict*, New York: Garland Publishing, 75.

[45] See http://114.xixik.com/gaokao/#anchor1, accessed 28 July 2021.

[46] Lixu, L. (2004), 'China's higher education reform 1998–2003: A summary', *Asia Pacific Education. Review*, 5, 14. https://doi.org/10.1007/BF03026275.

[47] http://old.moe.gov.cn//publicfiles/business/htmlfiles/moe/s3501/index.html, accessed 7 June 2021.

which, decision-making on resource allocation is held tightly in the hands of senior researchers and their bureaucratic allies.

Essentially, Chinese universities have a dual governance structure. The university president, although formally the leader and legal representative of the institution, shares authority with a CPC secretary, who in many cases is the chair of the university board and makes final decisions. Regulations on China's higher education remain extensive, and government approval is still required for many managerial decisions in universities.

China's large number of university graduates face an increasingly challenging job market as new technologies and innovations in automation and AI displace many jobs. The challenge for further higher education reforms is to educate students with new skills for new forms of economic activities and develop a workforce for an innovative China. Against this backdrop, China's Education Modernization 2035 was launched in 2019.[48] However, how this plan differs from the previous ones, especially in its implementation details, remains to be seen.

SOE Reforms

The Chinese state plays a direct role in promoting and influencing economic development through the country's large number of SOEs.

About 51,000 SOEs collectively worth $29 trillion employ about 20 million people.[49] Due to the support and protection of the government, many SOEs lack competitive pressures. This type of policy orientation can create inefficiency in resource allocation and weakened overall industrial competitiveness.

'SOEs are a special entity in China,' commented by an interviewee, a senior executive of a large multinational firm in China. 'SOEs sometimes have to carry out tasks for China's political agenda. In other words, SOEs play more a strategic role, than an independent economic entity purely for profit,' he added.

China began the first SOE reforms in the late 1990s. The reform separated the regulatory and business roles of some SOEs, and a number of large national SOEs were created through mergers and acquisitions. Many such SOEs are partially listed on major stock exchanges, and they epitomize China's form of state capitalism. Almost all major business sectors, such as energy, telecommunications, public transport, and other social infrastructure, are state monopolies. They are under the tight control of the government, as its top business executives are appointed by the state power. The state-owned sector in China does not equate to public goods. One interviewee commented, 'In SOEs, risks are shared by the public in a socialist way, but rewards from the capital market are privatized to executives who run the SOEs.'

---

[48] See http://en.moe.gov.cn/features/Specials_twoSessions/twosessions_Opinions/201903/t20190329_375938.html.

[49] OECD (2017), *The Size and Sectoral Distribution of State-Owned Enterprises*, Paris: OECD Publishing, doi: 10.1787/9789264280663-en.

SOEs have privileged access to resources in capital and policy support, consequently leaving fewer resources for innovation by other type of businesses. Most bank loans flow into SOEs. The government argues that, in order to maintain the monopoly in some industries, industrial policy has to impose restrictions on market access to discourage private enterprises. One consequence of this type of policy is that private enterprises are disincentivized to enter some areas in which innovation is most needed. The global financial crisis in 2008 strengthened the power of SOEs in comparison with the private sector.

One side effect of strengthened SOEs is that they create space for rent-seeking by private enterprises, which can profit by working with or alongside specific SOEs. A consequence of this is a reduced concern for innovation. For example, if an SOE is a customer of a private enterprise, product quality and innovation capability are subsidiary to the two parties having a good relationship. This can limit opportunities for those firms which invest to improve product quality and create cost advantages. The existence of SOEs reduces the degree of competition in the overall economy and can also lead to a lack of incentives to innovate in private enterprises.

As we have argued, China's policy framework is often broad-brushed strategic guidance to support certain industries. However, modern industries are often complex systems with many interconnected subsystems. For industrial policy to work, detailed implementation plans addressing each subsystem are needed. Those who are close to the market are better able to identify specific areas where capital, talent, and market protection is needed. On this front alone, private businesses have an important role to play in industrial development.

The central government has recognized this drawback and in 2019 started another round of SOE reforms. The reforms aimed to separate market-driven economic activities from SOEs. They aimed to enable market forces in resource allocation, provide a more level ground for private businesses to compete, and empower private enterprises to take a leading role in innovation. SOE reforms are part of China's economic structural reforms—promoting the diversification of ownership and encouraging the participation of non-state capital in SOEs, including in industries such as energy, transportation, telecommunications, and other non-natural monopoly industries. The reforms also aimed to abolish unreasonable regulations on the non-state run businesses, eliminate various hidden barriers that constrained private businesses, and strengthen the protection of property rights in all types of ownership structures.

It is expected that SOEs will retain an important role in China's economy, but fairer competition between SOEs and non-SOEs will occur, and the market will be empowered to select the most productive enterprises, regardless of their ownership. In market-driven sectors, state capital can become shareholders with privileged shares.

As an executive of a telecommunications operator commented:

In industries such as telecommunications, it is the first-time state capital let go its controlling power, transforming its role from management to investment. This reform is a smart way forward for SOEs. Telecommunication network operators carry strategic functions for the country by running the backbone networks, but they also need to face the demand from the market. Mixed ownership reform means Unicom still owns and runs the backbone networks, but the private firms run the network assets they invested in a joint venture with Unicom and other customer-facing businesses. The separation of the core and fringe businesses enables a reconciliation between the demand from the state and the consumers. This reform is a real institutional change. The reform will introduce market forces into the network operations, as private capital is now allowed to enter the non-backbone network operation businesses.

This reform has two advantages: mixed-ownership enterprises can engage in global activities without being considered as being a representative of the Chinese state; and capital from regional SOEs can be invested in other new and emerging industries. SOEs at all levels have accumulated large amounts of assets and profits from their often monopolistic positions and preferential policy support. Under the Government Guidance Fund scheme, SOEs are allowed to participate in equity investment.

Industrial Policy

Industrial policy in a broad sense refers to any policy that affects the industrial development or competitiveness of a country.[50] The consensus in developed countries is that, to be effective, industrial policies need to focus on market and systems failures to complement market forces. Industrial policies, however, play an important but different role in China, not just because of the large state presence in its economy, but also because of the imbalance between sectors and regions.[51] The visible hand in China aims not just to make up for market failures, but also to actively intervene in economic structural reforms, increase industrial competitiveness, and support strategic and emerging technologies.

Through multifaceted policy instruments in selected industrial sectors at different developmental stages, measures such as government investment, fiscal subsidies, low-interest loans, tax reductions and exemptions, low-cost land supply, and other mechanisms have been used. Government policy and SOEs play an especially active role in capital-driven, heavy industries which are considered significant for national defence and industrial infrastructure. The industrialization of heavy industries such

[50] J. Robinson (2011), 'Industrial Policy and Development: A Political Economy Perspective', in J. Y. Lin and B. Pleskovic (eds.), *Annual World Bank Conference on Development Economics Global 2010: Lessons from East Asia and the Global Financial Crisis*, Washington, DC: World Bank, 61–79.

[51] J. Y. Lin and B. Pleskovic (eds.), *Annual World Bank Conference on Development Economics Global 2010: Lessons from East Asia and the Global Financial Crisis*, Washington, DC: World Bank.

as chemical or steel making has benefited from such policies under the central-planning regime.

The number of industrial policy documents in China has increased significantly this century, and the content of policies has become more specific, with most measures being direct government interventions. Since 2001, China has issued more than 170 innovation support policies at the central level alone, and many more have been issued at the local level. Industry policies are formulated and implemented by at least twenty-four ministries and agencies. China's industrial policy development in the past forty years is summarized in Table 7.3 at the end of this chapter.

China's industrial policies are formulated by relevant government officials along with selected industry experts, but participation from industry and enterprises and other relevant stakeholders is relatively low. For a long time, industrial policy tried to restrict competition by designing entry barriers based on the ownership and scale of enterprises in selected industries. Such policies have caused market distortions and unfair competition, leading to inefficient resource allocation, which is contrary to the purposes of industrial policy.[52]

Another potential shortcoming is that policymaking focuses on formulation rather than on the supervision and evaluation of policy implementation. Local governments usually implement national industrial policies selectively according to local needs. Policies that conform to local interests will be amplified and implemented, and those that do not meet local needs will be deflated or selectively implemented. Although such flexibility may convey the advantages discussed in Chapter 6, it does limit the delivery of a whole of China approach.

With the improvement of the market economic system, industrial policy has the opportunity be more open, fair, and transparent. There are also advantages when industrial policy is linked with innovation policy, competition policy, fiscal policy, financial policy, and other relevant policies. To achieve this, further institutional reforms are needed.

The Functions of Industrial Policy at Different Developmental Stages

From the late 1970s, on the basis of the phased characteristics of economic development, China followed the industrial policies of Japan, South Korea, Singapore, and other catching-up countries. China's industrial policies gradually formed a huge and complex system composed of industrial structure policies, industrial technology policies, industrial organization policies, and industry-specific policies.

Industrial policy between 1978 and 1991 focused on adjusting the industrial structure when the market economy had yet been established. This visible hand played an important role in correcting the imbalance in industrial structure and promoting economic growth through direct interventions such as government investment, bank credit and taxation, supplemented by indirect interventions. From the late 1980s to the 1990s, for example, supporting policies for strengthening basic

---

[52] Robinson, 'Industrial Policy and Development'.

Table 7.3 The development of China's industrial policy in relation to innovation

Period	Key issues	Industrial policy guidance	Major policy instruments	Milestones
1978–91 Transition from central planning to market economy	• Imbalance in industrial structure	• Correcting major imbalance in industrial structure • Restoring economic growth	Direct interventions such as government investment, bank credit, taxation, supplemented by indirect interventions	• The Seventh Five-Year Plan (1986–90) in April 1986: for the first time, the term 'industrial policy' appeared in a national document • The Eighth Five-Year Plan (1991–2000) in March 1991: accelerating industrial structural reforms and improving economic efficiency, targeted at moving China towards modernization
1992–2011 Construction of early-stage market economy	• Regional disparity • 'Repeated construction of industrial capacity, the quality and efficiency of economic operations were low, and overcapacity in most industries was prominent.' • SOE reforms • Global financial crisis in 2008 • Increasing trade protectionism • Domestic economy downturn	• Adjusting industrial structure • Developing multilayered industrial structure. • Upgrading basic, pillar and high-tech industries • Upholding economic growth through technological investment • 'Quantity-oriented' growth giving way to 'quality-oriented' growth in industrial development • Developing indigenous innovation to enhance the competitiveness of Chinese industries in global value chains • Technological innovation, commercialization, and industrialization as new focus of growth • Developing dual-use technologies for both military and civilian use • Regional development plans	The use of direct interventions gradually giving way to indirect interventions, supplemented by economic, legal, and administrative measures	• In 1992, Deng Xiaoping's 'South Tour' speech: a new chapter in China's economic reforms • In March 1997, at the Fifteenth National Congress of the CPC, Jiang Zemin announced a new science and technology policy of 'fostering China's growth through promoting science, technology and education' (*Ke Jiao Xing Guo*) • The State Council's 'Government Work Report' in March 1999: SOE reforms and supporting the development of high-tech SMEs became a priority • In August 1999: 'Decision of the Central Committee of CPC and the State Council on Strengthening Technological Innovation, Developing High Technology, and Realizing Industrialization' • The Twelfth Five-Year Plan (2011–15) in March 2011: building a modern industrial system with high added value, strong employability, and upgrading of the manufacturing sector

| 2012–19 Construction of intermediate state market economy | • Industrial transformation and upgrading for high-quality growth
• Need for further institutional reforms
• Environmental challenges
• Growing urban–rural inequality widened.
• Emergence of digital economy | • Optimizing industrial structure
• Upholding economic growth through technological innovation
• 'Implement an innovation-driven development strategy.'
• Supporting strategic emerging industries
• Innovation clusters
• Accelerating industrial structural upgrades and transformation
• Supply side reforms
• Technological innovation for environmental protection | Industrial policies have paid more attention to the role of market, and measures through market mechanisms are used widely | • In November 2012, the CPC National Congress proposed 'adapting to new economic conditions at home and abroad, forming new development based on quality and efficiency and relying on all market players, and implementing innovation-driven development plan'
• In May 2015, *Made in China 2025* aiming to modernize China's industrial capability
• In October 2015, the Fifth Plenary Session of the Eighteenth Central Committee of the CPC: 'Innovation must be placed at the core of overall national development through continued effort in all kinds of innovation.'
• In December 2016, the Central Economic Work Force: the 'new normal' of economic development |

Source: Compiled by the authors from secondary sources, including the relevant government websites

industries and cultivating pillar industries promoted a rapid expansion of energy, steel, car-making, and other pillar industries, which in practice led to overcapacity in some industries.

After two decades of reforms, China accomplished its initial target of building a market logic into its economy. Its industrial policies thereafter shifted from quantity-oriented to quality-oriented industrial development and from the expansion of production capacity to creating industrial innovation capacity. Industrial policies have paid more attention to the role of the market, and market mechanisms are used widely, especially since 2006, with the aim of promoting indigenous innovation to increase the competitiveness of Chinese industries in global value chains.

The report of the Eighteenth National Congress of the CPC, for example, in November 2012 pointed out that China needs to pursue innovation-driven development by building a modern industry, noting: 'To achieve technological development by leaps and bounds, China must encourage technological innovation and develop its independent intellectual property rights in key areas and several frontiers of technological development.'

This report represented a policy shift which reflected the government's reactions to changing conditions domestically and globally. The aftermath of the global financial crisis imposed severe challenges for China's industrial progress. On the one hand, international market demand shrank, followed by global deflation and trade protectionism. On the other hand, the domestic economy faced a downturn, institutional and structural conditions continued to be a constraint for its industrial development, independent innovation capabilities were still weak, pollution was heavy after rapid industrialization, and urban-rural inequality widened. China's industrial policy at the time aimed to address the problems of unbalanced, uncoordinated, and unsustainable development by promoting accelerated industrial transformation and upgrading for high-quality growth.

New technologies characterized by digitalization, intelligence, networking, and environmental sustainability have called for further innovation in production methods, business models, and industrial ecosystems. To grasp this opportunity, the government reiterated the importance of innovation. An innovation-driven development strategy was outlined in the policy document by the Central Economic Work Force of the State Council in December 2016. The policy suggested that adapting to the new normal of economic development by enhancing 'supply-side structural reform' and promoting 'scientific and technological innovation' is critical for China's sustainable growth. The policy noted, 'It is necessary to focus on strengthening the new driving force of innovation-driven development, pay attention to exerting entrepreneurial talents, accelerate technological innovation, and strengthen product innovation, brand innovation, industrial organization innovation, and business model innovation.'

'Made in China 2025'

One industrial policy that has drawn considerable attention is *Made in China 2025*. China's unique geopolitical position as a manufacturing hub connecting innovation and capital in more developed countries with the supply of raw materials and labour from developing countries means China needs to have a complex industry policy to supply multilayered industries and multilevels of manufacturing capabilities. *Made in China 2025* is such a blueprint that its real transformative potential lies in its recognition of, and emphasis on, developing intangible assets such as intellectual property and technological standards.

Intangible asset investment is different from tangible investment in part because it is more difficult to value through traditional accounting methods and in part because it is more scalable (due to a lack of physical production constraints) and can generate less predictable productivity and economic value.[53] Therefore, intangible economy-based competition requires not only financial capital and well-organized regulation (for example, to enforce IPR), but also, importantly, enterprises that are able to generate ideas and research that can be commercialized into data, trade secrets, patents, brands, and the like. In many ways, the accumulation of intangible assets will determine China's future global competitiveness.

Industrial policy for a uncertain future

In 2020, in the light of the Covid-19 pandemic, China had the chance to review its *Made In China 2025* and the Thirteenth Five-Year Plan (2016–20) and proposed the outline of the country's Fourteenth Five-Year Plan (2021–6). The outline showed that policymakers recognize that 'industrial policies must ensure that the market mechanism is effective and leave all matters determined by the market'. The successes of Shenzhen as a Special Economic Zone and Shanghai Pudong New Economy Zone, as well as private enterprises such as Huawei, Alibaba, and Xiaomi, demonstrate that the market can solve structural problems well with little industrial policy intervention. Even if industrial policies are needed to make up for market deficiencies in certain areas, the implications of these successes are that they should be minimal and precise and use indirect guidance rather than direct interventions.

The outline also emphasized that, in the general competition field and outside natural monopoly industries, government-led resource allocation must be completely changed. The view expressed is that to avoid the possibility of rent-seeking behaviour, the government should not select winners and losers. The government should make more use of industrial policies inclusive of the private sector to provide necessary public services and infrastructure, to create a good market environment for industrial development.

China's economy has been deeply integrated into the world economy, with high degrees of interconnection with global industries, and as a result its status and influence globally have been greatly increased. To assume the responsibilities of an industrial superpower, China needs to shift its industrial policy from protection of its domestic industries and domestic markets to enhance the global competitiveness of

---

[53] J. Haskel and S. Westlake (2018), *Capitalism without Capital: The Rise of the Intangible Economy*, Princeton, NJ: Princeton University Press.

its enterprises in line with international rules. China's domestic competition has extended to the global market, and global competition has become more localized and regionalized. Thus, policymakers need to pay attention to the importance of compliance with international rules and consider foreign stakeholders when formulating and implementing industrial policies. This requires a new mind- and skill set in industrial policymakers.

Policy towards Green Growth

Another major policy thrust is directed towards environmental sustainability. China has declared it intends to become carbon-neutral by 2060, a decade later than nations such as the UK and Japan.

The nation is the world's largest emitter of carbon dioxide, emitting more than the US and EU combined.[54] Some immediate policy responses are being pursued, such as the push to encourage new energy vehicles (NEVs), which is described in the next section. The government has released a year-by-year schedule to phase out internal combustion engine vehicles (ICEVs). According to this plan, by 2050, the nationwide market share of ICEV new car sales will drop to zero.[55] China is also investing in long-term science and technology in fusion power (which has none of the safety and environmental drawbacks of fission nuclear plants). China has also made great strides in solar power. It is the world's largest market for photovoltaics and solar thermal energy and has the world's largest solar farm.[56] It makes more than 60 per cent of the world's solar panels.

The central government has shown its determination to rectify mistakes of the past, as seen in the establishment of the Ministry of Environmental Protection in 2008 (which became the Ministry of Ecology and Environment in 2018), an upgrade from an administrative bureau of environmental protection. This happened amid the general downsizing of government ministries, showing the government's determination. Chen Jining, the current mayor of Beijing, was appointed as the minister after serving three years as President of Tsinghua University. Trained as an environmental scientist at Imperial College London, Chen introduced advanced policy initiatives and was also instrumental in ensuring top-down policy implementation reform at the ministry. Advanced technologies have been used, for example, to monitor any underground practices in manufacturing facilities that cause damage to the environment. Despite these policy initiatives, the real issue in China's

[54] See R. Rapier (2018), 'China Emits More Carbon Dioxide than the U.S. and EU Combined, Forbes, 1 July, https://www.forbes.com/sites/rrapier/2018/07/01/china-emits-more-carbon-dioxide-than-the-u-s-and-eu-combined/, accessed 7 June 2021.

[55] Innovation Center for Energy and Transportation, June 2020. 'Update Timetable for phasing Out China's Traditional ICE Vehicles and Its Environmental Benefits Assessment', http://www.nrdc.cn/information/informationinfo?id=254&cook=1, accessed 27 July 2021.

[56] See C. Baraniuk (2018), 'How China's Giant Solar Farms Are Transforming World Energy', BBC, 4 September, https://www.bbc.com/future/article/20180822-why-china-is-transforming-the-worlds-solar-energy, accessed 7 June 2021.

environmental challenges lies in its local policy implementation. Local governments are policy implementers, but they also benefit from the immediate performance of the local economy, and following stringent environmental policy means sacrificing profitability. China's economic growth has been built at the cost of environmental damage in the past four decades; it will take as long or longer to rectify such damage, especially at the local level.

It is clear that, given the extent of the environmental challenges in China, a basket of policies not just from the energy supply side, but also aiming to change the dynamics of the demand side, needs urgent prioritization. Any future policies in science, technology, innovation, and industry designed to increase growth have to ensure that growth is environmentally sustainable. Most critically, as in any industries in China, market-driven reforms by demolishing state monopoly in a supportive policy environment will help China achieve its carbon-neutral target.

Industrial Policies in Car Industry

The car industry, as a pillar industry, has been the focus of much policy attention. The country is the world's largest and fastest-growing car market.[57] The best-selling makers of car are Volkswagen, Hyundai, Audi, and Honda, all of which entered China's market early and built JVs with local partners.[58] More than half of the cars on the roads in major cities in China are foreign makes.

Industrial policy aiming at developing China's car industry began in 1986. Starting from a very weak technological and industrial foundation, the policy adopted an approach to importing technologies in car parts and components manufacturing through its technology transfer scheme, which required foreign car-makers to form joint ventures with local parts and components manufacturers in order to enter the Chinese market. The policy hoped that through such a scheme, China would build its indigenous technology in car manufacturing by 'importing, absorbing, and re-innovating' foreign technologies. After decades of development, however, China's car market became large, but with little indigenous innovation in whole-car manufacturing. Market growth in China occurred though the use of older generations of imported technologies.

China's car industry did not develop its indigenous innovation capability as hoped. From the perspective of industrial policy, an endogenous ability in product development and production, especially in an industry as complex as car-making, requires the long-term accumulation of technological innovation capability and engineering know-how to achieve expected levels of quality and competitiveness. China's competitors in this industry possess these capabilities in abundance.

---

[57] Accenture, 2021, The Future of Automotive Sales in China. https://www.accenture.com/_acnmedia/PDF-147/Accenture-Study-The-Future-of-Automotive-Sales-in-China.pdf, accessed 27 July 2021.

[58] Economist (2020), 'China Has Never Mastered Internal-Combustion Engines', *The Economist*, 4 January, https://www.economist.com/technology-quarterly/2020/01/02/china-has-never-mastered-internal-combustion-engines, accessed 8 June 2021.

Changing to a New Technological Trajectory

The lessons from the failed catch-up in internal combustion vehicles are that acquiring advanced technological capability in a mature industry that has developed over many years is especially hard, and China has little time to accumulate it. At the same time as it was recognized that car industry policies had not achieved their objectives, the climate crisis caused by increasing carbon dioxide (CO_2) emissions called for new energy policies. This provided an opportunity for China to capitalize on the windows of opportunity opened by the emergence of a new technological trajectory in carmaking. China has bet on electric vehicles, reflecting the view that latecomers have a higher chance to lead on new trajectories than in catching up with old ones. It has introduced intensive policies and measures to support the development of new energy vehicles (NEVs).

In October 2007, the 'New Energy Vehicle Production Access Management Rules' were launched, which formulated the conditions for access to the production of new energy vehicles. To cultivate the NEV consumer market, in January 2009, the Ministry of Science and Technology and four other ministries and commissions launched the 'Ten Cities and Thousand Vehicles' energy-saving and NEV demonstration and application project. In 2010, the State Council identified NEVs as one of seven strategic emerging industries.

In June 2012, the State Council issued the 'Energy-Saving and New Energy Vehicle Industry Development Plan (2012–20)', clarifying that NEVs include pure electric, plug-in hybrid electric, and fuel cell vehicles. In 2013, conditions and subsidies for NEV demonstration cities were clarified. In 2014, the General Office of the State Council issued the 'Guiding Opinions on Accelerating the Promotion and Application of New Energy Vehicles', which outlined consumer subsidies for NEV purchases. Under this scheme, NEVs were exempted from vehicle purchase tax.

As a strategic emerging industry, NEVs have received a range of policy supports, including subsidies in R&D and production on the supply side and discounted charging operations, purchase subsidies, and tax reductions and exemptions on the demand side. On the supply side, domestic production of NEVs has entered a period of explosive growth. Between 2015 and 2020, at least 300 companies entered the car industry hoping to capitalize on the window of opportunity stimulated by the NEV policy, significantly increasing competition in the sector. Three categories of NEV makers have emerged in China:

- NEV car-makers: at present, these are represented by a group of start-ups such as Nio, Weltmeister (WM), and Xpeng that entered the industry with the view of running an internet business funded by VC/PE capital. They are still at the early stage of development and face challenges in meeting mass production targets.
- Foreign car-makers: these entered China's NEV market later than the new car-makers. At present, most foreign makes operate in China in the form of joint

ventures with local partners, such as Volkswagen with Jianghuai, BMW with Great Wall, and Mercedes-Benz with BYD.

- Traditional independent car-makers: at present, the domestic NEV market is still dominated by traditional car-makers such as Beijing Automotive Group, Shanghai Automotive Group, and BYD. According to statistics from the China National Machinery Centre, the top ten domestic NEV makers are all traditional car-makers.

Competition is intense between the new and traditional car-makers. Traditional car-makers, the latecomers in the NEV sector, possess advantages in mechanical technologies and processes compared to new car-makers; however, it is challenging for them to catch up in digital technologies such as AI and the internet of things. On the other hand, new car-makers, although heavily backed by investment from the capital market, have to rely on contract manufacturers for production, which makes them less capital-intensive but also yields less control over the production process.

On the demand side, often the most important incentive for consumers is that they can purchase NEVs without waiting for the vehicle registration licences which are offered to car buyers on a lottery system or by paying for high licensing costs in large cities. Passenger NEVs are largely sold in first- and second-tier cities, where restricted vehicle licences are implemented, but they are penetrating into third-tier cities. Sales of NEVs contributed only 4.5 per cent of the total vehicle sales in China, but their growth is accelerating. In 2010, the sales volume of NEVs was only 8,159 units and this reached 1.256 million units in 2018, more than 50 per cent of the world total. In 2018, the number of NEVs sold in Shanghai alone exceeded that of Germany, France, and the UK combined. The number of NEV sales in Hangzhou exceeds that of Japan. Half of China's NEV sales went to private buyers. The production and sales of NEVs continued to grow in 2020 despite Covid-19, reaching 1.366 million in production and 1.367 million in sales, 7.5 per cent and 10.9 per cent growth over the year before, respectively.[59]

Improvement of Industrial Policy in NEVs

China is not only the largest NEV market in the world, but it has strengths in advanced NEV technologies and supply chains. Industrial policy has played a central role in its development, although its subsidy scheme was criticized as a hotbed for rent-seeking behaviours such as corrupt and fraudulent subsidies. For example, some policies in NEVs were selective in that, in the absence of an effective competition policy, the 'visible hand' of the government selected the winners and technical standards in the industry, instead of letting the market decide.

---

[59] See https://www.argusmedia.com/en/news/2176409-chinas-nev-production-sales-rise-in-2020, accessed 28 July 2021.

To correct this distorted competition, Tesla's Gigafactory in Shanghai has become a market stimulus. It not only marked the end of restrictions on foreign shareholding of NEVs, but also exposed Chinese NEV makers to new competition. This policy, in the long run, will be beneficial to the development of the industry. The attraction of China for Tesla is not just its huge market and low-cost supply of parts and components, but also because China's manufacturing prowess helps Tesla overcome the production bottleneck it suffered. Another attraction is that China is likely to be ahead of the US in driverless vehicles.[60]

The government mandated that all NEVs sold in China from 2019 should be made with Chinese parts and components. Tesla has managed to the slash costs of its Model 3 made in its Shanghai factory by increasing the supply of localized components. The ratio of locally produced parts increased from 50 per cent at the end of 2019 to 70 per cent in October 2020. This will lead China to develop the world's most important supply chains for components of electric vehicles, potentially emulating its role in smartphones.

Tesla and other new makers of NEV, amid the rise of the internet, semiconductors, and other technologies, have blurred the industry boundaries of the car industry by reshaping the core value chain. The core value of the car industry will no longer lie with the engine and chassis, but with power storage, batteries, chips, and driving data. After ten years of planning and cultivation, China's NEV industry has built certain first-mover and scale advantages. China's forging ahead in the industry can be attributed to three windows of opportunity:[61] changes in the technological paradigm (from internal-combustion vehicles to NEVs), policy window (the government providing incentives for both the supply and demand side for NEV adoption), and changing demand conditions (some consumers have become more environmentally conscious, and some are responding to financial and other incentives for purchasing NEVs).

A New Era

The car industry possesses such significance in a country's economy that it often elicits political responses. In April 1990, when China faced sanctions from the West, the central government announced at the Shanghai Volkswagen General Assembly that China would open up to the outside world, and the then Premier Li Peng announced an agreement to speed up the development of the Shanghai Pudong New Area. This agreement marked China's willingness to open its market to foreign investment and technology. When China was facing an even more severe backlash in response to globalization and US sanctions against Chinese technology firms, the

---

[60]   Economist (2020), 'Cloning Tesla: Electric-Vehicle Wars in China', *The Economist*, 4 January, https://www.economist.com/business/2020/01/04/cloning-tesla-electric-vehicle-wars-in-china,   accessed   8 June 2021.

[61]   K. Lee and F. Malerba (2017), Catch-Up Cycles and Changes in Industrial Leadership: Windows of Opportunity and Responses of Firms and Countries in the Evolution of Sectoral Systems. *Research Policy*, 46(2), 338–51.

State Council approved the establishment of the Shanghai Free Trade Zone, which is four times larger than the Pudong New Area, and approved the establishment of Tesla's Shanghai Gigafactory as a wholly owned entity. Again, China chose to open its market to welcome foreign investment and technology. In the future, the government stated that in order to speed up the control of urban carbon emissions, it will ban the sale of vehicles using fossil energy, very likely around 2040. Given China's huge market size, the demand for NEVs is likely to shape the global automotive manufacturing landscape.

Lessons

Policy learning is a significant phenomenon in the transformation of China's innovation and industry.[62] This phenomenon is in sharp contrast to some commonly held (mis)understandings that policymakers are in a position, once and for all, to design a master plan that defines the optimal solutions to all problems. In all cases, an essential feature of effective policies associated with dealing with increasing challenges domestically and globally after the Covid-19 pandemic is the continued need for policy learning and adaptation as the challenges confronting the country change over time.

In the past, Chinese industrial policy has supported selected industries with direct policy and financial aid. In the future, there are advantages for industrial policy targeting enterprises by helping them develop innovation capabilities and improve their global competitiveness. In essence, this is a movement from industrial to innovation policy. In terms of institutional reforms, such a move would involve China enhancing the independence of regulatory authorities and further separating the government's regulatory functions from its ownership interests and policymaking.

A key challenge China is facing is ensuring that innovation independence will not undermine China's ability to benefit from open and collaborative innovation. Indeed, an open and globally integrated innovation system is critical to strengthening domestic innovation capacity and avoiding technologies that are only relevant in China.

As argued by the chief economist at the European Bank for Reconstruction and Development, after Covid-19 the big question is how the visible hand of the government will become a 'caring hand' by providing economic and social support without compromising private businesses or a 'grabbing hand' by which state capitalism is strengthened at the cost of private enterprises.[63] The consequence of this balance of institutional logics will have a profound impact on China's future.

We now turn, in Chapter 8, to how China manages the dialectic between chaos and order and assess the future for China's innovation machine.

---

[62] S. Gu and B.-A. Lundvall (2006), 'Policy Learning as a Key Process in the Transformation of the Chinese Innovation System', in B.-A. Lundvall, P. Intarakumnerd, and J. Vang (eds.), *Asia's Innovation Systems in Transition*, Cheltenham: Edward Elgar, 293–312.

[63] B. Javorcik (2020), 'Covid Has Made the State's Hand More Visible But There Are Risks', *The Financial Times*, 9 November, https://www.ft.com/content/c5295c0d-ab82-49fd-afb4-0edba303ac4d, accessed 8 June 2021.

8
Chaotic Order

"Utter chaos leads to great order under heaven."

Mao Zedong[1]

When Mao Zedong's position within the Communist Party of China was under threat, he regained his political legitimacy by stirring up mass political participation and nationwide chaos in the Cultural Revolution. This political philosophy—new order emerges out of chaos when the old order is demolished—has been the fundamental logic of dynasty changes in Chinese history for thousands of years. It is also the logic of the market economy with Chinese characteristics—order at the central and higher levels but lack of order at the local and lower levels. This logic also lies behind China's innovation machine. China is in transition from being a technological follower to a technological leader in the global arena. Given the international significance of this transition, much more needs to be understood about the chaos at the micro and component levels of the innovation machine and how patterns of order emerge at the macro and systemic levels.

In four decades, China's radical economic and institutional reforms transformed a central-planning economy into what is now a relatively mature mixed market economy second in size to that of the US. Technological innovation has been a major driving force behind China's growth. China's innovation performance results from the actions of innovators in its national institutional framework. Institutional reforms within this framework have played a critical role in China's advances in innovation. These reforms extend beyond SOEs and research institutions. They also include private enterprises and individual entrepreneurs, who were excluded from the country's innovation efforts before the reforms, and are an important addition, along with the SOEs and state-funded universities/research institutions, to what are commonly called national systems of innovation.

Research into national systems of innovation shows that the appetite and ability to innovate are deeply embedded within the particularities of countries. While many nations have similar institutional structures, technologies, and social and business mores, and some business behaviours are ubiquitous, countries differ in the way

---

[1] Author's translation. In Mao's letter to Madame Mao, Jiang Qing, dated 8 July 1966, Mao shared his opinions on the domestic and international situations and on the launching of the Cultural Revolution and said, 'Utter chaos leads to great order under heaven.' (Institute of History and Documentation of Chinese Communist Party, http://www.dswxyjy.org.cn/n/2013/0111/c244520-20169620.html, accessed 8 June 2021).

Demystifying China's Innovation Machine: Chaotic Order. Marina Yue Zhang, Mark Dodgson, and David M. Gann, Oxford University Press. © Marina Yue Zhang, Mark Dodgson, and David M. Gann 2022.
DOI: 10.1093/oso/9780198861171.003.0008

they encourage and apply innovations. They have different innovation machines. This relates to their distinct histories, politics, religions, and industrial and social structures. For this reason, China's innovation machine is significantly different compared to those of other nations.

As shown throughout this book, China's innovation performance cannot be explained simply as the result of government interventions. Rather than China's political or state capitalism being behind the nation's innovation successes, it is a result of the interplay of the state, enterprises, and entrepreneurs in a dynamic process. As Peck and Zhang summarize: 'If the awkward formulation of "state capitalism" reveals anything, it is that the recombinant Chinese state, which somehow holds together an unlikely marriage of entrepreneurial developmentalism with Leninist party discipline, remains the principal orchestrator of the country's development path.'[2]

We use the metaphor 'innovation machine' to describe China's innovation system, as it describes not only various elements in the system but also how they are connected in an active and dynamic way. It produces actions to a purpose, and these can include social and economic advance. The machine is comprised of numerous components, and its performance is optimal when they are all fully integrated and coordinated. Machines need to be powered (fuelled) and their operation needs to be eased (oiled), which can be allied in the metaphor to social and business relationships. The innovation machine both guides and is animated by the activities of innovation actors. On the other hand, machines can break down, quickly and unexpectedly, without continual maintenance and concern to build their resilience.

In China's complex innovation machine, actors in different subsystems develop deep specializations in any given area and form interdependent relationships. Although individual actors facing severe competition can be fragile, as this machine is so massive with countless actors in many subsystems, the machine is resilient. In other words, this innovation machine is an innovation ecosystem that, as a whole, is 'antifragile'.[3] Biological evolution is such that inheritable random variations at the individual level can be selected by nature and, thus, accumulate and amplify in the population. Like evolution in biology, in complex systems, as argued by Taleb (2012), bottom-up variations at the individual level, often in response to a certain level of stressors, may increase the resilience and even the antifragility of the collective whole. Antifragility is beyond robustness, which mitigates shocks and allows a return to the status quo, and rather has the capacity to make things better and stronger.

China's innovation machine has certain antifragile features; it not only resists shocks but also thrives under the right amount of stress and disorder. Antifragility in China's innovation machine has a property that allows the collective whole to deal with the unknown and to do things without a rule book or even understanding the

[2] J. Peck and J. Zhang (2013), 'A Variety of Capitalism…with Chinese |Characteristics?', *Journal of Economic Geography*, 13(3), 357–96.
[3] N. N. Taleb (2012), *Antifragile: Things That Gain from Disorder*, London: Penguin.

game it is playing. In other words, order emerges from chaos through bottom-up evolution. China's innovation machine is organic rather than mechanical, and it is a multilayered and complex ecosystem, the evolution of which follows some hidden rules. Its composition of multiple subsystems means that even if one part breaks down, the whole system will continue and potentially get stronger.

How China's innovation machine operates reflects the Chinese cultural roots of collectivism over individualism (e.g. group over individual) and holism over partition (e.g. state over local), as well as a high tolerance of ambiguity and uncertainty. Concerns about the fragility of Chinese innovation in the face of increasing protectionism and a potential technology cold war between China and the US need to account for the evolutionary view of its innovation machine and the potential, if certain conditions are met, that China will perform better facing such stressors. A disruptive black swan[4] event such as Covid-19 could cause the shutdown of a mechanical machine, but China's innovation machine built upon its organic structure moderated the shock, and there is evidence to suggest it became stronger. The resilience of this machine is shown in how China recovered rapidly in 2020 from the deep and profound impacts of the Covid-19 pandemic on its innovation capability, supply chains, and manufacturing sector.

Overall, innovation activities in China remain large but not uniformly strong. The lack of investment in basic science and weak independent innovation capability still limit China's development of cutting-edge industrial innovation power. There are many bottlenecks in elements of China's innovation machine, such as lithography, high-end IC chips, computer operating systems, mobile radio frequency devices, industrial software, and core algorithms for computing.[5] Building the antifragility of China's innovation machine requires resources and time and, most importantly, an open system that enables freedom to experiment at the individual level and distributed power to select winners and losers in the ecosystem.

Industrialization and the Democratization of Innovation

From the steam engine (first industrial revolution) to electricity and oil (second industrial revolution), and then to IC chips and internet technologies (third industrial revolution), and now to AI and integrated physical, digital, and biological technologies (fourth industrial revolution), technological advancement has driven industrial revolutions that have greatly increased the capacity for innovation and the efficiency of energy utilization and communications, which, consequently, have improved productivity and living standards. As a result of the third industrial

---

[4] N. N. Taleb (2007), *The Black Swan: The Impact of the Highly Improbable*, New York: Random House.
[5] A speech by Liu Yun, professor of the University of Chinese Academy of Sciences, at 2020 China Unicom Science and Technology Innovation Conference, November 2020: see http://www.techweb.com.cn/tech/2020-11-30/2814014.shtml, accessed 8 June 2021.

revolution, digitalization penetrated into all elements in industry value chains, and the fourth industrial revolution has empowered limitless possibilities for new combinations within value chains, which can create new industries within or across industry boundaries.

The advancement of information and communication technology, especially the development of the internet and mobile internet, has transformed people's lives through the recombination of data underlined by computer power and digital algorithms. This transformation has extended to connect online and offline spheres, enabling new lifestyles and the sharing economy, as well as smart manufacturing. Online and offline convergence has already had profound impacts on the economy, politics, and wealth creation. Empowered by platforms, individuals have a widened stage on which they can play important roles in innovation: they cluster by their common interests, not only by their geographic proximities, and, collectively, generate a disproportionally powerful influence in innovation compared to the simple addition of each individual.

Entrepreneurs and innovators from anywhere in the world can create and insert their designs into global value chains and can share their designs and collaborate with like-minded people in online communities. Using standard design files, entrepreneurs and innovators can send their unique design specifications to commercial manufacturers to be produced in any number. Digital tools enable individuals and organizations to create designs for new products and prototype them faster than ever, and these will be translated into customized mass production. This trend radically shortens the time from idea to entrepreneurship to commercialization, intensifying the innovation process.[6]

In summary, innovation has been decentralized and modularized, such that, in a sense, everybody can be an innovator. Using a web-based approach in manufacturing, for example, SMEs, micro-firms, or individuals can build a user community from which they draw inspiration for continued innovations, exploring variation and letting the market select the fittest.

The changing economics of value chains sees the boundaries between innovation in manufacturing and the consumption of technology becoming increasingly blurred. The third and the fourth industrial revolutions have not only increased production efficiency, but, more importantly, bring a paradigm shift from an industrial age to a digital and intelligent age, accentuating some of the features of innovation, including:

- Advances in digital technology, especially internet and mobile internet applications, have democratized innovation.
- Technological progress and innovation diffusion have rapidly accelerated in many fields.

---

[6] M. Dodgson, D. Gann, and A. Salter (2005), *Think, Play, Do: Technology, Innovation and Organization*, Oxford: Oxford University Press.

- Innovation has become an interdisciplinary process in an open system.
- Many innovations have become more complex and may require large-scale collaboration, often at the global scale.
- Innovation has self-generating and self-upgrading features in an open ecosystem.

In the industrial age, corporations built vertical value chains, the governance of which often followed a top-down approach. In the digital age, innovation occurs in an open ecosystem, and value chains are distributed in a network structure. In such a system, governance follows an adaptive approach of bottom-up innovation to create rules that may benefit the entire ecosystem. Digitalization and democratization of innovation open the door for spontaneous, organic, and constructive change driven from bottom-up, challenging the power of top-down design and governance.

As an example, there are 9 million sellers and over 500 million buyers in Taobao's e-commerce ecosystem, and daily transactions of tens of millions of US dollars. To create governance rules to maintain fair and safe transactions with cost and time efficiencies is difficult from the top down. Instead, Taobao designed a bottom-up approach allowing both sellers and buyers to evaluate each other after each transaction. Over time, each seller and buyer accumulates a credit score, which becomes the most critical governance mechanism in Taobao's e-commerce. As in the case of Taobao, in the digital age, important developments arise from the bottom up from which patterns emerge and trends evolve.

Schumpeter's creative destruction characterizes capitalism.[7] Digital technology empowers Schumpeterian entrepreneurs to innovate, allowing bottom-up changes which may lead to system-level evolution at the macro level. Digital technology has democratized innovation by giving power to individuals with creativity over the means of production that in the industrial age required corporate power.

China's 'mass entrepreneurship and innovation' initiative was a response to this paradigm shift. Within five years of the implementation of the policy, hundreds of millions of entrepreneurs and innovators, often educated with STEM degrees, started feeding China's innovation machine. However, China's comparative weakness in high-end manufacturing and certain core technologies can limit this bottom-up innovation approach, which raises the role of the state.

Developmental scholars, such as Justin Lin, the former World Bank chief economist, argue that China's future development in innovation and industry critically depends on further state-led improvements in research capabilities and industrial policies.[8] While this top-down view offers some insights, it has limitations. Particularly, it has missed the realities of the power of the digital age and the

---

[7] J. A. Schumpeter, (1934), *The Theory of Economic Development: An Inquiry into Profits, Capital, Credit, Interest and the Business Cycle*, Cambridge, MA: Harvard University Press.

[8] J. Y. Lin (2010), *New Structural Economics: A Framework for Rethinking Development*, Policy Research Working Paper No. 5197, Washington, DC: World Bank, https://openknowledge.worldbank.org/handle/10986/19919, accessed 8 June 2021.

complexity and dynamics of an open innovation ecosystem, boundary-spanning activities in innovation, and the exponential diffusion of knowledge in networks. Of most concern is the way the top-down approach might involve decisions based on political power, rather than the intrinsic value of innovations, in selecting winners and losers. In presuming the central position of the top-down approach, the roles of other actors and contexts and their interplay is systematically downplayed.[9]

Under any circumstances, entrepreneurs face uncertainties and high chances of failure, but through risk-taking trial and error, they create bottom-up innovation at the micro level, some of which can be selected by the market, amplified in interconnected networks, and enhance system-level performance. In an interconnected ecosystem, even failed entrepreneurial endeavours make contributions to system-level advantages, as their failures send signals to other actors in an interconnected system. In this and other ways, the scale of entrepreneurial activities matter.

An Evolutionary View of China's Innovation Machine

The evolutionary view of innovation focuses on the interactions of innovation actors and their environment. Moore[10] was the first mainstream business scholar who systematically discussed using the ecosystem in biology as an analogy to illustrate how enterprises in a business ecosystem form interdependent relationships. Since then this concept has been used to explain interrelations of actors in innovation networks, with each actor occupying a unique niche, and once the actor and the niche shifts, the change will have cascading impacts in the entire ecosystem.[11] While the evolutionary view of innovation is built primarily upon theories that treat innovation as a production-oriented process dominated by industrial innovators (corporates), it is highly relevant in open innovation systems in which multiple stakeholders (including entrepreneurs and individual innovators and users) contribute to innovation through digital technologies.

The evolutionary view of innovation ecosystems in the digital age is similar to 'Open Innovation 3.0' proposed by the European Union in 2013.[12] Based on this concept, a national innovation ecosystem as an open system includes four interconnected structures: government (public institutions), enterprises (industry), universities (research), and users (citizens). Although there is no consensus as to how to

[9] M. Srholec and B. Verspagen (2008), *The Voyage of the Beagle in Innovation Systems Land : Explorations on Sectors, Innovation, Heterogeneity and Selection*, UNU-MERIT Working Papers, Maastricht: United Nations University-Maastricht Economic and Social Research and Training Centre on Innovation and Technology.

[10] J. F. Moore (1993), 'Predators and Prey: The New Ecology of Competition', *Harvard Business Review*, 71, 75–83.

[11] M. Iansiti and R. Levien (2004), The Keystone Advantage: What the New Dynamics of Business Ecosystems Mean for Strategy, Innovation, and Sustainability, Cambridge, MA: Harvard Business Press.

[12] B. Salmelin (2013), 'Reflections from Open Innovation 2.0 Paradigm', European Commission. http://globalforum.items-int.com/gf/gf-content/uploads/2014/04/2_Bror_Salmelin_Global_Forum_Trieste.pdf, accessed 28 July 2021.

define a national innovation ecosystem, there are some common characteristics seen in China's case, including the interdependence of actors within and across subsystems, the diversity of actors, self-organization, and an open system with fluid boundaries.

Innovation is systemic. It is not a simple, linear progression from research to invention to commercialization within enterprise, industry, or national boundaries. Instead, mass actors (including both technology creators and users) work interdependently in a dynamic and sometimes recursive process, supported by multifaceted platforms, in which many elements of the economy and society interact to make innovation happen. Flows of technology, capital, and talent are intertwined and mutually reinforcing. In such systems, as Brian Arthur argues, technological innovation, like genetic mutation in natural ecosystems, creates itself following the rules of variation and selection.[13] In biological evolution, separation of a variation caused by genetic mutation from interbreeding of the dominant population is key to the accumulation of the variation. In human society, in contrast, being connected with other elements in a system is key for a variation caused by technological innovation to retain and expand its niche through co-creation and co-development.

In the digital age, the fittest variations are not necessarily the most efficient; instead, they are the most effective, occurring at the right time and in the right place. The most effective solutions are selected by customers in a niche first and then diffused into a larger community, and then onto the entire ecosystem through interconnectedness and interdependencies, and efficiencies will follow. In other words, it is the most connected that survive in an innovation ecosystem. In this collective process, innovations resulting from bottom-up trial and error among a large enough pool of actors are akin to genetic mutations of individual organisms that can be passed on through reproduction of the fittest to the benefit of the entire population.

This evolutionary process underlies China's innovation machine. Chinese innovation is not just about novelty or efficiency; it aims to provide the right solutions to a specific user group at the right time: innovations delivering effective solutions that will have a chance to be selected and amplified in markets. This effectiveness-driven model allowed latecomer Chinese firms with limited technological capability to catch up in market share with, and sometimes disrupt, incumbent multinational firms that have operated in China for decades.

Digital technologies have been used to improve flexibility and efficiency in production in China's manufacturing sector through continuous information sharing and learning through feedback mechanisms in networks. The often small firms that cannot afford advanced technologies achieve efficiency by specializing in clusters producing particular products that offer flexible system-level solutions. Their flexibility derives more from the interconnected ecosystem than the technology they use. China has many examples of advanced manufacturing clusters in highly specialized

---

[13] See W. B. Arthur (2009), *The Nature of Technology: What It Is and How It Evolves*, London: Penguin Books.

Evolution in a Biological Species   Evolution in an Innovation Ecosystem

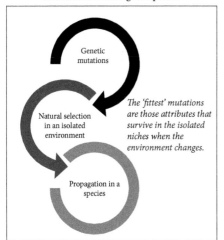
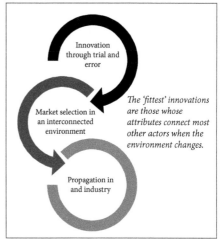

Figure 8.1 An evolutionary view of China's innovation machine

technologies that achieve scale and profits by being connected with larger upstream and downstream complementors in the interconnected ecosystem. In other words, in China's innovation ecosystems, system-level performance is built upon the contribution of each innovation actor, regardless of whether they are large or small, successful or unsuccessful. The dynamics of China's system are similar to those of Charles Darwin's theory of biological evolution according to which all species of organisms arise and develop through the natural selection of small, inherited variations that increase the population's chances of competing, surviving, and propagating. The difference is, in a digital world, the criterion for being 'the fittest' is the solution that has the most connections in the system.

Figure 8.1 illustrates innovation ecosystems in comparison with biological ecosystems. The high levels of connectivity in China's digital economy have implications for the theoretical understanding of innovation. The evolutionary economic theory of innovation, based around variation, selection, and propagation, needs to integrate the centrality of connections better, especially those facilitated digitally. An improved theory would incorporate variation, connection, selection, and propagation.

The Challenges Facing China's Innovation Machine

The biggest challenges facing China's innovation machine include the global economic downturn caused by Covid-19 and the impact of the trade war between the US and China. More profoundly, they involve ideological clashes with the West.

The Impact of Covid-19 on Globalization

The Covid-19 pandemic was 'a shared event with uneven impacts.'[14] Its business impact was deepest on those embedded in global supply chain networks. Consequently, in some spheres deglobalization, especially decoupling between China and the US, has accelerated.

Globalization is not the result of central planning; it has been an evolutionary process involving global flows of goods, capital, talent, and information. Global trade based on principles of the competitive and comparative advantages of nations has been one of the most significant engines of globalization. This led the developed countries, especially the US, to outsource low-end manufacturing jobs to countries such as China and to rely on long supply chains for their high-end manufacturing. One consequence of globalization was that countries with different endowments have been locked into relatively fixed positions in the global ecosystem of value chains: resource-rich countries in supplying raw materials, cheap labour countries in low-end manufacturing, and technologically advanced countries in design, technology, branding, and marketing at the other end of the upper stream of value added. China has secured its position in the global value chain as an international hub connecting developing countries with suppliers of raw materials and the more advanced countries with the supply of technology and brands. As discussed in Chapters 3 and 4, Western firms that have relocated production partly or entirely were attracted by lower labour costs in countries such as Vietnam and India for low-end manufacturing and the improvement of productivity enabled by automated manufacturing technologies such as 3D printing for high-end manufacturing domestically. Much relocated production, however, remains part of China's extended supply chain networks.

China has benefited greatly from its active participation in globalization, becoming an important hub for global supply chains as the 'world's factory' and 'the world's workshop'. In this process, foreign direct investment by multinational corporations has made a huge contribution to China's economic growth in general and technological innovation in particular. The Covid-19 outbreak forced those countries that relied on long global supply chains stretching internationally especially those in China, to consider reshoring or nearshoring options by relocating their critical supply chains and rebuilding their manufacturing capacity domestically or close to their home markets. Critical supply chains and manufacturing capacity include those related to national security and medical and healthcare products. Any relocation of those foreign companies that have invested in China will have a negative impact on China's competitive advantage in innovation.

The vast majority of Western multinational companies are not extensively relocating their supply chains and manufacturing from China following the Covid-19

---

[14] T. Nielsen, S. Smith, and H. LeHong (2020), 'The Postpandemic Planning Framework', Gartner Information Technology Research, 15 May, https://www.gartner.com/en/documents/3985245/the-postpandemic-planning-framework, accessed 9 June 2021.

pandemic. It takes time and capital to operationalize reshoring or nearshoring options despite the recommendations and financial incentives provided by their governments. Surveys by the American Chamber of Commerce and the European Union Chamber of Commerce suggest that only a small proportion of surveyed firms considered relocating some or all of their production from China as a result of the pandemic.[15] Most Western multinational companies remain in China because their products are primarily for the Chinese market and maintaining production close to their customers makes economic sense; additionally, they wish to continue to have access to China's vast supply chain networks and population of skilled labour.

China's trade data also showed that the world demanded more of its products amid the pandemic. China's global total trade volume for 2020 was 32.16 trillion RMB (about $4.97 trillion, while exports rose 4 per cent and imports fell 0.7 per cent from the year before). ASEAN was China's largest trading partners. Other major trading partners include the EU, the US, Japan and South Korea.[16] This strong growth momentum in global trade continued in the first half of 2021, where the trade surplus with the US widened to $164.92 billion in the first six months, despite the trade war between the two countries.[17]

The decoupling of China's supply chains from Western production systems had already begun before Covid-19, largely for economic reasons, but not as rapidly as expected. In the long run, self-reliance and safety of critical supply chains will be of higher priority for many countries following the pandemic. In the short run, developing regional supply chains will be of high priority. Trade deals, such as RCEP (Regional Comprehensive Economic Partnership)[18] and CPTPP,[19] will accelerate the transition from long supply chains to regional ones.

On the other hand, the Covid-19 pandemic highlights the importance of digital connectivity and digital infrastructure and has accelerated the digital transformation of many industries. New forms and models of digitalization have emerged. In both emerging and traditional industries, enterprises have started to pay attention to contactless ways of working and living, transferring activities in daily business and life into the digital space. With increasing hostility from the West towards China, the country has shifted the focus of its Belt and Road Initiative (BRI) towards the construction of digital infrastructure along the countries included in the initiative, with

[15] American Chamber of Commerce in China (2020), '2020 Business Climate Survey', https://www.amchamchina.org/press/2020-business-climate-survey-released/, accessed 4 June 2021; European Union Chamber of Commerce in China (2020), 'Business Confidence Survey 2020', https://www.europeanchamber.com.cn/en/publications-business-confidence-survey, accessed 4 June 2021.

[16] See http://www.xinhuanet.com/english/2021-01/14/c_139667906.htm, accessed 30 July 2021.

[17] See https://tradingeconomics.com/china/balance-of-trade, accessed 30 July 2021.

[18] The Regional Comprehensive Economic Partnership (RCEP), made up of ten South East Asian countries, as well as South Korea, China, Japan, Australia, and New Zealand, forms the world's largest trading bloc; see https://www.bbc.com/news/world-asia-54949260, accessed 9 June 2021.

[19] The Comprehensive and Progressive Agreement for Trans-Pacific Partnership (CPTPP) is a trade agreement between Australia, Brunei, Canada, Chile, Japan, Malaysia, Mexico, New Zealand, Peru, Singapore, and Vietnam. It evolved from the Trans-Pacific Partnership (TPP), which never entered into force due to the withdrawal of the United States; see https://en.wikipedia.org/wiki/Comprehensive_and_Progressive_Agreement_for_Trans-Pacific_Partnership, accessed 9 June 2021.

the potential to encourage growth of supply chains. Under the original BRI, China's large-scale infrastructure projects caused some resentment in local communities, but digital infrastructure projects are less visible and will have a quicker impact on local economies. This move has been labelled 'China's Digital Silk Road after the Covid-19 Outbreak' by a US think tank.[20] This shift has received support from countries in the region. The prime minister of Singapore, Lee Hsien Loong, for example, stated that his government supports the BRI, as 'We see it as a constructive mechanism for China to be positively engaged with the region and beyond.'[21]

Development on this front is uneven due to the varying levels of digital infrastructure in different countries. Countries with better digital infrastructure respond more quickly on the digitalization of medical and healthcare, education, remote working, and public services. Remote-working applications, for example, have been especially responsive and have experienced an exponential growth. Zoom's active users grew from 10 million in December 2019 to 300 million in April and 350 million in December 2020. Similarly, by the end of March 2020, Alibaba's Ding Ding, a mobile app for group meetings and communications, attracted 300 million individual users, 15 million enterprise users, including 140,000 schools, which operated over 3 million classrooms with 6 million educators/teachers offering classes to 130 million students across all age groups. Tencent Meeting, another mobile app for group conferences and online learning, attracted 10 million daily active users by May 2020.[22] Digital companies such as Alibaba and JD.com, using their cloud computing power and AI-enabled solutions, helped the government and communities track the spread of the virus and collect valuable data to fight against it. An experienced worker in a call centre can make about 200 phone calls in one day, compared to 1,000 per minute by AI-powered intelligent call machines in a call centre.[23] AI-powered call centres have not only reduced costs but also improved the quality of customer services.[24]

Covid-19 will not end globalization because of the dynamics of nations, industries, and firms becoming more interconnected, assisted by technologies such as AI, blockchain, cloud computing, and big data analytics. Furthermore, Covid-19 has accelerated global collaboration in science and technology, especially on R&D of vaccines against and medical treatment for diseases caused by the virus. There have been global efforts in allocating food and protective equipment to developing

[20] J. Blanchette and J. E. Hillman (2020), 'China's Digital Silk Road after the Coronavirus'. Centre for Strategic and International Studies, 13 April, https://www.csis.org/analysis/chinas-digital-silk-road-after-coronavirus, accessed 9 June 2021.

[21] Prime Minister Lee Hsien Loong's speech at the 2019 Shangri-La Dialogue, May 2019, https://www.channelnewsasia.com/news/singapore/lee-hsien-loong-speech-2019-shangri-la-dialogue-11585954, accessed 9 June 2021.

[22] Caijing (Finance) (2020), 'The Fission of China's Digital Economy amid the Covid-19 Pandemic', *Caijing Magazine*, June [in Chinese].

[23] Caijing (Finance) (2020), 'How China's Digital Economy Accelerates in Covid-19?', *Caijing Magazine*, June [in Chinese].

[24] See https://www.forbes.com/sites/insights-ibmai/2020/06/25/how-ai-is-revamping-the-call-center/?sh=59de9df034b2, accessed 9 June 2021.

countries in need as a call for humanity during the pandemic. The benefit of global-ization goes beyond immediate economic benefits and, as a result of the virus, governments around the world have the opportunity to rethink the long-term benefits of globalization for humanity, climate change, and sustainable development. This trend will be deepened with the availability and extensive applications of digital technologies.

Clashes in Ideology and Competition between Great Powers

The future of China's innovation machine is inextricably bound to global politics and economics. Although global trade from an economic perspective has been built on the principles of competitive and comparative advantages of different nations, from a geopolitical perspective, trust between trading partners within an agreed global framework such as the WTO is key to its success. Global trade transcends not just geographical distance, but also the political and cultural distances between nations. The trade war between China and the US has manifested this point, as a result of rising economic nationalism and protectionism. If such sentiments are not tamed, they could lead to clashes of ideologies and political values, and even military confrontations between the great powers.

'Let China sleep, for when she wakes, she will shake the world,' Napoleon is reputed to have said. When China began its opening-up policy and economic reforms in the 1980s, the West embraced China, expecting that economic development would lead the waking giant to eventually become a market democracy. Even in the 2010s, there was heated debate over whether China could catch up with the West and become a global citizen on the West's terms. More recently, as China marches on with its own developmental model and responds to external challenges and doubts with a more assertive attitude, the West has come to the realization that China has 'woken up' but without adopting Western ideology and values. The disparity between expectations and outcomes has caused a clash of values and beliefs between China and the Western democratic countries, especially the US. China's rise indeed worries the West, as this is the first time in human history that an Asian country with a different political regime and ideology has come so close to the centre of the world stage in modern times.

The trade conflict between the US and China goes beyond the two focal countries: there are interests of other countries in this important relationship. The more estranged the US and China become, the greater the stakes other countries have in this relationship and the greater the impact there will be on other stakeholders.[25] It is

---

[25] J. Lind (2019), 'The Rise of China and the Future of the Transatlantic Relationship', Chatham House, 29 July, https://www.chathamhouse.org/publication/rise-china-and-future-transatlantic-relationship, accessed 9 June 2021.

not just Japan and the EU countries that are important stakeholders, but also countries such as Australia, India, and Canada, are also part of this conflict. Each country has its own national interests to protect, feeding into the effects on China-US relations and the global order.

The challenge of this conflict is made stark in the case of Australia, which became trapped between the US and China, leading the country into a diplomatic impasse and trading difficulties with China. Political commentators have described Australia as the poor chicken that China has chosen to strangle to frighten the monkeys, but they have missed some important aspects of Chinese culture and history, which may add some nuance to their analysis. Historically, China, the 'middle kingdom' centred in East Asia and maintained its relationships with neighbouring nations through a tributary system—a loose network of international relations centred around China. This system facilitated trade and foreign relations in which China's predominant role in Asia was acknowledged and respected. Foreign nations sent tributary envoys to China on a schedule, who had to *kowtow* to China's emperors and come accompanied by gifts. Chinese emperors endowed those envoys with more valuable gifts in return and strengthened the mutual relationship on friendly terms. Such relationships were the foundation for those small nations to benefit from trade with China and, more importantly, receive military protection from China against other countries.[26] As the response of the Emperor Qianlong (b. 1711, d. 1799) to King George III of Great Britain (b. 1738, d. 1820) following the first British envoy's arrival indicated, China held a very inward-looking view of the world and believed in its superiority. The emperor said:

> I set no value on objects strange or ingenious, and have no use for your country's manufactures...Missions have been sent by Portugal and Italy, preferring similar requests. The Throne appreciated their sincerity and loaded them with favours, besides authorising measures to facilitate their trade with China...I confer upon you, O King, valuable presents in excess of the number usually bestowed on such occasions, including silks and curios—a list of which is likewise enclosed.[27]

What China expected in foreign relations was respect first and mutual benefits second. In this light, the Australian prime minister Scott Morrison's declaration that Australia will not side with either US or China during their trade war deeply hurt Chinese people when he further commented, 'You stand by your friends and you stand by your customers as well.' He was referring to the US as Australia's friend and China as its customer.[28] Although Chinese policymakers do not need to win support from citizens as leaders in democratic countries do, they pay attention to public opinion, especially regarding foreign relations. The rulers cannot be perceived by

---

[26] F. Zhou (2011), 'Equilibrium Analysis of the Tributary System', *The Chinese Journal of International Politics*, 4, 147–78.
[27] See https://china.usc.edu/emperor-qianlong-letter-george-iii-1793, accessed 9 June 2021.
[28] See https://www.sbs.com.au/news/china-customers-us-friends-morrison, accessed 9 June 2021.

their people as weak in the eyes of foreign nations when the president is promoting a Chinese dream for the people of righting the historical wrongs against the nation from the Opium Wars to the Japanese invasion. Public opinion, with or without government intervention, can grow out of control rapidly in the digital age. In a sense, China's 'wolf warrior' style of diplomacy is a response to the public opinion which provides an effective way to legitimize the CPC's rule. A powerful fight against the nation's enemy—be it a foreign entity or a natural disaster or a pandemic—has always been a useful tool for a ruling party to unite its people and strengthen its legitimacy.

A Canberra-based senior diplomat interviewee claimed that 'Australia's policy such as banning Huawei from 5G infrastructure and calling for an inquiry into the origin of Covid-19 irritated not just the CPC leadership, but also Chinese citizens.' On Chinese social media, Australia's approach was perceived as a betrayal, as it was considered as China's friend and ally. This was manifested most clearly when President Xi Jinping addressed Australia's parliament in 2014, a rare engagement by a Chinese leader that laid the groundwork for a trade deal between the two countries. Regular comments such as 'Chinese students should not go to study in Australia,' 'China should stop importing iron ore and coal from Australia,' and 'Chinese should stop drinking Australian wine and eating Australian beef and lobsters' appeared on China's social media, although mostly championed by those without vested interests in foreign relations with Australia.

One view on Australia's relationship with China was expressed by Geoff Raby, a former Australian ambassador to China: 'Australian foreign policy with respect to China has been weaponised.'[29] The wisdom of this has to be assessed in the light of the economic reality in Australia that 'The brutal reality is we simply do need China, more than they need us.'[30] China is Australia's largest trading partner for both exports (39 per cent of all goods exported went to China) and imports (27 per cent of all goods imported were from China) in 2019–20,[31] while trade with Australia accounted for less than 5 per cent of China's total trade. It is not surprising that for both the government and ordinary citizens, Australia seems insignificant. 'If you are not our friend and you are insignificant, why do we bother to have a relationship with you?' our interviewee commented. The trade conflict with Australia has forced China to look for alternative suppliers in iron ore, which is the most critical good China relies upon from Australia, which further reduced its significance. Every nation has the right to express its concerns about others, but even when these concerns are stark, they are best expressed diplomatically, in the context of mutual respect and historical friendship.

---

[29] J. Smyth, Financial Times, 17 December (2020), 'Australia's "Amateurish" China Diplomacy Sets Business on Edge', https://www.ft.com/content/843c9286-b135-4d39-acbd-dafd87f57e0c, accessed 9 June 2021.

[30] See https://www.abc.net.au/news/2020-12-10/china-australia-trade-war-your-questions-answered/12971434, accessed 9 June 2021.

[31] See https://www.abs.gov.au/articles/australias-trade-goods-china-2020, accessed 9 June 2021.

Competition between the US and China has three layers: on the outer layer, it is a trade war, in the middle layer it is the competition of technological leadership, and at its core it is the competition between incumbent and emerging great power: a 'Thucydides trap'.[32] China is different from any other great powers in history that challenged incumbents, the central motivation for which was either displaying military strength or desire for territorial expansion. China's rapid rise in economy and technology has greatly benefited from not just from its labour dividend and reform dividend, but also from a peace dividend: a comparatively long stretch of relative peace since the foundation of the PRC. More importantly, China and the US have developed interconnections in all aspects of their economies. The US and China are deeply intertwined with each other in ways that the US has never had with any other opponents such as the Soviet Union and Iran. The interrelations between the US and Chinese economies are complex and not easily disentangled. Despite great disquiet in the West about the Chinese approach to human rights and its activities in Hong Kong and the South China Sea, connections between the US and China deliver mutual benefits. Given this entanglement, although it will be very hard for both parties to accept a politically acceptable reconciliation, the idea of a Thucydides trap is unlikely.

The more likely scenario is that US and China continue to engage economically while disengaging politically—as distrust between the two governments increases. The conflict will manifest itself over control of not just technological standards and leadership, particularly digital technologies, but more fundamentally also over global rules and institutions: the global order maintained by international institutions. After the retreat from such institutions during the Trump presidency, their support by the Biden presidency will be a crucial contributor to resolving trade and political tensions.

When the US began to welcome China into the global order which it played a significant role in creating and maintaining since the Second World War, it believed that China would inevitably develop a need for democracy and adopt Western political values as its economy matured. This view was captured in Francis Fukuyama's 'End of History' essay in 1989.[33] The US has, however, miscalculated or underestimated the capacity of the Chinese political regime to retain control whilst developing its economy and managing technological catch-up.

As a former Trump Administration's policy adviser once said referring to the US-China conflict, 'This is a fight with a really different civilization and a different ideology, and the United States hasn't had that before. The Soviet Union and that competition, in a way, it was a fight within the Western family.' With China, in

---

[32] G. Allison (2017), 'The Thucydides Trap: When One Great Power Threatens to Displace Another, War Is Almost Always the Result—But It Doesn't Have to Be', *Foreign Policy*, 9 June, https://foreignpolicy.com/2017/06/09/the-thucydides-trap/, accessed 9 June 2021.

[33] F. Fukuyama (1989), 'The End of History?', *The National Interest*, 16, 3–18; P. Blustein (2019), Schism: China, America and the Fracturing of the Global Trading System, Kinston: McGill-Queen's University Press.

contrast, 'It's the first time that we will have a great power competitor that is not Caucasian.'[34] Indeed, it is not simply China's rise that creates the tension between the two great powers, but the means by which it has achieved the rise. The *Made in China 2025* proposal, for example, to encourage smart manufacturing using government subsidies for technological upgrading, has been perceived as violating the principle of fair trade.

The competition of institutions is not just about ideological philosophies; it is about how ideology is used in practical decision making, and especially the role played by the state in national economies with different institutional arrangements. From the US perspective, decision-making in Chinese institutions is seen to be complex and opaque, but from China's perspective it is about efficiency in using central power to make and implement decisions. In the Western political system, under the conventional rules of the market economy, government subsidy is politically questionable;[35] however, in China's political system, the government's intervention in innovation and industrial policies is a central component of its market economy with Chinese institutional logics, as discussed in Chapter 7.

It is inevitable that China will overtake the US to become the world's largest economy measured by GDP, and the question is not if but when. When that happens, there would be two significant changes in the global order. It would be the first time in the modern era that an Asian country becomes the greatest economic power in the world, moving the global economic centre of gravity. More significantly, this great power will lie in a country whose political and cultural values are very different from those of the previously dominant powers. According to one analysis, despite China's rise in economic power, it needs to develop four elements of structural power, which comprise (1) the capacity for the provision of security for oneself and for other actors in international affairs; (2) dominance in the production of goods and services; (3) the structure of finance and credit in the global economy; (4) the production of knowledge and ideas.[36]

Structural power in security in the digital age is very much related to a country's power in digital technology. The internet and global connectivity not only reshape the environment for competition but also are of the greatest importance to a country's national security. China, of course, possesses significant digital power, although its definition of security may involve what is seen in the West as infringements of human rights to privacy and data security in other nations. Of the four dimensions of a nation's structural power, China is strongest in its production power, which, as we have seen, is not simply a function of the size of the market and is inherently intertwined with the sophistication of its manufacturing structure and its centrality

---

[34] See https://www.nytimes.com/2019/08/02/us/politics/kiron-skinner-state-department-pompeo.html, accessed 9 June 2021.

[35] Stimulus investment in response to the Covid-19 pandemic bucks this conventional thinking.

[36] S. Strange (1989), 'Towards a Theory of Transnational Empire,' in E. O. Czempiel, and J. N. Rosenau (eds.), *Global Changes and Theoretical Challenges: Approaches to World Politics for the 1990s*, Lexington, MA: Lexington Books, 161.

in global value chains. China's structural power in finance and credit in the global economy remains weak, and China is gaining its power in knowledge by catching up in scientific research and technological innovation.

In many ways, China has become a great power in the world, but with power comes responsibility. China's leadership should acknowledge that the nation is no longer a poor country, but one with significant economic and technological influence. In the post-Covid-19 era, there would be much benefit if China took the initiative to shoulder more responsibilities in promoting international cooperation and amending the broken global order.

Will China be ready to take the responsibility bestowed with its rise under its current political regime? A world-leading power should start thinking about the interests of other countries, by, for example, providing access to its markets and respecting other nations' intellectual property. More importantly, a great power needs to establish real protection mechanisms for property rights and maintain just and fair market competition following the principles of the rule of law for its own citizens. It is this which will attract more foreign technology and investment into China's huge market. Institutional reforms that would produce a countervailing power against centralized political power include an independent judiciary system with impartial enforcement of the law and a free press. These institutional reforms and the creation of more of a civil society, where individuals and groups have the capacity to express common interests and shared activities, still have a long way to go in China.

Technology Decoupling and Technology Cold War

Ultimately, a country's ability to innovate and produce advanced technologies is the foundation of the country's economic strength and military power, and feeds its intangible global leadership. The West's, especially the US's, hard stance against China's technology intensified amid the Covid-19 pandemic. US sanctions against Huawei's access to US technologies have opened a chapter of technological decoupling between the two countries. In an increasingly volatile and complex geopolitical situation, competition in technological innovation will be a focal point of the competition between the great powers.[37]

The trade war between China and the US, as well as with its allies such as Australia, is not entirely about trade; rather, the tension goes far beyond economic issues and includes, crucially, technology. While the discussion on trade often refers to issues such as soya beans or blue-collar industrial jobs, more importantly it is

---

[37] See further Economist Intelligence Unit (2020), 'Geopolitics after Covid-19: Is the Pandemic a Turning Point?' 1 April, https://country.eiu.com/article.aspx?articleid=1339299717&Country=Albania&topic=Politics&subtopic=Forecast&subsubtopic=International+relations, accessed 9 June 2021; and B. Stauffer (2020), How the World Will Look After the Coronavirus Pandemic', *Foreign Policy*, 20 March. https://foreignpolicy.com/2020/03/20/worldorder-after-coroanvirus-pandemic/, accessed 9 June 2021.

about microchips, cloud computing, 5G, intelligence collected in Huawei's servers, or data on adolescent users gathered by TikTok. What is at stake is national security on the surface and technological leadership at the centre. Essentially, the competition over 5G between the US and China, for example, is about technological leadership in the next-generation digital infrastructure, with a focus on technological standards in the global order.

The decoupling of supply chains between China and the West has already started, and elements in the US have decided to rebuild their manufacturing onshore or nearshore. However, in reality, only those low-value-added assembly jobs or labour-intensive components in the industrial value chains have been moved to countries such as India, Sri Lanka, and Mexico. Such moves made economic sense for manufacturers, because, as we have seen, the labour force in those markets is younger and cheaper than in China. But, in a sense, the shift represents an extension of China's supply chains globally. Covid-19 has accelerated this trend. China's super supply chains were not built overnight, and it will not be easy for any country to replicate China's supply chains in scale and scope in a short time. Even if it is possible for multinational corporates to relocate their manufacturing facilities away from China, building self-sufficiency in entire supply chains is almost impossible in modern economies. For example, even for very simple products such as an ordinary cup of coffee, the industrial value chain can contain twenty-nine suppliers distributed in as many as eighteen countries.[38]

A more critical aspect in global supply chains is the high degree of technological interdependencies in almost all technology sectors. The Chinese technology sector has rapidly developed due to its supersize advantage in the domestic market, and its technology firms largely serve Chinese users. In contrast, most large US technology firms are global operators supplying international markets, including the Chinese. In their technology, these large firms are complementary with one another: US technology giants dominate industrial design tools and software, and Chinese firms enjoy unbeatable advantages in production at scale. China's current competitiveness in innovation, as argued throughout this book, is not in its technological breakthroughs; it is largely in the efficiency and scale of its applications, as well as in its agility in responding to diverse market demands and a rapidly changing environment.

These interdependencies are seen in the case of Huawei. Although Huawei has a plan for overcoming restrictions on its chip design and operating system, without chip design software it will not be able to design any new chips, and it will take a long time for the company and its partners to develop an entire ecosystem for its new operating system. On the other hand, US technology firms rely on China's manufacturing capability to translate their industrial designs into mass production with cost efficiency, as well as on China's super large market as a growth engine for further innovation. Without access to China's market, US chip companies such as Qualcomm and Micron will experience reduced revenue and require further investment, as high-tech products need to have scale to offset the risks involved in investment in R&D.

For these reasons, technological decoupling will be detrimental to the technology sector of both parties. More dangerously, decoupling in technology will potentially result in a two-track technological system, one dominated by China's firms and one by Western firms, led by the US. Examples of such inefficient, parallel, two-track technological systems such as the Betamax versus VCR for the video recording market and the first- and second-generation of mobile communications systems in the 1980s and 1990s were not constructive competition for the parties involved. Technology decoupling will be worse in today's environment, as technology is most useful when it is compatible across the global market.

Decoupling in technology will not necessarily benefit US national security because such a move will lead to a more concentrated effort in technological catch-up by Chinese technology companies. China's technology sector has learned hard lessons from Huawei's case: relying on imported core technologies seems an easy solution when the geopolitical situation is stable; however, when the wind changes, it could quickly cripple China's industrial development. This explains why China's industrial policy emphasizes independent innovation and self-sufficiency in technology. Doubtlessly, catching up in many core technologies will take years or even decades for Chinese companies, but it is not impossible, as China has attracted so much global R&D talent in AI, IC chip design, and memory chip design, mostly overseas returnees, to join Huawei and other Chinese technology firms.[39] Current US policies of decoupling in technology with China may in fact hurt the US far more than China on the investment side, as foreign direct investment from China in the US has almost halted.

Technology decoupling is in direct opposition to the direction of technology development which is based on interoperability and modularization. Closed systems are detrimental to all nations, and the dangerous bifurcation of global technologies and standards needs to be avoided through improved transparency and openness. There is much value in recalling Confucius' view that 'Superior people seek harmony with diversity (*jun zi he er bu tong*).'

The technology cold war between these two countries is a much more serious war than the trade war because whoever wins the technology war will also gain advantages on both economic and military fronts. This is because the technology competition and the bifurcation of technology sectors between the US and China is not just a matter of these two countries and influences the whole world.[40] At the

[39] A. Varas and R. Varadarajan (2020), 'How Restricting Trade with China Could End US Semiconductor Leadership', *Boston Consulting Group*, 9 March, https://www.bcg.com/publications/2020/restricting-trade-with-china-could-end-united-states-semiconductor-leadership, accessed 1 June 2021.
[40] P. Triolo (2020), *The Telecommunications Industry in US-China Context: Evolving toward Near-Complete Bifurcation*, Maryland: Johns Hopkins University Applied Physics Laboratory LLC.

very least, the conflict between the US and China amid the Covid-19 pandemic weakens the growth engine of the world economy. More profoundly, any structural and strategic decoupling of the two countries will impact the global order in innovation and industry, as decoupling in technology occurs not just in technological products and applications, but also in technological standards and supply chains, and even in the science and innovation behind product and production technology. There is much benefit for all nations around the world in avoiding a technology cold war.

The Future of China's Innovation Machine

Despite differences in governance and political ideology, China is a form of market economy albeit with its own characteristics. As a latecomer, China's catch-up has largely been due to a safe and peaceful environment over the past forty years. China's integration into the global value chain has been marked by a huge amount of foreign direct investment and technology transfer, which have helped China build its comprehensive supply chain network and mass manufacturing capabilities. China's innovation performance is not entirely driven by SOEs and state-funded research institutions; it is made possible by private enterprises such as Huawei, Xiaomi, DJ, BeiGene, and countless hidden champions discussed throughout this book.

The foundation of China's innovation machine and its resilience and antifragility are the strength of its comprehensive supply chain networks and its sophisticated manufacturing structure. Chinese supply chains balance efficiency and effectiveness substantiated by a massive number of specialized firms producing complementary products, connected by standard interfaces, and coordinated by regional clusters and digital platforms. Through such connections, Chinese supply chains maintain and manage the flow of products, services, capital, and data with very low costs but high efficiency and resilience. On the basis of such supply chains, China's manufacturing industry is transitioning from being the factory to being the workshop of the world. When the British prime minister Benjamin Disraeli first used the term 'workshop of the world' in 1838, he was referring to his nation's industrial and manufacturing capacity, what he called 'a gigantic development of manufacturing skill'. He was referring to its ability not only to manufacture for the world's markets, but also to design the means for that manufacture, alluding to the looms and steam engines that created the modern world. Disraeli also spoke, with great resonance for China today, about the challenges of distributing rewards across regions, alleviating the impact of change on citizen's skills, and the geopolitical consequences of industrial power. Through China's workshop, in 2020 China transformed the importation of 1 billion tons of iron ore, 500 million tons of raw oil, and 300 million tons of coal into products exported to the world including high-tech products worth $730 billion, clothes worth $120 billion, furniture worth $54 billion, and steel worth $53 billion.[41] Such scale inevitably brings the challenges to which Disraeli referred.

Despite the political centralization of China's governance, the country is actually highly distributed in technological development and innovation. Competition at the local, regional, provincial, or city level provides an effective mechanism for competition and counterbalance among local players, at least in economic and technological development. Under the guidance of the national strategy of building an innovative country, regions are developing their innovation clusters on the basis of their own unique conditions. Regional competition is intense, with each facing unprecedented opportunities and challenges.

There are a number of aspects of and around China's innovation machine that face challenges.

The central task for the CPC is to maintain economic growth and sustainable development in the decades to come. As President Xi has said, the world is 'undergoing changes not seen in a century' and 'in the current external environment of rising protectionism, downturn in the world economy, and shrinking global markets', China must give full play to the advantages of its massive domestic market and build a 'double loop' mechanism for economic growth: maintaining its export market whilst developing domestic consumption. Although China has the largest number of middle-class consumers in the world, around 400 million of its 1.4 billion population, it still faces an enormous domestic challenge of income inequality among its citizens. As Premier Li Keqiang said at the CPC's annual congress, China has 600 million people with a monthly income as low as 1,000 RMB (about $140).[42] For this reason, China must continue its growth through global trade.

A major component of its plan for growth lies in infrastructure investment. On 4 March 2020, the Standing Committee of the Political Bureau of the CPC Central Committee held a meeting and emphasized the need to speed up the progress of new infrastructure construction such as 5G networks and data centres. This meeting sent a strong signal to industry that post-Covid-19 pandemic investment in the development of digital infrastructure is an important prerequisite for the digital transformation that supports the nation's growth. This plan is called 'new infrastructure' initiatives.

The digital economy includes the industrialization of digital technology (i.e. expanding the digital part of the economy to industrial scale) and the digital transformation of traditional industry. There is no absolute distinction between the new and the old infrastructures. The upgrading of traditional infrastructure such as transportation and energy, for example, needs the support of digital technologies, such as large-scale data sharing, and platform interaction. China's new infrastructure initiatives aim to advance its interconnected and coordinated digital ecosystems

[41] See further http://www.customs.gov.cn/customs/302249/302274/302275/index.html, accessed 9 June 2021.
[42] See https://www.scmp.com/economy/china-economy/article/3086678/china-rich-or-poor-nations-wealth-debate-muddied-conflicting, accessed 9 June 2021.

and provide the technical foundation on which all kinds of industrial applications can work together.

China has made huge progress with its digital infrastructure, and the collaboration between technology companies and traditional industries has survived the test of Covid-19. However, the pandemic increased demand for infrastructure to support new applications and business models such as online conferencing, telecommuting, online teaching and medicine, and other applications.

In both emerging and traditional industries, enterprises have started to pay attention to contactless ways of working, transferring part of the activities in daily businesses to the digital space. Further changes are foreseen in the ways China's new infrastructure initiatives will lay a solid foundation for the digital transformation of industry. Industrial digital transformation is expected to create greater socioeconomic value as it increases consumption on digital platforms and transforms the entire value chains for more value creation. The industrial internet will support such digital transformation. According to an industry consulting report, by 2025, investment in new infrastructure initiatives such as 5G and the industrial internet will reach 10 trillion RMB (about $1.5 trillion), driving 17 trillion RMB ($2.6 trillion) of related investment.[43]

There are three aspects in the 'new infrastructure' initiatives which cover technologies in big data, cloud computing, artificial intelligence, the internet of things, blockchain, 5G, biomedicine, new materials, and new sources of energy production. Innovations that can potentially transform traditional industrial, transport, and urban infrastructure are also included in these initiatives, which will require an investment of trillions of dollars. Although these initiatives are called 'infrastructure', they do not involve constructions of bricks and mortar. The essence of these initiatives—and their investment and organizational model—is different from investments in traditional infrastructure. Government investment will not comprise the major source of funding for these projects; instead, favourable government policies will be key. These initiatives aim to attract private investments, and the benefits will be shared with investors.

The value of new infrastructure will result from enlarged data storage capacity, enhanced computing power, and improved communication efficiency through interfaces of human to human, machine to machine, and human to machine. Cloud computing is core to these functions. In 2020, Chinese technology firms such as Alibaba, JD, Tencent, and Huawei announced investment plans to strengthen their cloud computing power. For example, Alibaba Cloud announced that it would invest 200 billion RMB ($30 billion) in new infrastructure over the next three years; and JD.com announced that it would invest 500 billion RMB ($76.5 billion) over the next five years by launching the JD.com New Momentum Programme, which

---

[43] See further https://global.chinadaily.com.cn/a/202005/14/WS5ebcdf01a310a8b241155b32.html, accessed 9 June 2021.

aims to integrate JD's technology capabilities to provide infrastructure for digital transformation.

These initiatives represent a huge opportunity for both domestic and global firms to participate in and capitalize upon through innovation.

Can China Become a Responsible Global Citizen with Its Own Political Characteristics?

China's role is becoming ever more globally significant as its economic, technological, and military power increases. Neither money nor technology guarantees global leadership, however, which often relies on soft power, which can often reflect ideology. China's mode of development has clashed with the core values of Western democracy, and competition between what Milanovic[44] calls 'liberal' and 'political' capitalism and competition in ideology, technology, and geopolitical power are intensifying. China's participation in fighting against the common challenges humanity faces in the future, including emerging unknown viruses, climate change, terrorism, inequality, and sustainable development, using both hard and soft power, is critically important.

Beyond the business realm, Covid-19 highlighted that the only way for a sustainable future for humankind is through global cooperation. The challenge is how both China and the rest of the world adapt to the reality of China's rise. China needs to demonstrate to the world that its advance is benevolent not only through narratives, but also through actions. The rest of the world needs to better understand China's political systems and cultural values, including its institutional logics, advantages, and challenges. As Jeffery Sachs commented, 'China is not an enemy. It is a nation trying to raise its living standards through education, international trade, infrastructure investment, and improved technologies. In short, it is doing what any country should do when confronted with the historical reality of being poor and far behind more powerful countries.'[45]

Maintaining, repairing, and upgrading the global order is not only in China's best interests, but also in those of its trading partners. The upgraded global order should reflect China's more advanced state of development. The CPC's increasing control of all walks of life and growing nationalism when the country faces external enemies make this task more complicated. Holding different political values based on political rather than liberal capitalism does not help China under the CPC's reign to be perceived as a responsible and benevolent global power.

---

[44] B. Milanovic (2020), 'The Clash of Capitalisms: The Real Fight for the Global Economy's Future,' *Foreign Affairs*, January/February, https://www.foreignaffairs.com/articles/united-states/2019-12-10/clash-capitalisms, accessed 9 June 2021.

[45] J. Sachs (2019), 'China Is Not the Source of Our Economic Problems—Corporate Greed Is', 27 May, https://edition.cnn.com/2019/05/26/opinions/china-is-not-the-enemy-sachs/index.html, accessed 9 June 2021.

The interdependent relationships between China and the US in trade, investment, technology, and scientific research have become highly embedded. Such interdependence occurs not only at the national level, but, more importantly, at the organizational (corporate and research institution) and individual levels. It is in China's own interest to maintain and upgrade this type of interdependence. China needs the world, especially the US and other more advanced countries, as a market as well as a source of technology, in order to forge forward in innovation.

The issues of whether and how China will be integrated in the global order and develop certain new forms of leadership under its current political regime raise a number of specific questions. These include whether it is safe, politically and economically, for foreign firms to invest in China in order to benefit from its growing domestic market and to capitalize on its innovation power, and, if yes, when and how? On the other hand, is there a new model of globalization under which Chinese capital can invest in foreign entrepreneurial firms with advanced technologies in order to exploit market opportunities in China and globally?

As Abraham Lincoln said, 'The dogmas of the quiet past are inadequate to the stormy present. The occasion is piled high with difficulty, and we must rise with the occasion. As our case is new, so we must think anew and act anew.'[46] To rise with the occasion globally and domestically, China needs to think very carefully not just about its domestic policies, but also how it can further integrate into the global order. This will not merely be a temporary solution to patch the holes in the broken system: the new framework needs to involve revolutionary thinking and acting anew. If top leaders do not have the courage to launch a top-down reform, the bottom-up revolution will push for change. Ultimately, China's reforms in the past forty years have been a result of top-down adaptations to bottom-up pushes, and new ways of responding to those bottom-up pressures need to be devised.

For China to integrate into the new global order, or even participate in the making of the new global order, it needs to further its institutional reforms, such as IP protection and enforcement, fair competition by limiting the participation of the SOEs in global trade, and inclusive development that enhances the business environment for SMEs and micro enterprises. The nature of today's economy and technological innovation ensures mutual dependence between China and the rest of the world. China cannot afford to go back to its isolated past. To move forward, more profound reforms must be carried out in its economic structure and governance. It needs to promote international cooperation in the fields of public health, environmental protection, national security, and counter terrorism, and also further the liberalization and facilitation of global trade and investment.

To address whether China will maintain its innovation and economic growth performance in the future, we analyse the challenges and opportunities facing its innovation machine.

---

[46] From Lincoln's concluding remarks in his annual message to Congress in December 1862, in Washington DC.

Can China Deepen Its Institutions to Support Its Becoming 'an Innovative Country'?

There are many areas where China could make its innovation machine more efficient and resilient. The challenge China faces is whether the government can maintain institutional reforms and respond to the market forces that can deliver future growth. One of the analytical frameworks used in the book describes multi-institutional logics, and China operates with both central-planning- and market-led logics. The balance between these logics will profoundly affect the future of China's innovation machine. Confucian tolerance of ambiguity and emphasis on harmony help maintain authority whilst encouraging experiments, be they the promotion of technology entrepreneurship or local level interpretation and implementation of policy. Firms operating in this dual logic face the difficulty of managing informal and formal institutional logics, responding to market signals, and the necessity of building *guanxi*. This is especially challenging, as the balance between the logics is fluid, and, as was seen in the case of Ant Group and Didi, the primacy of government authority can be reasserted at any time. Further institutional reforms need to remove those institutional arrangements that impede innovation and to create a more inclusive, self-organizing, and autonomous market economy. They include:

Independent Innovation Capability and Basic Research

Several weaknesses in its innovation machine were exposed when China faced technology sanctions from the US. Reliance on imported technologies, especially IC chips, creates bottlenecks in China's manufacturing sector, and there are no shortcuts to overcoming them. Independent technological innovation capability and basic research are the keys to breaking the blockages in China's innovation machine. Technological breakthroughs in materials, production techniques, and design tools all rely on the results of basic science. China will benefit from strengthening its basic science research, and its investment in fusion energy research is an indicator of its preparedness to invest in very long-term experiments.

China's advantage in digital and smart manufacturing technologies has developed rapidly because China has a super-sized market, relatively low-cost skilful engineers, and advanced infrastructure. However, China's catch-up in this area is limited to the application and commercialization of Western technologies on a massive scale, but still lacks many critical technologies at the core of its digital systems. Digital networks have three technological levels: the core is the original technological innovation built on basic science, followed by innovation in technological applications in the middle, and commercialization of applications at the outer layer. Without its own independent technologies in these critical areas, and especially the core, China will always face a similar predicament to that found in its technological bottlenecks in high-end IC chips discussed in Chapters 2 and 5.

Basic science is often far away from the market. In the case of medical research, for example, research results are commonly at least ten to fifteen years away from commercialization. Chinese investment tends to avoid such risky and uncertain research, and so much of its focus remains distant from science. The traditional reward mechanisms and incentives in Chinese R&D have to be reformed. This involves not just increasing investment in basic science, but also reforming research institutions, including their funding strategy, governance, and performance indicators. Succeeding in the complex and emerging world of innovation and technology requires the freedom to diverge from norms and engrained practices, which is rare in China's current institutions.

The breakthrough in basic science will be key to sustaining China's manufacturing capacity. The advantages in China's manufacturing lie in its engineering excellence in translating designs into mass production and the resilience and flexibility in its supply chains. Yet China's manufacturing capacity needs to be applied to producing advanced technology in the global arena. In this way, China's overall industrial value can be maximized to benefit not only China, but also the world. At the same time, through the manufacture of the world's advanced scientific and technological products, it will transform from 'workshop-style' production to the smart manufacturing model under the *Made in China 2025* blueprint.

Continued Reforms in Innovation Policy

The government is not only a policymaker, but also a crucially important investor, innovator, and consumer in China's innovation machine, and has huge influence on its development. Chinese policies for science, industry, and innovation reflect the political structures of the nation and its progression from catch-up to independent innovation. Chinese policymaking has been highly pragmatic. Much has been learned, for example, from the geographical clustering of technology firms in Silicon Valley and Taiwan. China has learned about the transformation of SOEs by observing the South Korean *chaebol* and how to leverage FDI from nations such as Singapore. As the nation reaches technological frontiers, the need for policy learning is accelerating. The government needs to create a fairer competitive environment for firms regardless of the ownership structures of the actors in China's innovation machine, and especially support entrepreneurial SMEs and micro enterprises to participate in and contribute to the diversity and dynamics in China's innovation machine.

As well as reflecting strategic choices and directions, policies furthermore need to focus more on the supervision and evaluation of their implementation.

Policies have to adjust to the crucial role of intangible assets, needing to adjust, for example, to new international regimes in IP and technical standards. This will require sophisticated, internationally confident policymakers, a cohort that can take decades to mature. IP protection is especially important for innovators in some sectors who need to feel confident that their investment in R&D will be returned profitably. There would be much advantage if China improved not just its IP laws, but also law enforcement, to create a fair business environment for firms large or small, domestic or foreign, state-owned or privately owned. The challenge the government regulators face now is to balance limiting the monopoly of super platforms, on the one hand, and provide room for their continued investment and application of cutting-edge technologies to support China's fast-growing digital industry, on the other.

The Balance between Using Antitrust Law and Encouraging Innovation

Antitrust laws have been in place for decades in China, but have failed to protect fair competition, largely because SOEs are granted protected market positions, and in some areas monopoly positions which exclude the entry of non-SOE players. In recent years, with the development of China's digital super platforms, leaders in China's digital economy have gained a different type of monopoly. Practices such as coercing users to sign exclusive terms with platforms to exclude emerging competitors, differentiating customers on the basis of their consumption data analysis, over-charging those who are less price-sensitive, manipulating search results, and restricting online traffic have become questionable new ways for those super-platform firms to gain advantages in a 'winner takes all or most' competition. Towards the end of 2020, China's antitrust regulatory body indicated that the country would take antitrust law seriously, especially in regulating super platforms. This move is in alignment with the main anti-monopoly practice in Europe and the US which aims to protect grassroots entrepreneurship and innovation. These super-platform firms grew within a relatively relaxed policy environment. The government needs to find a balance that, on the one hand, controls the monopoly power of these firms and, on the other hand, encourages them to continue to innovate and to nurture entrepreneurship.

'From Chaos Comes Order'

This quotation is attributed to Nietzsche.[47] While its meaning is open to interpretation, it can be held to refer to a kind of generative power of all order that is founded in chaos. A similar philosophy is widely used in the daily life of Chinese people. For example, the aim of mah-jong, a popular tile-based game played by a group of four, is to create order out of chaos on the basis of the random drawing of tiles.

On the surface, China's bottom-up, broadly distributed, and entrepreneurial approach to innovation looks chaotic. This approach, involving massive numbers of people engaged in innovation in many locations and focusing on narrow niches is a reflection of 'crowd-accelerated innovation'. When these innovators have common

---

[47] Some believe that this quotation is not from Nietzsche. The most celebrated quotation from Nietzsche to that effect is 'One must face chaos to give birth to a dancing star.' Ordo Ab Chao (Order from Chaos) is from Freemasonry.

interests and their innovations can accumulate and propagate through rapid generational improvements in interconnected communities, the result is that the most connected variations will be selected, amplified, and rewarded by markets, which, in the long run, leads to the rise of an order in innovation.

The driving force of an innovation ecosystem lies less in a top-down master plan and more in the interplay of all subsystems and the interdependent relationships within each subsystem. In China's innovation ecosystem, the evolution from an orderless state to an orderly state, or from one orderly state to another, is the result of the interplay of bottom-up variations and top-down directions. Micro-level interactions of all elements through some hidden rules can enhance macro-level system performance and resilience, pushing the ecosystem to evolve from chaos to order.

Although not all actors in an ecosystem behave in a rational way or possess consensus as to what, how, and when to innovate, one actor's behaviour in an interconnected system can influence the rest of the system members directly or indirectly, as long as the system is large enough, the actors are diverse enough, and the time for the evolution of an innovation is long enough. If such conditions are met, the system often has self-generation, self-organization, and self-correction mechanisms. If the external environment, such as new technology, new information, new policy, or new demand conditions or competitors is volatile, ambiguous, and uncertain, the self-generation, self-organization, and self-correction mechanisms can bring the system back to balance and order even though subsystems may encounter instability and disorder. This is because actors that adjust their actions to fit the changing environment can cause structural disruptions of the system. Due to interconnectedness, instability in one subsystem can cause the entire ecosystem to develop from an old structure to a new one. An innovation ecosystem can, in theory, break the limitations imposed by uncertainties of technological innovation, inadequacy of indigenous innovation capability, and scarcity of innovation resources faced by individual actors. An ecosystem can, thus, help innovation actors build synergies by better utilizing external resources to achieve common innovation goals. However, it is important for such systems to encourage continuous self-correction at the individual and lower levels, but to avoid occasional overcorrections at the systemic and higher levels.

Chairman Mao's 'Great Leap Forward Campaign' in the late 1950s and early 1960s aimed to fast-track industrialization and is a stark example of such an overcorrection. Hundreds of millions of people were forced to be involved in this campaign, and the result was chaos that led to a national disaster. A sceptical view of China's 'mass innovation and entrepreneurship' policy compares it with this disastrous campaign and questions whether it is leading the country towards more chaos and disaster. In the late 1950s, however, China's industrialization was a very simple system, with linear value chains built upon the former Soviet Union's central-planning model. It was a fragile system and collapsed under shocks such as the sudden retreat of Soviet technological support and natural disasters such as famines. The weakness of vertical structures of industrial value chains was one of the reasons that the Japanese electronics industry lost its competitiveness to South Korean and Taiwanese competitors in the 1990s.[48] China's industry today is very different and is robust, as it has multilayered supply chains and complex manufacturing structures. And, most importantly, it is open and massive in scale and scope.

As argued throughout this book, China has created supply chains and manufacturing capacity that are unmatched in their scale, flexibility, agility, and robustness, and these characteristics are underpinned by standardization and modularity enabled by digital technologies. These technologies open the supply chains to greater diversity in suppliers, large and small, domestic and international, and minimize transaction costs. Behind China's massive supply chains and manufacturing capacity, there are 'industrial commons'[49]—the collective R&D, engineering, and manufacturing ability that can sustain innovation.

This strength exists within China's innovation machine—a seemingly chaotic system with multilayered actors and no rule books to follow. The power of this machine derives not from an ordered master blueprint of central political power; rather, it is from bottom-up innovation that drives the evolution of the entire system. In an innovation ecosystem, this happens through a process of experimentation and trial and error whereby beneficial variations are favoured by the market and harmful ones discarded. The mass entrepreneurship and innovation campaign continually refuels this machine every day. Just as the scale of the innovation machine continues to increase, its constitution changes as new innovative entrepreneurs and firms join the system and old and less competitive ones are forced out of business in the process of creative destruction.

China's innovation machine has grown and thrived in circumstances where traditional innovation models dominated by large corporates that control vertical integration of value chains are giving way to an emerging model of innovation ecosystems: networks of small but agile actors clustering around dominant platforms on which technology, talent, and capital co-develop. Although the government's role in China's innovation machine has to be recognized, innovation ecosystems (and many subsystems) are organic and follow seemingly random patterns, yet collectively drive the innovation performance of the entire system. Behind this organic force are hundreds of millions of Chinese aspiring to have a better life.

In this system, every consumer, business, bank, and investor is constantly receiving information, making their own judgements about the market, and then adjusting their strategies and trading with others in their own interests. Aggregated individual interactions influence the system, and the system has influence on individuals. Each individual will receive and interpret information they receive from the system differently and adapt to their perceptions of changing market conditions differently, which will lead to further changes in the market and the economy. It is an iterating and evolving process.

[48] T. Yunogami (2013), *Lost Manufacturing: How Japan's Manufacturing Sector Has Failed* [Chinese translation], Beijing: China Machinery Industry Press.

[49] G. P. Pisano and W. C. Shih (2009), 'Restoring American Competitiveness', Harvard Business Review, July-August, https://hbr.org/2009/07/restoring-american-competitiveness, accessed 9 June 2021.

When different individuals interact, if each individual follows certain simple rules, the aggregated effect of the group will be a complex pattern. This is an emergent phenomenon in an interconnected ecosystem, and it is difficult or almost impossible to foresee the consequences of any bottom-up innovation, a feature of economies characterized as complex adaptive systems.[50] Technological innovations often have unintended consequences, including changes in social and political spheres. AI technology, for example, can transform enterprises and can have an even greater impact in the social field. Currently, AI technology is used in education, medical and healthcare, social welfare, space research, and smart and safe travel, and so on. Even without social intentions, technological entrepreneurship may lead to social innovations as the indirect results of innovations in an innovation ecosystem. Such innovations can, of course, have negative social consequences, for example in restricting personal liberties.

Bottom-up change in a system can cause disruptive outcomes. History suggests that bottom-up evolution can be positive or negative—social media, for example, produces highly divergent outcomes—and top-down power, sometimes in the form of regulation, needs to intervene to keep the balance. For this reason, a developmental view that emphasizes top-down power in innovation and industrial development argues that it will always be needed because there is no guarantee bottom-up evolution in any free society will always play out well. Profit-driven enterprises or individuals, for example, pursue innovations with short-term benefits, ignoring those with long-term potential. Betting on short-term winners and losers by private investors or enterprises would have cascading effects in an interconnected ecosystem. Top-down planning, if done properly, is one of the balances that can overcome shortcomings in the market.

Government cannot, of course, simply produce Schumpeterian innovations. However, it is not the case that the best ideas and solutions to any problems arise spontaneously when top-down forces (i.e. governments) are not involved, as suggested by Ridley.[51] Due regard has to be placed on both bottom-up and top-down influences. As we argued in Chapter 7, whereas the Chinese government has certainly influenced science and technology development to a large extent, the nation's technological and scientific trajectory is hardly determined by the state. But the government can influence directions by channelling resources and influencing their allocation towards chosen routes. This top-down approach may contribute to developing indigenous innovation capabilities and fostering certain industries, as evidenced in Japan, South Korea, and Taiwan.

The policy of 'creative adaptation' for catching up with the world's leaders for the first two decades following the economic reforms was superseded in the following two decades by the 'creative innovation' policy for the development of indigenous

---

[50] E. Beinhocker (2007), *The Origin of Wealth: Evolution, Complexity, and the Radical Remaking of Economics*, Cambridge, MA: Harvard Business Review Press.

[51] M. Ridley (2015), *The Evolution of Everything: How New Ideas Emerge*, New York: Harper.

Chinese innovation capability and technologies. Key high-technology industries and projects such as AI research and applications and bioscience have been prioritized, and there has been massive investment in state-of-the-art laboratories and factories. Following the legitimation of technology markets in the 1980s, the nation's bottom-up policies of 'mass entrepreneurship and innovation' have seen the encouragement of technology start-ups and the creation of a number of world-leading companies. This policy shift reflects China's move to gradually introducing a market economy, albeit a different kind of market economy, with very strong state involvement. The visible hand of government and the invisible hand of the market connect as dual logics in influencing the nature and direction of innovation.

In practice, Chinese policymakers use general and ambiguous policy guidance in emerging fields, allowing the market to experiment and test different approaches at a localized level, before issuing detailed plans to implement at the national level. The case of mobile payments, which emerged in an institutional void, provides an example of top-down institutional arrangements and bottom-up innovation and entrepreneurship. Policy pragmatically responded and adapted as new business models in payment services emerged. Alipay and WeChat Pay created such useful and valuable platforms that policymakers responded iteratively. The relationship between market advance and policy development around technology and evolving innovation ecosystems is dialectic and recursive. In a sense, the development of governance and policy is the result of economic growth and technological advances which require better and more efficient governance. Therefore, government changes to fit such environmental changes.

As we have seen throughout this book, it has to be emphasized that the idea that China's innovation machine is constructed from highly centralized governance authoritatively mandating policies for science, industry, and innovation is a myth; no master plan can deal with the complexity and emergence of a modern economy. Reflecting the country's history and culture, policymaking is often a compromise between different political and economic interests. Policies are fluid and adaptable, balancing centralized directives and localized implementation, top-down strategic programmes and bottom-up entrepreneurship. The early development of industry was characterized by top-down, centralized power directed at social and land reforms. The prioritization of heavy industries in the early period of China's industrialization provided the foundations for more advanced industries. Since that time China's industry and innovation policies have pragmatically seen, on the one hand, top-down, strategic projects, 'concentrating strengths to do big things', and, on the other, the encouragement of technology entrepreneurship.

'From chaos comes order' reflects Chinese cultural values which are imprints of how China's innovation machine operates and how Chinese innovators think and practise. Children learn to live with contradiction and ambiguity from a young age. Developing compromised solutions is key. In other words, the Chinese believe that without chaos there would be no creation, no structure, or even no existence of life. After all, order is merely the repetition of patterns; chaos is the process that establishes those patterns. In this process, there is no rule book—interactions between members of society following sequences spontaneously. This self-generation of order and self-governance of maintaining order are not dictated by some central power or genius, but in Taoism; it belongs to the highest form of governance: 'governing without taking actions' ('*wu wei er zhi*') or 'managing with an invisible force' ('*da dao wu xing*'). Chaos and order are not contradictory, but complementary. China's innovation machine balances the chaos and order that is the basis of its success and resilience.

Bibliography

360doc, 2018, 'Who is Winning? Huawei's "Innovation-Industrialization-Trading" vs Lenovo's "Trading-Industrialization-Innovation"', http://www.360doc.com/content/18/0418/20/37113458_746730862.shtml, accessed 28 July 2021 [Chinese online library].

Accenture, 2021, The Future of Automotive Sales in China. https://www.accenture.com/_acnmedia/PDF-147/Accenture-Study-The-Future-of-Automotive-Sales-in-China.pdf, accessed 27 July 2021.

Adner, R. 2006. 'Match Your Innovation Strategy to Your Innovation Ecosystem', *Harvard Business Review*, 84, 98.

Adner, R. 2017. 'Ecosystem as Structure: An Actionable Construct for Strategy', *Journal of Management*, 43, 39–58.

Adner, R. and Kapoor, R. 2010. 'Value Creation in Innovation Ecosystems: How the Structure of Technological Interdependence Affects Firm Performance in New Technology Generations', *Strategic Management Journal*, 31, 306–33.

Ant's IPO prospectus (2020), https://www1.hkexnews.hk/listedco/listconews/sehk/2020/1026/2020102600165.pdf, accessed 28 July 2021.

AliResearch. 2017. *Inclusive Growth and E-Commerce: China's Experience*, https://unctad.org/meetings/en/Contribution/dtl_eWeek2017c11-aliresearch_en.pdf, accessed 4 June 2021.

Allison, Graham. 2017. *Destined for War: Can America and China Escape Thucydides's Trap?* Boston, MA: Houghton Mifflin Harcourt.

Allison, Graham. 2017. 'The Thucydides Trap: When One Great Power Threatens to Displace Another, War Is Almost Always the Result—But It Doesn't Have to Be', *Foreign Policy*, 9 June, https://foreignpolicy.com/2017/06/09/the-thucydides-trap/, accessed 9 June 2021.

Alper, Alexandra, Sterling, Toby, and Nellis, Stephen. 2020. 'Trump Administration Pressed Dutch Hard to Cancel China Chip-Equipment Sale', *Reuters*, 6 January, https://www.reuters.com/article/us-asml-holding-usa-china-insight/trump-administration-pressed-dutch-hard-to-cancel-china-chip-equipment-sale-sources-idUSKBN1Z50HN, accessed 1 June 2021.

Ahlstrom, D. Bruton, G. and Yeh, Y. 2007. 'Venture Capital in China: Past, Present, and Future', *Asia Pacific Journal of Management*, 24: 247-68. DOI: 10.1007/s10490-006-9032-1.

American Chamber of Commerce in China. 2020. '2020 Business Climate Survey', https://www.amchamchina.org/press/2020-business-climate-survey-released/, accessed 4 June 2021.

American Institute of Physics. 2018. 'Rapid Rise of China's STEM Workforce Charted by National Science Board Report', 31 January, https://www.aip.org/fyi/2018/rapid-rise-china%E2%80%99s-stem-workforce-charted-national-science-board-report, accessed 31 May 2021.

Arthur, W. B. 2009. *The Nature of Technology: What It Is and How It Evolves*. London: Penguin Books.

Autio, E., Nambisan, S., Thomas, L. D. W., and Wright, M. 2018. 'Digital Affordances, Spatial Affordances, and the Genesis of Entrepreneurial Ecosystems', *Strategic Entrepreneurship Journal*, 12, 72–95.

Autio, E. and Thomas, L. 2014. 'Innovation ecosystems', in M. Dodgson, D. M. Gann, and N. Phillips (eds.), *The Oxford Handbook of Innovation Management*. Oxford: Oxford University Press, 204–88.

Baldwin, C. Y. and Clark, K. B. 2000. *Design Rules*, i: *The Power of Modularity*, Cambridge, MA: MIT Press.

Baldwin, Richard. 2016. *The Great Convergence: Information Technology and the New Globalization*. Cambridge, MA: Harvard University Press.

Baraniuk, Chris. 2018. 'How China's Giant Solar Farms Are Transforming World Energy', BBC, 4 September, https://www.bbc.com/future/article/20180822-why-china-is-transforming-the-worlds-solar-energy, accessed 7 June 2021.

Beinhocker, Eric. 2007. *The Origin of Wealth: Evolution, Complexity, and the Radical Remaking of Economics*. Cambridge, MA: Harvard Business Review Press.

BEROE (2020). 'China CRO Market Intelligence', https://www.beroeinc.com/category-intelligence/cro-china-market/, accessed July 28 2021.

Blanchette, Jude and Hillman, Jonathan E. 2020. 'China's Digital Silk Road after the Coronavirus', Centre for Strategic and International Studies, 13 April, https://www.csis.org/analysis/chinas-digital-silk-road-after-coronavirus, accessed 9 June 2021.

Blustein, Paul. 2019. *Schism: China, America and the Fracturing of the Global Trading System*. Kinston: McGill-Queen's University Press.

Bogers, M., Sims, J., and West, J. 2019. *What is an Ecosystem? Incorporating 25 Years of Ecosystem Research*, Academy of Management Conference, August, Boston.

Breschi, Stefano, Malerba, Franco, and Orsenigo, Luigi. 2000. 'Technological Regimes and Schumpeterian Pattern of Innovation', *Economic Journal, Royal Economic Society*, 110(463), 388–410.

Caijing (Finance). 2020. 'The Fission of China's Digital Economy amid the Covid-19 Pandemic', *Caijing Magazine*, June [in Chinese].

Caijing (Finance). 2020. 'How China's Digital Economy Accelerates in Covid-19?', *Caijing Magazine*, 21 June [in Chinese].

Campbell, Matthew et al. 2021. 'Elon Musk Loves China, and China Loves Him Back—for Now', *Bloomberg Businessweek*, 13 January, https://www.bloomberg.com/news/features/2021-01-13/china-loves-elon-musk-and-tesla-tsla-how-long-will-that-last, accessed 1 June 2021.

Cantwell, J. 2017. 'Innovation and International Business', *Industry and Innovation*, 24, 41–60.

CB Insights, March 2020. 'The Complete List of Unicorn Companies', https://www.cbinsights.com/research-unicorn-companies, accessed 26 July 2021.

CCID (China Electronics and Information Industry Development Institute) 2020. 'White Paper for Manufacturing Industry Innovation centres' [in Chinese], Beijing, China. May 2020.

Chen, Y.-C. 2008. 'The Limits of Brain Circulation: Chinese Returnees and Technological Development in Beijing', *Pacific Affairs*, 81, 195–215.

Cheng, C. J. and Shiu, E. C. C. 2008. 'Re-Innovation: The Construct, Measurement, and Validation', *Technovation*, 28, 658–66.

China Academy of Information and Communications Technology (CAICT), July 2020. 'China's Digital Economy Whitepaper.' Beijing, China.

China Internet Network Information Center (CNNIC). 2020. 'The 46th China Statistical Report on Internet Development', http://www.cac.gov.cn/2020-09/29/c_1602939909285141.htm, accessed 20 July 2021.

China's Ministry of Commerce. 2019. 'China E-commerce Report 2019', http://www.199it.com/archives/1076562.html, accessed 5 June 2021.

China VC/PE Market Review 2018. Zero2IPO Research, February 2019. https://report.pedata.cn/1550832271140000.html, accessed 28 July 2021.

China's Science and Technology Statistics Yearbook, 2019. Beijing: China Statistics Press.

Chinese Torch Program Statistical Yearbook, 2019. Beijing: China Statistics Press.

Chinaventure Institute, 2020. 'White paper on investing in China's high-end manufacturing' (in Chinese). Beijing, China.

Chinese Academy of Engineering, State Industrial Information Safety Research Institution and Nanjing University of Aeronautics and Astronautics. 2020. '2020 China's Manufacturing Power Index'.

Christopher, Martin. 2011. *Logistics & Supply Chain Management*, 5th edn. London: Financial Times Prentice Hall.

Coase, R. H. 1937. *The Nature of the Firm*. doi: 10.1111/j.1468-0335.1937.tb00002.x.

Cohen, W. M. and Levinthal, D. A. 1990. 'Absorptive Capacity: A New Perspective on Learning and Innovation', *Administrative Science Quarterly*, 35, 128–52.

Cooke, P. and Morgan, K. 1998. *The Associational Economy*. Oxford: Oxford University Press.

Credit Suisse 2020. 'China Unicorns: Emerging from the Stables', *APAC Equity Research Reports*, 4 May, https://www.credit-suisse.com/cn/en/content-hub/equity-research.html, accessed 6 June 2021.

Cusumano, M. A., Gawer, A., and Yoffie, D. B. 2019. *The Business of Platforms: Strategy in the Age of Digital Competition, Innovation, and Power*. New York: Harper Business.

Dahlberg, T., Mallat, N., Ondrus, J., and Zmijewska, A. 2008. 'Past, Present and Future of Mobile Payments Research: A Literature Review', *Electronic Commerce Research and Applications*, 7, 165–81.

Deloitte, 2020. 'A Few Thoughts on China's 14th Five-Year Plan', May 2020.

Dhanaraj, C. and Parkhe, A. 2006. 'Orchestrating Innovation Networks', *Academy of Management Review*, 31, 659–69.

Diamandis, Peter H. and Kotler, Steven. 2020. *The Future Is Faster than You Think: How Converging Technologies Are Transforming Business, Industries, and Our Lives*. Exponential Technology Series. New York: Simon & Schuster.

Didi's IPO prospectus (2021) https://www.sec.gov/Archives/edgar/data/1764757/000104746921001194/a2243272zf-1.htm; 28 July 2021.

Dodgson, M. 2009. 'Asia's National Innovation Systems: Institutional Adaptability and Rigidity in the Face of Global Innovation Challenges', *Asia Pacific Journal of Management*, 26, 589–609.

Dodgson, M. and Gann, D. 2014. 'Technology and Innovation', in M. Dodgson, D. M. Gann, and N. Phillips (eds.), *The Oxford Handbook of Innovation Management*. Oxford, Oxford University Press, 3–25.

Dodgson, M., Gann, D., and Salter, A. 2005. *Think, Play, Do: Technology, Innovation and Organization*. Oxford: Oxford University Press.

Dodgson, M., Gann, D., Wladawsky-Berger, I., and George, G. 2013. 'From the Digital Divide to Inclusive Innovation: The Case of Digital Money.' Royal Society of Arts, https://www.thersa.org/globalassets/pdfs/reports/rsa-digital-money-report-june_2013.pdf, accessed 5 June 2021.

Dodgson, M., Gann, D., Wladawsky-Berger, I., Sultan, S., and George, G. 2015. 'Managing Digital Money', *Academy of Management Journal*, 58(2), 325–33.

Dodgson, M., Mathews, J., Kastelle, T., and Hu, M. C. 2008. 'The Evolving Nature of Taiwan's National Innovation System: The Case of Biotechnology Innovation Networks', *Research Policy*, 37, 430–45.

Dodgson, M. and Xue, L. 2009. 'Innovation in China', *Innovation: Management, Policy and Practice*, 11(1), 2–5.

Beinhocker, Eric. 2007. *The Origin of Wealth: Evolution, Complexity, and the Radical Remaking of Economics*. Cambridge, MA: Harvard Business Review Press.

Economist. 2019. 'A Transcript of Ren Zhengfei's Interview', *The Economist*, 12 September, https://www.economist.com/business/2019/09/12/a-transcript-of-ren-zhengfeis-interview, accessed 25 May 2021.

Economist. 2020. 'China Has Never Mastered Internal-Combustion Engines', *The Economist*, 4 January, https://www.economist.com/technology-quarterly/2020/01/02/china-has-never-mastered-internal-combustion-engines, accessed 8 June 2021.

Economist. 2020. 'China Takes Aim at Its Entrepreneurs: Private Enterprise Faces Formidable New Obstacles', *The Economist*, 12 November, https://www.economist.com/business/2020/11/12/china-takes-aim-at-its-entrepreneurs, accessed 7 June 2021.

Economist. 2020. 'Chip Wars: A New Escalation in the Tech Conflict Illustrates the Limits of American Power', *The Economist*, 21 May, https://www.economist.com/leaders/2020/05/23/america-is-determined-to-sink-huawei, accessed 30 May 2021.

Economist. 2020. 'Cloning Tesla: Electric-Vehicle Wars in China', *The Economist*, 4 January, https://www.economist.com/business/2020/01/04/cloning-tesla-electric-vehicle-wars-in-china, accessed 8 June 2021.

Economist. 2020. 'The Greatest (Trade) Show on Earth: China Is the World's Factory, More than Ever', *The Economist*, 29 June, https://www.economist.com/finance-and-economics/2020/06/23/china-is-the-worlds-factory-more-than-ever, accessed 4 June 2021.

Economist Intelligence Unit. 2020. 'Geopolitics after COVID-19: Is the Pandemic a Turning Point?' 1 April, https://country.eiu.com/article.aspx?articleid=1339299717&Country=Albania&topic=Politics&subtopic=Forecast&subsubtopic=International+relations, accessed 9 June 2021.

European Chamber of Commerce in China. 2020. 'Business Confidence Survey 2020: Navigating in the Dark', http://www.europeanchamber.com.cn/en/publications-business-confidence-survey, accessed 4 June 2021.

Fagerberg, Jan. 2006. 'Innovation: A Guide to the Literature', in Jan Fagerberg and David C. Mowery (eds.), *The Oxford Handbook of Innovation*. Oxford: Oxford University Press,

Fan Yifei, 'Analysis on the Policy Implications of the Positioning of Digital RMB M0', September 2020, https://blockcast.cc/news/fan-yifei-deputy-governor-of-the-central-bank-policy-perspective-analysis-of-digital-rmb-m0-positioning/, accessed 26 July 2021.

Financial Times. 2021. 'China's education sector crackdown hits foreign investors', https://www.ft.com/content/dfae3282-e14e-4fea-aa5f-c2e914444fb8, accessed 29 July 2021.

Fioretti, Julia. 2020. 'China's Star Board among the World's Top Three IPO Venues', *Bloomberg*, 3 August, https://www.bloomberg.com/news/articles/2020-08-03/china-s-star-board-among-world-s-top-three-ipo-venues-ecm-watch, accessed 6 June 2021.

Friedman, T. L. 2017. *Thank You for Being Late: An Optimist's Guide to Thriving in the Age of Accelerations*. London: Penguin Books.

Fu, Xiaolan. 2015. *China's Path to Innovation*. Cambridge: Cambridge University Press.

Fukuyama, Francis. 1989. 'The End of History?', *The National Interest*, 6, 3–18.

Fukuyama, Francis. 2020. 'The Thing That Determines a Country's Resistance to the Coronavirus: The Major Dividing Line in Effective Crisis Response Will Not Place Autocracies on One Side and Democracies on the Other'. *The Atlantic*, 30 March, https://www.theatlantic.com/ideas/archive/2020/03/thing-determines-how-well-countries-respond-coronavirus/609025/, accessed 25 May 2021.

Gao, J., Liu, X., and Zhang, M. Y. 2011. 'China's NIS: The Interplay between S&T Policy Framework and Technology Entrepreneurship', in S. Mian (ed.), *Science and Technology Based Regional Entrepreneurship: Global Experience in Policy & Program Development*. Cheltenham: Edward Elgar.

Garcia, R. and Calantone, R. 2002. 'A Critical Look at Technological Innovation Typology and Innovativeness Terminology: A Literature Review', *Journal of Product Innovation Management*, 19, 110–32.

Gawer, Annabelle and Cusumano, Michael A. 2013. 'Industry Platforms and Ecosystem Innovation', *Journal of Product Innovation Management*, 31(3), 417–33.

Geertz, Clifford. 1969. *Agricultural Involution: The Processes of Ecological Change in Indonesia*. Bekerley, CA: University of California Press.

Gewirtz Julian Baird. 2019. 'China's Long March to Technological Supremacy: The Roots of Xi Jinping's Ambition to "Catch Up and Surpass"', *Foreign Affairs*, 27 August, https://www.foreignaffairs.com/articles/china/2019-08-27/chinas-long-march-technological-supremacy, accessed 30 May 2021.

Gibson, J. J. 1979. *The Ecological Approach to Visual Perception*. East Susses, UK: Psychological Press.

Grassano, Nicola et al. 2020. 'The 2020 EU Industrial R&D Investment Scoreboard', 1 January. https://iri.jrc.ec.europa.eu/scoreboard/2020-eu-industrial-rd-investment-scoreboard, accessed 1 June 2021.

Gu, S. and Dodgson, M. (eds.), 2006. 'Innovation in China: Harmonious Transformation?' Special Issue, *Innovation: Management, Policy and Practice*, 8(1–2).

Gu, S. and Lundvall, B.-A. 2006. 'Policy Learning as a Key Process in the Transformation of the Chinese Innovation System', in B.-A. Lundvall, P. Intarakumnerd, and J. Vang (eds.), *Asia's Innovation Systems in Transition*. Cheltenham: Edward Elgar, 293–312.

Guo, L. Zhang, M. Y., Dodgson, M., and Gann, D. 2019. 'Huawei's Catch-Up in the Global Telecommunication Industry: Innovation Capability and Transition to Leadership', *Technology Analysis & Strategic Management*, 31(12), 1–17.

Guo, L., Zhang, M. Y., Dodgson, M., Gann, D., and Cai, H. 2019. 'Seizing Windows of Opportunity by Using Technology-Building and Market-Seeking Strategies in Tandem: Huawei's Sustained Catch-Up in the Global Market', *Asia Pacific Journal of Management*, 36, 849–79.

Hancock, Tom. 2019. 'AstraZeneca Backs $1bn China Biotech Fund', *Financial Times*, 5 November, https://www.ft.com/content/5727e4fc-ffe1-11e9-be59-e49b2a136b8d, accessed 6 June 2021.

Hansen, S. 2014. 'Techno-Nationalism in China's Rise: The Next Gunpowder Moment', *The Strategist*, Australia Strategic Policy Institute, 14 October, https://www.aspistrategist.org.au/techno-nationalism-in-chinas-rise-the-next-gunpowder-moment/, accessed 25 May 2021.

Haskel, J. and Westlake, S. 2018. *Capitalism without Capital: The Rise of the Intangible Economy*. Princeton, NJ: Princeton University Press.

Hayhoe, Ruth. 1996. *China's Universities 1895–1995: A Century of Cultural Conflict*. New York: Garland Publishing.

Herrigel, G., Wittke, V. and Voskamp, U. (2013). 'The process of Chinese manufacturing upgrading: Transitioning from unilateral to recursive mutual learning relations', *Global Strategy Journal*, 3, 109–125.

Hille, Kathrin. 2020. 'US "Surgical" Attack on Huawei Will Reshape Tech Supply Chain', *Financial Times*, 19 May, https://www.ft.com/content/c614afc5-86f8-42b1-9b6c-90bffbd1be8b, accessed 1 June 2021.

Hobday, M. 1995. 'East Asian Latecomer Firms: Learning the Technology of Electronics', *World Development*, 23, 1171–93.

Hu, A. G. and Jefferson, G. H. 2009. 'A Great Wall of Patents: What is behind China's Recent Patent Explosion?', *Journal of Development Economics*, 90(1), 57–68.

Hu, M.-C., Kastelle, T., and Dodgson, M. (eds.). 2013. 'Innovation in Taiwan', *Innovation: Management, Policy and Practice*, 15, 4.

Huang, Philip (1985), *The peasant economy and social change in North China*, Stanford, CA: Stanford University Press.

Huang, Philip (1990), *The peasant family and rural development in the Yangzi Delta, 1350–1988*, Stanford, CA: Stanford University Press.

Huang, Yiping. 2019. 'China 2049: What Has Been the Reason for China's Economic Success over the Past 40 Years?', https://ishare.ifeng.com/c/s/v0020X4-_DZacfQYcVcNC6O8H6mry282oWh14zT--IgNZo6DQ__?from=timeline&isappinstalled=0, accessed 6 June 2021.

Hucker, Charles O. 1975. *China's Imperial Past: An Introduction to Chinese History and Culture*. Redwood City, CA: Stanford University Press.

Hurun. 2020. 'Hurun Global Unicorn Index', https://www.hurun.co.uk/hurun-global-unicorn-index-2020-full-report.php, accessed 6 June 2021.

Iansiti, M. and Levien, R. 2004. *The Keystone Advantage: What the New Dynamics of Business Ecosystems Mean for Strategy, Innovation, and Sustainability*. Cambridge, MA: Harvard Business School Press.

IDC, 2020. 'Asia Pacific SME Digital Readiness Report'. Beijing, China.

IMF. 2019. 'China's Digital Economy: Opportunities and Risks'. IMF Working Paper.

Innovation Center for Energy and Transportation. June 2020. 'Update Timetable for Phasing Out China's Traditional ICE Vehicles and Its Environmental Benefits Assessment', http://www.nrdc.cn/information/informationinfo?id=254&cook=1, accessed 27 July 2021.

iResearch, 2019. 'China's path to smart manufacturing' (in Chinese), Beijing, China.

Jamrisco, Michelle and Lu, Wei. 2020. 'Germany Breaks Korea's Six-Year Streak as Most Innovative Nation', *Bloomberg Innovation Index*, 18 January, https://www.bloomberg.com/news/articles/2020-01-18/germany-breaks-korea-s-six-year-streak-as-most-innovative-nation, accessed 31 May 2021.

Javorcik, Beata. 2020. 'COVID Has Made the State's Hand More Visible But There Are Risks', *The Financial Times*, 9 November, https://www.ft.com/content/c5295c0d-ab82-49fd-afb4-0edba303ac4d, accessed 8 June 2021.

Jia, N., Huang, K. G., and Zhang, C. M. 2019. 'Public Governance, Corporate Governance, and Firm Innovation: An Examination of State-Owned Enterprises', *Academy of Management Journal*, 62(1), 220–47.

Khanna, T. and Palepu, K. G. 2010. *Winning in Emerging Markets: A Road Map for Strategy and Execution*. Boston, MA: Harvard Business School Press.

Kim, L. 1997. *Imitation to Innovation: The Dynamics of Korea's Technological Learning*. Cambridge, MA: Harvard Business School Press.

Kurlantzick, Joshua. 2020. 'Assessing China's Digital Silk Road: A Transformative Approach to Technology Financing or a Danger to Freedoms?', 18 December, https://www.cfr.org/blog/assessing-chinas-digital-silk-road-transformative-approach-technology-financing-or-danger, accessed 25 May 2021.

Kynge, James and Yu, Sun. 2021. 'Virtual Control: The Agenda behind China's New Digital Currency', *Financial Times*, 17 February, https://www.ft.com/content/7511809e-827e-4526-81ad-ae83f405f623, accessed 5 June 2021.

Lee, Aileen. 2013. 'Welcome to the Unicorn Club: Learning From Billion-Dollar Startups', *TechCrunch*, 3 November, https://techcrunch.com/2013/11/02/welcome-to-the-unicorn-club/?guccounter=1&guce_referrer=aHR0cHM6Ly93d3cuZ29vZ2xlLmNvbS8S&guce_referrer_sig=AQAAAMMzs85Ay-jXRbq9SnTHL_nJycN6RjT61LEPOaGSnFDWwCdxUETnlGP-Zs37uFpBEUuOGzI5VNshtcKXO-eB7oxn-aeAA9Plm2Ahin7qTtJizcUhHcowsxC-jeHoy5yU_mJKGnafLhgWfQgFqfTKFFaCqWiXYqQavuwoCA5m6raQV, accessed 6 June 2021.

Lee, Georgina. 2020. 'ChiNext, Star Market, China's Rival Tech Boards, Target Hong Kong "Red Chip" Secondary Listings as Competition Heats Up', *South China Morning Post*, 15 August, https://www.scmp.com/business/banking-finance/article/3097449/chinext-star-market-chinas-rival-tech-boards-target-hong, accessed 6 June 2021.

Lee, K. 2013. *Schumpeterian Analysis of Economic Catch-Up: Knowledge, Path-Creation, and the Middle-Income Trap*. Cambridge: Cambridge University Press.

Lee, K. and Lim, C. S. 2001. 'Technological Regimes, Catching-Up and Leapfrogging: Findings from the Korean Industries', *Research Policy*, 30, 459–83.

Lee, K. and Malerba, F. 2017. 'Catch-Up Cycles and Changes in Industrial Leadership: Windows of Opportunity and Responses of Firms and Countries in the Evolution of Sectoral Systems', *Research Policy*, 46(2), 338–51.

Lerner, J. and Tirole, J. 2013. *Standard-Essential Patents*. Cambridge, MA: National Bureau of Economic Research, https://www.nber.org/system/files/working_papers/w19664/w19664.pdf, accessed 31 May 2021.

Li, D. 2020, 'China is economically decentralized for competition among local governments [in Chinese]', see http://www.bjnews.com.cn/finance/2020/08/06/756083.html, accessed 27 July 2021.

Li. L. 2004, 'China's higher education reform 1998–2003: A summary', *Asia Pacific Education. Review*, 5, 14. https://doi.org/10.1007/BF03026275. (2004). 'China's higher education reform 1998–2003: A summary', *Asia Pacific Education. Review*, 5, 14. https://doi.org/10.1007/BF03026275.

Li, Z., Zhang, M. Y., and Zhang, H. 2020. 'Firm Growth Performance and Relative Innovation Orientation of Exploration vs Exploitation: Moderating Effects of Cluster Relationships', *Management and Organization Review*, 17(1), 1–30.

Lian, L. and Ma, H. 2010. 'Revaluation of FDI on the Economy Development of China—Is It an Entirely Unalloyed Benefit?', *International Journal of Business and Management*, 5, 184–90.

Lin, Justin Yifu. 2010. *New Structural Economics: A Framework for Rethinking Development*, Policy Research Working Paper No. 5197. Washington DC: World Bank, https://open-knowledge.worldbank.org/handle/10986/19919, accessed 8 June 2021.

Lin, Justin Yifu and Pleskovic, Boris (eds.). 2010. *Annual World Bank Conference on Development Economics Global 2010: Lessons from East Asia and the Global Financial Crisis*. Washington, DC: World Bank.

Lind, Jennifer. 2019. 'The Rise of China and the Future of the Transatlantic Relationship', Chatham House, 29 July, https://www.chathamhouse.org/publication/rise-china-and-future-transatlantic-relationship, accessed 9 June 2021.

Liu, James T. C. 1989. *China Turning Inward: Intellectual-Political Changes in the Early Twelfth Century*. Cambridge, MA: Harvard East Asia Center, Harvard University.

Liu, Yun. 2020. 'A Speech: China Unicom Science and Technology Innovation Conference', November, http://www.techweb.com.cn/tech/2020-11-30/2814014.shtml, accessed 10 June 2021.

Loch, Christoph and Kavadias, Stylianos (eds.). 2009. *Handbook of New Product Development Management*. Abingdon: Routledge.

Lundvall, B. A. 1992. *National Innovation Systems: Towards a Theory of Innovation and Interactive Learning*, London: Pinter.

McKelvey, M. and Jin, J. 2020. *Innovative Capabilities and the Globalization of Chinese Firms*. Cheltenham, Edward Elgar.

McMorrow, R. and Liu, N. 2020. 'How a Pandemic Led the World to Start Shopping on Alibaba.' *Financial Times*, 28 April, https://www.ft.com/content/4b1644b1-aeee-4d02-805a-c3ac26291412, accessed 10 June 2021.

Manyika, James et al. 2012. 'Manufacturing the Future: The Next Era of Global Growth and Innovation', McKinsey Global Institute, 1 November, https://www.mckinsey.com/business-functions/operations/our-insights/the-future-of-manufacturing, accessed 1 June 2021.

Mathews, J. A. 2006. 'Dragon Multinationals: New Players in 21st Century Globalization', *Asia Pacific Journal of Management*, 23, 5–27.

MIIT (Ministry of Industry and Information Technology), 2016. 'Implementation Guide of Building Manufacturing Innovation Centres' (in Chinese), Beijing, China.

MIIT (Ministry of Industry and Information Technology), 2018. 'Measures for Performance Assessment and Evaluation of the National State Manufacturing Innovation Centres' (in Chinese), Beijing, China.

Milanovic, Branko. 2020. 'The Clash of Capitalisms: The Real Fight for the Global Economy's Future,' *Foreign Affairs*, January/February, https://www.foreignaffairs.com/articles/united-states/2019-12-10/clash-capitalisms, accessed 9 June 2021.

Moore, J. F. 1993. 'Predators and Prey: The New Ecology of Competition,' *Harvard Business Review*, 71, 75–83.

Moore, Scott. 2020. 'China's Role in the Global Biotechnology Sector and Implications for US Policy,' Brookings Institute, April, https://www.brookings.edu/research/chinas-role-in-the-global-biotechnology-sector-and-implications-for-us-policy/, accessed 6 June 2021.

Nakamura, H. 1964. *Ways of Thinking of Eastern People*. Honolulu: University of Hawaii Press.

Nambisan, S., Lyytinen, K., Majchrzak, A., and Song, M. 2017. 'Digital Innovation Management: Reinventing Innovation Management Research in a Digital World,' MIS Quarterly, 41, 223–38.

National Intellectual Property Administration (2015). White Paper on the Intellectual Property Development. http://sipa.sh.gov.cn/annualreport/20191130/0005-28464.html, accessed 27 July 2021.

Naughton, B. 2011. 'China's Economic Policy Today: The New State Activism,' *Eurasian Geography and Economics*, 52(3), 313–29.

Needham, J. 1954. *Science and Civilisation in China*, I: *Introductory Orientations*, Cambridge: Cambridge University Press.

Needham, J. 1969. 'Science and Society in East and West,' *The Grand Titration: Science and Society in East and West*. 190–217. London: Allen & Unwin.

Negroponte, Nicholas. 1995. *Being Digital*. New York: Vintage Publishing.

Nelson, R. R. (1993), *National Innovation Systems: A Comparative Study*, Oxford: Oxford University Press.

Nelson, R. R. and Winter, S. G. 1982. *An Evolutionary Theory of Economic Change*. Cambridge, MA: Harvard University Press.

Nielsen, Tomas, Smith, Stephen, and LeHong, Hung. 2020. 'The Postpandemic Planning Framework,' Gartner Information Technology Research, 15 May, accessed 9 June 2021.

OECD. 2002. *National Innovation Systems*. Paris: OECD. https://www.oecd.org/science/inno/2101733.pdf, accessed 26 July 2021.

OECD (2014), *Recommendation of the Council on Digital Government Strategies*. https://www.oecd.org/gov/digital-government/Recommendation-digital-government-strategies.pdf, accessed 26 July 2021.

OECD. 2017. *The Size and Sectoral Distribution of State-Owned Enterprises*. Paris: OECD Publishing. doi: 10.1787/9789264280663-en.

Parker, G., Van Alstyne, M., and Choudary, S. P. 2016. *Platform Revolution: How Networked Markets Are Transforming the Economy and How to Make Them Work for You*. New York: W. W. Norton.

Peck, J. and J. Zhang, 2013. 'A Variety of Capitalism . . . with Chinese Characteristics?,' *Journal of Economic Geography*, 13(3), 357–96.

Peng, M.W., Sun, M.W., Pinkham, B., and Chen, H. 2009. 'The Institution-Based View as a Third Leg for a Strategy Tripod,' *Academy of Management Perspectives*, 23, 63–81.

Pisano, G. P. and Shih, W. C. 2009. 'Restoring American Competitiveness,' *Harvard Business Review*, July-August, https://hbr.org/2009/07/restoring-american-competitiveness, accessed 9 June 2021.

Pohlmann, T., Neuhäusler, P., and Blind, K. 2016. 'Standard Essential Patents to Boost Financial Returns,' *R&D Management*, 46, 612–30.

Prahalad, C. and Fruehauf, H. 2004. *The Fortune at the Bottom of the Pyramid*. Philadephia, PA: Wharton School Publishing.

Puffer, S. M., McCarthy, D. J., and Boisot, M. 2010. 'Entrepreneurship in Russia and China: The Impact of Formal Institutional Voids', *Entrepreneurship Theory & Practice*, 34, 441–67.

Rapier, Robert. 2018. 'China Emits More Carbon Dioxide than the U.S. and EU Combined', *Forbes*, 1 July, https://www.forbes.com/sites/rrapier/2018/07/01/china-emits-more-carbon-dioxide-than-the-u-s-and-eu-combined/, accessed 7 June 2021.

Redding, Gordon, 1990. *The Spirit of Chinese Capitalism*. Berlin: de Gruyter.

Ridley, M. 2015. *The Evolution of Everything: How New Ideas Emerge*. New York: Harper.

Robinson, J. 2010. 'Industrial Policy and Development: A Political Economy Perspective', in Justin Yifu Lin and Boris Pleskovic (eds.), *Annual World Bank Conference on Development Economics Global 2010: Lessons from East Asia and the Global Financial Crisis*. Washington, DC: World Bank, 61-79.

Rogers, E. M. 1995. *Diffusion of Innovation*, 4th edn. New York: Free Press.

Roy, Katica. 2019. 'How Is the Fourth Industrial Revolution Changing Our Economy?' *World Economic Forum*, 26 November, https://www.weforum.org/agenda/2019/11/the-fourth-industrial-revolution-is-redefining-the-economy-as-we-know-it/, accessed 31 May 2021.

Sachs, Jeffrey. 2019. 'China Is Not the Source of Our Economic Problems—Corporate Greed Is', 27 May, https://edition.cnn.com/2019/05/26/opinions/china-is-not-the-enemy-sachs/index.html, accessed 9 June 2021.

Salmelin, B. (2013), 'Reflections from Open Innovation 2.0 Paradigm', European Commission. http://globalforum.items-int.com/gf/gf-content/uploads/2014/04/2_Bror_Salmelin_Global_Forum_Trieste.pdf, accessed 28 July 2021.

Satell, Greg. 2021. 'How a Genius Thinks', *Forbes*, 1 June, https://www.forbes.com/sites/gregsatell/2014/06/01/how-a-genius-thinks/?sh=340132f40619, accessed 7 June 2021.

Saxenian, A. 2002. 'Transnational Communities and the Evolution of Global Production Networks: The Cases of Taiwan, China and India', *Industry and Innovation*, 9, 183–202.

Saxenian, A. and Hsu, J. Y. 2001. 'The Silicon Valley–Hsinchu Connection: Technical Communities and Industrial Upgrading', *Industry and Corporate Change*, 10, 893–920.

Schumpeter, J. A. 1934. *The Theory of Economic Development: An Inquiry into Profits, Capital, Credit, Interest and the Business Cycle*. Cambridge, MA: Harvard University Press.

Schwab, K. 2015. 'The Fourth Industrial Revolution', *Foreign Affairs*, 12 December, https://www.foreignaffairs.com/articles/2015-12-12/fourth-industrial-revolution, accessed 26 May 2021.

Schwab, K. (ed.). 2019. *The Global Competitiveness Report:2019*. Cologny, Switzerland: World Economic Forum, http://www3.weforum.org/docs/WEF_TheGlobalCompetitivenessReport2019.pdf, accessed 31 May 2021.

Shapiro, C. and Varian, H. R. 1998. *Information Rules: A Strategic Guide to the Network Economy*. Boston, MA: Harvard Business School Press.

Simon, Hermann, 2009. *Hidden Champions of the Twenty-First Century: The Success Strategies of Unknown World Market Leaders*. Bonn: Springer.

Sirekanyan, Tigran. 2021. 'World Order Established Following WWII Collapses—Former French PM Calls on to Understand Each Other on the Way to New World', *Armenpress*, 8 June, https://armenpress.am/eng/news/977753/, accessed 25 May 2021.

Smyth, Jamie. 2020. 'Australia's "Amateurish" China Diplomacy Sets Business on Edge', *Financial Times*, 17 December, https://www.ft.com/content/843c9286-b135-4d39-acbd-dafd87f57e0c, accessed 9 June 2021.

Sorace, C., Franceschini, I. and Loubere, N. (Eds.), *Afterlives of Chinese Communism: Political Concepts from Mao to Xi* (pp. 275-280). Australia: ANU Press.

Srholec, M. and Verspagen, B. 2008. *The Voyage of the Beagle in Innovation Systems Land: Explorations on Sectors, Innovation, Heterogeneity and Selection*, UNU-MERIT Working

Papers, Maastricht: United Nations University-Maastricht Economic and Social Research and Training Centre on Innovation and Technology.

State Council. 2012. 'Approving the Employment Promotion Plan (2011–2015)', http://www.gov.cn/jrzg/2012-02/08/content_2061241.htm, accessed 29 July 2021 [in Chinese].

State Council. 2014. http://www.gov.cn/xinwen/2014-05/13/content_2678979.htm, accessed 29 July 2021. 'Notice of the General Office of the State Council on Doing a Good Job in Organizing Entrepreneurship as an Employment Option for Graduates from Regular Colleges and Universities in the Country', http://www.gov.cn/jrzg/2012-02/08/content_2061241.htm, accessed 29 July 2021 [in Chinese].

State Council. 2015. 'Guiding Opinions of the General Office of the State Council on the Development of Makerspace to Promote Mass Entrepreneurship and Innovation', http://www.lawinfochina.com/display.aspx?id=21057&lib=law, accessed 28 July 2021.

State Council. 2019. 'Platform Economy to Be Promoted', 8 August, http://english.www.gov.cn/policies/latestreleases/201908/08/content_WS5d4bdd9bc6d0c6695ff7e685.html, accessed 5 June 2021.

State Council. 2020. 'Chinese University, College Graduates to Exceed 9 Million in 2021', 1 December, http://english.www.gov.cn/statecouncil/ministries/202012/01/content_WS5fc63051c6d0f72576941058.html, accessed 31 May 2021.

Stauffer, Brian. 2020. How the World Will Look after the Coronavirus Pandemic', *Foreign Policy*, 20 March, https://foreignpolicy.com/2020/03/20/worldorder-after-coroanvirus-pandemic/, accessed 9 June 2021.

Strange, S. 1989. 'Towards a Theory of Transnational Empire', in E. O. Czempiel, and J. N. Rosenau (eds.), *Global Changes and Theoretical Challenges: Approaches to World Politics for the 1990s*. Lexington, MA: Lexington Books, 16.

Taleb, N. N. 2007. *The Black Swan: The Impact of the Highly Improbable*. New York: Random House.

Taleb, N. N. 2012. *Antifragile: Things That Gain from Disorder*. London: Penguin.

Tan, Jessica and Ngai, Joe. 2018. 'Building a Tech-Enabled Ecosystem: An Interview with Ping An's Jessica Tan', *McKinsey Quarterly*, 4 December, https://www.mckinsey.com/featured-insights/china/building-a-tech-enabled-ecosystem-an-interview-with-ping-ans-jessica-tan, accessed 6 June 2021.

Teece, D. J. 2010. 'Business Models, Business Strategy and Innovation', *Long Range Planning*, 43(2–3), 172–94.

Triolo, Paul. 2020. *The Telecommunications Industry in US-China Context: Evolving toward Near-Complete Bifurcation*. Maryland: Johns Hopkins University Applied Physics Laboratory LLC.

US Department of Justice, 2020. 'Attorney General William P. Barr Delivers the Keynote Address at the Department of Justice's China Initiative Conference, Thursday, Washington, DC. February 6, 2020', https://www.justice.gov/opa/speech/attorney-general-william-p-barr-delivers-keynote-address-department-justices-china, accessed 30 May 2021.

Varas, Antonio and Varadarajan, Raj. 2020. 'How Restricting Trade with China Could End US Semiconductor Leadership', *Boston Consulting Group*, 9 March, https://www.bcg.com/publications/2020/restricting-trade-with-china-could-end-united-states-semiconductor-leadership, accessed 1 June 2021.

Wade, R. 2004. *Governing the Market: Economic Theory and the Role of Government in East Asian Industrialization*, Princeton, NJ: Princeton University Press.

Wang, H. 2012. *Globalizing China: The Influence, Strategies and Successes of Chinese Returnees*. Bingley: Emerald Group Publishing.

Weiying, Zhang and Lin, Yifu. 2016. 'Do We Need Industrial Policy', 9 November, http://www.xinhuanet.com/fortune/caiyan/ksh/193.htm, accessed 6 June 2021.

World Bank. 2019. 'Global Value Chain Development Report 2019: Technological Innovation, Supply Chain Trade, and Workers in a Globalized World', https://documents.worldbank.org/en/publication/documents-reports/documentdetail/384161555079173489/global-value-chain-development-report-2019-technological-innovation-supply-chain-trade-and-workers-in-a-globalized-world, accessed 3 June 2021.

World Bank Group. 2011. 'From Technological Catch-Up to Innovation: The Future of China's GDP Growth', https://openknowledge.worldbank.org/handle/10986/12781, accessed 30 May 2021.

World Bank Group. 2019. *Innovative China: New Drivers of Growth*. Washington DC: World Bank. doi: 10.1596/978-1-4648-1335-1.

World Economic Forum in collaboration with A. T. Kearney. 2018. 'Readiness for the Future of Production Report 2018', http://www3.weforum.org/docs/FOP_Readiness_Report_2018.pdf, accessed 2 June 2021.

World Intellectual Property Organization. 2017. 'Coffee: How Consumer Choices Are Reshaping the Global Value Chain', *World Intellectual Property Report*, Chapter 2, https://www.wipo.int/edocs/pubdocs/en/wipo_pub_944_2017-chapter2.pdf, accessed 9 June 2021.

World Intellectual Property Organization. 2020. 'China Becomes Top Filer of International Patents in 2019 amid Robust Growth for WIPO's IP Services, Treaties and Finances', 7 April, https://www.wipo.int/pressroom/en/articles/2020/article_0005.html, accessed 7 June 2021.

Wu Si. 2009. *Unwritten Rules* [in Chinese]. Shanghai: Fudan University Press.

Wu, X. 1997. 'The Evolutionary Process of Secondary Innovation', in D. F. Kocaoglu (ed.), *Innovation in Technology Management—The Key to Global Leadership*. PICMET '97, 183. doi: 10.1109/PICMET.1997.653308.

Yoo, Y., Henfridsson, O., and Lyytinen, K. 2010. 'Research Commentary: The New Organizing Logic of Digital Innovation: An Agenda for Information Systems Research', Information Systems Research, 21(4), 724–35.

Youlan, Feng. 1922. 'Why China Has No Science: An Interpretation of the History and Consequences of Chinese Philosophy', *International Journal of Ethics*, 32(3), 237–635.

Yunogami, Takashi. 2013. *Lost Manufacturing: How Japan's Manufacturing Sector Has Failed* [Chinese translation]. Beijing: China Machinery Industry Press.

Zahra, S. A. 2007. 'Contextualizing Theory Building in Entrepreneurship Research', *Journal of Business Venturing*, 22(3), 443–52.

'Top Ten Events in China's Venture Capital Market in 2006.' Zero2IPO Research, January 2007.

Zhang, M. Y. 2010. *China 2.0: The Transformation of an Emerging Superpower . . . and the New Opportunities*. Singapore: Wiley & Sons.

Zhang, M. Y. 2014. 'Innovation Management in China', in M. Dodgson, D. M. Gann, and N. Phillips (eds.), *The Oxford Handbook of Innovation Management*. Oxford: Oxford University Press, 355–74.

Zhang, M. Y. 2016. 'Meso-Level Factors in Technological Transitions: The Development of TD-SCDMA in China', *Research Policy*, 45(2), 546–59.

Zhang, M. Y. and Dodgson, M. 2007. *High-Tech Entrepreneurship in Asia: Innovation, Industry and Institutional Dynamics in Mobile Payments*, Cheltenham: Edward Elgar.

Zhang, M. Y., Dodgson, M., and Gann, D. 2021. 'Entrepreneurship and Knowledge Flows in China's Supply Chains: The Roles of Platforms' Academy of Management Conference.

Zhao, T. Y. 2016. *The Making and Becoming of China: Its Way of Historicity* [in Chinese]. Beijing: CITIC Press.

Zhao, Y. F. and Lin, S. L. 2015. 'National Institutions and Governance: China's Logics', *Chinese Public Administration* 359(5) [Chinese journal].

Zhou, F. 2011. 'Equilibrium Analysis of the Tributary System', *The Chinese Journal of International Politics*, 4, 147–78.

Zhou, X. G. 2010. 'The Institutional Logic of Collusion among Local Governments in China', *Modern China*, 36(1), 47–78.

Zhou, X. G. 2012. 'Rethinking about China's Institutional Logics: Political Campaigns', *Open Times*, 9, 105–125 [Chinese journal].

Zhou, X. G. 2017, *Institutional Logics of Chinese Governance: An Organizational Perspective* [in Chinese]. Beijing: Sanlian Press.

Zhou, Y., Zhu, S., Cai, C., Yuan, P., Li, C., Huang, Y., and Wei, W. 2014. 'High-Throughput Screening of a CRISPR/Cas9 Library for Functional Genomics in Human Cells', *Nature*, 509, 487–91. doi: 10.1038/nature13166.

Zhu, F., Zhang, Y., Palepu, K., Woo A., and Dai, N. 2019. 'Ant Financial (A)', Harvard Business School Case 617-060, https://www.hbs.edu/faculty/Pages/item.aspx?num=52493, accessed 6 June 2021.

Zhu, H., Zhang, M. Y., and Lin, W. 2017. 'The Fit between Business Model Innovation and Demand-Side Dynamics: Catch-Up of China's Latecomer Mobile Handset Manufacturers', *Innovation: Organization & Management*, 19(2), 146–66.

Ziyi, Tang and Xiaoli, Xue. 2020. 'Four Things to Know about China's $670 Billion Government Guidance Funds', *Caixin*, 25 February, https://www.caixinglobal.com/2020-02-25/four-things-to-know-about-chinas-670-billion-government-guidance-funds-101520348.html, accessed 6 June 2021.

Zott, C. and Amit, R. 2007. 'Business Model Design and the Performance of Entrepreneurial Firms', *Organization Science*, 18, 181–99.

Zott and Amit (2008), 'The fit between product market strategy and business model: Implications for firm performance', *Strategic Management Journal*, 29, 1-26.

Zott, C. and Amit, R. 2010. 'Business Model Design: An Activity System Perspective', *Long Range Planning*, 43(2–3), 216–26.

Zweig, D. 2008. 'A Limited Engagement: Mainland Returnees from Canada', Asia Pacific Foundation of Canada Research Reports, https://www.asiapacific.ca/sites/default/files/file-field/ChinaReturnees.pdf, accessed 7 June 2021.

Index

For the benefit of digital users, indexed terms that span two pages (e.g., 52–53) may, on occasion, appear on only one of those pages.